New Canadian Readings

CONTEMPORARY APPROACHES TO CANADIAN HISTORY

New Canadian Readings

CONTEMPORARY APPROACHES TO CANADIAN HISTORY

Edited by
Carl Berger

Copp Clark Pitman Ltd.
A Longman Company
Toronto

ISBN   0-7730-4642-9

Editing: Barbara Tessman, Nicholas M. Stahl
Design: Kathy Cloutier
Cover Illustration: Julia Veenstra
Typesetting: Compeer Typographic Services Limited
Printing and Binding: Webcom Ltd.

Canadian Cataloguing in Publication Data

Main entry under title:
Contemporary approaches to Canadian history

(New Canadian readings)
Bibliography: p.
ISBN 0-7730-4642-9

1. Canada — Historiography. I. Berger, Carl, 1939–
II. Series.

FC149.C66 1987   971'.007'2   C86-094771-8
F1024.C66 1987

Copp Clark Pitman Ltd.
495 Wellington Street West
Toronto, Ontario
M5V 1E9

Associated companies:
  Longman Group Ltd., London
  Longman Inc., New York
  Longman Cheshire Pty., Melbourne
  Longman Paul Pty., Auckland

Printed and bound in Canada

FOREWORD

New Canadian Readings is an on-going series of inexpensive books intended to bring some of the best recent work by this country's scholars to the attention of students of Canada. Each volume consists of ten or more articles or book sections, carefully selected to present a fully-formed thesis about some critical aspect of Canadian development. Where useful, public documents or even private letters and statistical materials may be used as well to convey a different and fresh perspective.

The authors of the readings selected for inclusion in this volume (and all the others in the series) are all first-rank scholars, those who are doing the hard research that is rapidly changing our understanding of this country. Quite deliberately, the references for each selection have been retained, thus making additional research as easy as possible.

Like the authors of the individual articles, the editors of each volume are also scholars of note, completely up-to-date in their areas of specialization and, as the introductions demonstrate, fully aware of the changing nature of the debates within their professions and genres of research. The list of additional readings provided by the editor of each volume will steer readers to materials that could not be included because of space limitations.

This series will continue into the foreseeable future, and the General Editor is pleased to invite suggestions for additional topics.

J.L. Granatstein
General Editor

CONTENTS

INTRODUCTION

The last twenty years have witnessed a virtual revolution in historical writing about Canada. This change was most obvious in the enormous expansion of the historical profession and a vast increase in research and publication; it was evident also in the emergence of new fields of study and the relative decline of national history. Up to the mid-1960s, successive generations of historians had concentrated upon the origins, evolution, and character of Canada as a national community. They surveyed the rise of self-government and relations with Britain and the United States, and they traced the unique patterns in the country's economic development. In the 1950s and the 1960s, historians devoted their best efforts to political biography as a vehicle for examining the nation-building process and the maintenance of national unity. This tradition was hardly homogeneous, for it contained competing points of view on the nature of Canada's national experience, as well as a rich diversity of themes and subjects. Still, it did highlight political events and personalities.

This tradition of historical writing came under criticism in the mid-1960s by historians who were in some respects representatives of it. Both J.M.S. Careless and Ramsay Cook censured the preoccupation with nation-building and national unity, not only as wishful thinking, but also for obscuring the complexity of the past. And both urged historians to pay greater attention to the more "limited identities" of regions and provinces and the distinct worlds of working people, women, and ethnic groups other than those of French or British origin. These critics recognized the beginning of tendencies already underway, and correctly anticipated the themes that would dominate the "new" history of the 1970s.

The emphasis upon regionalism was hardly an abrupt break with previous historical writing. French-Canadian historians had persistently focussed upon the origins of a separate national collectivity. As far back as the mid-1940s, William L. Morton had protested against one rendition of Canada's history, which accorded priority to the businessmen and politicians of the St. Lawrence system in creating the country, and which relegated the West to the status of a peripheral hinterland. And as Allan Smith's essay on British Columbia illustrates, that province's history had been the subject of long-standing investigation. What was novel about regional and provincial studies in the 1970s was the intensity of enthusiasm for these fields and the explicit and sometimes strident justifications for the approach. The exponents of regional studies accepted as an axiom that "Canada is a country of regions. Whether one is referring to historical development or to current realities, it is a truism to observe that Westerners, Ontarians, Quebeckers, and Maritimers are products of distinctive regional communities whose differences from one another often seem more striking than their similarities."* Others went much further by reasserting the claim that certain parts of the country — usually the

---

*Peter Oliver, *Public and Private Persons: The Ontario Political Culture* (Toronto, 1975), 2.

West and the Maritimes — had paid an inordinate price for national unity and continued to do so.

This renewed appreciation for regional history involved much more than a change of fashions in historical scholarship. The regionalism of the historians reflected a more general, positive appreciation for localities as centres of loyalties and identities, and a feeling that their histories were as important as what had happened in distant places. The acknowledged importance of these limited identities was sustained, too, by the recognition that provincial governments had become far more powerful and prominent in Canada in the years after 1960. Historians (and historical geographers) who were not primarily concerned with discovering regional character also reinforced this tendency towards the local by examining social groups through community studies. The net impact of these influences was to impart to regional studies a legitimacy and purpose. The recovery of distinct regional perspectives was not an end in itself: it was rather a step towards bringing those perspectives into general histories of Canada in a more integrated and sustained fashion.

The readings in Section 1 of this collection suggest the numerous influences that impinged on regional studies, present the distinct historical problems that have preoccupied historians of specific areas, and allude to common themes linking them together. These papers also implicitly illustrate the varied meanings and definitions of region that historians have assumed and employed, and invite the reader to consider whether "region" has become as much an abstraction as "nation" once was.

The second, and closely related, dimension of the new history has been the rise of social history, an approach that has been defined and practised in quite different ways. Some historians have emphasized the analysis of anonymous processes and structures in the material foundations of life and the ways in which these shaped behaviour, perceptions, and class relations. A very few have applied statistical analysis to information derived from census documents to isolate patterns in social mobility, marriage, and family composition. On the whole, however, social history in Canada has been cultivated as a series of distinct subfields devoted to the working class, native peoples, women, ethnic groups, urban centres, and education. Historians who write about these subjects were initially moved by an impatience with accounts of the past that dwelt upon the activities of exceptional members of elites, especially politicians, and they were determined to understand the conditions of life of "ordinary" people who had figured only fleetingly, if at all, in received history. They have shown how groups once considered passive historical actors possessed a certain autonomy and ability to shape their own lives. Social historians in general had an acute sensitivity to dominance and conflict in class and ethnic relations, and to the repressive functions of such institutions as the public school.

As the essays in Section 2 indicate, each of the sub-themes in social history possessed its own rationale and research agenda. Indeed, in one case, that of labour history, two approaches diverged rather drastically. These essays, however, are apt to convey an exaggerated impression of differences and fragmentation. For they are not merely reflections on the new subject matter of history or progress reports calling attention to significant trends: they are also, to varying degrees, justifications for certain lines of inquiry. The divisions within social history were the necessary result of specialization; but they were magnified by the process by which certain subjects attained scholarly recognition and legitimacy. The fragmentation of social history was much more pronounced in essays in historiography than in such syntheses as *The Canadian Prairies* (1984) by Gerald Friesen, or *Quebec: A History, 1867–1929* (1983) by Paul-André Linteau, René Durocher, and Jean-Claude Robert. It is instructive, also, to consider how many times certain key books are judged in these essays to constitute fundamental additions to several of the subdivisions of social history.

The following essays represent approaches to the past that most emphatically differentiate current work from what existed before. It would be quite wrong, therefore, to conclude that the so-called traditional fields of biography or political history have vanished from the scene. It is simply that historians working within established conventions feel less need to explain or justify what they do than those who seek to break the hold of custom. It is worth keeping in mind, too, that more books have in the last two decades been published on military than on women's history, and, as the papers in Section 3 indicate, the study of politics has hardly remained frozen in the mold of the 1950s.

In spite of the obvious biases of these articles, they provide a guide to aspects of the transformation in recent historical writing and contain hints and clues that help us come to terms with the central themes in the history of history—why do historians' viewpoints change at all, and why have the subjects explored since the mid-1960s become so important?

SECTION 1
REGIONS

"LIMITED IDENTITIES" IN CANADA†

J.M.S. CARELESS

A suitable text for the present disquisition may be found in a review article by Professor Ramsay Cook discussing some works of 1967 that deal with Canada's perennial problem, its lack of national unity and identity. On this topic Professor Cook remarks: "Perhaps instead of constantly deploring our lack of identity we should attempt to understand and explain the regional, ethnic, and class identities that we do have. It might just be that it is in these limited identities that 'Canadianism' is found, and that except for our over-heated nationalist intellectuals Canadians find this situation quite satisfactory."[1] What follows here, then, is a commentary on this theme in twentieth-century Canada: if one nation, eminently divisible.

Canadian historiography has often dealt too wishfully with nationalism — and *ergo*, with unification — thus producing both expectations and discouragements out of keeping with realities. We may be somewhat past the colony-to-nation epitome of the Canadian story ("and with sovereignty, everybody lived happily ever after — see Africa"), but we are still considerably hung up on the plot of nation-building. There are the good guys and the bad, the unifying nation-builders and their foes; though one trouble is that the characters often change hats and whiskers in the French-language version. There are also the good eras and the bad, largely seen in terms of nation-building. In this sense, during the twentieth century, Canada's years before the testing of World War I were golden years of national expansion; the twenties a decade where blotchy prosperity was further marred by the federal government abdicating national leadership; the depressed thirties a time of crisis in federal, more than class, relationships; the forties an era of national triumph arising out of national trial; and the booming fifties a new noonday of nation-building, unity, and harmony — after which the darkening discord of the sixties follows as a decided shock.

Now I would not seek to deny a good deal of validity even to this oversimplified, partial version of the nation-building account. I mean rather to say that it is merely one assessment, which does not necessarily have to be equated with the working out of historical destiny for Canada. This is not to condemn it as too readily subjective — and thereby enter into the bottomless debate as to whether there is objective history. It is to assert instead that the theme of nation-building has an unfortunately teleological cast. One looks for the end to be achieved; one measures developments, pro or con, in terms of the goal — a strong, united nation. One anticipates the re-enactment of the American success story and, when it does not come, particularly blames the presence of the huge American neighbour itself. Again this is not to deny all validity to that account. Obviously, a transcontinental Canadian union has been established and has been constantly

†*Canadian Historical Review* L, 1 (March 1969): 1–10. An earlier version of this paper was presented to a meeting of the American Historical Association held in Toronto, December 1967.

subjected to powerful American influences. But it still can be contended that the nationbuilding approach to Canadian history neglects and obscures even while it explains and illuminates, and may tell us less about the Canada that now is than the Canada that should have been — but has not come to pass.

Viewed in a different context, accordingly, the years of the early twentieth century can appear as the period when a vigorous new western region emerged to join the existing coterie of Canadian regions; the twenties, as the time when forces of modern industrial society began to shape the present powerful provincial empires; the thirties, when class and ethnic strains proved at least as potent in disrupting the Canadian political fabric as the constitutional decisions of the Judicial Committee of the Privy Council; the forties, when external crisis undoubtedly brought resurgent national sentiment — but two nationalisms, in two Canadas; the fifties, an era when rapid industrial and urban growth greatly strengthened regional orientations and ethnic pressures — and helped bring on the divisions of the sixties as a natural consequence.

This is not an attempt to replace a success story with a failure story — nor, indeed, is it very new, since it essentially puts forward elements long recognized. What may be newer, however, is the notion that if the Canadian people have fallen short of the Canadian dream (held, that is, chiefly by historians and intellectuals) it could be because their interests were elsewhere — and that they nevertheless shared in a viable Canada, if not that laid up in heaven for them. Accordingly, it might be worth investigating what their Canadian experience was, observing that it did not greatly focus on Ottawa and the deeds of hero federal politicians, or on the meagre symbols of some all-Canadian way of life.

How, then, is this Canadian experience to be discerned and defined? Some of it is doubtless common to all as citizens in one political sovereignty, with many economic and social interconnections besides. But much of it surely lies in the "limited identities" of region, culture, and class referred to by Professor Cook. These represent entities of experience for Canadians no less than the transcontinental federal union; indeed, it is largely through them that Canadians interpret their nation-state as a whole. Of course — emphatically — regional, ethnic, and class factors apply in other national histories; and of course they have scarcely gone unnoticed in Canada as well. But what still is needed is more study of their roles in this country of relatively weak nationalizing forces: a land of two languages, pluralized politics, and ethnic multiplicity, yet all so far contained within one distinctive frame of nation-state existence.

It is impossible to do more here than sketch some outlines of this study or, because of the limitations of space, to go much beyond one aspect of the limited identities, the regional, while touching on ethnic and class factors in passing. It may be hoped, however, that enough can be done to make plain the significance of such a view of Canada throughout its development as a nation-state.

In taking up a theme of regionalism, one is conscious that it may suggest a somewhat dated environmentalist approach by analogy with the history of the United States. There, it can bring to mind implications of Turner and the frontier school: of the pouring of people into sectional moulds to harden in the frontier's advance across the various physiographic regions of the continent. Through the inevitable workings of revision in American history, from critics of Turner who urged other factors than the moulding power of the frontier environment down to Louis Hartz, whose special stress on cultural importation leaves little to the landscape, a regional treatment can come to seem rather old-hat, tending perhaps to the parochial or antiquarian.[2] This may be so, to an extent, for a country where national forces have worked mightily, the powers of One Big Market, One Big Government, and the Americanizing Dream having proved so paramount. But the Canadian context is almost antithetical. Whether one moves, accordingly, with Turnerian or Hartzian waves, the experience of regionalism remains prominent and distinctive in Canadian history — and time has tended less to erode it than to develop it.

Most of the reasons here are oft given and obvious: the geographical segmentation and encumbrances of the country; the north-south orientation of many regional economic patterns and the related problem of sustaining east-west lines; the Anglo-French duality; and the lack of positive popular commitment to a strong federal union, despite the intentions of the framers of Confederation. Whatever their ideas or assumptions, in fact, the union of 1867 was in large degree a coming together of regions and so has remained: regions articulated or integrated under a central regime, but surely not reduced or unified thereby.

Yet there are other factors that must also enter to explain this persistence of regionalism. After all, the United States had a mass of geography too, not all of it advantageous, and a strong American union was not born but was made in history, in the very growth of popular commitment. Nor can the Anglo-French duality in Canada, however intrinsic, be found sufficient reason in itself for e pluribus non unum; there are also several English Canadas, not just one. A further fact, instead, is that the social patterning of Canada particularly tends to favour regional commitment. There is a relationship here between regional identification and broader social values that deserves investigation.

John Porter makes the essential point when he observes: "Unlike the American value system, which has always emphasized the idea of the equality of peoples within a new nation, the Canadian value system has stressed the social qualities that differentiate people rather then the human qualities that make them the same."[3] Porter discusses the point chiefly in regard to the persistence of immigrant groupings in Canada, where ethnic fragmentation is more the mode than assimilation and is expressed in the ideal of the mosaic instead of the melting pot. But this Canadian tendency to treat people as groups and communities rather than as individuals and citizens pertains to more than the fairly recent development of the ethnic mosaic. Its roots run deep in history.

French Canada's social values found their origins in the corporate authoritarian traditions of the seventeenth century. English Canada's were shaped in the organic, pragmatic, Victorian liberalism of the nineteenth century. In other words, one may follow Louis Hartz on the power of transferred cultural fragments to mould new societies, yet contend that for English Canada the formative power lay not in the weak remnants of eighteenth-century American empire but in the swamping force of earlier nineteenth-century British immigration. At any rate, neither French nor English Canada knew eighteenth-century rationalist democracy, as did the United States, with its generalized precepts on the equality, rights, and powers of men as men. In the Canadian scheme of values there was no all-embracing sovereign people but rather particular societies of people under a sovereign crown. They were exclusive rather than inclusive in viewpoint. Their guide was adapted organic tradition more than the innovating power of the popular will. And they stressed the nearer corporate loyalties of religious and ethnic distinctions — Scots, English, and Irish, as well as French — instead of broad adherence to a democratic state.

Though self-government came, it developed in terms of the Canadian perception and experience, as did federal union. And while the Fathers of Confederation might devise a strong union under the crown, designed indeed to counter claims for states' rights, they could not invoke for it the power of the American belief in the sovereign people. As subsequent demands for provincial rights arose, federal leaders dealt with them pragmatically, rather than seek some broad, national counter-response. Indeed, Canadian particularist habits of mind largely favoured impulses to state sovereignty over sovereignty of the people — so that, in the Canadian union of the twentieth century, one might almost witness the gradual victory of the long defunct Confederate States of America.

Furthermore, the crown, whose supremacy the fathers of 1867 might count on to obviate pretensions of founding power in the provinces, had its place within the spheres of provincial government as well as federal. Drawing on the traditional symbol, provinces might well aspire to the rank of co-ordinate kingdoms; and most had existed as entities under the crown before the creation of the federal state. In the twentieth century, the growing demands on government in an industrializing, urbanizing society of course greatly enlarged the activities of the provinces; but, not less significantly, the process strengthened their identification with the particularist societies of Canada. They grew in status as well as function. It is not only evident that federal-provincial conferences have acquired something of the atmosphere of diplomatic exchanges between states, but it is also not inexpressive of Canadian conditions that heads of powerful provincial regimes may use the title of prime minister for their office — as in the current advance of the kingdom of British Columbia to co-equal dignity.

Accordingly, while it would be absurd as well as unnecessary to deny historical evidence of Canadian sentiment for the union and the country as a whole, the fact remains that basic schemes of values in both English and French Canada accord more readily with smaller, differentiated provincial or regional societies. In French Canada, too, sentiment is far more strongly focussed on the corporate Quebec community than on the whole extended French-Canadian segment of the union; it is even a question whether separatism is not best conceived as the height of Quebec communalism. As for English Canada, the habitual emphasis on particularized social groupings rather than mass citizenship, on pragmatically nearer community interests instead of some generalized, idealized, national way of life, effectively ministers to strong identification with regions or provinces delineated by geography, economics, and history.

That pervasive twentieth-century process, urbanization, has also reinforced regional identities in Canada. It was after World War I that the Canadian population became more than 50 percent urban; by the 1960s the proportion was over 70 percent. One might conjecture that the long decline of an older, more isolated rural Canada, one of the most notable features of this century, would foster nationalizing forces—and no doubt this has been true in some degree. But the significant aspect for this study is the way in which the rise of dominant urban centres or metropolises has also aided regional orientation and the shaping of provincial power structures.

One may note that all across the country major metropolitan centres have organized broad regional hinterlands about themselves, thanks to their dominance of communication nets and of market, manufacturing, or financial facilities that serve the region. Again, this is a world as well as a North American phenomenon and has been going on in Canada for quite some time. Even in the relatively static Atlantic provinces, Halifax achieved metropolitan dominance in Nova Scotia in the later nineteenth century, largely through the building of railways; and through railways Saint John widened its commercial sway in New Brunswick. As for Quebec, another old port city—of hallowed antiquity by North American standards—its political role and cultural hold as the capital of French Canada maintained its special regional dominance, however much it continued economically to fall behind its upriver rival, Montreal. Leaving Montreal for the moment, Toronto was fully established as the metropolis of prosperous agricultural and industrial southern Ontario by the end of the nineteenth century; and in the twentieth, it added control of the huge mineral resource area of northern Ontario, so that successive opulent suburbs of Toronto spell out a veritable progression of northern mining booms.

In the West, Winnipeg's hold spread across the prairies with the wheat boom of the early twentieth century and the transcontinentals that funnelled down to its yards. Its growth was slower after World War I, as the opening of the Panama Canal route tapped off some of its western hinterland to the Pacific. But it retained an influential position as a major regional focus, even when newer western metropolises developed: Calgary with the oil boom after World War II; Edmonton with its drive to the northern hinterland of the Peace, and by air, railroad, and barge to the very shores of the Arctic. Westward again, there was Vancouver, the transcontinental outlet, soaring with its own ever-richer Pacific hinterland of lumber, minerals, and water power.

All these cities were centres of regional dynamism, identified with the economic leadership and welfare of vast sections of the country; centres, often, of political as well as of business elites, foci of public opinion in their regions, of chief media instruments like newspapers and television, seats of major provincial educational or cultural facilities. And the evergrowing pattern of urban concentration in the highway and apartment age has simply strengthened the focussing of Canadian regions around their chief metropolitan cities.

To admit the obvious once more, the metropolitan centres of the United States have grown in similar fashion — to still greater wealth and size — yet the result has not been comparable in the regionalizing of the nation. The fact is, however, that while the phenomenon of metropolitan–regional growth is wholly apparent in the United States, there are offsetting factors in that country; and it is these that are notably less evident in Canada.

For one thing, the American urban pattern is far more complex, containing many counter-pulls — with more sizable cities and tiers of cities, more regions and subregions, and also more states. There is not the relative simplicity of the Canadian scene, where a few large cities dominate huge sweeps of territory, sometimes within one provincial jurisdiction, and that perhaps centred within the city itself. For another thing, the overmastering role of the chief or "national" metropolis is not really comparable. Naturally, Montreal is Canada's closest equivalent to New York, the greatest head-office centre, key to the national transport system, the final capital of the country's economic life. This may be so economically. But in socio-cultural terms — in "national regard," if one may use the phrase — Montreal is not a single great metropolis but the split capital of two Canadas: for the one, yielding to Quebec in some aspects; for the other, to Toronto and elsewhere; perhaps finding general national regard only at extraordinary occasions like Expo 67. Montreal does not fill the metropolitan headship role held by the huge American conurbation. In Canada, people do tend far more to look to their regional metropolitan centres than to Montreal — or else to New York, Chicago, or Los Angeles. As for Ottawa, as a purely political capital, a weaker Washington in a less consolidated country, its presence does not greatly alter the Canadian particularist tendency to focus on to the regional metropolis.

In the main, therefore, the growth of urbanism and metropolitanism has largely worked to confirm regional identities in twentieth-century Canada. One can identify the West Coast culture of Vancouver, for example, far more explicitly than the traits of national culture, just as one can more easily depict an Albertan or a Maritimer than a Canadian. About the only strongly identifiable national urban propensity, in fact, is the wide eagerness to scorn Toronto, which is consoled by its inherent belief that all Canadian cities really do aspire to be Toronto, if they are good.

One could go on noting still more factors making for regional identification — the ethnic mosaic, for example, built up in the waves of twentieth-century immigration. Each region has virtually a distinctive ethnic composition of its own, according to the proportion and variety of immigrants it has received, with consequent effect on its political as well as cultural responses. Once more this might be said of the United States, where assimilation may be the ideal more than the complete achievement. Nonetheless, how different is the degree, when in Canada the ideal, or plain acceptance of fact, is the survival of ethnic diversity, where there is a declared distinction between "founding peoples" and later arrivals — and where "ethnic" has vulgarly become a noun to signify a member of one of the contingents of the non-French, non-British third force in Canada. Of course, acculturation has nevertheless proceeded among immigrant elements, from the mid-nineteenth-century "famine Irish" to the mid-twentieth-century Hungarian refugees. Still, the ethnic persistence fostered by Canadian socio-cultural values plainly intensifies regional differentiation, quite aside from the special French and English identifications of Quebec and Ontario. Compare the largely "old-Canadian" make-up of the Maritimes, for example, with the strong non-British, if English-acculturated component in plains society, the significance of Ukrainians in Manitoba, of Italians in urban Ontario, or the still more cosmopolitan mixture of West Coast society.

Then too, class patterns may be observed as varying from region to region in Canada, no doubt complying with differing regional economic scales. At any rate, industrialism and urbanism have not yet here created strong national awareness of common class interests. Socio-economic strains have tended to be expressed in largely regional terms, or at most in non-enduring regional alliances of disadvantaged elements. This may be said of Progressivism in the twenties, a class-oriented movement which foundered amid regional diversity; of the CCF of the thirties and forties, which largely failed, beyond its western bases, to make lasting inroads on the eastern working classes; of Social Credit in the fifties and after, which essentially stayed dependent on sure provincial bailiwicks in Alberta and British Columbia. And today class discontents are still largely expressed in regional or provincial stances, as in the Maritimes, or in Quebec communalism. As for socialism, one might feel that if the hopefuls of the Second International ran headlong into nationalism, so in Canada its proponents still have to face the divisive force of regionalism.

These threads, of course, should be followed further; but for now one may assert that regional, ethnic, and class identities have all tended to fit together more than to develop national identification in Canada. The ultimate conclusion, indeed, might seem to be that the true theme of the country's history in the twentieth century is not nation building but region building. But here it is necessary to make one final point. All this does add up to a characteristic and persisting Canadian pattern, largely differentiated from the United States — and the whole may indeed be greater than the sum of its parts, producing through its internal relationships some sort of common Canadianism. At least this is the contention here: that the distinctive nature of much of Canadian experience has produced a continent-wide entity identifiable in its very pluralism, constraints, and compromises.

A key word is articulation. What has been sought, and to some degree achieved, is not really unification or consolidation, but the articulation of regional patterns in one transcontinental state. In this process, it may be said, the implicit aim of every regional community has been maximum autonomy for itself consonant with the maximum advantage to be gained from an overriding central regime. In this, indeed, these communities were simply manifesting the historical behaviour exemplified in Canadian relations with British imperial power, where the essential process was the gradual maximizing of autonomy rather than a doctrine-based conflict over sovereign independence. But the concept of autonomy involves notions of both practical adjustment and continuing association. The analogy may not be precise between the external and internal processes in Canada — at any rate, in honesty, one knows where the former led — but the real fact is, it does fit the particularist, pragmatic tradition of the Canadian communities.

And the result may be that each of them, in whatever varying degree, could exhibit something common, to be called Canadianism, as they viewed the whole country from their own regional, ethnic, or class position, seeing it largely in their own perspective but accepting its limitations and need of continual adjustment, while also feeling the shared benefits it provided. All, indeed, have tended to make a virtue of their own regional or provincial willingness to "sacrifice" to maintain Canada and most have found the concept of the general union necessary as a context for their own aspirations and desires. In any case, by pursuing a line largely of socio-cultural enquiry, one may hope to uncover satisfactions in the limited identities named by Professor Cook that have added up to some positive balance of satisfaction with Canada itself.

Notes

1. G.R. Cook, "Canadian Centennial Cerebrations," *International Journal* XXII (Autumn 1967), 663.

2. Louis Hartz, et al., *The Founding of New Societies in the History of the United States, Latin America, South Africa, Canada and Australia* (New York, 1964).

3. John Porter, "The Human Community" in *The Canadians, 1867-1967*, edited by J.M.S. Careless and R.C. Brown (Toronto, 1967), 396. See also John Porter, *The Vertical Mosaic* (Toronto, 1965), 60-73.

IN SEARCH OF A POST-CONFEDERATION MARITIME HISTORIOGRAPHY, 1900–1967†

E.R. FORBES

. . . The emphases in Canadian historical writing, at least until the 1950s, tended to enrich Maritime historiography in the pre-Confederation period while diverting attention away from it thereafter. The focus on French-English relations encouraged a host of amateur and professional historians such as Francis Parkman, James Hannay, D.C. Harvey, and Archibald MacMechan to examine the Acadians, their conflict with the English, and their ultimate expulsion. Naomi Griffiths has noted over two hundred works on the expulsion alone.[1] But English Canadian historians appeared to lose all interest in the Acadians after the deportation; those concerned with the problems of Francophone minorities directed their attention almost exclusively to Ontario and the West. Similarly the theme of Canada's step-by-step growth from colony to nation — the other primary preoccupation of Canadian historians at the beginning of this century[2] — encouraged imperialist and liberal-nationalist scholars alike, such as James Hannay, D.C. Harvey, Chester Martin, W.R. Livingston and J.A. Roy, to explore a variety of Maritime topics relating to constitutional development, including the "struggle" for responsible government and the "achievement" of Confederation, and to develop a cult of Joseph Howe, hero of the fight for responsible government and anti-hero in the conflict over Confederation. But after Confederation the road to nation and commonwealth by-passed the Maritimes entirely in a focus on trade policy, imperial conferences and external affairs. For constitutional historians the Maritimes had virtually ceased to exist.[3] This was in conspicuous contrast to the Prairies whose historians, led by the ubiquitous Chester Martin, found a parallel to Canada's struggle for autonomy in their own evolution to "full" provincial status. This approach served to express sectional grievances and even suggested a rationale for securing increased subsidies from federal governments.[4]

The shift in interest from British-Canadian to Canadian-American relations after the World War helped the student of the modern Maritimes only a little. Boundary disputes in the region were settled in an earlier era. J.B. Brebner confined his thesis of Nova Scotia as an extention of New England to the Acadian and Revolutionary periods. Even the voluminous Carnegie series yielded but scattered bits of information, largely confined to population movement, fisheries disputes, and the timber industry.[5] The view of Canada's history as the story of the development of a series of staples for export, which also became fashionable in the inter-war period, contributed only slightly more. Accounts of the fur trade touched on the Maritimes only in the earliest period; those of the timber trade largely petered out with Confederation.[6] Harold Innis' *Cod Fisheries* devoted but

†*Acadiensis* VIII (Autumn 1978): 3-21.

two chapters of fifteen to the Atlantic fishery after 1867, and studies of the wheat economy ignored the Maritimes entirely.[7]

The frontier approach, which also diverted attention away from the Maritimes in the modern era, paradoxically contributed substantially to the image of the region which did emerge. Frederick Jackson Turner's essay of 1893 set out the hypothesis of a frontier moving in stages westward through the United States with the availability of free land. This frontier provided a "crucible" in which "immigrants were Americanized, liberated, and fused into a mixed race." The ideas of social stratification were sloughed off with other cultural baggage and from this process came a dynamic for social and material progress, democracy, and nationalism.[8] It was a thesis that, with a few adjustments for differences in westward development, could readily be applied to Canada.[9] The thesis had tremendous appeal to those who could still see themselves or their region as close to the frontier stage. After all, it implied that they were progressive, democratic, and represented the true essence of the nation. But it was difficult for Maritimers to perceive themselves as part of a frontier society. The Maritimes were the only provinces lacking huge territories in the process of settlement or other forms of primitive development. And even a cursory examination suggested that here the process of cultural fusion was neither rapid nor complete. In short, the "frontierist" approach implied that for an understanding of the progressive dynamic animating Canada in the late nineteenth and early twentieth centuries, one should look westward to Ontario, to the Prairies, to British Columbia and to the North. The Maritimes were of interest only as a foil against which to demonstrate the validity of the frontier approach; simple logic suggested that, if the frontier encouraged progressive, egalitarian and democratic attitudes, then that part of the country furthest removed from the frontier stage must be conservative, socially stratified and unprogressive.

It would be simplistic, however, to attribute the pervasive frontierist influence in Canadian writing merely to a conscious acceptance of the theories outlined by Turner. In 1970 Michael Cross commented that "an avowed 'frontierist' is hardly to be found in a day's walk. Yet evidence of the frontier approach is to be discovered in the writings of a great many historians, many of whom would take umbrage at having this fact drawn to their attention."[10] Perhaps the latter were unaware of any debt to Turner because they were influenced more by the popular ideas in which Turner's work had its roots. Often the "greatest" and certainly the most popular historians are those who express clearly ideas and emotions implicit in the local folk culture.[11] Henry Nash Smith in *Virgin Land: The American West as Symbol and Myth* suggested such a role for Turner. The principal ingredients of Turner's hypothesis — the focus on the West, pride in democracy, the provision for new opportunities and the emphasis on agricultural settlement — were already very much a part of the Americans' view of their country when Turner presented his paper. Canadians too developed a myth of the West similar in essence to that of the Americans. Professor Gerald Friesen has outlined the principal ingredients of that myth, which portrayed the West as a source of individualism, new opportunities, virility, co-operative ideas, democracy, cultural fusion, and material and social progress.[12] Undoubtedly, Turner's contribution to the formulation and articulation of this myth was significant; one suspects, however, in view of the all-pervasive expression of these ideas in popular culture and the emotional satisfaction which they provided for so many Canadians, that a similar myth would have evolved even had Turner remained a journalist.[13]

In any case, the "myth of the West," as Professor Friesen has noted, "captured" English Canada before the end of the First World War. The popular view that western development and the wheat economy were the keys to Canada's current and future prosperity suggests an underlying economic motive in the myth's triumph. In a bid for immigrants, government, railway, and board of trade propaganda portrayed Canada as a frontier community. The ideals of the western myth — democracy, cultural fusion, agrarianism, and progress — had become so firmly rooted in British, American, and Canadian traditions that most English-Canadians delighted in ascribing them to their country.[14] The popular literature of the day, including the work of Canadians Ralph Connor and R.J.C. Stead, and Americans widely read in Canada, such as Zane Grey, trumpeted the virtues of the frontier *ad nauseum*.[15]

In the western myth's capture of Canadian historians the key factor was probably personal contact with the Prairies. Westerners espoused their myth with a passion and commitment that was contagious. In the early decades of the twentieth century those who took their news from the Winnipeg *Free Press*, attended the sermons of a William Ivens, J.S. Woodsworth, or other Prairie social gospel preachers, and rubbed shoulders with the enthusiasts of the grain-grower co-operatives could hardly have avoided a warm glow of satisfaction that they too were involved in a dynamic experiment which would lead the way to a prosperous and morally superior nation. One of the striking facts revealed in Berger's survey [Carl Berger, *The Writing of Canadian History: Aspects of English-Canadian Historical Writing*, 1900–1970 (Toronto, 1976)] was the number of Canada's leading historians of the first half of the century who taught on the Prairies at formative stages of their careers. These included Chester Martin, Frank Underhill, A.R.M. Lower, W.A. MacIntosh, D.C. Masters, and sociologist S.D. Clark. Not surprisingly, some of the leading Canadian exponents of frontierism came from this group. Both Frank Underhill, who lectured at the University of Saskatchewan from 1914 to 1926, with only a brief interruption, and A.R.M. Lower, who taught at Wesley College in Winnipeg until his call to Queen's in 1947, proclaimed a version of Canadian history in which the ideas of Turner and the western myth were prominently featured, and a version of Canadian history in which the Maritimes virtually ceased to exist after the union. As Underhill succinctly put it, "As for the Maritime provinces, nothing, of course, ever happens down there."[16] A.R.M. Lower, who had enthusiastically espoused the Turner thesis from the beginning of the 1930s, made the same point more subtly by entirely ignoring this period of Maritime history in his *Canadians in the Making*. Although Lower was already showing interest in the role of the metropolis when this text appeared in 1958, the following excerpt reveals his continued commitment to the myth of the West and his disdain for the Maritimes:

> There is an ocean of difference between the relatively mature localism of a secondary urban community and the air that blows through the national

capital, Ottawa. This air begins to blow at Montreal, where the meeting of the two cultures makes for unwilling breath. It strengthens in Ottawa, whose major reason for existence is the duty of seeing in all directions. A current from it runs down to Toronto and the western peninsula of Ontario (only three chapters ago this was "western Canada"), both of which are rescued from parochialism by the scope of their economic activities. But it is at the head of the lakes that the air begins to blow strong, for with Port Arthur the traveller is in another world, the West. From Lakehead to the Pacific coast, the same air blows. The same kind of observation could be made as one goes northward, for here too there is another world. The atmosphere is similar to that of the West. It has the geographical emancipation, the hope, energy, lack of convention, readiness to accept all comers and on equal terms, that mark new societies wherein, the old moulds having been broken, the pieces are set loose and shaken up into new patterns.[17]

As the Western myth grew in popularity Maritimers became increasingly conscious of the need to assert a regional perspective of their own. This was the goal of the semi-scholarly historical and literary journal *Acadiensis*, established in 1901, and the popular *Busy East of Canada*, founded in 1910.[18] Writing in the latter, R.V. Sharp of Sydney most clearly articulated the Maritime dilemma. If the Western myth were allowed to define the nation — a myth which set such un-Maritime criteria for nationalism as rapid cultural fusion and unrelieved agrarianism — how then could Maritimers identify themselves as Canadians? They would, Sharp argued, have to assert their own version of Canadianism — a Maritime Canadianism.

A country such as these Maritimes, a race of Canadians such as these eastern men of pioneer breed, have no need to turn to the provinces of the melting pot for their conceptions of Canada and Canadians. It is time the east came out from behind the skirts of the west and made it clear to the world that there is more to Canada than gigantic farms, more than great sweeps of prairie, more than Rocky Mountains and mushroom cities and immigrant citizens — that there is a Canada, distinct and individual from this, a Canada with a definite past as old as any in America, a Canada with a definite future which is not at all the future of the country of golden grain. Canada cannot be served by bending the old to the new. Each must go its way; and the east must realize itself, even as the west has done.[19]

In the 1920s the leaders of the Maritime Rights Movement became aware of the deficiencies of Canadian historiography regarding national commitments allegedly made to their region at Confederation and in subsequent decades. Sporadically they published pamphlets and magazine and newspaper articles to show the historical background of their grievances. A.P. Patterson, wholesale grocer from Saint John, turned out a lengthy pamphlet entitled *The True Story of Confederation*, a second edition of which was circulated by the New Brunswick King's Printer in 1926. Dartmouth journalist H.S. Congdon produced a spate of articles on the historical basis of the Maritimes' claims to Canada's winter trade. F.C. Cornell, the freight-rate expert employed by the Maritime Transportation Committee, dug up considerable information of the history of transportation policy in the region. Constant appeals to Dominion statistician R.H. Coates for data led to the publication of historical profiles on the Maritimes in 1927, 1934, and 1948.[20] Literally dozens of studies commissioned for or prepared as submissions to a proliferating number of provincial and federal royal commissions attempted to show the historical background of Maritime problems. None of these, with the exception of S.A. Saunders' *Economic History of the Maritime Provinces* (Ottawa, 1939), merits serious attention as historical literature on the Maritimes.[21] But their accumulation, along with the other material mentioned above, revealed a pressing desire by Maritimers to understand their recent past, the nature of their industries and society, and their role in the Canadian nation. In meeting this need they were poorly served by the Canadian historical community.

Even historians within the Maritimes tended to pursue other interests. At Dalhousie University, George Wilson, a progressive in his youth who turned to history for an understanding of society and a guide for future reform, found Canadian history dull, and having contributed a dull book of his own on Robert Baldwin and responsible government, escaped to the more exhilarating clime of the French Revolution.[22] At Acadia R.S. Longley produced a biography of Francis Hincks, and at Mount Allison D.G.G. Kerr laboured on the biography of a colonial governor. Nova Scotia's provincial archivist D.C. Harvey was prolific and varied in his choice of topics on Prince Edward Island, Nova Scotia and the region as a whole, but steadfastly adhered to the earlier period, at least until the twilight of his career.[23]

New Brunswick was the scene of the most promising attempt to develop an indigenous historiography of the modern Maritime period. In 1927, J.C. Webster of Shediac produced a pamphlet entitled *The Distressed Maritimes* in which he castigated the country in general and the Maritimes in particular for their neglect of culture and education, and identified this neglect as the most critical of Maritime problems.[24] Webster was in a strong position to criticize. A gentleman and scholar in the British liberal tradition, Webster wrote history on the Acadian period, invested his personal fortune in the collection of books and manuscripts which would otherwise have been lost, at least to New Brunswick, and served as patron to the New Brunswick Museum.[25] In 1934, acting on his own initiative, he attracted to the museum a most promising scholar in A. G. Bailey, and managed to secure grants for his sustenance from the Carnegie Foundation. Meanwhile, A. P. Patterson, now Minister of Education in the Dysart government, still sought to carve out a Maritime perspective in Canadian historiography and establish once and for all the "true" story of Confederation. Distrusting the traditional "ivory tower" concept of the university, and influenced by theories of adult education then current, Patterson proposed to establish Bailey in a chair of Maritime history directly responsible to the Minister of Education. From this position the incumbent might be expected to produce a suitable version of Canadian history which he would then disseminate at university and in lectures and study groups throughout the province. As an independent scholar, Bailey was less than enthused. Aided by Webster's influence with other cabinet ministers, he secured instead an appointment to a new chair in history at the University of New Brunswick, a chair supported but not controlled by the provincial government.[26]

Professor Bailey took seriously the responsibility of helping to develop the history of the constituency which his university served. He prepared a series of essays on New Brunswick and Confederation but, much to A.P. Patterson's disgust, instead of serving as a basis for regional propaganda as had Chester Martin's early work on the West, they proved a model of scholarly detachment.[27] Bailey also launched what was intended to be a wholesale attack on the lamentable lack of historical literature on his province. Drawing up a list of some thirty thesis topics which stressed economic, social and cultural history, he eventually secured a grant from the Rockefeller Foundation to fund graduate students and the publication, under his editorship, of expanded versions of their theses. The first of these studies, a solid examination of the development of the New Brunswick school system by Katherine MacNaughton, broke the Confederation barrier by carrying its analysis forward to 1900.[28] Unfortunately, the first study published was also the last, as Bailey was sucked into the maw of academic administration. In 1946 he passed on his mantle as regional historian to W.S. MacNutt. But MacNutt decided that the pre-Confederation period would have to be re-worked before one could hope to understand the later period.

When major academic studies of the post-Confederation Maritime provinces finally did materialize in the 1950s and 1960s they came not from historians but political scientists. The "Government of Canada" series edited by Nova Scotia-born R. MacGregor Dawson yielded studies of political institutions in each of the three provinces.[29] Frank MacKinnon's *The Government of Prince Edward Island* (Toronto, 1951), J. Murray Beck's *The Government of Nova Scotia* (Toronto, 1957), and Hugh Thorburn's *Politics of New Brunswick* (Toronto, 1961) contained sufficient historical perspective to make them the most important contributions to the modern historiography of each province up to that time. Although concentrating on the contemporary politics of New Brunswick in the 1950s, Thorburn examined the traditional, regional and ethnic divisions in the province and provided a brief synthesis of the chiefly French-language literature on the Acadian renaissance. MacKinnon's work on the Island was a study of governmental institutions from their colonial origins through the modern era. Beck's study followed a similar format, but with much richer historical detail and analysis, especially for the later period. Indeed, although not technically fitting the scope of Berger's study, this is one work which perhaps should have been included for its monumental contribution to a neglected field of Canadian history.

Yet from the historian's viewpoint all three works had their limitations. They were narrowly political; they were written before much private political correspondence was available; and they relied to a significant degree on each author's personal acquaintance with his province and on confidential interviews with unnamed politicians and other prominent citizens. Writing after a period of more than two decades of Liberal ascendancy in provincial and federal politics, Beck frequently repeated the Liberal mythology, although not necessarily endorsing it as factual.[30] His scholarship appeared to be tinged also with a barely suppressed indignation at what he considered the conservatism of his province's leaders in failing to develop innovative legislation and to protect provincial and regional interests at the federal level. He so stressed, for example, the "omnipresent caution" of Premier Murray's long regime (1896–1923) that the province's participation in reforms of North America's "progressive era" — including its pioneering role in technical education — went quite unnoticed.[31] His claim that "Nova Scotian members of Parliament have followed a thoroughly conservative course, never resorting to the radical procedure of threatening to break up a government or even deviating from the party line to strengthen their bargaining position" has not been sustained by subsequent investigation.[32] Nevertheless, his general picture of overriding political conservatism has gone unquestioned by Canadian historians, for it fitted perfectly the ultraconservative stereotype already firmly established for the region.

Logically deducible from the frontier thesis, the popular stereotype had received a strong boost from the Prairie's disappointment at the Maritime's rejection of their leadership in the Progressive movement. Refusing to admit that Maritime interests differed in any way from their own, Prairie Progressives ascribed their failure in the region to one factor — the innate conservatism and traditional partisanship of the people.[33] Residents of the Central Canadian metropolises were also happy to attribute the destruction of the Maritime economy to the generally unprogressive nature of the Maritime character — a cause for which they could in no way be held responsible. According to R.L. Calder, a Montreal barrister, instead of trying to help themselves, Maritimers preferred "to sit on the country store steps...chew apples and talk politics." Or, as Harold Cunningham put it in an article in *Maclean's Magazine*, the Maritime Provinces were like a housewife who having married for money which failed to materialize "neglected her housework, went down to the seashore...watched the ships go by and pouted."[34]

While it is not surprising in view of the paucity of research, that contemporary stereotypes should provide historians with explanations for Maritime behaviour, it is ironic that one of those who relied on the stereotype was W. L. Morton, who had stressed distinct regional perspectives in his 1946 critique of the Laurentian school of Canadian historians. In 1950 Morton himself gave an effective affirmation of the Prairie regional perspective in his *Progressive Party in Canada* (Toronto, 1950). But in this and in his later works he appeared to draw his interpretations of Maritime behaviour from the Winnipeg *Free Press*. Having established the Progressive Party as the product of a unique economic base — the "political expression of the monolithic wheat economy" — he then explained its failure in the east by a wholly gratuitous invocation of Maritime conservatism.[35] His oft-cited article, "The Bias of Prairie Politics," minimized the effectiveness of separate political movements by exaggerating Maritime gains from working within the traditional party framework — an exaggeration which was a standard ploy by the Prairie press and politicians in demanding more for their region.[36] The shaky foundations of Morton's generalizations about the modern Maritimes are most clearly revealed, however, in a highly misleading statement in the *Kingdom of Canada*, where he informs the reader that in the 1920s "Maritimers refrained from protest or talk of secession as in the past. They generally put their faith in the Liberal party and followed the veteran Fielding and the young J. L. Ralston in seeking relief by pressure on that party. In 1926 they were rewarded by the appointment of a royal commission on Maritime claims."[37] This, of course, was the period of the Maritime Rights Movement, the secession resolution of H.W. Corning, and the overwhelming Conservative victories in the region in three provincial and two federal elections.

Similar distortions can be found in other monographic literature. In 1950 Catherine Cleverdon's *Woman Suffrage Movement in Canada* provided a more balanced regional study of a nation-wide movement. Each of the traditional regions received a separate chapter. But despite the regional approach, the traditional myth of the frontier and the Maritime stereotype continued to dominate. The overriding thesis was apparent in the chapter subheadings. Ontario was the "Pioneer" which "bore the brunt of pioneering for women's rights." Then the Prairies, which represented "Democracy's 'Grass Roots'," took the lead in giving full political privileges to women, an action "typical of western progressiveness." The Maritimes, "Stronghold of Conservatism," afflicted by a "weight of indifference" and an "atmosphere of conservatism" brought up the rear, at least for English Canada.[38] Cleverdon's Maritime chapter is a classic example of begging the question and using emotive language to support a weak thesis. The suffrage movement in Canada, as Cleverdon portrays it, was a narrow middle-class crusade involving no more than a tiny minority of women in each province. This fact is mentioned as a neutral piece of information in the chapters on each of the other regions, but in the Maritimes the non-involvement of the majority of women becomes a critical factor in demonstrating regional conservatism. In her discussions of New Brunswick and Nova Scotia women, Cleverdon manages to use the words "indifference" or "indifferent" nine times, "conservative" or "conservatism" eight times, and adds, perhaps for stylistic variation, the terms "disinterest," "apathy," "hostility," "contempt," and "ultraconservative."

What evidence is there to justify the thesis of a greater Maritime conservatism in women's rights? For New Brunswick and Nova Scotia before 1912 there seems to be none at all. Indeed, Maritime women appear to have led the agitation for admission to universities. In 1846 a pamphlet by a Halifax lady scathingly asked: "Who gave you men the right to establish Colleges and Universities, at which to educate your sons, in all the substantial sciences . . . while woman, hedged about on every hand by the guardianship of a governess, is taught . . . the whole science of composing and scrawling billet-doux after the most approved method. . . ?"[39] A later pamphlet berated Joseph Howe for his failure to take up the cause and in 1859 Mount Allison University admitted its first women students to a degree program. Most other Maritime universities soon followed. Cleverdon portrayed E.H. Stowe of Toronto as the heroic pioneer of the Canadian feminist movement, citing particularly her influence in securing the admission of women to the University of Toronto in 1886. This "triumph" came eleven years after Mount Allison had granted the first Bachelor of Science degree awarded to a woman in the British Empire.[40] For Halifax, at least, the suffrage movement of the 1880s and 1890s marked the culmination of nearly half a century of vigorous debate on woman's place in society.[41] And for those two decades the agitation in the two larger Maritime provinces followed a pattern similar to that of the other provinces—a pattern characterized by a plethora of bills, supported by a comparable number of petitions and meeting an identical lack of success.

Defeated in every province by the end of the 1890s, the movement entered what Cleverdon called a "breathing period" from which it would not emerge until 1912. The tardiness by two of three years of Nova Scotia and New Brunswick women in actually securing the vote hardly justifies the image of an all-pervasive indifference or hostility to the feminist movement arising from an innate regional conservatism.

Morton and Cleverdon were but the first of many historians to invoke the stereotype as the explanation of supposedly deviant behaviour by Maritimers. Sometimes the evolution of the stereotype involved a co-operative effort by several historians. This seems to be the case in the field of labour history. A multi-volume series on Social Credit included D.C. Masters' study of the Winnipeg General Strike which suggested a greater militancy and radicalism among labour in western Canada. S.D. Clark's "Foreword" took the process a step further by setting the One Big Union in "the tradition of American frontier radicalism."[42] With the west more radical than Ontario all that was needed was a conservative Maritimes to round out the familiar frontier model. In his survey of labour unrest in Canada, S.M. Jamieson initially shied away from the western myth by stressing the importance of the industries involved rather than the regions in which they were located. But when he came to the Maritimes he reverted to the traditional pattern. Since there was no research to indicate radical labour activity in the Maritimes outside of the coal-mining areas, he readily concluded that there was none. Maritime labour was "exceedingly conservative in political and other orientations,"[43] Certainly if he knew anything about Amherst's version of the One Big Union or the T.L.C.'s expulsion of the Nova Scotia Federation of Labour in the reaction against industrial unionism, he made no mention of them.[44] British Columbia's Martin Robin took the final step and excluded even the coal miners on the assumption that nothing radical of a political nature involving labour had ever developed in the conservative Maritimes. Thus his *Radical Politics and Canadian Labour* omitted all mention of the protracted struggles between "radicals" and "progressives" for control of District 26 of the United Mine Workers of America, the largest geographically cohesive block of organized labour in the country. In 1922 the radicals endorsed a program that included the statement that "we proclaim openly to all the world that we are out for the complete overthrow of the capitalist system and capitalist state, peaceable if we may, forceable if we must" and elected their slate of candidates to the executive by majorities of approximately four to one.[45] That the radicals did not succeed in their goal of linking up with the Red International and ultimately succumbed to a concerted effort of repression from the U.M.W. International, the British Empire Steel Corporation, and the local government does not erase the significance of their victory. Labour in the Maritimes did not achieve a revolution, or even come close, but then where in North America did they do so?

Accumulated ignorance also contributed to the stereotype of religious conservatism in the Maritimes. First, the author of a University of Toronto M.A. thesis on the social gospel in the Methodist church suggested, without any reference to Maritime sources, that the social gospel had little impact on the church there. Stewart Crysdale and E.A. Christie noted the hostile response by the Halifax

Presbyterian *Witness* to labour's tactics in the Winnipeg General Strike. Apparently guided by such comments, the western myth, and the overriding stereotype of Maritime conservatism, Richard Allen rashly concluded that the Maritimes was "a part of the nation where the social gospel had made virtually no impact whatsoever."[46] Not only was this conclusion inconsistent with Allen's own thesis that the movement in Canada was a product of broad intellectual currents, but it ignored the fact that all of the major Protestant denominations in the Maritimes formally endorsed social gospel principles and that clergymen from the Maritimes were active in the movement at the national level.[47]

Practical considerations, closely related to the theoretical, also inhibited the development of modern Maritime historiography. By their judgments and interests historians influenced what archivists collected, and the availability of source material in turn influenced historians' interests and the direction of their research. Since historians were primarily concerned with the early Maritimes, this was the period for which papers were collected, catalogued and even published by the Public Archives of Nova Scotia, the New Brunswick Museum and the Public Archives of Canada. Materials of a later period languished in private attics or government offices, forgotten or destroyed as fate might decree. In the late 1960s when this author sought the proceedings of the 1926 federal royal commission on Maritime claims, the archivists at the Public Archives of Nova Scotia and Public Archives of Canada had no idea where they were located. The former turned up a copy a few years later; the latter, according to a recent note in the *Canadian Historical Review*, located a set last year.[48] The attitudes of historians found echo even in the archival finding aids. One such aid on the R.B. Hanson papers at the PAC informed the reader that only papers of national significance were microfilmed; Hanson's legal papers and Maritime correspondence had been returned uncopied! It was particularly ironic that when two successive Nova Scotia archivists finally turned to a post-Confederation topic, a biography of W.S. Fielding, it should be the cause of blocking rather than facilitating the research of others; the Fielding papers, one of that archives' most important political collections, remained closed until the biography was completed. Thus, it is understandable that a historian undertaking the study of a national movement should gratefully seize upon the stereotype rather than attempt the difficult, expensive and probably frustrating task of trying to locate the materials necessary to develop a genuine appreciation of the region.

It is not the purpose of this paper to develop a new myth of a dynamic and progressive Maritimes. What the paper is trying to show is that we really know very little about the Maritimes in the post-Confederation period. Much of the so-called "knowledge" we do have is highly suspect, having in many cases been deduced from the frontier myth supported by contemporary attitudes, or a repetition of the stereotype seized upon as a convenience by the researcher, who boggled at the task of having to open a neglected field as only a small part of a major study. With repetition in so many books on so many topics, the stereotype has become an accepted historical "fact." It should not be necessary to point out the danger of dealing in stereotypes, be they regional, racial or national. It is not that the stereotype is entirely false, although, on occasion, that may be the case. The danger lies in an acceptance of a point of view in which fact and fiction are jumbled together without critical analysis. The term "conservative" is particularly unfortunate since it is a comparative term which has little meaning unless the point of comparison is clearly indicated. In many cases "conservative" was used by Maritimers themselves to compare the Maritimes, less to some other region, than to their own ideal of what their region should be. In this sense, the term becomes a statement of social criticism. That appears to be the way it was used in the various comments of Maritimers employed as evidence by Cleverdon. One suspects that there was also an element of social criticism in Beck's ringing indictment of Nova Scotia's leaders for their excessive caution in domestic legislation and their failure to protect regional interests at the federal level.

Another danger of the stereotype, towards which historians in particular should be alert, is its static image which does not allow for chronological variation. Perhaps there were periods in the Maritimes' history when a careful and specific comparison with other regions would show them to be more conservative in certain respects. By the end of the 1930s, for example, the Maritimes had endured two decades of depression — one more than the rest of the country. Successive attempts at political and social protest had failed.[49] Their people had reason to be pragmatic, cautious, and sceptical — especially of the ready solutions to their problems offered by outsiders. Thus it is perhaps not surprising that some Maritimers who lived through this period have been quick to brand people of their region as conservative and have found it difficult to imagine the optimism of an earlier age. Perhaps too it explains the comments of some visitors to the region in this period. Although here one has to be careful that "conservative" does not merely mean "different" — something outsiders may in their arrogance not fully understand.

The criticism given above is directed at the "bad old days" of Canadian historiography. Canadian graduate studies are no longer under the control of a few "great" men in one or two central Canadian universities and no single journal can now pose as the arbiter of what constitutes "national" significance in historical writing. In the 1960s student militancy and preoccupation with "relevance" and the universities' concern for numbers swept many cobwebs out of the system, making universities more responsive to student demands regarding curriculum. This has contributed to expanding enrolments in Canadian courses, which tend to be offered earlier in the students' program and to focus more intensively on the modern period. Student interest has thus reinforced a focus on "limited identities."[50] In the Maritimes, students reflect the continued desire by Maritimers to understand the society with which they most closely relate — a desire also suggested by the success of popular history on the region.[51] During the expansion of Maritime universities in the late 1960s and early 1970s, almost all hired regional specialists, nearly half of whom were working on the modern period. Archives have proliferated and benefitted from the competition. A regionalized national museum lent encouragement to work in the modern period. Both the articles and the review articles of a revived *Acadiensis* reflect a wide variety of approaches by regional scholars — approaches and ideas drawn from a broad international community.

But although the outlook of modern Maritime studies is promising, the effects of the long period of neglect and stereotyping will continue to be felt for years to come. Many scholars working both within and outside the region now ignore the old stereotypes, basing their analysis on a rigorous assessment of evidence. But analyzing the Maritimes is still no easy task, especially for those for whom that complex region is not a primary focus. It is still much easier to make a token reference to the stereotype, toss in a few anecdotes about quaint Maritime customs, and then shift the discussion back to the "important" regions. More serious, however, than such simple failings of human nature is the extent to which the stereotype of Maritime conservatism is embedded in the classics of Canadian historical literature. How can the student be expected to read these without unconsciously absorbing the false picture of the Maritimes which they tend to convey? Obviously he or she cannot. Thus it becomes the duty of authors and teachers of Canadian history to force a critical assessment of the Maritime stereotype wherever it may be encountered.

Notes

1. Naomi Griffiths, "The Acadian Deportation: A Study in Historiography and Nationalism" (M.A. thesis, University of New Brunswick, 1957), 3.

2. Carl Berger, *The Writing of Canadian History: Aspects of English-Canadian Historical Writing, 1900-1970* (Toronto, 1976), 17. See also J. M. S. Careless, "Frontierism, Metropolitanism, and Canadian History", *Canadian Historical Review* (hereafter *CHR*) XXXV (1954): 1-21.

3. In Chester Martin, *Foundations of Canadian Nationhood* (Toronto, 1955), the Maritimes receive no mention in the last 117 pages except for the usual brief note on the entry of Prince Edward Island into Confederation.

4. Chester Martin, *The Natural Resources Question: The Historical Basis of Provincial Claims* (Winnipeg, 1920); C.C. Lingard, *Territorial Government in Canada: The Autonomy Question in the Old North-West Territories* (Toronto, 1949); L. H.Thomas, *The Struggle for Responsible Government in the North-West Territories* (Toronto, 1959).

5. M.L. Hansen and J.B. Brebner, *The Mingling of the Canadian and American Peoples* (New Haven and Toronto, 1969); L.B. Shippee, *Canadian-American Relations, 1848-1874* (Toronto and New Haven, 1939); C. Tansill, *Canadian-American Relations 1875-1911* (Toronto and New Haven, 1939).

6. See A.R.M. Lower's *Settlement and the Forest Frontier in Eastern Canada* (Toronto, 1936); *The North American Assault on the Canadian Forest* (Toronto, 1938); and *Great Britain's Woodyard* (Toronto, 1973). *The North American Assault* did include a sketchy article-length survey of forest industries in the Maritimes after Confederation by S.A. Saunders.

7. H. Innis, *The Cod Fisheries: The History of an International Economy* (New Haven, 1940); V.C. Fowke, *The National Policy and the Wheat Economy* (Toronto, 1957). That such a topic might have been extended to include a Maritime perspective is not as ridiculous as it might appear on the surface. Maritime development, especially that of its major cities, was fundamentally altered by an attempt to participate in both the national policy and the wheat economy, as a soon-to-be completed study by Elizabeth McGahan will show.

8. *The Early Writings of Frederick Jackson Turner*, Essay Index Reprint Series (Freeport, N. Y., 1938), 211.

9. Chester Martin, *Foundations*, 271-5.

10. M.S. Cross, ed., *The Frontier Thesis and the Canadas* (Toronto, 1970), 1.

11. H.N. Smith, *Virgin Land: The American West as Symbol and Myth* (New York, 1950), 293. In *Frederick Jackson Turner, Historian, Scholar, Teacher* (New York, 1973) Turner's biographer, R.A. Billington, stresses the "indelible impressions" made by Turner's boyhood experiences in a frontier community and

outlines the conjunction of circumstances which made his work popular. Not the least of these was the revolt of the Midwest against the cultural domination of New England (pp. 17 and 112). To these factors Richard Hofstadter added the emotional needs of the progressives. "At last the democratic middle-class reformers, especially those rooted in the agrarian traditions of the Middle West, were beginning to find a historical basis for their politics," *The Progressive Historians* (New York, 1968), 86.

12. G.A. Friesen, "Studies in the Development of Western Regional Consciousness" (Ph.D. thesis, University of Toronto, 1973), 110.

13. In 1919, Turner conceded the same point regarding the United States. Quoted in Billington, *Frederick Jackson Turner*, 112.

14. Friesen, "Studies in the Development of Western Regional Consciousness," 109.

15. See for example, Ralph Connor, *The Man From Glengarry* (London, 1901); R.J.C. Stead, *The Cowpuncher* (Toronto, 1918); Zane Grey, *The Light of the Western Stars* (New York, 1913); Zane Grey's more than two dozen novels, many of which explicitly developed the theme of the superiority and reforming influence of the western frontier, were available from T. Eaton catalogues on into the 1950s.

16. F.H. Underhill, The *Image of Confederation* (Toronto, 1964), 63; also cited in Rawlyk, "A New Golden Age," 55.

17. A.R.M. Lower, *Canadians in the Making* (Toronto, 1958), 358. In his autobiography Lower was more explicit. The Maritimes were "the most conservative parts of English Canada . . . . It is in the less restless, less dynamic nature of their society that Maritimers differ from other parts of English Canada," *My First Seventy-Five Years* (Toronto, 1967), 226.

18. P.A. Buckner, "Acadiensis II," *Acadiensis* I (Autumn 1971): 3–9. *The Busy East* later became the *Atlantic Advocate*.

19. R.V. Sharp, "Do You Know Who We Are," *The Busy East of Canada* (December 1919): 9–13.

20. [H.S. Congdon], *The Maritime Provinces Claim Their Rights Under the Act of Confederation: The Right of Maritime Ports to the Transatlantic Trade of Canada* [Dartmouth, 1923]; "Proceedings of the Board of Railway Commissioners for Canada," 1926, vol. 262, Public Archives of Canada (Cornell's findings received their widest distribution in Nova Scotia's published submission to the Duncan Commission); *The Maritime Provinces Since Confederation* (Ottawa, 1927); *The Maritime Provinces in Their Relation to the National Economy of Canada* (Ottawa, 1934 and 1948).

21. Sixteen major federal and provincial royal commissions investigated Maritime problems between 1925 and 1967. Each received up to several dozen submissions.

22. G.E. Wilson, *Robert Baldwin, A Study in the Struggle for Responsible Government* (Toronto, 1933). The comments on Wilson are based largely on recollections of his statements in lectures, which this author attended in 1965, and in his informal discussions with graduate students. Wilson loved his students but had little interest in the region in which they resided, "Never did I think that my life would be spent in the Maritime Provinces," he wrote in his autobiography (G.E. Wilson, *All for Nothing* ([Halifax], 1973), 39–40. "That was a part of the Dominion about which I knew little and cared less. All my life had looked westward. Canada extended to the Pacific and all movement was towards the sunset. The three Atlantic Provinces were a curious enclave that history had made part of the country but which were of little importance. It was the last place a boy raised in Ontario expected to go." That he remained in the region more than half a century he attributed to "lack of initiative" and the freedom from supervision or pressure to publish, which he enjoyed at Dalhousie University. See also G.E. Wilson, "Have I Anything to Declare?" *Transactions of the Royal Society of Canada* LVI, series III (1962): 81–92.

23. R.S. Longley, *Sir Francis Hincks, A Study of Canadian Politics, Railways and Finance in the Nineteenth Century* (Toronto, 1943); D.G.G. Kerr, *Sir Edmund Head, a Scholarly Governor* (Toronto, 1954). Harvey began the project of a biography of W.S. Fielding which was later taken over by his successor at the Public Archives of Nova Scotia, C.B. Ferguson. See Carman Miller's review of the first volume of this work in *Acadiensis* I (Spring 1972): 91–98. Harvey's papers at the PANS provide an extensive, although incomplete, bibliography of his published works.

24. J.C. Webster, *The Distressed Maritimes: A Study of Educational and Cultural Conditions in Canada* (Toronto, Ryerson Essay No. 35, 1926).

25. G.F.G. Stanley, "John Clarence Webster: The Laird of Shediac," *Acadiensis* III (Autumn 1973): 59–60.

26. A.G. Bailey, "Origins of the Study of History at the University of New Brunswick" (manuscript at UNB Department of History), 3 and 23, supplemented by an interview with the author, April 1978. See also Alfred G. Bailey, "Retrospective Thoughts of an Ethno-historian," *Historical Papers* (1977): 15–29.

27. A.G. Bailey, *Culture and Nationality* (Toronto, 1972), chaps. 5, 6 and 7.

28. K.F.C. MacNaughton, *The Development of the Theory and Practice of Education in New Brunswick 1784–1900* (Fredericton, 1947).

29. Dawson was born and attended high school in Bridgewater, Nova Scotia. He studied and later taught at Dalhousie University — one of several university appointments before entering the Department of Political Science at the University of Toronto in 1938. Lunenburg *Progress-Enterprise*, 23 July 1958. (Citation courtesy of Dr. Ron Macdonald, who has investigated Dawson's career for the National Historic Sites and Monuments Board.)

30. See, for example, his treatment of Maritime attitudes on the tariff and the role of the 1926 Duncan Commission. Beck, *The Government of Nova Scotia*, 340–41.

31. According to Beck, under Murray "the Ontario statute book became the utmost limits to which Nova Scotia might hope to aspire in many matters" (Beck, ibid., 201; see also on Murray's caution 161–2, 166–7, 189–90, 202, 203, 204, 209, 257). The Murray government's program of technical vocational education introduced in 1907 was reputed to be the first in Canada, *Canadian Annual Review*, 1907, 620-21 and Halifax *Daily Echo*, 24 May 1913. While Murray's "progressive" reforms were far from radical and were probably dictated more by the interests of capital than labour, in this, as the works of Gabriel Kolko, James Weinstein, and H.V. Nelles suggest, they conformed to a pattern which appears to have had few exceptions on the North American continent. See Gabriel Kolko, *The Triumph of Conservatism* (New York, 1963); James Weinstein, *The Corporate Ideal in the Liberal State, 1900–1918* (Boston, 1968); H.V. Nelles, *The Politics of Development: Forests, Mines and Hydro-Electric Power in Ontario 1849-1914* (Toronto, 1974).

32. Beck, ibid., 170. While it is difficult to prove what threats may or may not have been made in the secrecy of cabinet and caucus, Maritime MPs did "bargain tough" on several occasions. For example, in 1876 they appeared to have blocked the rising surge of protectionist sentiment in the national Liberal Party, and in 1884, after several separate caucuses and Macdonald's complaints of "blackmailing," secured a commitment to a CPR "Short Line." Naturally, as their percentage of seats declined, the number of opportunities for them to exert such pressure declined accordingly. D.C. Thompson, *Alexander Mackenzie: Clear Grit* (Toronto, 1960), 260; M.E. Angus, "The Politics of the Short Line" (M.A. thesis, U.N.B., 1958), 62 and 67; and D.G. Creighton, *John A. Macdonald: The Old Chieftain* (Toronto, 1968), 416.

33. E.R. Forbes, "Never the Twain Did Meet: Prairie-Maritime Relations," *CHR* LIX (1978), 28. The terms "conservative" and "conservatism" as employed by contemporaries and later historians, are negative and critical epithets equivalent to "backward," "cynical," "timid," or "unprogressive"; any resemblance to any political or social philosophy living or dead is probably coincidental.

34. Quebec *Telegraph*, 12 October 1926; *Maclean's Magazine*, 15 October 1926.

35. W.L. Morton, "Clio in Canada: The Interpretation of Canadian History" in *Approaches to Canadian History*, edited by Carl Berger (Toronto, 1967).

36. W.L. Morton, "The Bias of Prairie Politics" in *Historical Essays on the Prairie Provinces*, edited by Donald Swainson (reprinted Toronto, 1970), 296.

37. W.L. Morton, *The Kingdom of Canada* (Toronto, 1963), 445.

38. C.L. Cleverdon, *The Woman Suffrage Movement in Canada* (reprinted Toronto, 1974). See especially 24, 44, 49 and chap. 6. In his introduction, Professor Ramsay Cook did not help to correct the stereotype when he disenfranchised the women of New Brunswick and Nova Scotia until the "early 1920s" and then sought new reasons to account for their conservatism. Ibid., xv.

39. *Essays on the Future Destiny of Nova Scotia, Improvement of Female Education and on Peace* (Halifax, 1846). A subsequent essay ascribed to "An Anonymous Lady" had written immediately thereunder with a quill pen the inscription "by an insane female." Unfortunately this pamphlet, which this author read in the open stacks of the Dalhousie University Library in 1965, can no longer be located.

40. R.S. Harris, *A History of Higher Education in Canada, 1663–1960* (Toronto, 1976), 11; V.J. Strong-Boag, *The Parliament of Women: The National Council of Women of Canada, 1893–1929* (Ottawa, 1976), 12-13.

41. Robert Sedgewick, *The Proper Sphere and Influence of Women in Christian Society* (Halifax, 1856); John Munro, *The Place and Work of Women in the Church* (Halifax, 1877); J.S. David, *A Reply to "The Place and Work of Women in the Church"* (Halifax, n.d.); *Debates and Proceedings of the House of Assembly of Nova Scotia, 1886*, 506.

42. D.C. Masters, *The Winnipeg General Strike* (Toronto, 1950), viii.

43. S.M. Jamieson, *Times of Trouble: Labour Unrest and Industrial Conflict in Canada, 1900-66* (Ottawa, 1968), 25 and 100.

44. Nolan Reilly, "The Origins of the Amherst General Strike, 1890-1919" (paper presented to the annual meeting of the Canadian Historical Association, 1977).

45. Martin Robin, *Radical Politics and Canadian Labour* (Kingston, 1968); *The Workers' Weekly* (Stellarton), 30 June and 25 August 1922.

46. M.V. Royce, "The Contribution of the Methodist Church to Social Welfare in Canada" (M.A. thesis, University of Toronto, 1940), 238; E.A. Christie, "The Presbyterian Church in Canada and its Official Attitude Towards Public Affairs and Social Problems" (M.A. thesis, University of Toronto, 1955); Stewart Crysdale, *The Industrial Struggle and the Protestant Ethic in Canada* (Toronto, 1961), 83.

47. Richard Allen, *The Social Passion: Religion and Social Reform in Canada 1914-28*, 110; see my extended review of the above in *Acadiensis* II (Autumn 1972): 94–99, and E.R. Forbes, "Prohibition and the Social Gospel in Nova Scotia," *Acadiensis* I (Autumn 1971): 15–29.

48. *CHR* LVIII (March 1977), 109.

49. E.R. Forbes, *The Maritime Rights Movement: A Study in Canadian Regionalism* (Montreal and London, 1978).

50. J.M.S. Careless' "Limited Identities in Canada," *CHR* L (1969): 1-10 gave a kind of pontifical sanction to the process already underway. See also Michael Cross, "Canadian History" in C.F. Klinck, *The Literary History of Canada* (Toronto and Buffalo, 1976), III: 63–64.

51. Arthur Doyle's *Front Benches and Back Rooms* (Toronto, 1976) sold more than 7,000 copies in its first year of publication.

THE HISTORIOGRAPHY OF NEW FRANCE, 1960–1974: JEAN HAMELIN TO LOUISE DECHÊNE†

SERGE GAGNON

In one of his essays, Professor J.R. Hexter[1] has questioned the validity of applying the sociology of knowledge to the study of historians and their craft. His basic premise is that historians can be judged only by their peers, that the society of historians has an exclusive claim to pass judgment on the strengths and weaknesses of its members. In so arguing, Hexter suggests that the attempt to find relationships between historiography and society as a whole has no particular value or relevance — or at least this appears to be implied by his criticism of the ideas of E.H. Carr. Since I, on the other hand, take a great interest in the impact of society on knowledge and vice versa,[2] my first reaction to Hexter's views was a negative one. Having overcome this initial response, however, I recognized a possible basis for agreement.

History has now acquired the status of a "scientific" activity, the validity of which is comparable to that of any other field of knowledge. It is thus the responsibility of professional historians to determine whether their work represents an accurate analysis and factual account of past societies. In general, such judgments are passed in the book review sections of scholarly journals, or in the evaluations of a jury during a thesis defence. Does the candidate deserve to be a member of the historians' guild? Did she or he successfully apply the methods and tools of her or his science? The fact remains, however, that the historian's decision to study one subject as opposed to another reflects, to some degree, a connection between his or her field of investigation and some aspect of current public thought or opinion.[3] Of course, some inquiries into the past bear little, if any, direct relation to the current ideologies of the historian's own society. The influence of climate on crops is a good example of such a study, but social historians usually put very little emphasis on the apparently neutral aspects of life.

The work of historians, then, is determined, at least to some degree, by their personality and social environment. Nor does this influence necessarily call into question the excellence of their work as a genuine contribution to knowledge. Would one, for example, condemn a sociologist because in studying the characteristics of underdevelopment he or she implicitly or explicitly compared the society under observation to the standards of the industrialized world? In so doing, however, the social scientist passes judgment on the values of Western civilization. To cite a further instance from the field of natural science, it has

†From Serge Gagnon, *Quebec and its Historians: The Twentieth Century* (Montreal: Harvest House Ltd., 1985): 53–80, 181–89. A version of this article originally appeared in the *Journal of Canadian Studies* 13, 1 (Spring 1978): 80–99.

been revealed by psychoanalysis that Jean Rostand's interest in the study of monster frogs was in some way linked with the monsters created by his dramatist father, a possibility which Rostand himself admitted. Would biologists therefore conclude that Rostand is a poor scientist? In effect, then, the sociology of knowledge and the evaluation of research results are distinct but not necessarily opposite dimensions of science.

It is with these considerations in mind that I shall proceed with the first part of this review of recent historical literature on New France. It is not my intention to cover everything that has been published. Good bibliographies are available in the *Canadian Historical Review* and, since 1967, in the *Revue d'histoire de l'Amérique française*. I have chosen, instead, to draw the reader's attention to a number of the major debates or conflicting interpretations in the field. To begin with, I will attempt to demonstrate the close connection between debates among historians and the evolution of French Canada in recent years. Secondly, I will examine a new variety of historiography, characterized by the attempt to write a more "scientific" history.

Contemporary Quebec and Its Historians

Since the beginning of the twentieth century, the province of Quebec has experienced cultural changes rooted in demography and economics. The migration of rural French Canadians to the industrial cities led ultimately to a decline in the birth rate, thus threatening their survival as a distinct "national" group. New values gradually replaced old ones. The process of secularization which followed urbanization undermined the once powerful role of the church. In the 1950s, a new group of leaders emerged in Quebec society. The newcomers, many of whom had been educated abroad in the social sciences, began to accept the idea that the future of Quebec was irrevocably bound to the new industrial age, while the traditional elite, composed of or trained by the clergy, never really acknowledged the social impact of industrialization. Because Quebec has been and continues to be economically dominated by outsiders of English cultural background, the new "lower middle class" attempted to explain why French Canadians had not assumed control over the development of the "national" territory. Why, in effect, was there not a significant group of powerful French-Canadian entrepreneurs among Quebec businessmen?[4] The two explanations that have been offered place the blame either on the clergy or on the minority position of French Canada.[5]

Professional historians in Quebec were deeply involved in the debate. Whereas the traditional elite group had seen the conquest of Canada by the British as part of a providential design to save the French Catholics from the evils of the French Revolution, some of the new secular minds began to argue that 1760 had, in the long run, deprived the French of their entrepreneurs in North America. As Richard Colebrook Harris wrote:

> The conquest has always loomed over the literature on the French regime, and the most recent historiographic manifestation of the conquest psychosis is the debate over the role, if any, of a Canadian bourgeoisie. An earlier Quebec looked back to a golden agricultural age. An urbanized Quebec

which has pulled up its rural roots . . . is inclined to see, if it looks back at all, an age when French Canadians controlled the commerce of the lower St. Lawrence.[6]

And, in fact, during the last two decades an increasing number of French Canadian intellectuals have come to view the Conquest as an irreparable disaster. During the same period, another school of thought argued that the British conquerors were by no means responsible for the fact that French Canadians had played such a minor role in their own economic development, a fact which they argued must be attributed to France, or to the French Canadians themselves. New France had never had a group of solid entrepreneurs who might have been capable of maintaining control of the commerce of the colony after the Conquest.[7]

The controversy over the bourgeoisie in New France arose in the fifties, and continued to enliven historical debate throughout the sixties. The conclusion of Jean Hamelin's *Économie et société en Nouvelle-France* of 1960 can be considered the springboard for those who did not believe in the existence of a powerful bourgeoisie during the French regime. In 1965, "La Bourgeoisie canadienne-française et ses fondements historiques" was the theme of a symposium held at Laval University in Quebec.[8] Like Guy Frégault and Michel Brunet, Cameron Nish attempted to disprove Hamelin's thesis. His *Les Bourgeois-Gentilhommes de la Nouvelle-France* (Montreal: Fides, 1968) actually involved much more than the thesis of the existence of a bourgeoisie: Nish pointed out that the notion of the landed aristocracy as a rural community collecting rents was false. The seigneurs in fact lived in towns and many of them had acquired their fortunes in commercial ventures. Nish's seigneurs were thus entrepreneurs rather than nobles disdainful of business. Hence his title, *Les Bourgeois-Gentilhommes*. Nish's argument was supported by the many marriages arranged between members of influential families from both groups in order to acquire still more wealth or prestige and/or the protection of the state in the fur trade. But above all, Nish wanted to prove that Jean Hamelin and Fernand Ouellet[9] had been wrong, and that there had, in fact, been a viable entrepreneurship in the French colony.[10]

Since 1968, Nish's thesis has been challenged many times. His critics contend that Nish has supported his argument for the existence of great entrepreneurs by reference to a few cases of individuals involved in big business. But had there been a social group capable of overthrowing the non-bourgeois values which were dominant in colonial politics? Was capitalism strong enough to overcome the social values of the Old Regime? Did the businessmen of the colony really reject the way of life of the Old Regime aristocracy? Here the support for Nish's thesis was weak. Since he was only interested in establishing the existence of individuals who made profits, he did not examine the values or the world view of his entrepreneurs. It must also be remembered that some of his great merchants ultimately lost their fortunes, hardly an indication of a healthy bourgeoisie. Y. F. Zoltvany's "Some Aspects of the Business Career of Charles Aubert de la Chesnaye (1632-1702)" contained a major attack on Nish's thesis. Zoltvany suggested that Hamelin was probably right in stating that there had been no powerful business community in New France:

The story could have been different had la Chesnaye succeeded in building a large fortune in Canada. For this might have encouraged other important businessmen to invest in the colony and a class of powerful Canadian *entrepreneurs* might then have emerged. La Chesnaye, however, had failed. His debt in 1702 amounted to 408,000 *livres* while his assets consisted of little more than his Quebec house, a few seigneuries, 43,000 *livres* of *rentes* and accounts receivable of which 200,000 *livres* had to be written off as bad debt. Such a discouraging precedent might explain the subsequent reluctance of private enterprise to risk capital in Canada, which, in turn, forced the state to expand its economic role. If this should be the case, la Chesnaye's failure would not merely be that of an individual but, more basically, that of a type of entrepreneurship.[11]

The controversy over the bourgeoisie did not end with Nish and Zoltvany in 1968. In the same year, Denis Vaugeois introduced new evidence on the Conquest period in *Les Juifs et la Nouvelle-France* (Trois-Rivières: Boréal Express, 1968), part of which was devoted to a narrative account of the role of the Jews in the war economy of the 1760s. In 1970, at the annual meeting of the Institut d'histoire de l'Amérique française, many historians were again engaged in the debate.[12] More recently, José Igartua has argued that "patronage relationships between British military officials and British traders . . . deprived the Canadians of an equal chance in the competition for furs" after 1760 in Montreal.[13] It may well be, as Louise Dechêne has pointed out, that the question is nothing but a "superficial argument about poorly defined concepts."[14] In so far as the contribution to knowledge is concerned, Professor Dechêne is probably right. However, the prominence of the issue in historical discussion reflects the importance of current ideologies in contemporary Quebec: why *is* it that the French province is underdeveloped, or developed by outsiders? The nationalist argument assumes that the economic assets of New France were sound and that the British conquest then deprived the French Canadians of their businessmen.[15] The contemporary nationalist school of historians has thus argued against the liberal tradition which, since Parkman, has contended that New France was an authoritarian, hierarchical society. They have attempted to establish the existence of what Rosario Bilodeau has referred to as the "economic and political freedom of the Canadians under the French regime."[16] On the opposite side of the debate, liberal historians such as Fernand Ouellet argued (and in so doing perpetuated a long liberal tradition in English-Canadian historiography) that the existence of monopolies, state control over the economy, and the involvement of military and civil administrators in fur trading were factors which stunted the growth of a national bourgeoisie. Moreover, he contended that those engaged in business were attracted by the noble way of life, and tended to squander their profits on personal luxuries rather than invest their gains in profitable enterprises.[17]

The election of Jean Lesage's Liberal government in 1960 opened a new era in Quebec history, popularly known as the "Quiet Revolution," in which liberalism flourished throughout Quebec society. The intellectuals of the fifties, who had been labelled anti-clericals, atheists, or communists,[18] could now rely on the provincial government, within the limits of its jurisdiction, to protect individual freedom against the power of the Catholic church, which had hitherto controlled social life in Quebec. In fact, the emergence of the welfare state under the Lesage government signified a radically altered status for the church in Quebec.[19] In the field of education, a department of education was established, encroaching directly upon the empire of the church. Similarly, in the realm of health, social welfare, and public services in general, the state took effective control away from the Catholic clergy. The secularization of Quebec, a process that had begun long before the early 1960s, called for political initiatives to promote civil liberties. Laws providing for civil marriage and divorce were enacted. The rights of non-Catholic minorities to have their own schools were recognized, and the state began to acknowledge the pluralistic character of Quebec society. As one might expect, the church did not give up without a fight. But ultimately the supremacy of the state triumphed over the greatly diminished power of the clergy.

The social conflicts resulting from these events put an end to consensus historiography.[20] The battle profoundly influenced the study of the church's role in the past. Whereas the traditional historians had taken pleasure in depicting the French Canadian habitant as obedient to the morality taught by the priests, the new generation of scholars shifted their focus to less docile peasants. The new trend is best exemplified by Robert-Lionel Séguin.

In the fifties, Séguin began to write essays questioning the high degree of "moral hygiene," as Canon Lionel Groulx put it, of the *habitant canadien* in New France. Three of Séguin's works that should be mentioned in this connection are *La Sorcellerie au Canada français du XVIIe au XIXe siècle* (Montreal: Ducharme, 1961), *Les Divertissements en Nouvelle-France au dix-septième siècle* (Ottawa: Musée national du Canada, 1968), and *La Vie libertine en Nouvelle-France au dix-septième siècle* (Montreal: Leméac, 1972). In the first book, Séguin demonstrated that there was superstition and sorcery in New France, whereas previous writers had stated that the colony's Catholicism had been uncontaminated by such unorthodox beliefs and practices. In *Les Divertissements*, the French-Canadian of the seventeenth and eighteenth centuries dared to break the rules of the church by drinking and dancing, despite the warnings of the curé and the bishop. In *La Vie libertine*, the habitant violated the marriage laws of the Catholic church, apparently without remorse.

Originally, *La Vie libertine* was a doctoral dissertation presented at the University of Paris. Although Séguin's thesis obtained for him the distinction *summa cum laude*, one may question the degree to which it really contributed to a better understanding of the society of New France. In general, the book did not add up to much more than a collection of facts. Séguin made no effort to measure the degree of sexual license among the habitants. Moreover, the periodic interjection of value judgments weakened his case. At one moment, the author seemed rather amused that a peasant should make love to his neighbor's wife, while at another he denounced homosexuality or bestiality. It is obvious that Séguin did not pay much attention to the critical tradition of historiography. Nor was the statistical treatment of the facts in the last part of the book of any redeeming value, as in fact it constituted a very poor example of quantitative history.

What, then, is the significance of the book? Its contribution to genuine knowledge is quite slim. However, Séguin's desire to prove that French-Canadian mores in the seventeenth century were different from those propounded by the church and praised by traditional historians puts him squarely in the new secular camp. Such histories are therefore useful for the study of "liberalism" in contemporary Quebec, but because they do not attempt to distinguish "normal" from "marginal" behavior, they do not lead to any deeper understanding of the Old Regime.

Other books have been written expressing similar views. Micheline Dumont-Johnson's *Apôtres ou agitateurs: La France missionnaire en Acadie* (Trois-Rivières: Boréal Express, 1970), belongs in the same category. The apostles so dear to traditional historiography were suddenly accused of political agitation and (to contemporary secular minds) betrayal of their specific role of preserving faith and morality. Like Séguin's work, *Apôtres ou agitateurs* is useful primarily as a reflection of secularization in contemporary Quebec.

Despite the increasingly secular mood of recent years, the area of religious history has continued to attract many historians. For the English-speaking reader, H. H. Walsh's *The Church in the French Era, from Colonization to British Conquest* (Toronto: Ryerson Press, 1966) is a useful recent survey. Dr. Lucien Campeau has undertaken the publication of documents and narratives on the Jesuit missions in New France,[21] although his article about Bishop Laval does not provide much new insight.[22] Pierre Hurtubise is the only historian in a century-old tradition who has attempted to understand the controversial bishop within the context of his times.[23] Of the few doctoral theses on the religious history of New France written during recent years, one by Noel Baillargeon has been published in Canada,[24] while another by Guy Plante was published in Europe.[25] Parts of the two others have been published by Jean Blain and Cornelius Jaenen.[26]

Amerindian studies have traditionally been popular in North America, and thanks to anthropologists such as Bruce Trigger[27] and historians such as André Vachon[28] and Cornelius Jaenen,[29] the tradition has recently been revived. Jaenen has recently published a book consolidating the results of his long-term research in the field.[30]

The liberal mood in historiography is also exemplified by recent studies of the judicial practices of New France, which assume that the forms of punishment in the colony were very cruel.[31] One wonders, however, to what extent such anachronistic assumptions are really valid and whether the historian is in fact justified in making this kind of judgment.

Toward a More Scientific History

In recent years, a new historical school has emerged in Quebec in opposition to positivist traditions and present-minded historiography. As one might expect, the new approach did not originate in Quebec, but was imported, chiefly from France. During the last fifteen years, French historians such as Robert Mandrou, Georges Duby, Pierre Goubert, Fernand Braudel, Ernest Labrousse, Pierre Vilar, Albert Soboul, and others have been visiting professors in many French-Canadian universities. Moreover, some Canadian historians acquired their degrees in Paris, so that the influence of the *Annales* school has played an important part in recent revisionism.

It is unnecessary to describe here the essence of the French approach, which has been ably summarized for the North American audience by Professor Isser Wolock, who refers to it as "the French school of history."[32] In a 1972 issue of the *Journal of Modern History*, John Hexter has given a detailed presentation of "Fernand Braudel and the *Monde Braudellien* . . ." for the American reader. In fact, the following summary does not apply only to the French historians. What is now called the New History in the United States as well as in the United Kingdom has spread throughout the West. What is specific about Quebec is that historians of New France have learned it from the pioneers of the New History: the French.

Let me simply recall here that quantification (the study of social groups through systematic inventories of series of documents such as notarial or judicial records) is used to reconstruct the daily life of both elite groups and the common people. Great events dominated by prominent individuals are no longer the historian's major preoccupation. Investigation of the *longue durée* replaces the old chronicles. Although much attention is devoted to the slow process of structural change, the new historiography is also concerned with more short-term matters like fluctuations in prices, profits, and wages, the indicators of economic conditions (depression, inflation, etc.) or, as the new historians say, with cycles or the *conjoncture*. The ultimate ambition of the new approach is to examine the totality of a society, therefore preventing the historian from making the more or less arbitrary choice of one aspect of it. Hence the classical organization of the French thesis: geography, demography, economy, society, mentality. Although the French historians themselves are modest about their claims to achieve what they call *histoire totale*, they have nonetheless initiated an important movement toward a more scientific study of the past. Before attempting to establish whether the most recent essays on New France conform to these criteria,[33] I should point out that this type of historiography is quite different from what has been called interdisciplinary history.[34] Based as it is on theory derived from the study of contemporary societies, the latter variety of history is prone to all types of anachronisms, and is, to say the least, not always very historical. In fact, it is a rather North American way to practise the New History.

As Jean Blain has remarked, the new economic and social history had not yet taken hold in Quebec in the 1950s.[35] At that time, the canons of critical historiography were either imported from the United States, or were the remnants of an older tradition which would soon cease to be of great interest to the majority of professional historians. Historical works written under the influence of this tradition took the form of descriptions and/or narrative accounts of New France in terms of the actions of great men and great events; the *Annales* school called it *histoire evénémentielle* or *histoire historisante*. Even in the early sixties, this style of historical writing was still very much in evidence in Canada and, indeed, the majority of historical works over the last fifteen years have followed in this tradition. It is by no means my intention to detract from the value and merits of the older generation of historians. In fact, the new variety of history has been made possible by the narrative and institutional history of the colony, and the works of such historians as Gustave Lanctôt, W. J. Eccles, and Marcel Trudel thus remain essential contributions to the knowledge of the past.[36] Their critical general histories are the starting point for more specialized studies. Moreover, Trudel and Eccles have shown in their recent writings that they are full acquainted with the new history.[37]

Others who have attempted this shift of historical method, however, have had less success. In *La Civilisation traditionelle de l'"habitant" aux 17e et 18e siècles* (Montreal: Fides, 1967), Robert-Lionel Séguin tried to make use of some of the new kinds of sources (notarial deeds), but was unable to classify his evidence according to social strata. M. E. Arthur wrote about the book:

> In the first place, the heavy reliance upon notarial documents— agreements, inventories, and so forth—is dictated by the decision to concentrate upon social history. In dealing with these documents, Dr. Séguin sometimes blurs the lines between country and town dwellers on the one hand and between social classes on the other. One is often led to question whether the "habitant" of the title was exclusively the "type terrien bien particulier" [the actual farmer] or any inhabitant of the colony, irrespective of his residence or rank in society. The inclusion of catalogues of goods owned by various seigneurial families and by scarcely typical bourgeois . . . suggests a greater affluence among the *censitaires* and a greater fluidity in social classes than may have existed. Only rarely, as for example in the discussion of the wearing of mourning, is the point made explicit that a custom belonged principally to one class . . . . The feeling of uneasiness increases as lists of luxury goods belonging to seigneurial and bourgeois families are examined. Then appears the conclusion that the *habitants* spent a disproportionate part of their income on wearing apparel.[38]

Cameron Nish gave evidence of a very different problem in *Les Bourgeois-Gentilhommes*. Richard Colebrook Harris was correct in his comments on Nish's misuse of quantitative analysis:

> His method is to amass data in support of a particular proposition, but not to give the data any quantitative measure. It is one thing to show that some merchants behave in a certain way, and quite another to show that the group with such behaviour was a certain percentage of all merchants. . . . In some cases, as when Professor Nish discusses the extent of intermarriage among the elite, his evidence is ample enough to be fairly convincing; in others, as when he compares the commercial vigour of Canada and the English colonies, the evidence is so thin and the many assumptions so tenuous that few readers will be convinced. Whatever the weight of the evidence, almost all of it appears to have been selected to prove a point. . . . The chapter on the seigneurial system is a good example of the basic problem. It is true, as professor Nish points out, that in the 1730s, 1740s and 1750s a substantial group, most of whom had interests in commerce, government, or the military, received seigneuries; but it is equally true that almost all of these seigneuries were entirely unsettled and, even at the end of the French regime, furnished no revenue for their seigneurs. Professor Nish demonstrates that some seigneurs held more than a single seigneurie; true enough, but many more held only a fraction of one. Some seigneurs undoubtedly lived in the towns, and Professor Nish has listed some forty who lived there in 1744. At this date there were over two hundred rural

seigneuries. Is one, therefore, to conclude that 80 percent of the seigneurs did not live in towns, or that the list is seriously wanting? Some seigneurs did sell their seigneuries, but in relation to the number of seigneuries, sales were strikingly few and far between. In short, a few examples do not make a case.[39]

These remarks by Harris (who himself made such successful use of statistical analysis in his masterly work, *The Seigneurial System in Early Canada: A Geographical Study*),[40] could apply to many other recent essays. Not only do some historians misuse the tools, but many of them fall into what the American sociologist Sorokin has called "quantophreny." In fact, the French school of historians has had a great many poor imitators on this side of the Atlantic. The many volumes and booklets published by Roland Lamontagne since 1962 are a most striking example of yet another such failure. Nish and Séguin were not disciples of the French school, but Lamontagne has laid claim to this prestigious title, his supposed master being none other than Fernand Braudel.[41] The work of this self-proclaimed disciple of Braudel has created confusion and doubt about the real possibilities of the new history, to the extent that some historians trained in the traditional pattern have, not surprisingly, questioned its validity altogether.[42]

Économie et société en Nouvelle-france, published in 1960 by Jean Hamelin, was the first essay written by a historian[43] using the French methodology. The conclusion of the book relates to the ideological controversy on contemporary Quebec, but the study as a whole raised relevant questions about the past. The inaccuracy of some of Hamelin's conclusions in the essay was largely a result of the type of evidence on which the study was based.

Reviewers accustomed to the old ways of writing history failed to grasp the importance of Hamelin's revisionism. Having studied at the École pratique des hautes études in Paris, the author was a foreigner among his Canadian peers. Of the latter, William J. Eccles praised the new approach as a means of producing "a clear picture of Canadian society, in any period,"[44] but on the whole, the most favorable and sound reviews were not published by historians.[45]

As a result of Hamelin's study, there was a perceptible shift of focus among professional historians. One of them had learned to work through hypotheses rather than being "blindly" guided by primary sources. Hamelin's survey dealt mainly with *structures*; however, one chapter was devoted to *conjoncture* (the other favorite concept of the new historians)[46] through an analysis of series of wheat prices. The purpose of the book was to explain the failure of economic development in New France. Statistical information combined with analysis of administrators' correspondence showed that a lack of currency, capital, and skilled manpower[47] had precluded a "take-off" in the colonial economy. The methods Hamelin used to estimate the quality of manpower were particularly novel. Of course some of Hamelin's generalizations were weak but, nevertheless, the scientific spirit had invaded the field of historical studies. Systematic explanation had replaced implicit or explicit value judgments. The generous use of evaluative terms would no longer suffice as the stuff of history.

During the last twenty years, the economy and society of New France have been subjects of increasing interest to many historians. André Vachon's *Histoire du notariat canadien, 1621-1960* (Quebec: PUL, 1962) combined the traditional with the new approach, while a number of short essays by younger historians were more obviously products of the new history. André Lachance's article, "Le Bureau des pauvres de Montréal, 1698-1699: Contribution à l'étude de la société montréalaise de la fin du XVIIe siècle," *Histoire sociale/Social History* (Nov. 1969): 99-110, is a good example. In the field of social history, the most valuable example of the new historical mode was *L'Hôpital général de Québec, 1692-1764* (Montreal: Fides, 1971) by Micheline D'Allaire. However, neither Lachance nor D'Allaire went beyond the level of institutional history and they made virtually no attempt to refer to the social structure of the colony. Their studies can be considered to offer only a partial view of what is, in the full sense, social history. There remains much to be done in the reconstruction of social strata before institutional history can be placed in its proper social context.[48]

A number of studies in the history of commerce and industry are worth mentioning in this connection. J.F. Bosher,[49] James Pritchard,[50] and Jacques Mathieu[51] have already offered glimpses of the results of their long-term research and of their prospective publications.

The social history of political life has been initiated by Jean-Claude Dubé's very thorough biography: *Claude-Thomas Dupuy, intendant de la Nouvelle-France, 1678–1738* (Montreal: Fides, 1969). Using the methodological principles formulated by French historian Roland Mousnier, Dubé is currently working on a history of the office of the intendant during the entire colonial period.[52] His biography of Claude-Thomas Dupuy is a good example of the way in which the new economic and social history can transform the biographical approach to history. Dupuy is examined in the context of the French *intendance* and, through his connections in society, is established as representative of a particular social "type" in the colony. By comparison to Dubé's biographical approach, the limitations of the heroes of Thérèse Prince-Falmagne,[53] Antoine Champagne,[54] and Maurice Filion[55] are particularly apparent, although Champagne's work is in any case only partly a classical biography and in equal part panegyric. Filion, on the other hand, shows signs of adapting to the new history. In fact, the new trend is now so well established that recent works following the traditional pattern are occasionally reviewed in terms of the canons of the new historical science.[56]

Louise Dechêne of McGill University is the only Canadian historian who has fully applied the best of French methodology. In 1971, she challenged traditional interpretations of the seigneurial regime in a short essay, "L'Évolution du régime seigneurial au Canada; Le Cas de Montréal aux XVIIe et XVIIIe siècles."[57] The notion that the seigneurs were agents and entrepreneurs of settlement was claimed to be proven false. So too was the "frontier thesis" as an explanation of the distinctive features of the institutions in New France; in fact, the Sulpicians, seigneurs of the Island of Montreal, managed their fief in the traditional French manner. Nor did the presumed friendship between seigneurs and censitaires correspond to the facts. As for the notion that the intendant was an arbitrator whose role was to protect the censitaires, Louise Dechêne showed that, in fact, the intendant was consistently on the side of the seigneurs. The generous concessions of land allotted during the founding of the colony were quietly replaced by contracts in which obligations and constraints became increasingly burdensome. During the eighteenth century, contracts tended to be two or three pages long, whereas intitially one page had sufficed. And the habitant reacted against these increasing restrictions, belying the traditional image of the peasant as an independent, prosperous, and happy farmer. As Dechêne remarked, "The habitants complained about levies being too onerous; they accused the seminary of enriching itself at their expense, and considered the burning of their mills providential."[58]

In 1973, Dechêne's essay, "La croissance de Montréal au XVIIIe siècle"[59] offered a few hints about her forthcoming book. Some elements of the article should be noted here. Prior to the publication of this essay, historians had generally believed that the colony was characterized by rapid urban growth, basing this assumption on the intendants' denunciation of poverty and idleness in urban areas. However, through analysis of census records, Dechêne demonstrated that "ruralization" rather than urbanization characterized the evolution of the colony. The tiny city of Montreal, for example, was a source of recruits for land settlement.

This short essay, which dealt with demography, occupations, economy, and way of life, was but a small-scale sample of Louise Dechêne's subsequent book, *Habitants et marchands de Montréal au XVIIe siècle* (Paris and Montreal: Plon, 1974), based on her doctoral dissertation defended at the University of Paris. In the latter work, Dechêne adopted the traditional organization of French theses devoted to *l'histoire totale*: geography, demography, economy, society, world view, and *mentalité* (i.e., the study of beliefs and cultural values as revealed by the organization of families, etc.). Following the French methodology, and focussing principally on the rich but not easily elicited evidence offered by notarial documents, she chose to study a small area, the island of Montreal, over an extended period of time. She compiled and computed her evidence with an unusual degree of precision and was then able to compare the behavior of the different social groups in that part of the colony with that of their counterparts in France. For the most part, she was successful in reconstructing the process by which the social structures of France were transplanted and/or adapted in Montreal, and, in some cases, throughout the whole St. Lawrence valley. She pointed out in her introduction that: "Step by step, we must follow the evolution of a society that has left traces other than the impressions of a handful of administrators, memoir-writers who paid little attention to everyday life, or visitors in search of the picturesque — impressions which are repeated over and over again, arranged to suit the purposes of whomever is writing" (p. 7).

This program was indeed an ambitious one, to say nothing of its implied condemnation of the work of most of her predecessors! However, she was correct to the extent that previous writers were not, in fact, much concerned with observing the structural *process*. When they did attempt to describe patterns of daily life, they tended to take snapshots based chiefly on impressionistic views, or on the comments of politicians, clerics, or "tourists."[60] As the psychology of testimony and the sociology of knowledge tell us, diaries rarely give accurate views about behavior, influenced as they are by the values, prejudices, and limitations of their authors (p. 299). As for the correspondence of governors, intendants, and the like, it, too, tends to reflect the preoccupations, fears, and aspirations of those of their own status, rather than the ordinary behavior of different social groups (see, for example, her comments on Jean Talon, the "Great Intendant," p. 302, n. 8). In short, therefore, while all these testimonies are useful in the study of the opinions and thought processes of a minority in the top social strata, they are frequently of no value for understanding the life of the common people. Moreover, because historians have, until recently, observed the French colony through the eyes of its rulers, they tend either to endorse or condemn the prejudices of those rulers. Liberal historians thus identify with such writers as the famous Baron de Lahontan, while the conservatives are inclined to prefer the impressions of missionaries and the like. Prior to the publication of *Habitants et marchands*, these types of primary sources were the substance from which historical portraits of the habitant, the trader, the seigneur, and so forth had been drawn. Little wonder that such histories have repeated the same old clichés about New France from generation to generation throughout the last century of historiography.

Dechêne's book divided the history of the settlement of New France into three major elements: (1) the motives of emigrants for leaving France; (2) the geographic and social origins of the settlers; (3) the structure of the colonial population, and the pattern of its growth. Most of the settlers in New France had suffered hardships, chiefly economic ones, prior to emigrating from France. However, there was no clear indication that they were driven from France by an actual economic crisis, as Robert Mandrou suggested in 1959.[61] The small number of immigrants (10,000 for the whole colony up to 1760), was not surprising as, at the time, France was a highly "populationist" country.

Louise Dechêne devoted particular attention to those settlers referred to as *engagés* (pp. 50–77). No idleness was permitted these quasi-slaves, she emphasized. After studying their working and living conditions, she rejected "the idyllic image of old and new *engagés* working side by side, eating at the same table, with no barrier to the new arrival being integrated into a family" (p. 62). Through an examination of judicial records, she showed that severe punishment threatened those (they were too poor to pay fines) who failed to fulfil the duties prescribed by their contracts (pp. 69ff.).

Little was said about female immigration. Dechêne suggested, however, that on the whole, woman settlers were far from the "call girls" Lahontan depicted. On the other hand, she judiciously noted that there were two sorts of women immigrants: those destined for marriage to the common settlers, and those intended for the military officers. "There were two parallel immigrations, of which contemporaries were well aware" (p. 80).

Dechêne's study of the military establishment followed the approach suggested by W.J. Eccles.[62] She focussed particular attention on the proletarian status of soldiers working for officers as *engagés*, under the benevolent eye of the colonial authorities (pp. 85–88). The chapter on immigration ended with an analysis of the distribution of population according to geographic origin and rate of illiteracy (pp. 95ff.). In a chapter on the structure of the population, Dechêne dealt with various aspects of historical demography. But here, as in the case of many other realms of social life in that pre-statistical era, quantitative data had proven difficult to collect. Some of her more interesting findings in this area should, however, be mentioned. Administrators (and therefore historians relying on the records of this group) repeatedly observed that the natural growth of the population was inhibited by the substantial number of *coureurs de bois*. By studying the seasonal birthrate in the colony, however, Louise Dechêne disproved this notion:

> The fact that children were conceived between April and August refutes the widely held view that the habitants abandoned their land to be *coureurs de bois*. The journey west took place mainly between May and August, and it is clear that the large majority of married men were co-habiting with their wives [p. 114].

In fact, the figure given on page 113 of Dechêne's book indicates that the level of fecundity tended to be higher or at least as high during the very months when the men were supposedly in the wilderness.

According to some superficial observers cited by Dechêne, such as the intendant Desmeules and Marie de l'Incarnation (p. 115), high death rates did not appear to have been a problem characteristic of New France. Even demographers have underestimated the situation by failing to take into account the large number of deaths which were not recorded at the time.[63] Despite the problem of collecting adequate data, Dechêne argued, through an ingenious process of calculation, that one quarter of the newborn died before their first birthday.

The chapters devoted to commerce began with a study of the elements of the market economy as exemplified in the colony. Many of the assumptions made by Jean Hamelin in *Économie et société en Nouvelle-France* were shown here to be rather weak or clearly obsolete. For example, Dechêne showed that, contrary to Hamelin's point of view, the currency in New France was not overvalued in order to keep a sufficient supply of money in circulation,[64] but rather to increase the profits of merchants (pp. 131ff.). In another instance, the *Compagnie des Indes occidentales*, concerned with its monopoly position and the duties collected on fur exports, had requested Frontenac's permission to search every household in the colony for hidden beaver pelts. Hamelin (p. 32) had assumed that Frontenac's action in refusing permission for the search implied that peasants were, in fact, hoarding pelts. By examining a significant number of inventories taken after death, Dechêne suggested that this assumption was false. Furthermore, the "courtier governor," as Eccles called Frontenac,[65] wished to "prevent the Company agents . . . from seizing the skins which several merchants, including his own associates, were smuggling to Europe" (p. 135).

One further insight in Dechêne's analysis of commerce in New France related to the level of profits from the fur trade. In reality, as she showed through a careful analysis of net return, profits were not as high as most historians, Hamelin included (*Économie et société*, pp. 51ff.), have calculated, but actually averaged between ten and fifteen percent on invested capital.

In a chapter entitled "Production Relationships" (pp. 171–230), Dechêne analysed the relationships among the groups of participants in the fur-trading economy. Here, too, her emphasis was on social and economic structures. Beginning as a random process, the commercial activity of the colony gradually acquired a structure by the end of the seventeenth century. At that point, the roles were well defined along capitalist lines. Professionalism had become the rule: the *coureur de bois* was replaced by the professional *voyageur*, while merchants, allied with and protected by the *gentilhommes*, had taken control of the whole process of production. The fortunes of the entrepreneurs, as revealed by twenty-one inventories taken after death between 1679 and 1712, consisted of a small amount of currency, between one-half and two-thirds pelts in stock, and various accounts owing, divided into good and bad debts. The *voyageurs* and *engagés* (the white manpower involved in the fur trade) represented only a small minority of the working population of New France (pp. 220ff.) and were often the products of families which had been exclusively involved in the fur trade for generations. They worked hard for a modest earning (pp. 226–39): "It was a hard trade, which did not employ very young men and scarcely provided enough income for early retirement."

According to Dechêne's account, therefore, the traditional portrait of the *coureur de bois* as a social type belonged to fiction. "For the historians of New France, massive participation by the population in this activity is taken for granted, as well as certain characteristic behavior usually associated with it, such as leaving the land, poor farming habits, insubordination, and immorality" (p. 217), and to these traits we can add their supposed tendency to spend money without stint (Hamelin, p. 57). As Pierre Goubert wittily remarked in a review of *Habitants et marchands*, Dechêne's thesis suggested that the historians who wrote about them were perhaps more numerous than the *coureurs de bois* themselves.[66]

In the conclusion of her analysis of commercial activity, Louise Dechêne questioned the validity of the famous "staple" theory as a tool for explaining the development of New France.[67] In fact, the fur trade involved only a small proportion of the colony's labor force, the majority of which was isolated from the sphere of international trade and absorbed in the founding of a largely self-sufficient agricultural society.

Following a study of the seigneurial regime on the island of Montreal, Louise Dechêne carefully examined the habitant on his land. She argued that the accepted portrait of an improvident, careless, and independent peasantry, spending lavishly and improvising farming methods, was a product of romanticism and liberalism, rather than an accurate description of the farm economy.[68] Bringing land into cultivation was a long and arduous task. Once the habitant was ready to sow a part of his lot, he followed the traditional pattern of French agriculture (pp. 303ff.) which he had brought with him from the Old World. The fact that he did not grow large quantities of wheat was not, however, the result of poor agricultural methods. There simply was not a market for a substantial surplus production. Moreover, the superficial observations of the Swedish traveler Pehr Kalm in 1749, and of historians who relied on him, have led to the conclusion that crop rotation was unknown to Canadian peasants. Dechêne attempted to show this assumption to be false by examining a significant number of farm leases (p. 303). Robert-Lionel Séguin, basing his conclusions on the declarations of politicians, created the impression that the number of horses per farm was rather high in the colony.[69] As usual, his somewhat random quantitative documentation failed to give a correct account of the situation, and he took for granted the supposed accuracy of the intendants' observations on the subject. In the specific case of Montreal, Louise Dechêne calculated that, in fact, the number of horses per farm was not particularly high. Indeed in the 1730s, the number of horses per habitant was still below the quota imposed by Raudot in 1709! The supposed "conspicuous consumption" was thus not evidenced by the numbers of livestock, despite the fact that administrators were shocked: "Here are these peasants, mounted like only officers used to be" (p. 319).

Dechêne's study of agricultural productivity (pp. 324–30) was intended to demonstrate that, in the Montreal area, it was comparable to average farm productivity in France. In effect, she aimed to destroy "the stereotyped image . . . of the irresponsible settler, who had only a secondary interest in farming, and who passively accepted the land offered, ruined it through negligence, and abandoned it at the first opportunity to become a *coureur de bois*.[70] Some may indeed have fitted this description, but there were many who were busy taming the countryside, building a family asset, and recreating a more or less familiar way of life, if possible, in the hope that the old habits and work patterns would bring security" (pp. 269ff.).

Going beyond the occupational distribution of the population, Dechêne reconstructed the class structure of society. The seigneurial system, which began merely as a form of organization imposed on the settlement, gave birth to a seigneurial class (the Sulpicians in Montreal) whose increasingly high rents provided an economic foundation for their status and power. Indeed, if there was any "conspicuous consumption" in New France, it was an indulgence of the nobility rather than the habitants as so many historians have thought. The evidence provided by inventories taken after death indicates that the nobility was, in fact, the only group in the colony which indulged in the purchase of luxuries. The records show that the merchants, by contrast, owned no expensive furniture, nor in fact any possessions beyond the requirements of comfort (pp. 390 ff.). It thus appears that, contrary to the view of Cameron Nish, it was necessary to distinguish between bourgeois and *gentilhommes* in New France, in so far as the records of their way of life and their habits of saving and expenditure would indicate.

At the opposite extreme, the peasantry lived in small cabins of 18 by 20 feet, "space necessarily being sacrificed for warmth" (p. 400), and in general, had a very modest standard of living. The habitant's furniture and clothes were scarcely adequate, still less luxurious (pp. 400 ff.). His supposed delusions of grandeur appear to be a figment of the imagination of some historians.[71]

Dechêne's brief examination of craftsmanship (pp. 392-94) referred to some sound research undertaken by Peter Nicholas Moogk.[72] Her conclusions on social mobility suggested that in the Montreal area, such mobility was high, although generally directed *down* the scale of social strata rather than upwards. In this context, she also argued that purchasing land was not a source of social prestige for merchants, as so many historians from both France and Canada have thought; it was, in fact, viewed merely as a business operation (pp. 410 ff.). The last two chapters of *Habitants et marchands* dealt with the family and religion, and here, too, Dechêne offered new insights to whet the historian's appetite. It was unfortunate that the book had no index, as it will undoubtedly serve as a fundamentally important study of New France for many years to come. For Canadian historians, the publication of Dechêne's work was a turning point comparable to what has been called the "Ouelletist revolution," which began with the publication of Fernand Ouellet's masterly *Histoire économique et sociale du Québec — Structures et conjoncture* (Montreal: Fides, 1966). In so far as methodology and new evidence are concerned, *Habitants et marchands* is among the most genuinely original historical works produced in Canada in recent decades. Its overall impact has been to cast serious doubt on the validity of such widely held theories as the "frontier thesis" and the "staples approach."

If I had to summarize the orientation of *Habitants et marchands*, I might suggest that it could be considered a slightly Marxian response to the dominant liberal interpretation in Canadian historical writing. Unlike many North American historians, however, Dechêne does not treat Marxism simply as an ideology, and indeed, her work bears no resemblance to that of Marxist historians who speak the language of politicians. Instead, through careful analysis of a rich body of evidence, she renews the exploration of the relations involved in the process of production, an exploration which distinguished Marx himself as a social scientist.

Dechêne's criticism of liberal historiography can be characterized by a few examples. There was little industrial development in New France, which was primarily an agricultural and commercial colony. While liberal historians held mercantilism and the nature of colonial government responsible for retarding "development," Louise Dechêne pointed out that, in fact, merchants in the colony had established their fortunes in international trade, and thus had little incentive to encourage the growth of domestic industry. Some historians[73] have tried to account for the lack of industrial development in New France by distinguishing between two categories of merchants, the French and the Canadians, and by arguing that competition from the former inhibited the capital accumulation necessary for industrial growth. This nationalist and liberal account does not appear to correspond to what actually occurred in New France or, at least, in Montreal, in the seventeenth century. As Dechêne pointed out, the merchants of the island of Montreal had no such liberal and national consciousness. Most were capitalists whose activities were based on a market that spanned the Atlantic.

Some historians have stressed the importance of state controls on the economy, exercised through the granting of monopolies and trade licences, as well as through the participation of public officials in the fur trade. However, following the recent interpretation of J.-F. Bosher,[74] Dechêne argued that "it is irrelevant to denounce the 'corruption' of this or that official; what is important is a closer examination of the administrative structure of the Old Regime, where private enterprise progressed alongside and merged with the public sector" (p. 174, n. 4). Whereas such state intervention as price controls on bakers, butchers, and the like has been denounced as inconsistent with the liberal principles of a market economy, Dechêne pointed out that consumer protection was an established responsibility of the state under the Old Regime (p. 394).

Similarly, the law of primogeniture did not exist in New France, where the principle of equal portions for all children ruled inheritance. Liberal historiography has condemned such practices, holding them responsible for poor agricultural productivity because of their tendency to promote the fragmentation of farms. Dechêne noted, and implicitly praised, the egalitarian character of such customs. However, she proceeded to show that while every descendant had the right to claim his share, in fact only one member of the family continued to exploit the farm, paying his due to his brothers and sisters (pp. 294-98, and the chapter on the family). The only disadvantage of this practice was that the peasant of each new generation was saddled with a heavy burden of debt for many years of his working life.

Among the many reviews of *Habitants et marchands*, those by Fernand Ouellet and Hubert Charbonneau were particularly articulate.[75] Their criticisms may be summarized, like the book itself, under the headings of population, economy, and society.

Both reviewers argued that the number of *coureurs des bois* in the colony was probably much higher than Louise Dechêne's estimate, and Charbonneau's statistical argument seemed particularly convincing.[76] As for Fernand Ouellet, he contended that notarial deeds were not a useful indicator of the number of *voyageurs* and *engagés*, and his own figures seem to confirm that Dechêne may have underestimated the proportion of the population involved in the fur trade. Ouellet pointed out two other weaknesses in Dechêne's demographic calculations: the fact that the size of the total population remains unknown renders statistics on births, marriages, and deaths virtually meaningless; and the fact that the population was, in any case, a constantly changing and unstable one falsifies her analysis, since the classical demographic methodology she employs is applicable only to stable populations.

In the area of economic life, Ouellet contradicted Dechêne's thesis about the wealth of the habitants. Both historians relied on inventories taken after death to prove or disprove that the *censitaires* possessed currency. Four habitants cited by Ouellet did in fact possess large amounts of currency at the time of their deaths (about 1760). As for agricultural techniques, Ouellet argued that the fact that crop rotation was explicitly stipulated as a condition of farm leases proved that such practices were not, in fact, common.

Ouellet cast doubt on Dechêne's description of social classes in New France. According to him, the bourgeoisie were greatly influenced by aristocratic values and imitated the nobility in the consumption of luxury goods as in many other ways. Nor did he accept Dechêne's description of habitant life:

> This is an almost idyllic picture. . . . This traditional habitant, no worse than elsewhere, experienced an egalitarian way of life . . . and his practices for handing on property breathed generosity. . . . But the author does not bring out this aspect, which contradicts the idea that "time is a leveler in rural society" [p. 485]. Even if society was becoming more and more rural, the rural world in the eighteenth century was increasingly diversified as a result of the commercialization of agriculture. The presence of merchants in rural areas, the increasing number of villages and craftsmen, all these things

figure in a long-term context that created inequalities, even within the peasant group. . . . Rural society tended to stratify, making such egalitarianism a mere figure of speech.

Ouellet also pointed out that, for the colony as a whole and in the *longue durée*, the notion of a rural society based on uniform, small land holdings was entirely false, partly because—and here he agreed with Dechêne—land was not divided through the inheritance process. In the long run, "landed property was not destined to remain in the same hands, was not equally divided between individuals and . . . was subject to movements that created inequality, and that would give priority to grouping property at one moment, while at another deciding to parcel it out."

On the whole, Ouellet's review was harsh, but many of his criticisms were sound, rooted as they often were in his own impressive command of primary sources. But the ideology implicit in his convictions about the backward agricultural methods of the habitants, their way of life, and their relation to commercial activity in New France, placed him squarely in the old liberal tradition of historiography.[77] Therefore, it was not surprising to discover that he himself described writers like Louise Dechêne as the spiritual heirs of the old nationalist agriculturalist ideology. In 1975 he wrote:

> Can one go as far as to say that nationalism has been rooted out of the historian's work? One need not look far to find new and unconscious idealizations. When, for example, in reading some of the recent studies by either amateur or scientific historians, we find an almost uniform picture of the oldtime habitant emerging—independent, no worse than elsewhere, aware of the market, egalitarian, tolerant, free-thinking, and revolutionary —then we know that such writers are not advocating an old-fashioned return to the soil; rather, it reveals the existence among us of petit bourgeois who have adapted to urban living but find the noise and pollution distressing, and who feel a nostalgia for the rural life, expressed through their ideologically biased reconstructions of the past.[78]

Nevertheless, if the history of New France is to be fully re-examined, it is undoubtedly sources like notarial documents[79] that offer the present generation of historians the greatest opportunity to grasp the reality of the daily routine of life among the different social groups, in terms of the value system prevailing at the time. It currently appears that Montreal will be singled out for this kind of systematic inquiry.[80] Before Louise Dechêne, Marcel Trudel had already examined marriage contracts in the Montreal region as a basis for his essay, "The Beginnings of a Society: Montreal 1642–1663."[81] In the same manner that ordinary behavior may be revealed by notarial records, the judicial records of the colony should permit an accurate understanding of crime considered in sociological terms—that is, as the nonconformity to social norms. Such articles as those of Jacques Mathieu (see n. 21) and John A. Dickinson[82] suggest the possibilities of exploration in the area. Beyond the period under study here, two scholars have published one book each in the field: André Lachance, *La Justice criminelle du roi au Canada au XVIIIe siècle* (Quebec: PUL, 1978); John A. Dickinson, *Justice et justiciables, La Procédure civile à la prévôté de Québec, 1667–1759* (Quebec: PUL, 1982). Despite the sharp distinction that I have drawn in this chapter between "scientific" historians and more present-minded ones, the historical profession in Canada is not really divided into such opposite camps. Besides, it must be remembered that classical training in the critical tradition was a prerequisite for what I have identified as the new scientific spirit. If I have drawn the reader's attention to the achievements of the second variety of history, it is because I firmly believe in the future of history as one of the social sciences. I remain conscious, however, that classical scholarship, as applied to the study of prominent figures, will survive alongside enquiries into social groups involving the analysis of large quantities of numerical data.[83] History is not art, nor science, but a combination of both.

The whole debate over the existence of a bourgeoisie in New France is a good example of the hybrid nature of history. The question was originally raised by historians in response to a contemporary controversy concerning the causes of the economic inferiority of the French in Quebec. But if Nish's conclusions, for example, have proven partly false, the reason is not simply the distortions introduced into the process of historical interpretation by current political and intellectual debates. Faulty historical methodologies are equally to blame for dubious conclusions. In the end, books written by historians like Nish or Robert-Lionel Séguin may belong to scientific literature, but they are vulnerable to the distorting influence of contemporary ideologies because of their authors' lack of adequate methodological tools. For historians like Louise Dechêne, on the other hand, a comparison with the Jean Rostand case referred at the beginning of this chapter seems more appropriate. Her analysis of the social structure of the island of Montreal in the seventeenth century is very successful, but her emphasis on the common people and her criticism of political leaders are inspired by a purely twentieth-century fascination with ideas like participatory democracy. Could it be that works like *Habitants et marchands* herald a general embrace of socialism by Quebec intellectuals?

Notes

1. "The Historian and His Society: A Sociological Inquiry — Perhaps," *Doing History* (Bloomington and London: Indiana University Press, 1972), chap. 3.

2. See my book, *Man and His Past: The Nature and Role of Historiography* (Montreal: Harvest House, 1982).

3. As illustrated in the collection of writings edited by Robert Allen Skotheim, *The Historian and the Climate of Opinion* (Addison-Wesley, 1969).

4. For more information, see Norman Taylor, "A Study of French Canadians as Industrial Entrepreneurs" (Ph.D. thesis, Yale University, 1957). Parts of the study have been published: "French Canadians as Industrial Entrepreneurs," *Journal of Political Economy* 68, 2 (Feb. 1960): 37-52; "The Effects of Industrialization: Its Opportunities and Consequences upon French-Canadian Society," *Journal of Economic History* 20, 4 (Dec. 1960): 638-47.

5. See Conrad Langlois, "Cultural Reasons Given for the French-Canadian Lag in Economic Progress," *Culture* 21: 152-70.

6. See Harris's review of Cameron Nish, *Les Bourgeois-Gentilhommes de la Nouvelle-France, 1729–1748* in the *Canadian Historical Review* (hereafter *CHR*) L, 4 (Dec. 1969): 449.

7. This school of thought was led by historians like Marcel Trudel, Jean Hamelin, and Fernand Ouellet, discussed more fully in Serge Gagnon, "Historians and the Quiet Revolution: A Look at the Debate of the Mid-Sixties" in *Quebec and Its Historians: The Twentieth Century* (Montreal: Harvest House, 1985), 5–30. See also my chapter in André Beaulieu, Benoît Bernier, and Jean Hamelin, *Guide d'histoire du Canada* (Quebec: PUL, 1969), 33–52.

8. André Garon, José Igartua, and Jacques Mathieu have summarized the debate in *Recherches sociographiques* (hereafter *RS*) 6,3 (Sept.–Dec. 1966) 305–10.

9. See Fernand Ouellet, "M. Michel Brunet et le problème de la conquête," *Bulletin des recherches historiques* (hereafter *BRH*) 62, 2 (Apr.-June 1956): 29-101. His *Histoire économique et sociale du Québec 1760–1850* (Montreal: Fides, 1966) gives a more detailed account of his assumptions.

10. The first chapter of the book is devoted to the historiography of the problem. The conclusion, "Une Bourgeoisie coloniale: Une Thèse," 173–84, sums up the argument. For a summary of the whole discussion, see Nish, *The French Canadians, 1759–1766: Conquered? Half-Conquered? Liberated?* (Toronto: Copp Clark, 1966). In "Une Question historiographique: Une Bourgeoisie en Nouvelle-France?" Robert Comeau and Paul André Linteau have examined the arguments of both schools of thought. R. Comeau, ed., *Économie québécoise* (Montreal: PUQ, 1969), 311–24.

11. The Canadian Historical Association, *Historical Papers* (1968), 22–23.

12. A discussion report has been published in *Revue d'histoire de l'Amérique française* (hereafter *RHAF*) 24, 1 (June 1970): 79–81.

13. José Igartua, "A Change in Climate: The Conquest and the 'Marchands' of Montreal," Canadian Historical Association, *Historical Papers* (1974): 125–26. Igartua argues that the traditional nationalist conviction about the Conquest's harmful effect on the French-Canadian merchants is probably well-founded. See also his Ph.D. thesis, "The Merchants and 'Negociants' of Montreal, 1750–1755: A Study in Socio-Economic History" (Michigan State University, 1974).

14. *Habitants et marchands de Montréal au XVIIe siècle* (Paris and Montreal: Plon, 1974), 488, n. 7.

15. Such was the argument at the beginning of the discussion. See Michel Brunet, "La Conquête anglaise et la déchéance de la bourgeoisie canadienne, 1760–1793," *La Présence Anglaise*, 49–112.

16. *RHAF* 10, 1 (June 1956): 49–68. The article by Bilodeau is the summary of a Ph.D. thesis presented at the University of Montreal.

17. See n. 9.

18. See Robert Rumilly, *Les Socialistes dominent le réseau gauchiste* (Montreal: Robert Rumilly, 1959). In some ways, the condition of intellectual life at the time could be compared to what happened in the United States during McCarthy's anti-Red-Peril crusade. However, it should be noted that Quebec remained a "priest-ridden" province for more than a century. After the failure of the rebellion of 1837, the clergy took over the national leadership of French Canada. A clergy-owned school system began to expand. Colleges and universities under their control trained the professional and political leaders of French Canada. Apart from a few liberal minds, ultramontanism, the set of values which it implied, and the network of social institutions which it favored, flourished in the province of Quebec. Land settlement, schools, hospitals, and trade unions became more and more controlled by the church. The dominant position of the Catholic church has been seriously jeopardized only since World War II. Until then, Quebec had a social organization resembling that of Spain, hardly challenged by five decades of industrialization.

19. Defined by a group of intellectuals in Marcel Rioux, et al., *L'Église et le Québec* (Montreal: Les Éditions du Jour, 1961).

20. These concepts (applied to American historiography) are taken from J. Rogers Hollingsworth's review: "Consensus and Continuity in Recent American Writing," *South Atlantic Quarterly* 1, 6 (Winter 1962): 40–50. The consensus school of the 1950s "described an America with a unified past. As classes, sections, and ideologies have melted into myths, a history characterized by consensus and continuity has emerged." The opposite school of thought, represented by writers like Turner, Beard, and Parrington, "had stressed conflict as a basic theme in the American past by emphasizing section versus section, class versus class, ideology versus ideology, agrarianism versus industrialism." When I refer to traditional or consensus historiography, I mean the kind of history that prevailed during the century-long domination of the clergy over the intellectual life of French Canada. The historians of that period praised the role of the Catholic church in New France, and the moral conduct of settlers and political leaders as well as the seigneurs. The only strong criticism was directed toward the businessmen of the early colonial period. In

sum, there was a sense of consensus and continuity between church-oriented historians, the political, seigneurial, and religious leaders of the early colonial period, and the obedient peasant.

21. *Monumenta Novae Franciae*, vol. 1, *La Première Mission d'Acadie, 1602–1616* (Quebec: PUL, 1967), 276, 719. Professor Campeau is sometimes biased when he studies the value systems and religious beliefs of the Amerindians. Lucien Campeau, *La Première mission des Jésuites en Nouvelle-France (1611–1613) et les commencements du Collège de Québec, 1626–1670* (Montreal: Bellarmin, 1972).

22. "Mgr de Laval et le Conseil souverain, 1659–1684," *RHAF* 27, 3 (Dec. 1973): 323–59.

23. "Ni janséniste, ni gallican, ni ultramontain: François de Laval," *RHAF* 28, I (June 1974): 3–26. "Aspects doctrinaux de la dévotion à la sainte famille en Nouvelle-France," *Eglise et théologie* 3 (1972): 45–68, is another valuable contribution to history by Pierre Hurtubise.

24. *Le Séminaire de Québec sous l'épiscopat de Mgr de Laval* (Quebec: PUL, 1972).

25. *Le Rigorisme au XVIIIe siècle: Mgr. de Saint Vallier et le sacrement de pénitence* (Gembloux, Belgium: Duculot, 1970). For other essays in the field, see Nive Voisine, "La Production des vingt dernières années en histoire de l'Église du Québec," *RS* 15, 1 (Jan.–Apr. 1974): 991–03.

26. Blain, "Les Structures de l'Église et la conjoncture coloniale en Nouvelle-France, 1632–1674," *RHAF* 21, 4 (Mar. 1968): 749–56. Jaenen, *The Role of the Church in New France* (Toronto: McGraw-Hill Ryerson Ltd., 1976).

27. *The Huron: Farmers of the North* (New York: Holt, Rinehart, and Winston, 1969).

28. "L'Eau de vie dans la société indienne," *Canadian Historical Association Annual Reports* (hereafter *CHAR*) (1960). In the recent issues of *Les Cahiers des Dix*, André Vachon has published other essays in the field. Vachon is well acquainted with the findings of cultural anthropology.

29. "The Frenchification and Evangelization of the Amerindians in Seventeenth-Century New France," *Canadian Catholic Historical Association Report*, English-Language section (1968): 57–71. This essay follows and completes the one written by Vachon in 1960. "Amerindian Views of French Culture in the Seventeenth Century," *CHR* 55, 3 (Sept. 1974): 261–91, is a sound interpretation of intercultural relationships.

30. Cornelius Jaenen, *Friend and Foe — Aspects of French Amerindian Cultural Contact in the Sixteenth and Seventeenth Centuries* (Toronto: McClelland and Stewart, 1976).

31. Raymond Boyer, *Les Crimes et les châtiments au Canada français du XVIIe au XXe siècle* (Montreal: Le Cercle du livre de France, 1966). For the most part, Boyer deals with New France records. André Lachance, *Le Bourreau au Canada sous le régime français* (Quebec: La Société historique de Québec, 1966). In "Les Causes devant la prévôté de Québec," *Histoire sociale/Social History* (hereafter *HS/SH*) 3 (Apr. 1969): 101–11, Jacques Mathieu tried to avoid value judgments. But, as Louise Dechêne has pointed out, "Studies of criminality are currently in fashion — an interesting area, no doubt, but a dangerous one so long as we do not know what the norms were" (*Habitants et marchands*, 414).

32. "French Economic and Social History," *Journal of Interdisciplinary History* 4, 3 (Winter 1974): 435–57.

33. Robert Mandrou has reviewed the recent production according to these criteria in "L'Historiographie canadienne-française: Bilan et perspectives," *CHR* 51, 1 (Mar. 1970): 5–20.

34. During the last decade, one long-term research project in interdisciplinary history has been launched by a group of specialists in the fields of demography and history at the University of Montreal. Hubert Charbonneau, Jacques Légaré, René Durocher, Gilles Paquet, and Jean-Pierre Wallot, "La Démographie historique au Canada — Un Projet de recherche," *RS* 8, 2 (May–Aug. 1967): 214–17; H. Charbonneau and Yolande Lavoie, "Introduction à la reconstruction de la population du Canada au XVIIIe siècle. Étude critique des sources de la période 1665–1668," *RHAF* 24, 4 (Mar. 1971): 485–511; Charbonneau, Lavoie, and Légaré, "Le Recensement nominatif du Canada en 1681," *HS/SH* 7 (Apr. 1971): 77–98; Charbonneau, Légaré, and Lavoie, "The Early Canadian Population: Problems in Automatic Record Linkage," *CHR* 53, 4 (Dec. 1972): 427–42.

35. "Économie et société en Nouvelle-France: L'Historiographie des années 1950–1960," *RHAF* 28, 2 (Sept. 1974): 163–86. Frégault, a major figure of the 1950s, and "a convert to positivist methods, sought to impart them to his students by distributing a handbook on methodology entitled *A Guide to Historical Methods*, edited by the Jesuit Gilbert J. Garraghan, and published by Jean Delanglez. It was based on old German models of the late nineteenth century, which relied almost entirely on heuristic argument and the criticism of sources" (169).

36. The Eccles-Lanctôt-Trudel trio belongs to the tradition of "national" historians. Many of their books are devoted to general history and have been translated for the common reader in one of the two major languages of the Canadian community. Their most important studies published during the last fifteen years are: (1) Eccles: *Canada under Louis XIV, 1663–1701* (Toronto: McClelland and Stewart, 1964); *The Canadian Frontier, 1534–1760* (New York: Holt, Rinehart, and Winston, 1969); *Canadian Society during the French Regime* (Montreal: Harvest House, 1968); *France in America*, The New American Nation series (New York: Harper and Row, 1972). (2) Lanctôt: *Canada and the American Revolution, 1774–1783* (Harvard University Press, 1967); *Montreal under Maisonneuve, 1642–1665*, 3 vols. (Toronto: Clarke Irwin, 1963). (3) Trudel: *Histoire de la Nouvelle-France*, vol. 1, *Les Vaines Tentatives, 1524–1603*, vol. 2, *Le Comptoir, 1604–1627* (see chapter 2 of Serge Gagnon, *Quebec and Its Historians. The Twentieth Century* (Montreal: Harvest House, 1985) for a discussion); *The Beginnings of New France, 1524–1663* (Toronto: McClelland and Stewart, 1973); *Introduction to New France* (Toronto: Holt, Rinehart, and Winston, 1968); the last title is mainly devoted to the history of institutions and is more complete than André Vachon's *L'Administration de la Nouvelle-France, 1627–1760* (Quebec: PUL, 1970).

37. See for example Marcel Trudel, *La Population du Canada en 1663* (Montreal: Fides, 1973). His *L'Esclavage au Canada français: Histoire et conditions de l'esclavage* explored a relatively new field (see Gagnon, *Quebec and Its Historians*, chap. 1, n. 39, and discussion in chap. 2, ibid.). Eccles's "The Social, Economic, and Political Significance of the Military Establishment in New France," *CHR* 52, 1 (Mar. 1971): 1-22, is a sound revisionist essay. One of the more recent books by Marcel Trudel, *Les Débuts de régime seigneurial au Canada* (Montreal: Fides, 1974), is a very detailed statistical description of land ownership up to 1663.

38. *CHR* (Mar. 1969): 89.

39. *CHR* (Dec. 1969): 449ff.

40. Richard Colebrook Harris, *The Seigneurial System in Early Canada: A Geographical Study* (Madison, Milwaukee, London, and Quebec: The University of Wisconsin Press and PUL, 1966). On this very important book, the reviews by Fernand Ouellet, *HS/SH* 1 (April 1968): 152–59, and Jean Blain, *RS* 9, 3 (Sept.–Dec. 1968): 319-22, should be consulted.

41. Even though Braudel prefaced some of his works, Roland Lamontagne never really applied his mentor's methodology. Titles published by Lamontagne are: *La Galissonnière et le Canada* (Montreal: PUM, 1962); *Chabert de Cogolin et l'expédition de Louisbourg* (Montreal: Éditions Leméac, 1964); *La Vie et l'oeuvre de Pierre Bougues* (Montreal: PUM, 1964); *Succès d'intendance de Jean Talon* (Montreal: Éditions Leméac, 1964); *Aperçu structural du Canada au XVIIIe siècle* (Montreal: Éditions Leméac, 1965); *L'Atlantique jusqu'au temps de Maurepas* (Montreal: PUM, 1965); *Ministère de la marine Amérique et Canada, d'après les documents Maurepas* (Montreal: Éditions Leméac, 1966); *Problématique des civilisations* (Montreal: PUM, 1968); *Textiles et documents Maurepas* (Montreal: Éditions Leméac, 1970); *Maurepas et Pellerin d'après les sources manuscrites* (Montreal: PUM, 1972).

42. For a good example of the scepticism of senior scholars regarding new methods, see the comment of André Vachon, "La Restauration de la Tour de Babel ou 'La Vie à Québec au milieu de XVIIe siècle'," *RHAF* 24, 2 (Sept. 1970): 167–250) on the "provocative" essay by Jacques Mathieu, "La Vie à Québec au milieu du XVIIe siècle: Étude de sources," *RHAF* 23, 3 (Dec. 1969): 404–24.

43. Other essays on New France published before 1960 with a "scientific basis" belong to interdisciplinary history; they were not written by historians as such.

44. *CHR* 42 (1961): 336.

45. For example, Fernand Dumont, *RS* 1, 2 (Apr.–June 1961), 263ff. The best review was done by an economist, Pierre Harvey, in *AE* (Oct.–Dec. 1961): 537–48.

46. The word *structure* refers to the economic and social structure of a given society, its forms of economic organization, social strata, etc. Structural changes are usually slow. *Conjoncture* refers to more short-term economic and social trends or circumstances: economic cycles, crisis, growth, inflation, and so forth. Historians study these by means of series of price and wage statistics, many of which they must laboriously reconstruct themselves. In fact, however, such series reflect the same realities as the consumer price index, the unemployment rate, and the like, in our own society.

47. This aspect has been challenged by Peter Nicholas Moogk (see n. 72).

48. See also Micheline D'Allaire, "Conditions matérielles requises pour devenir religieuse au XVIIIe siècle," in *L'Hôtel-Dieu de Montréal, 1642–1973* (Montreal: Éditions HMH, 1973): 183–208.

49. J.F. Bosher, "French Protestant Families in Canadian Trade, 1740-1760," *HS/SH* 7, 14 (Nov.

1974): 179–201; "Le Ravitaillement de Québec en 1758," *HS/SH* 5, 9 (April 1972): 79–85.

50. At the 1972 meeting of the Canadian Historical Association, Pritchard read a paper entitled, "Maritime Traffic Patterns Between France and New France to 1760"; see also his "Voyage of the *Fier*: An Analysis of a Shipping and Trading Venture to New France, 1724–1728," *HS/SH* 6, 11 (Apr. 1973): 75–97.

51. See his *La Construction navale royale à Québec, 1739–1759* (Quebec: La Société Historique de Québec, 1971). For Mathieu, the low quality, scarcity, and cost of Canadian wood prove that the type of ships built in Quebec at the request of the metropolis were not those which matched Canadian resources. In the history of international trade, Mathieu wrote a suggestive article: "La Balance commerciale en Nouvelle-France–France–Antilles au XVIIIe siècle," *RHAF* 25, 4 (Mar. 1972): 465–497.

52. One can get an idea of Dubé's approach to the subject in "Origine sociale des intendants de la Nouvelle-France," *HS/SH* 2 (Nov. 1968): 18–33.

53. *Un Marquis du Grand Siècle: Jacques-René de Brisay de Denonville, gouverneur de la Nouvelle-France, 1637–1710* (Montreal: Éditions Leméac, 1965).

54. *La Vérendrye et le poste de l'ouest* (Quebec: PUL, 1968); *Nouvelles études sur les La Vérendrye et le poste de l'ouest* (Quebec: PUL, 1971).

55. *Maurepas, ministre de Louis XV, 1715–1749* (Montreal: Éditions Leméac, 1967). *La Pensée et l'action coloniales de Maurepas vis à vis du Canada, 1723–1749* (Montreal: Éditions Leméac, 1972).

56. For example, the review of Lionel Laberge's *Rouen et le commerce du Canada de 1650 à 1670* (Quebec, 1972), by Jacques Mathieu, *RHAF* 26, 3 (Dec. 1972): 437.

57. *RS* 12, 2 (May–Aug. 1971): 143–83.

58. Ibid., 177.

59. *RHAF* 27, 2 (Sept. 1973): 163–79.

60. A good example of this is Raymond Douville and Jacques Donat Casanova, *La Vie quotidienne en Nouvelle-France — Le Canada, de Champlain à Montcalm* (Paris: Hachette, 1964).

61. "Les Français hors de France aux XVIe et XVIIIe siècles," *Annales*, E.S.C. (Oct. 1969): 671.

62. "The Social, Economic, and Political Implications of the Establishment in New France," *CHR* 52, 2 (Mar. 1971): 1–22.

63. Jacques Henripin, *La Population canadienne au début du XVIIIe siècle: Nuptialité, fécondité, mortalité infantile* (Paris, 1954).

64. Jean Hamelin, *Économie et société en Nouvelle-France* (38). Hamelin echoes the assumptions of administrators.

65. *Frontenac, The Courtier Governor*, first published in 1959, is perhaps the best book ever written by Eccles.

66. *Le Monde*, 1 Nov. 1974.

67. "Following the great work of Herold A. Innis, *The Fur Trade in Canada: An Introduction to Canadian Economic History* (Toronto, 1927), the economic history of Canada has regularly been written in terms of the rise (and occasionally, fall) of her exported staple product. What is a staple? It is a product with a large natural resource content. Some part of its fabrication must take place at the spot even if only in the trivial sense of seizing it away from Nature. The staple is a product which does not require elaborate processing involving large quantities of labor or rare skills. . . . The staple is a product which will bear transport charges and which is in international demand." Richard A. Caves and Richard H. Holton, *The Canadian Economy: Prospects and Retrospects* (Harvard University Press, 1959), 31.

68. Marcel Trudel, *Introduction to New France*, chap. 6.

69. R.-L. Séguin, *La Civilisation traditionnelle de l'habitant*, 538–41.

70. A few pages were devoted to land mobility (287ff). Louise Dechêne studied the parish of Pointe aux Trembles. She concluded that a great geographic stability existed among the peasants. Perhaps the sample was rather too small for the conclusion to be applied to the whole colony. Marcel Trudel's important book, *Les Débuts du régime seigneurial au Canada*, came to different conclusions through a very detailed collection of data for the whole community. The contradictions between the two writers may be explained by the fact that they worked in different periods: 1627–1663 for Marcel Trudel, and 1642–1731 for Louise Dechêne. Trudel agreed that almost all seigneury owners kept their *censive* during the founding decades.

71. For such statements, see Eccles, *The Canadian Frontier, 1534–1760* (Toronto, 1969), 94.

72. Peter Nicholas Moogk, "The Craftsman in New France" (Ph.D. thesis, University of Toronto, 1973); some of the findings have been published: "Apprenticeship Indentures: A Key to Artisan Life in New

France," Canadian Historial Association, *Historical Papers* (1971), 65–83; "In the Darkness of a Basement: Craftsmen's Associations in Early French Canada," *CHR* 57, 4 (Dec. 1976): 399–439.

73. Like Hamelin (*Économie et Société*) and Eccles (*The Canadian Frontier*). See Dechêne, *Habitants et Marchands*, 215, n. 136.

74. "Government and Private Interest in New France," *Canadian Public Administration* 10 (1967): 244–57.

75. Fernand Ouellet, *HS/SH* 8, 16 (Nov. 1975): 372–82; Hubert Charbonneau, "À Propos de démographie urbaine en Nouvelle-France . . ." in *RHAF* 30, 2 (Sept. 1976): 263–74.

76. According to the 1681 census, "There are many more young women than young men between twenty and thirty years of age, particularly in the areas where the most coureurs de bois are recruited," that is, the Montreal and Trois-Rivières districts. The figures were as follows: District of Montreal: 66.3 males to 100 females; outside the city limits, the ratio was 46.3 males to 100 females. The difference between sexes was not so high in the Trois-Rivières region — 83.8 males for 100 females, but one can conclude that a large number of young men from the rural area participated in the fur trade. Charbonneau writes: "It follows that only the difference in emigration can explain these figures."

77. Once more exemplified by Jacques Mathieu's recent survey of New France. See Jean Hamelin, et al., *Histoire du Québec* (Toulouse: Privat, 1976), chap. 4, 5, and 6.

78. Fernand Ouellet, "Historiographie canadienne et nationalisme," *Transactions of the Royal Society of Canada*, 4th ser. (Ottawa, 1975), 13: 36ff.

79. These sources are not, however, without their own limitations. For a critique of the use of inventories after death, for example, see Jean-Pierre Wallot and Gilles Paquet, "Les Inventaires après décès à Montréal au tournant du XIXe siècle: Préliminaires à une analyse," *RHAF* 30, 2 (Sept. 1976): 176–82.

80. Louis Lavallée, Jean Blain, Louis Michel, and others have also undertaken new research based on notarial documents. See Louis Lavallée, "Les Archives notariales et l'histoire sociale de la Nouvelle-France," *RHAF* 28, 3 (Dec. 1974): 395–403.

81. *RHAF* 23, 2 (Sept. 1969): 185–207.

82. "La Justice seigneuriale en Nouvelle-France: Le Cas de Notre-Dame-des-Anges," *RHAF* 28, 3 (Dec. 1974): 323–46.

83. *The Dictionary of Canadian Biography*, published by the University of Toronto Press, is a huge collective effort by professional historians to publish critical biographies. In so doing, historians participate in shaping the collective memory of the nation. The first three volumes deal with New France: vol. 1 (1967) covers the years 1000–1700; vol. 2 (1969), 1700–1740; and vol. 3 (1974), 1740–1770.

Recent Historical Writing on the Prairie West†

Gerald Friesen

The prairie West has long been a favourite subject of Canadian historians. Substantial volumes on the region's history appeared as early as the 1880s and 1890s and many more were added in the first half of this century. But, despite the long list of historical works published before 1960, the flood of publications after that date is still remarkable. A recent western Canadian bibliography listed four thousand items, of which at least two-thirds bore imprints from the 1970s, and the pace has quickened since its appearance. Community-sponsored local histories alone sustain a small industry. Government-funded research projects, such as those of Parks Canada and the provincial departments of culture, have also added new sources of funding for prairie historical study. If historical writing is a measure of cultural maturity, the region has been blessed in the decades after 1960.

Early prairie scholars were especially interested in the fur trade. They favoured the French, the North-West Company, or the Hudson's Bay Company, depending upon their predilections and their patron. The Hudson's Bay Company sponsored its own publishing venture—the Hudson's Bay Record Society—and they viewed the West as a distinct theatre of British imperial history. The great achievement of this research was Arthur Silver Morton's *A History of the Canadian West to 1870–71*.[1] Next in importance as a field of study was the era of transition to Canadian rule, including the Mounted Police, the railway, and the disturbances associated with Louis Riel. The era of agricultural settlement received special attention because of the Canadian Frontiers of Settlement series, a multivolume project undertaken by the American Geographical Society and the Social Science Research Council in the 1930s. The political behaviour of Albertans, in particular, became the object of a similarly ambitious research project in the 1940s, the Social Credit in Alberta series directed by S.D. Clark. The eight volumes of the Frontiers group and the ten volumes related to Social Credit represented a very large proportion of prairie scholarship on twentieth-century topics. Thus, the selection of these subjects for special attention by funding agencies determined, to a large degree, the shape of pre-1960 prairie scholarship.[2]

The historical discipline changed considerably after 1960. New approaches, especially the widespread interest in social history as opposed to political and economic analysis, happened to become popular just as Canadian universities were growing rapidly and training increasing numbers of history specialists. After a generation when national topics were the chief concern of Canadian historians, regional, class, and ethnic subjects were coming into vogue. The result was a dramatically revised version of western Canadian history.

†From R. Douglas Francis and Howard Palmer, eds., *The Prairie West: Historical Readings* (Edmonton: Pica Pica Press, 1985): 5–18.

Native history or ethnohistory, ignored to a large degree by such scholars as A.S. Morton, achieved prominence in the 1970s. The landmark work on the western interior was A.J. Ray's *Indians in the Fur Trade*,[3] but this one volume was complemented by Ray's and Donald Freeman's *Give Us Good Measure*,[4] Abe Rotstein's dissertation on the relationship between native trade and diplomatic alliances,[5] Charles Bishop's study of the northern Ojibway,[6] the reissue of David Mandelbaum's *Plains Cree*,[7] and John Milloy's "The Plains Cree"[8] These authors had in common a determination to examine pre-treaty, pre-reserve native history from the native perspective and thus, like their counterparts in recent working-class studies, to examine an entire and distinctive society. They demonstrated that there was considerable native cultural and economic autonomy in the first years of contact with whites. They showed, too, that the Indians of the western interior, unlike some of their eastern counterparts, were partners of the Europeans in the fur-trade for several centuries. Indians adapted slowly to the introduction of European trade goods, in this view, and retained considerable independence for at least a century and a half after serious trading began in the 1680s. By examining native population movements before and after white contact, these recent historical works demonstrated how the European trade could be integrated into native culture without drastic dislocation and, indeed, that particular native alliances were able to control the direction and pace of the trade.

Contemporaneous with their revisions of native history, scholars also established new approaches to fur trade company studies. Where H.A. Innis, A.S. Morton, and E.E. Rich were concerned with company organization, market share, geographical determinants, and the effect of reliance upon staple exploitation, recent works by Van Kirk, Brown, and Foster concentrated upon the traders in the field.[9] A most important change in perspective resulted: the fur posts were no longer regarded merely as isolated extensions of Britain or Canada; rather, these scholars were suggesting that the native-white relationships constituted a distinctive society in the western interior—a "fur trade society"—which encompassed traders, labourers, hunters, wives, and children. This society had several variants—the Hudson's Bay Company, the North West Company, and the French models—with different patterns of upward mobility in the fur-trade hierarchy, different relationships with natives, particularly with native women, and different patterns of family stability and of child-raising. The history of this society acquired its own chronology, too, based upon the eras when native women were favoured as wives (before 1780), when Métis women were preferred (1780–1830) and, finally, when a few influential white women were introduced (1820–50). What was striking about this chronology or periodisation was that it parallelled changes in the position of natives and whites in the trade, where three eras also had been delineated: first, when Indian customs dominated trade practice (before 1770); second, when trade reflected a combination of European and native customs (1770–1820); and, third, when European direction became overwhelming (post–1821).

Little attention has been paid to the question of when this fur trade society gave way to the recognizably "modern" agricultural society. The delination of a brief era of transition, seen most clearly in Professor W.L. Morton's work, suggested that the transition from old order to new occurred between 1857 and 1870.[10] Recent interpretations blurred this picture, it would seem, and yet promised a new and fascinating consensus. Sylvia Van Kirk, for example, suggested that the European wives who arrived in the western interior in the 1830s and 1840s had a significant impact upon fur trade society because they relegated native and Métis women to a distinctly inferior position. Similarly, Frits Pannekoek emphasized the arrival in the same era of European clergy, Protestant and Catholic, but especially those from the Church Missionary Society, and argued that they created instability in Red River that could lead only to social disintegration.[11] Irene Spry and Carol Judd preferred to concentrate upon economic factors, particularly the quest of the Métis for economic opportunity and upward mobility, in their treatment of the events that brought about the transformation of prairie society.[12] Doug Owram discussed the conscious campaign of a handful of Ontario expansionists to change the image of the West from wilderness to promised land in the 1856–60 era.[13] These interpretations had in common an emphasis upon the changing cultural perspective of Europeans, Canadians, and some mixed bloods. These recent historians have implied that coexistence with native society in an unchanging fur economy was no longer acceptable to Europeans whose views were shaped by nineteenth-century industrial capitalism. Thus, like the studies of eastern Canadian workers by H.C. Pentland and Gregory Kealey,[14] these historical works pre-figured a new consensus in Canadian history. Based upon developments in the social history of England and Europe, in which the Industrial Revolution assumed a centrality once reserved for the Renaissance and the rise of the nation-state, this consensus divided the history of the nation, and of the western interior, at some point near the middle of the nineteenth century when the industrial capitalist way of life became the dominant social force in Canada.

The transition which began in the decades around the middle of the nineteenth century proceeded with amazing rapidity. For Indians, the story included treaty-making,[15] economic crises,[16] government, church and police activities to facilitate native adaptation,[17] and the native response to these developments.[18] Recent analysis of Métis society has also resulted in important new interpretations. The conventional wisdom of past generations, created by Marcel Giraud and George Stanley, emphasized French-English differences in the mixed-blood population and argued that the French Métis, in particular, who were said to be closer to their native cultural roots, found it difficult to make the shift from fur trade to agriculture and experienced serious conflicts with the incoming civilization.[19] W.L. Morton emphasized the Canadian context of the Red River resistance of 1869, suggesting that the French Métis were merely resisting Ontario English-speaking newcomers; that is, though Morton rejected the thesis of a clash between frontier and civilization, he did not revise the broader picture of French-English differences among the Métis.[20] This consensus has been challenged by Douglas Sprague, whose quantitative analysis of account books, land registers, and the census suggests that economic patterns in the French and English parishes were identical. In his view the French and English communities, like villages within two nations, were physically separated from each other but their social structures were remarkably similar.[21] The Red River communities were suddenly confronted with Ontario troops and a new political order in 1870. According to Sprague, the subsequent "government lawlessness" drove many Métis from their farms. This was not a voluntary exodus, he argued, but was the result of violence and illegality.[22] This theme of Métis struggle and eventual flight was evident in other recent work which suggested that the French and English-speaking mixed-bloods of Manitoba's "old order" made common cause in defence of their interests until the collapse of their political coalition in 1879.[23]

A striking reinterpretation of the 1885 uprising was also presented in recent years. Where earlier discussions of the uprising juxtaposed Riel's madness and territorial political and economic grievances,[24] Thomas Flanagan treated Riel as a prophet and the rebellion as a millenarian movement.[25] As in fur trade studies, so this new view of Riel brought western Canadian historical scholarship into contact with international currents in the social sciences and demonstrated that mutually enriching insights could be achieved in the process. By emphasizing the social context of Riel's visions, Flanagan implied that the rebellion of 1885 should be seen as the product of many causes and that the Métis and Cree uprisings were very different expressions of concern about the adjustment to Canadian rule.

The imposition of a Canadian institutional and economic structure upon the western interior was controlled largely by the federal government and, as historians have recognized for many years, its central features were the treaties, the Mounted Police, and the Pacific railway.[26] The customary interpretations of the National Policy described it as a positive element in western development.[27] The first challenge to this view was presented by V.C. Fowke, who characterized these policies and the protective tariff which accompanied them as an instrument created by eastern Canadian imperialists to exploit a western hinterland.[28] John Dales raised further discussion by suggesting that the three pillars of the National Policy, taken together, constituted neither an integrated nor a positive contribution to Canadian economic development.[29] But the vexing question as to why, with an institutional structure in place, the West failed to experience a sustained boom in the last quarter of the nineteenth century was not discussed except by reference to the international depression of 1873–96. Having discredited that concept of a monolithic depression, recent economic histories re-examined the timing and nature of western settlement, and after an interesting and fruitful dialogue, produced elements of a new consensus.[30] According to Kenneth Norrie, the National Policy did *not* significantly affect the rate and timing of western settlement; the crucial factors, instead, were the exhaustion of the preferable subhumid lands in the United States, the development of dry-farming techniques, the post-1896 rise in world wheat prices, and the movements of relative real wages in Canada, the United States, and the United Kingdom.[31]

Another apsect of this discussion raised the possibility that the National Policy, especially free land and railway land grants, actually induced settlement and rail construction before it was economically viable and thus resulted in the "misallocation of scarce resources" and a good deal of human misery.[32] These significant revisions of the conventional wisdom were reinforced by two empirical studies, one by Donald Loveridge, who examined the settlement process in the Rural Municipality of Sifton, 1880–1920,[33] and a second by Lyle Dick, who studied two blocks of townships near Abernethy, Assiniboia, 1880–1900.[34] Forerunners of serious quantitative analysis of settlement strategy, these works suggested there were no simple answers to the question of why individuals selected their particular plot of land, but they also argued that federal policies might well have resulted in the inefficient allocation of resources.

Debate over the rate and timing of western settlement was accompanied by an equally stimulating dispute in which economic historians questioned the regional consequences of the National Policy. The alleged "central Canadian imperialism" of Macdonald's policy was the focus of interest in this debate. As in the discussions of the rate of settlement, the discussion began in the work of Creighton, Fowke, and Dales. The traditional view of the matter, as presented in Creighton's works, was that the National Policy created the framework for an integrated, prosperous national economy. Fowke argued instead that the Ottawa government viewed the West as a resource hinterland subservient to the commercial and industrial interests of the East and, thus, that individual incomes on the prairies were lower than would have been possible under an alternative policy structure. Dales suggested simply that the National Policy was a "dismal failure" because it created an inefficient and inappropriately sized Canadian economy. Until very recently it was customary, in prairie academic circles at least, to endorse a version of the Fowke interpretation.[35] But Kenneth Norrie challenged this convention in an important series of articles. He agreed that the issue of "regional impacts of national economic policies" was important and should be examined, but he concluded that individuals resident on the praires did not suffer unfair "economic and non-economic costs of adjustment solely because of their geographical location." Moreover, he argued that the absence of industrial development on the prairies, a crucial matter in today's debates about the future of Confederation, was not the result of Ottawa's tariff and rail freight rate policies. Finally, he suggested that, though the tariff did redistribute income among regions (*to* manufacturing and *from* resource regions), it did not redistribute income among regions in an unfair fashion.[36] Norrie's argument rested on his definition of economic and political justice: he assumed that tariffs were in place before settlement began and thus were part of the economic calculation of the immigrant. He did not suggest that westerners were misguided in their attempts to change federal tariff policy or to alter freight rate structure. After all, prairie success in these protest campaigns would increase the relative income of prairie citizens. But, Norrie continued, these prairie people did not suffer, as was often alleged, "actual out-of-pocket transfers"; rather they failed to appropriate capital gains on a regional basis. Though he did not convince his colleagues on all points, Norrie established the terms for the debate on the National Policy. Local empirical studies may take over from macroeconomic analysis in the discussion of the rate, timing, and strategy of settlement, but new social science techniques such as econometric models and new approaches such as counterfactual propositions will now be the prevailing approaches to the debate over prairie economic structure. Norrie's refreshing insistence upon the use of the concept of "comparative advantage" when dealing with the failure of the prairies to achieve significant industrial development will undoubtedly shape the thinking of his future critics.

The era of transition from a non-industrial to an industrial capitalist society in western Canada extended from some point around the mid-nineteenth century to about the last decade of the century. By the 1890s, the native way of life had been altered irrevocably, the Métis had lost political power, and the economic structures and intellectual assumptions of a western European and, more precisely, a British-Ontario society had been set in place. The new West differed sufficiently from its parents to warrant description as a distinct region, but the elements it shared with its founding societies were profound. Of these, the most important was prairie acceptance of a local version of industrial society's class structure. Thus, Rod MacLeod's study of the North West Mounted Police, Alan Artibise's work on Winnipeg, and David Breen's work on ranchers,[37] to cite just three recent contributions to this theme, emphasized that prairie social leaders assumed they were part of the "better element" and that they must control the "lower elements" around them. From their selection of house type and creation of segregated residential districts to their foundation of historical societies, schools, private clubs, and other voluntary agencies of cultural improvement, the members of the respectable class set the proper tone for prairie life.[38] The danger they anticipated was not class war of the Marxian type but an Indian uprising or frontier violence or disrespectful — even downright disgusting — public behaviour. Thus, the recent literature demonstrated that class affiliation and class ideals were very much a part of prairie society and played an important role in the social history of the last two decades of the nineteenth century. Though the definition of these class assumptions was far from satisfactory, the presence of such class lines was no longer disputed.

The prairie world changed drastically around the turn of the twentieth century. Population numbers rose sharply, ethnic diversity became almost unmanageable — or so it seemed to many — and the conventions of the preceding generation, including worker-management relations, the place of the prairie farmer in the national economic and political order, the place of women in the home and in public life, and even the structure and role of the churches, were called into question. Recent scholarship reinforced the thesis of a sharp change in prairie society around 1900. Many of the recent studies began in the 1890s or in the first decade of the twentieth century and, by implication, suggested sharp differences between the western interior in, say, 1886, and that same territory in the decades after 1905. This was particularly true in Saskatchewan and Alberta, where the population influx simply inundated the small society of the pre-1900 era, but it was also applicable in Manitoba, where the impact of post-1898 immigrants upon Winnipeg and rural districts alike was quite extraordinary.

The important social changes were not simply the result of demographic factors. They were also evident in the rise of a myriad of social and economic reform movements which produced intense debate about the appropriate distribution of wealth and exercise of power in prairie and, indeed, Canadian society. City government reform, women's suffrage, direct legislation, prohibition, progressive education, co-operative elevators, and similar issues were aspects of a drive to make government more democratic, to make the distribution of wealth more equitable, and to ensure that the new Canada would be a more decent and humane society than other parts of the nation and the world. Recent historical writing focussed upon these social and political tensions with results that were extremely interesting. They can be discussed under four headings: first, where western political protest had once been described as agrarian, recent work emphasized the importance of the construction camp and the company town; second, where prairie society had been seen as primarily agricultural, recent studies on urban centres demonstrated the importance of cities and towns in the social fabric; third, the study of rural ideas and farm protest — once included in institutional analysis of the Progressives and the co-operatives — itself moved to another level with the adoption of the concept of populism to describe the tactics and goals of these organizations; fourth, ethnic group history came of age and transformed our impressions of pioneer days.

Camp and company-town life, wherever these phenomena existed in Canada, were distinguished by sharp class divisions and by wretched living and working conditions for the labourer. Scholars debated the root cause of western labour radicalism — the national policy, the stifled hopes of immigrants, socialist agitation — but the importance of the protest movements was plain: the experience of the miner, the timber-worker, and the construction crew member was an integral part of the history of the western interior. To what end? Bercuson had once argued that the western labour movement was betrayed by a handful of radicals in 1919.[39] This was not so clear after further scholarly work was completed. Avery and McCormack demonstrated the depth and extent of worker dissatisfaction; Bercuson himself chronicled the rise and collapse of the workers' "revolutionary" vehicle, the One Big Union.[40] Several authors suggested that the radical leadership was actually overtaken by the tide of worker unrest in 1919.[41] Rather than being able to direct the workers' energies toward an eventual revolution, these works argued, the leaders of the militants were forced to go along with the ill-prepared strikes which broke out after the declaration of the Winnipeg general strike. Left-wing factionalism, arrests, government intervention, AFL re-organizing efforts, and business resistance, as Professor Bercuson demonstrated, did the rest.[42] The radical movement never came together again.

Recent work on the urban scene complemented this perspective. As Artibise demonstrated in the case of Winnipeg, businessmen dominated civic governments and determined the policies of the city councils.[43] This business influence accounted for the politicians' interest in immigration and cheap electricity and their failure to respond to the need for public housing, public health measures, and social amenities for the urban labourer. And, as Bercuson suggested, the roots of the Winnipeg general strike lay not simply in the wartime and post-war situation, but in social conditions and labour-management relations that had been breeding class division for at least two decades.[44] Finally, J.E. Rea demonstrated conclusively that the Winnipeg strike simply hardened these class lines so that over the next 50 years — indeed to this day — Winnipeg political support was divided into two camps along class and neighbourhood lines.[45]

An allied area of concern to historians was the middle-class reform movement. Recent investigation of the social crises in the cities concentrated upon the role of the social gospel in Canadian Protestant churches.[46] It also noted the emergence of a "culture of professionalism" in business and education and government.[47] Scholars contended that the religious revival and the human and social sciences produced an extraordinary range of important reform movements. John Thompson singled out the prohibition and women's suffrage movements for special attention, and by so doing demonstrated how important was urban British-Canadian support for the achievement of their goals. Other historians discussed technical high schools and the child-welfare system but, in the process, made the same point that Thompson had emphasized; a city-based professional class had emerged in prairie society just as it had in the rest of North America.[48]

Studies of the professional class, political reform, and radicalism may lead to a reconsideration of the Progressive revolt of 1919–25. The Progressive movement had once been seen as the culmination of grain growers' unrest in western Canada.[49] Thus, despite their obvious support in the Maritimes and Ontario and among urban reformers in the West, the Progressives were described as a regional and occupational protest movement. As a result of recent contributions, progressivism has been placed in a broader context. Forbes revised eastern Progressive history[50] and a number of scholars discovered that "populism," as defined by Lawrence Goodwyn in particular, provided an interesting context for political reform movements on the Prairies.[51] Rather than confine their discussions to group government and co-operatives, these students apparently concluded that both farm and city reform movements were built upon a widespread dissent from industrial capitalism and that both groups, like the revolutionary labourers, wanted to build an alternative society. Thus, adopting Goodwyn's definition of the American Populist movements of the 1890s, these scholars suggested that the various types of Canadian progressive envisioned "a new society based on decentralized political and economic institutions, direct democracy, and a co-operative ethos."[52] In the view of recent scholarly writers, the co-operatives, the United Church, the Wheat Pool, and the prohibition movements shared a critique of contemporary North America and a vision of an ideal alternative.[53]

Revision of progressive historiography led in turn to reconsideration of Social Credit and the Co-operative Commonwealth Federation. The most important contribution to this discussion was John Richards and Larry Pratt's *Prairie Capitalism*, which took up the old chestnut of prairie studies, "why did Saskatchewan go socialist and Alberta Social Credit?" Their interesting solution was to suggest that western Canada experienced two variants, a left and a right-wing of the populist strategy: the left supported farm-labour alliances against capitalists; the right preferred a regional common front of all classes; the left attacked all sectors of corporate capitalism whereas the right concentrated its attention upon banks; the left relied heavily upon co-operatives as the basis for an alternative economic system and happily advocated government regulation or ownership; the right, on the other hand, had few links to the co-op movement and preferred open competition except where banks were concerned. The authors did not suggest that the prairie political movements were consistently "left" or "right" but they did suggest that, by the accidents of political history, new provincial governments came from the right in Alberta and from the left in Saskatchewan.[54] One might add, judging from John Kendle's recent study of Premier John Bracken, that Manitoba farm protest was less ideological than that in Alberta and Saskatchewan. Bracken established a pragmatic government with no ideological commitment beyond the maintenance of the status quo at minimal cost to the taxpayer.[55] These recent works suggested that a reexamination of prairie Progressivism was under way and that the story of reform politics in the 1920 and 1930s, particularly the striking differences in the three provincial political systems, would soon appear in a new light.[56]

An examination of trends in prairie historiography in the early twentieth century within the categories of frontier resource communities, urban society, and populism, neglects a fourth vital strand of historical writing, that dealing with ethnic groups. As in native history, so in ethnic history, scholars provided two different perspectives upon their subject: some were most concerned to address the evolution of the ethnic group itself;[57] others preferred to examine the reaction of Canadian society to the presence of these newcomers.[58] These works suggested a different rhythm and a different periodisation for every ethnic community and every wave of immigration. They suggested, too, that the transition from parent to prairie society must be the first theme in the story.[59] They would soon be able to compare rates and processes of adaptation.[60]

The second perspective upon ethnic history, that from the host Canadian society, became clearer with every passing year. Not only did individual ethnic histories touch upon relations with the larger society, but a number of general works dealt precisely with attitudes to ethnic minorities. As the writings of J.S. Woodsworth revealed long ago, there was a continuum from the welcome extended to Scandinavians, at one extreme, to the hostility expressed towards Orientals, at the other.[61] The story was more descriptive of the host than of the newcomer, to be sure, but it did suggest the context within which the immigrant encountered Canadian society.

Just as the nature of prairie society changed in the mid-nineteenth century and again at the end of the century, so it altered during the course of the twentieth century. In his discussion of recent events in the western interior, W.L. Morton distinguished the era after 1947 from the one before, thinking perhaps of the oil bonanza in Alberta;[62] John Thompson noted that, in 1941, for the first time, half of prairie farms had tractors;[63] J.H. Archer was impressed by the fact that Saskatchewan elected a CCF government in 1944;[64] others noted that rural-to-urban migration became a significant social phenomenon in the 1940s.[65] Each of these indices, in brief, suggested that the 1940s should be the point of demarcation between the third and fourth eras of prairie history.

Not surprisingly, the historiography of the modern era was sparse. Oil inspired a number of volumes but, aside from the very important Richards-Pratt study of Alberta and Saskatchewan resource politics, was not the subject of significant business histories. The modern grain trade was, remarkably, almost untouched; students of these two topics turned to international journalism — to Anthony Sampson's *Seven Sisters* and Dan Morgan's *Merchants of Grain* — to learn a little more about the operation of these important industries.[66] There was one thorough study of grain trade policies, one survey of the farm scene and several valuable histories of the pools and co-ops but, given the role of agriculture in the prairie West, this was a remarkably brief list.[67] Social studies were more numerous, especially those dealing with ethnic groups, but their conclusions did not readily fit into a synthesis upon ethnicity in the west.[68] Native politics, though an ideal subject for study, were little discussed in scholarly publications.[69] Literary criticism prospered but the relationship between literature and history was not clear-cut; indeed, some scholars contended that fiction created the environment and, thus, that historical events were of little importance in shaping prairie literature.[70] The gaps in the scholarly literature, as is apparent, were considerable.

Western political behaviour and the issue of "western alienation" did receive a great deal of scholarly attention. One of the broadest of the recent political studies was Roger Gibbins' *Prairie Politics and Society: Regionalism in Decline*.[71] Gibbins contended that the prairies had ceased to be a political region and, instead, like central Canada, consisted of several provincial empires fighting for advantage in a federal state. His conclusion was useful because it impressed upon the reader that regions were not static places with fixed boundaries. Rather, they were communities which coalesced and disappeared with changes in the political, economic, and intellectual environment.[72] And, as the writing of provincial histories suggested, provincial identities were replacing regional loyalties in the post-1940 prairie West.

Recent historical writing has produced significant new perspectives upon the prairie West. Not that it is "better" than the scholarship of the preceding generations, for it is not; contemporary historians will have difficulty matching the great accomplishments of A.S. Morton and V.C. Fowke, to cite just two of many examples. But every generation writes its own history and, in doing so, responds to the changing interests and values of its age. In recent work, prairie scholars were more concerned than their predecessors with social and cultural themes. As a consequence, "ordinary people" and literary and artistic production appeared more often in their work. If the frontier myth of social equality was sometimes applied to the prairie West in earlier decades, the concepts of social hierarchy and social class were more influential in recent scholarship. The concept of a prairie region, once a static and environmentally determined approach, became a flexible descriptive device. Above all, the prairie West was the subject of vigorous debate and serious interest in these decades as it had been for almost a century.

Notes

1. A.S. Morton, *A History of the Canadian West to 1870–71*, 2nd ed., edited by Lewis G. Thomas (Toronto, 1973; first published 1939).

2. Surveys of this writing are L.G. Thomas, "Historiography of the Fur Trade Era" and T.D. Regehr, "Historiography of the Canadian Plains after 1870" in *A Region of the Mind*, edited by Richard Allen (Regina, 1973).

3. Arthur J. Ray, *Indians in the Fur Trade: Their Role as Hunters, Trappers and Middlemen in the Lands Southwest of Hudson Bay* (Toronto, 1974).

4. Arthur J. Ray and Donald Freeman, *"Give Us Good Measure": An Economic Analysis of Relations between the Indians and the Hudson's Bay Company before 1763* (Toronto, 1978).

5. A. Rotstein, "Fur Trade and Empire: An Institutional Analysis," (Ph.D. dissertation, University of Toronto, 1967).

6. Charles A. Bishop, *The Northern Ojibwa and the Fur Trade: An Historical and Ecological Study* (Toronto, 1974).

7. David G. Mandelbaum, *The Plains Cree: An Ethnographic, Historical Comparative Study* (Regina, 1979; first published in 1940).

8. John S. Milloy, "The Plains Cree: A Preliminary Trade and Military Chronology 1670–1870" (M.A. thesis, Carleton University, 1972).

9. Sylvia Van Kirk, *"Many Tender Ties": Women in Fur Trade Society in Western Canada, 1670–1870* (Winnipeg, 1980); Jennifer S.H. Brown, *Strangers in Blood: Fur Trade Families in Indian Country* (Vancouver, 1980); J.E. Foster, "The Origins of the Mixed Bloods in the Canadian West" in *Essays on Western History*, edited by L.H. Thomas (Edmonton, 1976).

10. W.L. Morton, *Manitoba: A History* (Toronto, 1957).

11. Frits Pannekoek, "The Anglican Church and the Disintegration of Red River Society, 1818–1870" in *The West and the Nation: Essays in Honour of W.L. Morton*, edited by Carl Berger and Ramsay Cook (Toronto, 1976).

12. Carol Judd, "Native Labour and Social Stratification in the Hudson's Bay Company's Northern Department, 1770–1870," *Canadian Review of Sociology and Anthropology* 17, 4 (1980): 305–14 and "Mixt Bands of Many Nations: 1821–1870" in *Old Trails and New Directions: Papers of the Third North American Fur Trade Conference*, edited by Carol M. Judd and Arthur J. Ray (Toronto, 1980): 127–46; Irene M. Spry, "The Private Adventurers of Rupert's Land" in *The Developing West: Essays on Canadian History in Honor of Lewis H. Thomas*, edited by John E. Foster (Edmonton, 1983): 49-70.

13. Doug Owram, *Promise of Eden: The Canadian Expansionist Movement and the Idea of the West* (Toronto, 1980).

14. Gregory S. Kealey, "H.C. Pentland and Working Class Studies," *Canadian Journal of Political and Social Theory* 3, 2 (1979): 53–78.

15. John Leonard Taylor, "The Development of an Indian Policy for the Canadian North-West 1869–79" (Ph.D. dissertation, Queen's University, 1975); Jean Friesen, "My Birthright and Land: The Making of Treaty 3" (forthcoming).

16. Noel E. Dyck, "The Administration of Federal Indian Aid in the North-West Territories 1879–1885" (M.A. thesis, University of Saskatchewan, 1970).

17. A.J. Looy, "The Indian Agent and his Role in the Administration of the North-West Superintendency 1876–1893" (Ph.D. dissertation, Queen's University, 1977); Jacqueline Gresko (Kennedy), "Qu'Appelle Industrial School: White Rites for the Indians of the Old North West" (M.A. thesis, Carleton University, 1970).

18. John Tobias, "Subjugation of the Plains Cree 1876-1885," *Canadian Historical Review* LXIV (1983): 519–148.

19. Marcel Giraud, *Le Métis Canadien: Son Role dans l'Histoire des Provinces de l'Ouest* (Paris, 1945); George F.G. Stanley, *The Birth of Western Canada: A History of the Riel Rebellions* (Toronto, 1936, 1960).

20. W.L. Morton, ed., *Alexander Begg's Red River Journal* (Toronto, 1956).

21. D.N. Sprague and R.P. Frye, comps., *The Genealogy of the First Métis Nation: The Development and Dispersal of the Red River Settlement 1820-1900* (Winnipeg, 1983).

22. D.N. Sprague, "The Manitoba Land Question 1870–1882," *Journal of Canadian Studies* 15, 3 (Fall, 1980): 74–84.

23. Gerhard Ens, "Métis Lands in Manitoba," *Manitoba History* 5 (1983): 2–11; Gerald Friesen, "Homeland to Hinterland: Political Transition in Manitoba, 1870 to 1879," Canadian Historical Association, *Historical Papers* (1979): 33–47.

24. Lewis Herbert Thomas, *The Struggle for Responsible Government in the North-West Territories 1870-97* (Toronto, 1956, 1978); Stanley, *Birth of Western Canada*.

25. Thomas Flanagan, *Louis "David" Riel: "Prophet of the New World"* (Toronto, 1979).

26. Donald Creighton, *Dominion of the North* (Toronto, 1944).

27. Donald Creighton, *John A. Macdonald. Volume II, The Old Chieftain* (Toronto, 1955).

28. Vernon C. Fowke, *The National Policy and the Wheat Economy* (Toronto, 1957).

29. John H. Dales, "Some Historical and Theoretical Comments on Canada's National Policies," *Queen's Quarterly* LXXI, 3 (Autumm 1964): 297–316.

30. Kenneth H. Norrie, "The National Policy and the Rate of Prairie Settlement: A Review," *Journal of Canadian Studies* 14, 3 (Fall 1979): 63–76.

31. Kenneth H. Norrie, "The Rate of Settlement of the Canadian Prairies, 1870–1911," *Journal of Economic History* XXXV, 2 (June 1975): 410–27.

32. Kenneth H. Norrie, "National Policy and Rate of Prairie Settlement," 72.

33. Donald Merwin Loveridge, "The Settlement of the Rural Municipality of Sifton 1881–1920" (MA thesis, University of Manitoba, 1977).

34. Lyle Dick, "A Social and Economic History of the Abernethy District, 1880–1920," Parks Canada Manuscript Series (forthcoming).

35. See the Introduction to *Canada and the Burden of Unity*, edited by David Jay Bercusson (Toronto, 1977, 1985), 1–18.

36. Kenneth H. Norrie, "The National Policy and Prairie Economic Discrimination, 1870–1930" in *Canadian Papers in Rural History* 1, edited by Donald H. Akenson (Gananoque, 1979).

37. R.C. Macleod, *The NWMP and Law Enforcement* (Toronto, 1976); Alan F.J. Artibise, *Winnipeg: A Social History of Urban Growth 1874–1914* (Montreal, 1975); David H. Breen, *The Canadian Prairie West and the Ranching Frontier 1874–1924* (Toronto, 1983).

38. Gerald Friesen "The Manitoba Historical Society: A Centennial History," *Manitoba History* 4 (1982): 2–9; A.A. den Otter, *Civilizing the West: The Galts and the Development of Western Canada* (Edmonton, 1982).

39. David J. Bercusson, "Western Labour Radicalism and the One Big Union: Myths and Realities" in *The Twenties in Western Canada*, edited by S.M. Trofimenkoff (Ottawa, 1972): 32–49.

40. David J. Bercusson, *Fools and Wise Men: The Rise and Fall of the One Big Union* (Toronto, 1978); A. Ross McCormack, *Reformers, Rebels and Revolutionaries: The Western Canadian Radical Movement 1899–1919* (Toronto, 1977); Donald Avery, *"Dangerous Foreigners": European Immigrant Workers and Labour Radicalism in Canada 1896–1932* (Toronto, 1979).

41. Gerald Friesen, " 'Yours in Revolt': The Socialist Party of Canada and the Western Canadian Labor Movement," *Labour/Le Travailleur* 1 (1976): 139–57.

42. Bercusson, *Fools and Wise Men*.

43. Artibise, *Winnipeg*.

44. David Jay Bercusson, *Confrontation at Winnipeg: Labour, Industrial Relations, and the General Strike* (Montreal, 1974).

45. J.E. Rea, "The Politics of Class: Winnipeg City Council, 1919–1945" in *The West and the Nation: Essays in Honour of W.L. Morton*, 232–49.

46. Richard Allen, *The Social Passion: Religion and Social Reform in Canada 1914–28* (Toronto, 1971), and Richard Allen, ed., *The Social Gospel in Canada* (Ottawa, 1972).

47. David C. Jones, Nancy M. Sheehan, and Robert M. Stamp, eds., *Shaping the Schools of the Canadian West* (Calgary, 1979). For an American example, see Burton J. Bledstein. *The Culture of Professionalism: The Middle Class and the Development of Higher Education in America* (New York, 1976).

48. John Herd Thompson, *The Harvests of War: The Prairie West, 1914-1918* (Toronto, 1978).

49. W.L. Morton, *The Progressive Party in Canada* (Toronto, 1950).

50. Ernest R. Forbes, *The Maritime Rights Movement, 1919–1927: A Study in Canadian Regionalism* (Montreal, 1979).

51. Lawrence Goodwyn, *The Populist Moment: A Short History of the Agrarian Revolt in America* (Oxford, 1978).

52. Ian MacPherson, "Seiected Borrowings: The American Impact upon the Prairie Co-operative Movement, 1920-1939," *Canadian Review of American Studies* X, 2 (Fall 1979).

53. Ian MacPherson, *Each for All: A History of the Co-operative Movement in English Canada, 1900–1945* (Toronto, 1979).

54. John Richards and Larry Pratt, *Prairie Capitalism: Power and Influence in the New West* (Toronto, 1979).

55. John Kendle, *John Bracken: A Political Biography* (Toronto, 1979).

56. Carlo Caldarola, ed., *Society and Politics in Alberta: Research Papers* (Toronto, 1979); Evelyn Eager, *Saskatchewan Government: Politics and Pragmatism* (Saskatoon, 1980); Lewis H. Thomas, "The CCF Victory in Saskatchewan, 1944," *Saskatchewan History* XXXIV, 1 (Winter 1981): 1–16; David E. Smith, *Prairie Liberalism: The Liberal Party in Saskatchewan 1925–71* (Toronto, 1975); Thomas Peterson, "Manitoba: Ethnic and Class Politics" in *Canadian Provincial Politics: The Party Systems of the Ten Provinces*, edited by Martin Robin, 2nd ed. (Scarborough, 1978), 61–119; J.F. Conway, "The Prairie Populist Resistance to the National Policy: Some Considerations," *Journal of Canadian Studies* 14, 3 (Fall 1979): 77–91.

57. Alan B. Anderson, "Prairie Ethnic Studies and Research: Review and Assessment," *Prairie Forum* 7, 2 (Fall 1982): 155–70; Howard Palmer, "Canadian Immigration and Ethnic History in the 1970s and 1980s," *Journal of Canadian Studies* 17, 1 (Spring 1982): 35–50.

58. Howard Palmer, *Patterns of Prejudice: A History of Nativism in Alberta* (Toronto, 1982).

59. Orest T. Martynowycz, "Village Radicals and Peasant Immigrants: The Social Roots of Factionalism Among Ukrainian Immigrants in Canada, 1896–1918" (M.A. thesis, University of Manitoba, 1978).

60. Alan B. Anderson, "Linguistic Trends Among Saskatchewan's Ethnic Groups" in *Ethnic Canadians: Culture and Education*, edited by Martin L. Kovacs (Regina, 1978); Ross McCormack, "Cloth Caps and Jobs: The Ethnicity of English Immigrants in Canada, 1900–1914" in *Ethnicity, Power and Politics in Canada*, edited by Jorgen Dahlie and Tissa Fernando (Toronto, 1981).

61. James S. Woodsworth, *Strangers Within Our Gates: or Coming Canadians* (Toronto, 1909, 1972).

62. W.L. Morton, "A Century of Plain and Parkland" in *A Region of the Mind*.

63. Robert E. Ankli, H. Dan Helsberg, and John Herd Thompson, "The Adoption of the Gasoline Tractor in Western Canada" in *Canadian Papers in Rural History* II, edited by Donald A. Akenson (Gananoque, 1980): 9–39.

64. John Archer, *Saskatchewan: A History* (Saskatoon, 1980).

65. Marc-Adelard Tremblay and Walton J. Anderson, eds., *Rural Canada in Transition* (Ottawa, 1966); Barry Wilson, *Beyond the Harvest: Canadian Grain at the Crossroads* (Saskatoon, 1981).

66. Anthony Sampson, *The Seven Sisters: The Great Oil Companies and the World They Shape* (New York, 1975); Peter Foster, *The Blue-Eyed Sheiks: The Canadian Oil Establishment* (Toronto, 1979); J.D. House, *The Last of the Free Enterprises: The Oilmen of Calgary* (Toronto, 1980); Dan Morgan, *Merchants of Grain* (New York, 1979, 1980).

67. C.F. Wilson, *A Century of Canadian Grain: Government Policy to 1951* (Saskatoon, 1978); Wilson, *Beyond the Harvest*; G.E. Britnell and V.C. Fowke, *Canadian Agriculture in War and Peace 1935-1950* (Stanford, 1962).

68. Leo Driedger, "Multicultural Regionalism: Toward Understanding the Canadian West" in *Papers of the Western Studies Conference 1983*, edited by A.W. Rasporich (forthcoming); J.E. Rea, "The Roots of Prairie Society" in *Prairie Perspectives*, edited by David P. Gagan (Toronto, 1970), 46–57.

69. J. Rick Ponting and Roger Gibbins, *Out of Irrelevance: A Socio-Political Introduction to Indian Affairs in Canada* (Toronto, 1980); Ian A.L. Getty and Antoine S. Lussier, eds., *As Long As The Sun Shines and Water Flows: A Reader in Canadian Native Studies* (Vancouver, 1983).

70. Dick Harrison, *Unnamed Country: The Struggle for a Canadian Prairie Fiction* (Edmonton, 1977); Laurence Ricou, *Vertical Man/Horizontal World: Man and Landscape in Canadian Prairie Fiction* (Vancouver, 1973); Eli Mandel, *Another Time* (Erin, Ont., 1977); Gerald Friesen, "Three Generations of Fiction: an Introduction to Prairie Cultural History" in *Eastern and Western Perspectives*, edited by David Jay Bercuson and Phillip A. Buckner (Toronto, 1981).

71. Roger Gibbins, *Prairie Politics and Society: Regionalism in Decline* (Toronto, 1980); David E. Smith, *The Regional Decline of a National Party: Liberals on the Prairies* (Toronto, 1981); Larry Pratt and Garth Stevenson, eds., *Western Separatism: The Myths, Realities and Dangers* (Edmonton, 1981).

72. Roger Gibbins, *Regionalism: Territorial Politics in Canada and the United States* (Toronto, 1982).

The Writing of British Columbia History†

ALLAN SMITH

I

Few collections of historical literature demonstrate more clearly than the work produced by British Columbia's historians the truth of the proposition that historians' vision of the past results from a complex process of interaction involving their own intelligence, the changing character of the reality they contemplate and the conceptual lens through which they view it. Each of the three main divisions into which historical writing about British Columbia falls must, in consequence, be defined not only in terms of the structure given it by the varying phenomena of which the historians producing it found it necessary to take account, but also by the manner in which their sense of what formed an appropriate subject of investigation was shaped by the changing framework of assumption, hypothesis, and value within whose confines they operated. What follows, then, at once records the shifting picture of the British Columbia past painted by its historians and attempts to explain how that picture acquired the balance and composition that set it apart. In so doing—the point should be made clear at the outset — it makes no attempt to examine exhaustively the body of historical writing dealing with British Columbia, but concentrates instead on work that seeks to make a comprehensive statement about its subject or contributes importantly to the articulation of a significant point of view about that subject.[1]

II

The first generation of British Columbia's historians approached their task through the agency of conceptual tools drawn directly from the values and experience of bourgeois Victorians. Human activity, they believed, was to be judged in terms of the extent to which it released the wealth of the world, created moral communities, and illustrated the truth that the individual was the master of his fate. In British societies, moreover, such activity had also to stand up under the scrutiny of those who sought to satisfy themselves that the interests of an entity of worldwide scope were being served.

On all of these counts the shape and content of the British Columbia experience did more than meet the test, for nothing seemed clearer than that the province was a place of wealth and splendour whose inhabitants were daily advancing themselves and their community down the road to development, the fulfillment of its imperial responsibilities, and moral perfection.

It helped, of course, that the province's inhabitants had been given much with which to work. The generation of British Columbia's historians active from the

†*BC Studies* 45 (Spring 1980): 73-102.

1880s to World War I was, in fact, struck more forcibly by the abundance of its material resources than by any other single factor in its character. Extravagantly endowed with land and fisheries,[2] in possession of vast mineral and timber reserves,[3] it seemed truly a land of plenty.[4] One could, indeed, hardly exaggerate its potential. It comprised, noted two early students of its past, "an empire equal in area to a third of Europe, and, though still in a state of savage nature, rich beyond measure in political and industrial possibilities."[5] Even reference to the immense difficulties geography had placed in the way of realizing that potential — the work, noted provincial librarian and archivist E.O.S. Scholefield, was "herculean" in its proportions[6] — served only to magnify the already considerable scope of what was being accomplished. As Scholefield himself insisted, the province's "progress within the fifty years succeeding the fur-trading era is the most remarkable in history."[7] Taking their cue from this stupendous fact, moving forward to consider what lay in front of them, the province's historians advanced as one to follow the lead given by Ontario immigrant and popular historian Alexander Begg in his efforts "to place on record . . . the rise and progress of British Columbia from its earliest discovery to the present. . . ."[8]

There was, inevitably, disagreement concerning which events in the province's history were to be assigned special status in its march towards greatness. Some thought it had all begun with the discovery of gold;[9] others took the view that the land-based fur trade precipitated the development of the colony;[10] all, however, agreed that whatever the significance of these early events, the coming of the CPR had been decisive. More than any other, that event had opened the way for unimagined growth and even the assumption by the province of a role of truly global significance.[11]

If the province's material progress had been extraordinary, there was, its historians insisted, equally compelling evidence that what it had experienced in the field of moral improvement was no less worthy of note. The action of Douglas in dealing with the American miners of the gold rush period offered one clear indication that standards of morality and order prevailed, but those wishing to prove how civilized life in British Columbia was found no need to stop short after having cited that familiar example. Few commentators, in fact, hesitated to speak in sweeping and all-inclusive terms of the striking contrast they saw between peaceful and law-abiding British Columbia and the settlements to be found on the American frontier. "In British Columbia," reported R.E. Gosnell, the province's first provincial librarian and archivist, "towns of the coast society were leavened with an especially religious and moral element,"[12] while, emphasized Scholefield, "even when Barkerville reached its high-water mark of prosperity, the population was generally distinguished for its sobriety and orderliness."[13]

Commentators, in fact, found a number of indications that life in British Columbia had attained a quality and perfection unmatched elsewhere. Schooling, noted Scholefield, "with all its softening and cultural influences"[14] had early been introduced into the life of the province, a point that the American historian H.H. Bancroft emphasized in closing his volume with a lengthy chapter on "Settlements, Missions, and Education 1861–1866."[15] Technology, too, had been instrumental in improving the quality of life. "Victoria city," noted Gosnell, "was one of the first cities in America to be lighted by electric lights," and the existence of its people had also been eased by trolley systems and hydroelectric power.[16] Even coal mining in British Columbia had a purer and less debilitating character than was the case elsewhere. "Beautifully situated with bright skies [and] pure air . . . [Nanaimo]," Bancroft claimed, "presents little of that sooty, opaque appearance, either physical or moral, so common to the colliery villages of England."[17] How, enthused Begg, could one doubt that in British Columbia there was much indeed to "delight the gaze of the enraptured visitor."[18]

This model society, insisted its historians, at once owed much to, and offered a nearly perfect environment for, the activities of the individual. While few commentators linked the themes of individualism and progress so explicitly as Gosnell and Scholefield — they entitled the sections of their history which contained biographical sketches of the province's great men "Sixty Years of Progress" — most were quite as concerned to make the point that the good society could have no real existence apart from the individuals who had shaped it. Captain Vancouver and Alexander Mackenzie, the voyageurs of fur-trading days and the prospectors of the gold rush, the officials of the Hudson's Bay Company (HBC), and the businessmen at the end of the nineteenth century were alike portrayed as men embodying the classic virtues of will, initiative, character, and pluck. Some, like Vancouver[19] and Douglas,[20] were celebrated for having lifted themselves far above the common level; others, such as the voyageurs[21] and the gold prospectors,[22] exemplified an anonymous populist virtue; still others — the words are Gosnell's, describing Judge Matthew Begbie — were seen as "men who left strong finger marks on the history of British Columbia in the plastic day of its first growth."[23] In each case, the message was the same: much of what was valuable and important in the history of the province had been created by self-reliant and enterprising individuals. The British Columbia experience, as Gosnell put it, was "illustrative of a phase of Canadian individual enterprise that in recent years has evolved so many men of large affairs out of the rugged elements of Canadian life and produced so much wealth from the resources of a country rich in opportunity and rapid in development."[24]

Important as it was, this emphasis on the individualist theme did not wholly supplant other ways of assessing the elements of provincial growth. Given the province's geography and early dependence on external markets and transportation links, it was, indeed, hardly possible to ignore the fact that what happened to the province and its people had much to do with circumstances beyond the control of any one individual. "Success," as Gosnell put it, "was in a general way dependent upon railway construction and communication with the outside world. . . ." In making possible the development of the interior, allowing commercial contacts with the rest of the Dominion, and opening direct trade with the Orient and Australasia, this mode of development had done much to make possible the great work of the province's citizens.[25] Even as they wrote of the individual's power, commentators thus devoted no small degree of attention to at least one part of the context within which the individual and the community were working out their destiny.

The American Bancroft was, paradoxically, one of the most determined of this group of historians to insist on the reality and importance of British Columbia's association with Canada. The province's imperial orientation did not escape his notice, but he was equally anxious to stress the fact that "we must . . . consider [B.C.] as linked with her sister colonies, with Vancouver Island as one with herself, and with the Dominion of Canada. . . ."[26] Begg, very much concerned to introduce British Columbia to eastern Canadians, was similarly anxious to locate it in a Canadian context. The CPR, he conceded, might have an imperial dimension, but its construction had also made possible the "Union of East and West," a fact the meaning of which had been underscored by the visits of the Governor General to British Columbia, all of which Begg chronicled in detail.[27]

Other commentators were, however, less sure that the Canadian link was to be given pride of place. Mindful of the province's maritime origins, aware of the role played by the HBC in the formative years of its history, and much impressed by the fact of Britain's imperial power in their own day, it seemed to these observers that the province's relationship to Canada was to be conceived largely in terms of its provincial and imperial relevance. This did not mean that British Columbia's links with the Dominion were held to be of no importance: Gosnell and his collaborator in writing the life of James Douglas, for example, took the effective development of British Columbia to have begun with the commencement of North West Company activities on the Pacific Coast. They pointed out that Douglas had considered after 1859 that the province's population would be built up by settlement from Canada rather than Britain, and they reminded their readers that the westernmost part of the continent had played an important part in the development of North America as a whole.[28] What received consistent emphasis was, nonetheless, British Columbia's isolation from what lay to the east. In terms both of its population and its external links, Scholefield insisted, mid-nineteenth-century British Columbia was an imperial community completely lacking "any relations whatever with any other portion of British North America. . . ."[29] Even after the eastern provinces joined together, the west coast remained isolated. "Geographically," noted Gosnell, "[it] was far removed from the seat of [federal] Government. An almost insuperable barrier of mountains cut it off from the rest of the British possessions. . . . The country . . . was in every sense foreign to Canada."[30] What was more, suggested one-time journalist and Speaker of the B.C. Legislature D.W. Higgins, the feeling was mutual: the British Columbia delegates sent to Ottawa to negotiate terms were regarded "as visitors from one of the heavenly planets, who, having ventured too near the edge of their world, had missed their footing and, falling into space, had landed at the federal capital."[31] This meant, insisted Gosnell, that union with Canada was in no sense a foregone conclusion. What produced it was, in fact, a quite rational calculation of provincial interest coupled with a strong sense that such a move had an important imperial relevance. It was, indeed, unlikely that in the absence of such a relevance, matters would have proceeded, for "throughout the length and breadth of the Empire there is no part where the people as a whole are so wholly and unreservedly devoted to the ideal of imperial unity and to British institutions as in British Columbia."[32] This meant that matters affecting the province were to be assessed in terms of their impact on it as part of the empire. The CPR, certainly, was very much to be viewed as having an imperial rather than a merely national role to play. The driving of the last spike, asserted Coats and Gosnell, "was a grave moment in the history of Canada and the British Empire. . . . The gateway to the Orient had been opened at last by land."[33] Even the Panama Canal was to be judged in terms of its capacity to allow British Columbia to move towards the assumption of a British-like status in world affairs. That remarkable engineering feat, predicted Gosnell, "will inevitably build up an industrial and mercantile Britain on the British Columbia coast, corresponding in all material respects to the Great Britain of many centuries old. . . ."[34] British Columbia, its historians insisted, was thus very much an imperial rather than a Canadian province, firmly rooted in a larger world. Having, as Gosnell put it, "interests which are *sui generis* in a degree greater perhaps than is true of any province of Canada," it had perforce to deepen its sense of its destiny, enlarge its understanding of the direction in which the unfolding of the historical process was taking it, and so avoid the dismal and pedestrian fate of becoming content with provincial status in a mere agglomeration of other and lesser jurisdictions.[35]

III

For all that they were concerned with painting the history of British Columbia in the brightest and most flattering colours, the early historians of the province were not entirely unaware that by the end of the nineteenth century the study of history had become a disciplined and critical undertaking. Begg, to be sure, was largely a compiler of other historians' work, but Bancroft displayed a Rankean enthusiasm for original sources and the kind of truth that flowed from them,[36] Gosnell was familiar with the germ theory of historical development and had some awareness of the relativity of historical judgment,[37] and both he and Scholefield were fully alive to the importance of documentary evidence.[38] It was, nonetheless, only after the Great War that historians of British Columbia developed an approach to their subject which, in moving them away from the special pleading on behalf of development, empire, and self-made men which had characterized so much of the early work, showed that they were prepared to take matters of perspective, analysis, and objectivity with due seriousness. What they wrote could hardly lose all trace of its ideological cast — as time passed it in fact more and more assumed the informal duty of rationalizing the claims of the regional interest groups that became steadily more prominent in both the economy and the government — but overall it acquired a noticeably more rigorous, disciplined, and methodologically sophisticated quality.[39]

The fact that growth and development were basic realities in the province's life insured, of course, that they would continue to receive attention, a guarantee also offered by the prevailing conceptual wisdom, which, in emphasizing geographical determinants, made it virtually impossible to ignore the important role played in the shaping of the province's history by exploitation of its resources. None of this was, however, incompatible with the taking of a more rounded and analytical view of the province's economic history. On the contrary, the application of environmentalist concepts to the study of British Columbia's evolution reinforced the moves in the direction of adopting a more critical perspective that had been encouraged by society's maturing and the emergence of history as a university-based discipline.[40] These developments, moreover, were in their turn powerfully reinforced by the growth of a reformist critique of big business which, in conjuction with the onset of the Great Depression, stimulated the impulse to observe the province's growth from something other than a blandly approving point of view.[41]

Even, in consequence, as commentators continued to place emphasis on the ruggedness of the environment and the difficulties it put in the way of road and railway builders[42] they focussed attention on such technical details as the difficulties created for the timber industry by the immense size of British Columbia logs[43] and began the process of reexamining the province's early economic history, paying particular attention to the relative importance of the land-based and maritime fur trades.[44] Notwithstanding the persistence of familiar lines of argument — the University of British Columbia's W.N. Sage, for example, never really abandoned his judgment that "it was the production of gold in British Columbia which in the end determined the future of both colonies"[45] — other elements in the province's economic life thus began to receive systematic consideration.

The single most important conceptual innovation in these years was undoubtedly that derived from the work of the staple theorists. Economist W.A. Carrothers' early work on the timber industry clearly betrayed the influence of the idea that B.C. development was best understood through the technique of relating it to the evolution of resource-based industries,[46] an approach he pursued in his examination of the fishing industry.[47] The leading national exponents of staple theory also interested themselves in the structure of the B.C. economy. A.R.M. Lower included Carrothers' work on the B.C. forest industry in his *North American Assault on the Canadian Forest*, while H.A. Innis examined mining in the Kootenays,[48] emphasized the links between the forest industry and the autonomist outlook of British Columbia,[49] and noted the particular character which its land-oriented, inshore nature had given the province's fishing industry.[50]

In all of this work there was a clear concern not simply to emphasize the importance of staple production but also to provide a more fully articulated view of economic development than had previously been made available. At the same time that investigators provided gross accounts of production and growth, they also, therefore, tried to characterize the activity with which they were dealing. Carrothers, certainly, emphasized the peculiar technology that terrain and size made it necessary for the forest industry to develop,[51] while Margaret Ormsby's reminder that agricultural activity was firmly rooted in the province's economic history drew particular attention to the role played by both technological and institutional innovation in that field.[52]

The more careful look at the province's economic life inspired by the economic and intellectual history of the interwar period not only resulted in a body of work that presented the province's history as the consequence of the exploitation of a series of staples; it also stimulated an attempt — never, regrettably, carried to fruition — to view the province's social and political life as a function of these activities. Innis himself, of course, played a key role in this process. His classic *Fur Trade in Canada* (Toronto, 1930) outlined the case for viewing geography and economics as the vital determinants of the political framework within which B.C. had come to operate, while in later work he drew attention to the manner in which the production of new staples had enhanced the strength of centrifugal forces in Canadian federalism, thereby strengthening autonomist tendencies in British Columbia as elsewhere.[53] Historians closer to home also made contributions in this area. In 1937 Sage suggested the existence of linkages between mining activity in the province and its peculiar outlook,[54] while by 1942 Judge F.W. Howay could emphasize the fur trade's preparation of the ground not only for settlement but for political division as well.[55]

More far-reaching in its impact on the writing of the province's historians—in fact a fundamental component of it — was the attention paid to the matter of situating the province in its appropriate context. Concern with this issue was not, it need hardly be said, new, but where the first generation of historians had been led by its emphasis on steam technology and its sentiment for empire to emphasize the province's imperial orientation, the decline of the empire coupled with the new investigators' concern with staples and markets led them to pay close attention to its regional character and its continental connections.[56] They had, indeed, already been pointed in this direction by their adoption of the frontierist modes of thought still fashionable in North American scholarly circles in the 1920s. Much influenced by H.E. Bolton and F.J. Turner, Sage noted in 1928 that "Canadians have not as a rule regarded their history from the North American point of view, still less from the standpoint of an historian of the Americas who sketches the evolution of the twin continents from the North Pole to Cape Horn."[57] When, he continued, they did look at it from this vantage point they would discover that their history could not be separated from that of the continent as a whole. Particularly concerned to insist on the existence of a single North American frontier,[58] Sage found his belief in its reality leading him to support André Siegfried's view that the natural divisions of the continent ran north and south and that, in consequence, "each of the settled regions of Canada is more closely in touch with the adjoining portion of the United States than with the next region of Canada."[59] The lesson to be extracted from this was clear — "If Canadian historians are to present in the future a more balanced picture it is essential that they should keep the whole development of the nation and of the five cultural regions more constantly before them"[60] — and Sage did not hesitate to apply it. In doing so he did not deny the importance of the orientation to the nation, to the empire and to the Pacific, that history had given B.C.,[61] but he was even more anxious to underscore the fact that geography had made a contribution of its own: "The isolation of the province from the rest of Canada," he informed his readers, "is an essential fact. British Columbians are Canadians with a difference."[62]

Utilizing this perspective, and hearkening back to the role markets and the structure of the economy played in the orientation of societies, political scientist H.F. Angus was led in 1942 to conclude that the province was, in fact, part of no single geographical or economic system. There had, it was true, been much economic involvement with the U.S., but the creation of political boundaries had created rival economies and so made it "quite wrong to consider the Pacific slope as constituting a single economic area."[63] Equally, however, no integrated national economy had developed, for the 1920s had seen the province's export markets oriented increasingly towards foreign buyers. "British Columbia's economic interests had," in consequence, "become independent of those of Canada."[64] That the province had links in several quarters but was pointed clearly in none seemed clear to Canadian-born historian James T. Shotwell: "Although still separated from the East by over a thousand miles of prairie and a wilderness untamed except by the national railway system, British Columbia found in federal union with the provinces farther east, a safeguard for the essentially British character of its traditions and institutions. At the same time its contacts with the western states increased."[65]

The uncertainty to which adoption of the regional-continental perspective had led was unwarranted to some — Innis had little patience with it[66] — but the difficulty of locating B.C. in the proper context remained. Even Margaret Ormsby's work demonstrated a degree of ambivalence on the matter. Very much committed to a fixed and unchanging view of the character of the province's internal life — she placed much emphasis on coast-interior rivalries, on the character of the valley communities, and on the shaping influence of Anglo-Irish and Canadian elements[67] — she resolved the larger problem of B.C.'s place in the world only with the passage of time. Preoccupied with purely regional concerns in the 1930s, war-time centralism, her sojourn in Ontario, and the influence of the Rowell-Sirois approach to national issues moved her for a period in the direction of a centralist view of the nation's history and British Columbia's relation to it.[68] Once back in British Columbia, however, she returned to a more fully province-centred view of the region's relationship to the country at large.

Central to her later work — and in this her essential regionalism plainly revealed itself — was the conviction that functions vital to the life of the province were rooted in the province itself. "From this time on," suggests John Norris, "there is observable in her writings a growing emphasis on the importance of the province as the true centre of cultural and social function. The Canadian union was increasingly viewed as a permissive entity, allowing variation — ideally, a loose federation permitting unity in emergencies."[69] As Ormsby herself put it in her 1966 Presidential Address to the Canadian Historical Association, "the fact of the matter was that, in nation-building, the nation would have to take much of its energy from tension. It would be desperately difficult to secure the articulation of regional economies and disparate cultural traditions."[70]

This Sage-like emphasis on the fundamental importance of regionalism in Canada did not, however, imply a Sage-like continentalism. Where Sage sought to work against the victory of a narrow provincialism by emphasizing the province's continental situation, Ormsby moved towards the same end by drawing attention to its British and imperial character. As she argued as late as 1960, only if the region were viewed in this context could its nature be fully understood. "Above all," as she put it, "we need to put the colonies on the Pacific seaboard into the setting of empire, since, forgetting that they were merely part of a greater whole, we are still too much inclined to think of them as isolated political units."[71] The province, to quote John Norris once more, was thus to be seen as "a British community whose provincialism is rooted in the large cosmopolitan civilization of a world-wide empire."[72]   While, then, the middle period has seen historians of

British Columbia move away from the earlier emphasis on progress, development and individualism, it also — as Ormsby's call to remember the imperial dimension in the province's past made clear — witnessed an important degree of continuity. Ormsby's own work laid undiminishing emphasis on the British and imperial background, and economic development — albeit viewed through different spectacles than in the earlier period — remained very much in the forefront as well. Overall, however, the fact of change was in the air. The impact of environmentalist modes of thought had been considerable, and, as Ormsby's work — synthesized in her 1958 *British Columbia: A History* — itself made clear, much new light had been shed on the province's character and development by considering its internal geography, its location in space, and the rivalries of its people. It would, a double set of events in the life of the province ensured, be this thrust in the direction of change which would be carried forward in the future.

IV

Just as the changing conceptual framework of British Columbia's historians after World War I had combined with alterations in the nature of the world in which they lived to displace the early emphasis on empire, progress, and individualism in favour of a concern with geographical and economic determinants, so by the 1960s another conceptual shift and further changes in the nature of reality were moving the focus of investigation in yet another direction. The complex process, to speak concretely, by which North American historians discovered that society, possessed of its own structure and dynamic, could not be understood solely in terms of the impact on it of the primary environment, stimulated an unprecedented interest on the part of British Columbia historians in the British Columbia variant of that phenomenon.[73] At the same time the changed position of Indians and orientals in British Columbia society, the arrival of significant numbers of European immigrants, and the clear emergence of a class-based politics created conditions which, in attracting attention to phenomena which could only be understood as components of society, invited the deployment of modes of analysis appropriate to their study.

Moves in the direction of dealing with themes in the history of society in British Columbia did not, of course, involve an absolute break with what had gone before. Even work which continued to concern itself with the familiar themes of development, growth and external links came, however, to possess a new cast. Not only did it offer a more nuanced look at such matters as investment patterns and the orientation of the economy — making the point that American involvement had not been so clearly dominant as had earlier been thought[74] — it also drew on the concepts of urban historians such as Lampard and Warner to begin the process of anatomizing the British Columbia city, providing a picture of urban growth, and specifying the role in it played by the various groups involved.[75]

For all, however, that changes in approach and emphasis could be discerned in these areas, it remained true that the most dramatic evidence that new developments were occurring came in other fields. One of them had, indeed, long profited from the attention paid it by the social scientists. In making their extraordinarily fruitful investigations into the lives and culture of the Northwest Coast Indians, the anthropologists had not, however, produced much that historians found worthwhile. Those commentators, sharing the perspective of the worthies whose exploits in civilizing the province they were recounting, were prevented by the world view in terms of which they operated from seeing the native population as anything other than a pitiful obstacle to progress and development, doomed to eclipse by the movement of history. When, therefore, the first generation of the province's historians did not ignore Indians altogether it dealt with them in the accents — disgust, superiority, paternalist condescension — of the civilization whose accomplishments it was recounting.[76]

As the movement of time made clear the magnitude of the European triumph over the native population and so diminished any sense that it was to be seen as a barrier on the path to progress, historians began to moderate their judgments. It became possible to view the native Indians first as an object of sympathy[77] and then, the passage of still more time having removed them yet further from the sight of the society from which historians took their cue, to see them as an irrelevance which, having in relative terms hardly figured in the province's past, need scarcely be mentioned at all.[78] At length the wheel came full circle. The very fact that Indians had almost disappeared from sight underscored the circumstance that their conqueror lived in a society founded on their displacement. The emerging realization that this was so — in part stimulated, be it said, by a new militance on the part of the Indians themselves — led to a developing interest in the process which had produced so devastating a result. It was at this juncture that the relevance of work done in the social sciences finally commended itself to historians, disciplining their inquiry and suggesting — as the emergence of the field of ethnohistory had already made clear — that they need not seek to make amends for past neglect by indulging in a naïve and guilt-ridden romanticization of the Indians' experience. Students of the British Columbia past, like students of North American history in general, thus found themselves taking a wholly new view of the Indian component of it.

This shift in perspective was simple but decisive. Once Indian societies began to be viewed as entities possessing societal integrity and coherence, the character of their relationship with the incoming Europeans assumed a much different aspect than it had been earlier thought to have. The components of Indian society were now seen to have formed a tough and cohesive whole which had been far from passive in its contacts with the Europeans. This was, to be sure, a point the burden of making which was still largely assumed by the anthropologists,[79] but by the 1960s there was clear evidence that historians had begun to take up the task. One of the most remarkable incidents in the history of contact in British Columbia could, in fact, be viewed by an historian of the Victorian world with quite remarkable results. William Duncan's success in building his model village at Metlakatla had, Jean Usher could insist, as much to do with the Tshimshians' own powers of adaptation and with Duncan's willingness to adjust his plans to meet their needs as it did with his determination and the power of the civilization he represented.[80] That the native population had been anything but supine during much of the contact period was demonstrated with particular force by Robin Fisher. The Indians' response to the arrival of the whites was,

Fisher argued, in no small measure to be understood "in terms of the priorities of their own culture." Before 1858, the year the fur trade ceased to be the dominant element in the province's economy and society, "Indians and Europeans shared a mutually beneficial economic system"[81] in which the integrity of Indian civilization was not seriously affected; only after that year, with the advent of settlement, did the Indians lose their capacity to control in some measure what was happening to them.

If the Indians' changing relationship to white society played a part in preparing the way for a new view to be taken of them, broadly similar alterations in the oriental's position led to much the same result. So long as the Asian immigrants remained a largely alien presence in a society still very much in process of formation — a presence linked, moreover, to exotic civilizations with whom neither British Columbia nor Canada at large had significant contact — discussion of them aroused intense feelings. Most of those who commented on the oriental's life in British Columbia in fact found it impossible to avoid participating in the controversy to which that life had given rise. This was true of the early historians whose anxiety to support the building of a British society led them to approve the racial exclusivism they regularly noted,[82] it was true of Chinese historian Tien-fang Cheng's plea for fair treatment for his compatriots,[83] it was true of Lower and Woodsworth's concern over the relationship a Japanese presence on Canada's west coast might bear to Japanese expansion,[84] and it was true, thanks to their approval of restrictions on oriental immigration and their advocacy of a quota system, of the work of the first sociologists to investigate the problem.[85]

With, however, the defeat of Japan, the fact of war-time co-operation with China, and the ongoing acculturation of the Japanese in Canada, the revulsion against racism produced by Nazi excesses could act with the continuing work of the social scientists to produce conditions in which it was possible to take a less heated view of the Asian minorites in British Columbia. The results the adoption of such a perspective might yield had indeed been anticipated before the war in the fact that the 1933 study undertaken by sociologists Charles H. Young and Helen R. Y. Reid did not simply implicate its authors in the controversy by virtue of the policy recommendations it made, but actively sought to locate the roots of racism itself by drawing on conceptual tools — especially those dealing with the effects in multicultural societies of competition for status and subsistence — developed by Robert E. Park and others.

The key developments, however, came after 1945. Writing in the immediate post-war period, sociologist Forrest LaViolette showed how observers might begin to view white-oriental relations by the expedient of attempting, at least for purposes of analysis, to distance themselves from direct involvement in them. Conceding that "race prejudice most certainly does have an economic component," he nonetheless argued that "more than mere economic competition and its associated processes" were involved in the generation of anti-oriental feeling in British Columbia.[86] A fuller explanation, he suggested, lay in the peculiar circumstances of the British Columbia community itself. There the problems of community building and integration always present in new societies were compounded by geographical isolation, concern about American expansionism, and a desire to remain British. These factors, joined to the relative absence of a creed which, in emphasizing individualism and citizenship, would have facilitated integration into the community of peoples of diverse backgrounds, ensured that highly visible and culturally distinct elements in the population would be perceived as posing a particularly sharp threat to the building of a unified community and so would become objects of discriminatory behaviour and policy.

By the 1970s a new generation of historians, contemplating the changed nature of the white-oriental relationship, inhabiting a climate of opinion which did not involve them in the old controversies about racism, and sensitized to the perspectives of the social scientists, were developing a genuine sympathy towards the idea that white-oriental relations could be best comprehended by employing a way of viewing behaviour which insisted that all facets of it — however strong the feelings of sympathy or revulsion they might arouse — were, in Durkheim's famous formulation, social facts, rooted in, and intelligible in terms of, a complex social whole to the comprehension of which a rigorously objective viewpoint was essential.[87] To be sure, Ken Adachi's account of the Japanese-Canadian experience,[88] for all that it provided a valuable insight into the factors inducing the Japanese-Canadians to accept their fate, remained essentially an indictment of white attitudes and policies, and in that sense did no more than Barry Broadfoot's popular account to grapple with the causes of racism.[89] Patricia Roy's sympathy with the more disciplined and critical approach of the social scientist was, however, clearly evident in her impatience with those who, preferring to see prejudice as the property of the perverse and wrong-headed, showed little disposition to understand its roots. She insisted, too, on the necessity of getting a sense of the time in which the events under study took place, and, no less importantly, on the need to go beyond simple economic explanations for anti-oriental feeling in favour of an insistence on the central role of the irrational.[90]

Carrying forward LaViolette's emphasis on the role a concern to consolidate and integrate the community in support of a specific set of values and modes of behaviour had played in creating anti-oriental feeling, and insisting, like Roy, on the centrality of the irrational, historian W.P. Ward made effective use of the concepts of social psychologist Gordon W. Allport in pointing to the tensions engendered between whites and orientals by British Columbia's existence as a pluralist society. The province's whites — thanks, Ward argued, to the important role stereotypical thinking played in such circumstances — could do no other than perceive the orientals as a threat to their values and a serious obstacle to the building of a homogeneous society. "Cultural pluralism," he argued, "was unacceptable to the white community . . . [for] the plural condition generated profound, irrational racial fears [and] stirred a deep longing for the social cohesion which could only be achieved, it seemed, by attaining racial homogeneity."[91]

The experience of Indians and orientals notwithstanding, acquisition over time of a lower profile was only one way in which different elements of the community might find themselves being viewed in a new way. The assumption by certain groups of a more obvious role in the life of the province could, it soon became clear, have precisely the same result. Where, accordingly, the relative absence of continental European stock in the province's population had allowed the first two generations of historians to indulge their British bias freely — as late as 1937 Sage could identify the province as "distinctly British"[92] — by 1970 historian Norbert MacDonald found it necessary carefully to underscore the role European immigration had played in the growth of its largest urban centre.[93] The interest in articulating the multicultural character of British Columbia to the growth of which MacDonald's work pointed was, of course, in part a manifestation of the concern — widespread in the decades after World War II — to build a strong and integrated community by making all its members feel that they had a place in it. One of the first attempts to focus systematic and organized attention on the province's ethnic groups was made in connection with the 1958 centennial,[94] while John Norris' 1971 account of the ethnic presence in British Columbia took form as part of the one-hundredth anniversary celebration of the province's entry into Confederation.[95] Even, however, in devoting itself to the task of redefining the character of the province's life in a way that legitimized the presence in it of many ethnic and racial groups, this work exposed to view many of the factors — prejudice in the host society, the immigrants' pre-migration background, their expected roles and statuses in their new country — governing the ethnic experience in British Columbia as elsewhere. Attention was not, however, focussed only on those adjustments which had been made relatively painlessly; in some instances the character of the immigrant experience made it necessary for historians to draw particular attention to the kind of conflict which the clash of cultures produced by that experience could create. In their study of one of the most difficult of these cases, George Woodcock and Ivan Avakumovic sought to explore the tension which resulted when an intensely self-conscious minority — the Doukhobors — determined to maintain its identity collided with a majority no less firmly committed to enforcing what it viewed as minimum standards of conformity.[96]

The rise to prominence of the ethnic fact in British Columbia's life was not the only new reality demanding attention in these years. The social, economic, and political divisions which seemed to acquire the status of permanent and central features in the province's life after 1945 also did their share in producing an altered picture of the province's character. There was, of course, nothing novel about the fact of conflict itself, for union activity, strikes, and a radical politics had been features of British Columbia's life since the late nineteenth century. The general shape of the province's history and, more especially, the peculiar configuration of its political life had, however, conspired to shift attention to other matters and so allowed these to sink into a general and all-encompassing oblivion. Where, that is to say, in other British North American and Canadian communities the clash of rival groups soon became institutionalized in clearly comprehensible political formations, conflict in British Columbia manifested itself in a less coherent rivalry between island and mainland, in faction-forming based on attitudes towards the federal tie, and in a politics of personal attachment and ascendancy of a distinctly eighteenth-century sort, a circumstance which led to a clear tendency to characterize the province's politics as without form and substance. As Coats and Gosnell, reflecting this tendency, put it, "a lack of leadership and even of constructive party organization . . . has been a feature of the politics of British Columbia. . . . [T]o make the obvious comparison with the eastern colonies, there was here no feud of ruling races to allay, no Family Compact to uproot, no Clergy Reserve to divide, no complicated fiscal policy to arrange."[97]

Even when party lines did emerge, in 1903, they appeared to delineate divisions among the members of the province's leading groups which seemed, if anything, more random and indeterminate than those to be found between Liberals and Conservatives in other parts of the country. "An examination of party platforms, resolutions of local and provincial Associations, speeches from the Throne, [and] debates in the legislature," Edith Dobie's 1936 survey of the first three decades of party history in British Columbia noted, "reveal[s] almost complete agreement between Liberals and Conservatives both in theory and in policies."[98]

Where, then, the clearly demarcated struggles between Reformers and Tories in Upper Canada or the clash of rival interests on the prairies invited the writing of a history that focussed on the activities of distinct political alternatives definable at least to a point in terms of real differences in outlook, the apparently vague and indeterminate character of conflict in British Columbia elicited only cursory and uncomprehending looks from those hurrying by to consider what seemed the manifestly more important, and certainly more readily understood, matters of growth and development. Even so astute an observer as Gosnell could make little sense of what he saw,[99] while later observers were content to repeat D.W. Higgins's attempts to introduce the categories of whig history into their discussion of the province's politics[100] or deal with such major events as the introduction of party politics in terms of its character as a stabilizing measure in a chaotic and volatile situation.[101]   The clear emergence in the 1930s of socialism as a key element in the province's political system forced a reconsideration of the character of that system which, thanks to the Beardian categories employed by its creator,[102] stressed both conflict and the existence of a relationship between economic interest and political behaviour, but by 1948 Sage, returning to a discussion of politics before 1903, abandoned this line of analysis in favour of one cast largely in terms of the conviction that "provincial politics in British Columbia was largely a game of the In's and Out's and a struggle between the Mainland and the Island."[103] Neither John Saywell's 1951 discussion of the relationship between economic interest and political organization in the early history of socialism in British Columbia[104] nor Margaret Ormsby's account of the difficulties economic geography and sociological background placed in the way of effective political organization by British Columbia's farmers[105] committed the same oversight, but what resulted from their work was, nonetheless, only a partial account of the manner in which division and conflict had manifested itself in the province's life.

If this absence of any sustained and comprehensive discussion of conflict in British Columbia society had meant only that students of the province's history were being spared what Donald Creighton once referred to as the "colossal tedium" of dealing with it in terms of the pseudo-struggles of party,[106] it might have been no bad thing; but it meant also that British Columbia's historians — with the exceptions above — maintained a peculiar blind spot when it came to social and economic conflict in general. The result was to reinforce the tendency to eschew discussion of the structure of the province's society in favour of situating it spatially, celebrating its growth and development, and concentrating attention on the great individuals who had contributed so much to its making. Captives of the obvious, enmeshed in the surface of events, British Columbia's historians not only failed to generate anything approaching the work of a Morton, a Lipset, or a Macpherson; they did not even duplicate L.G. Thomas's achievement in writing the history of an established party.[107]

That this was an unsatisfactory state of affairs seemed more than clear by the 1960s. The presence of division and conflict in the province's life had been made obvious both by the character of its politics and by the strength of its labour movement, facts which almost literally cried out for discussion and analysis. It was, appropriately enough in view of the awareness she had earlier shown of the relationship between politics, interest group membership, and the character of the economy, Margaret Ormsby who in 1960 made it clear that understanding of a whole dimension of the province's life was lacking. "We are ignorant," she wrote, "of the mainsprings of our political development. We can name our premiers, describe their careers, and recount their legislative enactments; but, as yet, we have not probed deeply enough to explain the basis of our early non-party tradition or the basis of the schisms and the realignments which have occurred since parties were first established."[108]

The convergence of a clear need to deal with these matters with the realization by Canadian scholars that the concept of class could be a useful one in the analysis of the historical process did much to ensure that the task would be carried out largely through the agency of that analytical tool. Where class and the conflict flowing from it could once have been dismissed as a kind of infantile disorder bound to disappear with the passage of time — "Nowhere in Canada," observed Coats and Gosnell in 1909, "have industrial disputes been waged with greater bitterness and violence than in British Columbia. This, however, is but to say that the province . . . is still in its infancy as an industrial community, and that the impulse which it obeys is western"[109] — the new circumstances did not allow it to be set aside so easily, for even the most casual observer could see that the province's political and industrial life had come to be affected in what seemed a fundamental way by a species of class activity. The peculiar militance of the British Columbia working class now, indeed, became a subject of discussion in its own right. Labour economist Stuart Jamieson, seeking in 1962 to locate its sources, found them in factors — the province's frontier character, its strike-prone type of industry, the influence of conditions in the United States, the structure of the province's labour legislation — specific to British Columbia,[110] while Paul Phillips, preferring to explain its existence in terms of more general factors, emphasized the role played in the rise of a militant labour movement by the unstable character of the market for labour in an economy dependent on primary products for export, the impact of technology, and the effect of social and economic dislocation.[111] This, it should be noted, did not mean that Phillips rejected out of hand the idea that class-based organizations in British Columbia had a particular character. For him, however, that special character was to be seen not so much in the circumstances that had given rise to those organizations as in the fact that their members had become more politically active than their counterparts in other sections of the country. In seeking anti-oriental legislation, protection for workers against exploitation by employers, and economic planning that would reduce the instability inherent in a resource-based, export-oriented economy, British Columbia workers, Phillips suggested, had early learned the value of political action and so were more fully influenced than other Canadian workers by the socialist ideology that was "in the air" at the turn of the century and after.[112]

That the British Columbia political system as a whole was class-based became the governing assumption of the most ambitious examination of the linkages between the province's politics, society, and economy so far undertaken. Arguing that the "nonpartisan" character of British Columbia's politics, the nature of its radicalism and the ascendancy of Social Credit were all linked to the character of the province's social and economic life, political sociologist Martin Robin's semi-popular account of the province's political growth sought to show that the presence of large enterprises in the timber and mining industry, the growth of a wage-earning class, the emergence of a petite bourgeoisie oriented mainly towards the service sector, and the absence of a significant number of independent commodity producers had produced a political system characterized by a succession of groupings, parties, and coalitions through the agency of which the large interests could maintain their influence, by an anti-capitalist rather than an anti-eastern protest tradition, and ultimately by a brand of populism whose petit bourgeois base made it first the enemy and then the ally of the large concentrations of power that dominated the economic life of the province.[113]

What Robin's work demonstrated — that the British Columbia political experience was, like other departments of the province's life, susceptible of analysis in terms of perspectives drawn from the social sciences — dramatically underscored the fact that discussion of the province's character and history had come to occupy ground far different than that on which it had earlier stood. How long scholars would continue to find the components — ethnic, racial, and class — of which society consisted an appropriate object of investigation would depend, as always, on what resulted from the interplay between the data historical reality presented for consideration and the conceptual tools by means of which those data were perceived and assessed; at the end of the 1970s there was, however, little evidence that this critical process was altering the framework within the confines of which those concerned with the British Columbian past had been working for much of the preceding two decades. The focus of study, it seemed likely, would remain firmly fixed on society and its nature.

V

For all that the perspective on the province's past employed by British Columbia's historians altered through time, one element in the changing picture they painted remained fixed and constant. Whether they placed emphasis on the province's imperial and national linkages, on its geography, on its orientation towards external markets or on its intelligibility in terms of concepts based on the experience of society at large, they demonstrated a strong and consistent commitment to the idea that British Columbia could not be understood without taking full account of its relationship to the world around it. Even as the regional focus of their activities anticipated Canada's national historians in underscoring the legitimacy of the regional approach, they thus avoided falling victim to a narrow provincialism.[114]

This did not mean that they knew at all times to what larger entity—nation, continent or empire—the province was linked; it certainly did not mean that they had a clear sense of the major realities—the individual, class—animating its internal life; least of all did it mean that they were able to produce a fully realized vision of the province's character and history. What, however, it did signify was that the province's most able and representative historians—no matter in what period they wrote— never fell victim to the illusion that the community of which they spoke could be understood in terms of anything other than its place in a larger world. The result was a body of writing which, in its attempts to grapple with problems of context, orientation, and social dynamic, at all times showed its authors anxious—within the conceptual limits specified above—to situate British Columbia in an appropriately comprehensive framework of analysis and discussion. At the same time that it demonstrated the complex nature of the relationship between the historian's circumstances, the reality she or he contemplates, and the work that results, that writing thus also made plain the cosmopolitan thrust of those who concerned themselves with the past and the character of Canada's westernmost province.[115]

Notes

1. For a good general bibliography of B.C. history, see H.K. Ralston, "Select Bibliography on the History of British Columbia," in *Historical Essays on British Columbia*, edited by J. Friesen and H.K. Ralston (Toronto: McClelland & Stewart, 1976), 281–93. For an excellent discussion of the work of some of the province's leading historians, see J. Friesen, "Introduction," ibid., vii–xxv.

2. Hubert Howe Bancroft, *History of British Columbia 1872–1887* (San Francisco, 188?), 743–48.

3. R.E. Gosnell, *A History of British Columbia* ([Vancouver?], 1906), 273, 289.

4. The maker of these remarks was D.W. Higgins, one-time editor of the Victoria *Colonist* and a former speaker of the B.C. Legislature, who contributed to Gosnell, *A History of British Columbia*. For the comments referred to here, see 122.

5. Robert Hamilton Coats and R.E. Gosnell, *Sir James Douglas* (Toronto, 1909), 94.

6. E.O.S. Scholefield, "Part One," in E.O.S. Scholefield and R.E. Gosnell, *A History of British Columbia* (Vancouver and Victoria, 1913), 156. "No other part of Canada," Scholefield emphasized, "had so much to contend with in this particular as had the Colony of British Columbia" (187).

7. Ibid., 67.

8. Alexander Begg, *History of British Columbia From its Earliest Discovery to the Present Time* (Toronto, 1894), 7.

9. Bancroft, *History of British Columbia*, 758; Scholefield, "Part One," 153.

10. "The sailor," wrote Coats and Gosnell, "showed the way, but it was the overland traveller who entered and took possession." (Coats and Gosnell, *Sir James Douglas*, 49–50.)

11. "The period from 1886 to 1892," noted D.W. Higgins, "was one of unexampled prosperity . . . throughout the province." Coats and Gosnell claimed that "the completion of the Canadian Pacific Railway marks from many points of view the beginning of a new era in the development of British Columbia" and Gosnell himself argued in 1913 that "progress . . . since the CPR has been completed, has been rapid and during the last decade phenomenal." See Higgins, in Gosnell, *A History of British Columbia*, 141; Coats and Gosnell, *Sir James Douglas*, 328; and R.E. Gosnell, "Part Two," in Scholefield and Gosnell, *A History of British Columbia*, 3.

12. Gosnell, *A History of British Columbia*, 7.

13. Scholefield, "Part One," 174.

14. Ibid., 180.

15. Bancroft, *History of British Columbia*, 707–39.

16. Gosnell, "Part Two," 178.

17. Bancroft, *History of British Columbia*, 574.

18. Begg, *History of British Columbia From its Earliest Discoveries to the Present Time*, 7.

19. Ibid., 50–51.

20. Coats and Gosnell, *Sir James Douglas*, 353.

21. Gosnell, *A History of British Columbia*, 39.

22. Ibid., 100–01; Bancroft, *History of British Columbia*, 758; Scholefield, "Part One," 178.

23. Gosnell, *A History of British Columbia*, 94.

24. Gosnell, "Part Two," 186n.

25. Ibid., 13, 4.

26. Bancroft, *History of British Columbia*, viii–ix.

27. Begg, *History of British Columbia From its Earliest Discoveries to the Present Time*, 457, 434–40, 509–45.

28. Coats and Gosnell, *Sir James Douglas*, 56–57, 253–54, 2.

29. Scholefield, "Part One," 179.

30. Gosnell, *A History of British Columbia*, 200–01.

31. Higgins, in Gosnell, *A History of British Columbia*, 123.

32. Gosnell, "Part Two," 5.

33. Coats and Gosnell, *Sir James Douglas*, 326. See also Gosnell, "Part Two," 114.

34. Gosnell, "Part Two," 196–97. See also Gosnell, *A History of British Columbia*, 295–96.

35. Gosnell, "British Columbia and British International Relations," *Annals of the American Academy of Political and Social Science XLV* (1913), 2.

36. "The simple truth in plain language was all," he once wrote, "I aimed at, and if any doubted my judgment or questioned my inferences, there before the reader should be the sources of my information from which he might draw his own conclusions." Hubert Howe Bancroft, *Retrospection: Political and Personal* (New York, 1912), 324.

37. Gosnell, "A Greater Britain on the Pacific," *Westward Ho! Magazine* II, 1 ([January?]) 1908), 8; Gosnell, "Prefatory," in Scholefield and Gosnell, *A History of British Columbia*.

38. "Many hundreds," reported the editor, "indeed thousands, of authorities and original sources of information — represented in individual recollections, old manuscripts, diaries, official documents and state papers, magazines, newspapers, pamphlets and books — were consulted." See "Editor's Foreword," Scholefield and Gosnell, ibid.

39. This shift was not equally clear in all quarters. F.W. Howay, one of the middle period's most prolific historians, continued to trade very largely in the intellectual commodities of the pre-war era. The Victorian certitudes that informed his major work, written in collaboration with Scholefield and published in 1914, were equally in evidence in what he produced in later years. He was particularly captivated by the myth of the self-made man. Cook, he would assert in 1928, was "the son of a day labourer . . . [who] by sheer industry and merit . . . rose rapidly," while David Thompson was also "a wonderful example of a self-made man." He continued, too, to believe that the province's history could best be written around the theme of progress, a fact underscored by the title of his 1930 contribution to the *Cambridge History of the British Empire*. Even University of British Columbia historian W.N. Sage, very much alive to new currents of thinking, did not wholly escape the influence of the old. His 1930 biography of Sir James Douglas showed him to be still very much impressed by the role the individual could play in the historical process — Douglas, he wrote, was "a great man, the greatest in the history of British Columbia" and has done much to shape its future — and as late as 1946 he was prepared to advance the proposition that the history of the province's largest city could be usefully approached in terms of the concept of progress. See E.O.S. Scholefield and F.H. Howay, *British Columbia from the Earliest Times to the Present*, 4 vols. (Vancouver, 1914); F.H. Howay, *British Columbia: The Making of a Province* (Toronto, 1928), 15, 60; F.H. Howay, "The Settlement and Progress of British Columbia, 1871–1914," *Cambridge History of the British Empire*, vol. 6 (Cambridge, 1930); Walter N. Sage, *Sir James Douglas and British Columbia* (Toronto, 1930), 347; and Walter N. Sage, "Vancouver — 60 Years of Progress," *British Columbia Journal of Commerce Yearbook, 1946* (Vancouver, 1946).

40. What H.F. Angus had in mind when he suggested in 1929 that the time had come for historians and social scientists to consider in a close and detailed way the province's social and economic history, focussing, in particular, on the experience of representative communities in order to get a sense of the manner in which the community as a whole had developed. See H.F. Angus, "A Survey of Economic Problems Awaiting Investigation in British Columbia," *Contributions to Canadian Economics* II (1929), 47.

41. By the early 1940s Angus could dismiss the overweening concern with development that had been characteristic of British Columbia's businessmen at the turn of the century as the outcome of a "predatory psychology," while ten years after that Margaret Ormsby balanced what John Norris called her "hinterlander's" approval of development as something that brought "comfort, leisure, education, and civilization" against the fact that such development was often uneven in its impact, and, in consequence, productive of serious social and economic inequities. See F.W. Howay, W.N. Sage, and H.F. Angus, *British Columbia and the United States* (Toronto and New Haven, 1942), 379, and John Norris, "Margaret Ormsby," in *Personality and History in British Columbia: Essays in Honour of Margaret Ormsby*, edited by John Norris and Margaret Prang (Victoria, 1977), 17.

42. Especially noticeable in such works as Noel Robinson, "Mining, Roads, and Development," in *Builders of the West: A Book of Heroes*, edited by F.W. Howay (Toronto: Ryerson Press, 1929), 218–31, but also to be seen in Howay, Sage, and Angus, *British Columbia and the United States*, 302.

43. A theme developed by W.A. Carrothers, "Forest Industries of British Columbia," in *The North American Assault on the Canadian Forest*, edited by A.R.M. Lower (Toronto and New Haven, 1938), 246, reference to which is also made in Howay, Sage, and Angus, *British Columbia and the United States*, 302.

44. In which work Howay took great interest. For a summary of his views, see F.W. Howay, *British Columbia: The Making of a Province* (Toronto, 1928), 90.

45. Sage, *Sir James Douglas and British Columbia*, 237.

46. Carrothers, "Forest Industries of British Columbia."

47. W.A. Carrothers, *The British Columbia Fisheries*, foreword by H.A. Innis, University of Toronto Political Economy Series No. 10 (Toronto, 1941).

48. H.A. Innis, *Settlement and the Mining Frontier* (Toronto, 1936). Published in one volume with A.R.M. Lower, *Settlement and the Forest Frontier in Eastern Canada* (Toronto, 1936).

49. H.A. Innis, "Editor's Preface," in A.R.M. Lower, *The North American Assault on the Canadian Forest*, vii-xviii.

50. H.A. Innis, "Foreword," in Carrothers, *The British Columbia Fisheries*, v-xii.

51. Carrothers, "Forest Industries of British Columbia," 246.

52. "It was," she wrote, "in the field of specialized agriculture and experimentation in controlled marketing that British Columbia was to make its unique contribution to Canadian agriculture." See her "Agricultural Development in British Columbia," *Agricultural History* XIX, 1 (Jan. 1945): 11, and her "The History of Agriculture in British Columbia," *Scientific Agriculture* XX, 1 (Sept. 1939): 61-72, where these points are first outlined. For another commentator's view of the importance of agriculture in the province's development, see G. Neil Perry, "The Significance of Agricultural Development and Trade in the Economic Development of British Columbia," *Scientific Agriculture* XX, 1 (Sept. 1939): 73-86.

53. Innis, "Editor's Preface," in Lower, *The North American Assault on the Canadian Forest*, vii-xviii.

54. W.N. Sage, "Geographical and Cultural Aspects of the Five Canadas," Canadian Historical Association, *Annual Report* (1937), 34.

55. Howay, Sage, and Angus, *British Columbia and the United States*, 41.

56. Their preoccupation with its imperial sitatuion had not, of course, completely blinded the first generation of historians to the fact that the province had a continental dimension to its experience. Bancroft had seen it as part of the civilization of the Pacific slope, Okanagan historian J.A. MacKelvie had emphasized the manner in which its interior geography had linked it to the United States— "stretching from the Peace River to the Gulf of Mexico," he noted, "is a general succession of valleys and plains lying in a continental depression behind the coast range of mountains, and of this chain the Okanagan forms an important link" — and even Gosnell made it clear that he found geography to have tied B.C. closely to the continent as a whole. In the main, however, the realities of the age in which these figures lived combined with the conceptual tools in terms of which they operated to ensure that their attention would be focussed elsewhere. See Bancroft, *History of British Columbia 1872-1887*, MacKelvie, "The Development of the Okanagan," in Scholefield

and Gosnell, *A History of British Columbia*, 211, and Gosnell, "British Columbia and British International Relations," 3.

57. W.N. Sage, "Some Aspects of the Frontier in Canadian History," Canadian Historical Association, *Annual Report* (1928), 62.

58. Ibid., 63. In a 1940 revision of this article, Sage stressed the interconnectedness of the two societies even more strongly. *"This interlacing of the frontier,"* he wrote, italicizing his words for emphasis, *"is most important."* See W.N. Sage, *Canada From Sea to Sea* (Toronto, 1940), 32.

59. Sage, "Geographical and Cultural Aspects of the Five Canadas," 28.

60. Ibid., 34.

61. There were, he freely conceded in 1932, forces within British Columbia itself which had impelled the colony in the direction of union with the rest of British North America, and by 1945 he could advance the argument that the early years of the twentieth century had seen British Columbia—thanks largely to changes in the character of its population and the links provided by the CPR—integrated into the Dominion. The CPR, he wrote elsewhere—and here his emphasis on the imperial tie was clear— had in fact been not only "the iron link of Confederation" but also "of great strategic importance to the British Empire," while the Pacific, he continued, "is at [British Columbia's] door and the orient just beyond." See Walter N. Sage, "The Critical Period of British Columbia History, 1866–1871," *Pacific Historical Review* I, 4 ([Autumn?] 1932): 424-43; Walter N. Sage, "British Columbia Becomes Canadian 1871–1901," *Queen's Quarterly* LII, 2 (Summer 1945): 168–83; Walter N. Sage, "Five Canadas," 34. See also Walter N. Sage, "British Columbia," in *The Story of Canada*, edited by George M. Wrong, Chester Martin, and Walter N. Sage (Toronto, 1929), 347, 351.

62. Sage, "Five Canadas," 33.

63. Howay, Sage, and Angus, *British Columbia and the United States*, 380.

64. Ibid., 388.

65. Shotwell, "Introduction," in ibid., vi.

66. See his review of ibid., *Canadian Historical Review* (hereafter *CHR*) XXXV, 3 (Sept. 1943): 311–12.

67. Ormsby's emphasis on the heterogeneous character of British Columbia society had been anticipated by Sage's remark that "Geographically there are six or seven British Columbia's. . . . The centres of population are on the coast and many portions of the vast interior are exceedingly sparsely settled. The division of the province into coast and interior is vital. The older division of island versus mainland still exists. . . ." Assessments of this kind were in fact common enough even in the writing of the first generation of historians, but Ormsby's special feeling for the interior communities allowed her to elaborate the point in a wholly unprecedented way. Her general history made frequent reference to the valleys and their people, and part of the strength of her Presidential Address to the Canadian Historical Association derived from the attention it gave the British Columbia character as a phenomenon rooted in the small communities of the province. Even her discussion of Susan Allison's life in British Columbia focussed on the nature of life in the hinterland communities rather than the experience of pioneer women; here, too, as John Norris suggests, Ormsby was concerned to portray the Similkameen and Okanagan settlements Allison inhabited as "examples of the warm, intimate communities which provide the basic strength of a society in any era. . . ." Sage, "Five Canadas," 33–34; Ormsby, *British Columbia: A History* (Toronto, 1958), 440; Ormsby, "A Horizontal View," Canadian Historical Association, *Historical Papers* (1966), 11; Ormsby, *A Pioneer Gentlewoman in British Columbia: The Recollections of Susan Allison* (Vancouver, 1976); John Norris, "Margaret Ormsby," 26.

68. "Prime Minister Mackenzie, the Liberal Party, and the Bargain with British Columbia," *CHR* XXVI, 2 (June 1945): 148–73; "Canada and the New British Columbia," Canadian Historical Association, *Annual Report* (1948): 74–85.

69. Norris, "Margaret Ormsby," 24–25.

70. Ormsby, "A Horizontal View," 8.

71. Ormsby, "Neglected Aspects of British Columbia's History," *British Columbia Library Quarterly* XXIII, 4 (April 1960): 10.

72. Norris, "Margaret Ormsby," 15.

73. The conviction that society is a phenomenon possessing its own structure and dynamic and can usefully be approached carrying the tools of the social scientist did not, of course, impress itself on all North American historians with equal force. For a comment on its failure, in the early stages of its development in

the U.S., to do so there, see A.S. Eisenstadt, "American History and Social Science," *The Centennial Review* VII (Summer 1963): 255–72. In the next year, however, a group of American historians could co-operate in the writing of a volume intended to acquaint their colleagues in the field with the utility of this approach; by the early 1970s interest in it had grown to the point where, in Samuel P. Hays' view, there was as much of a need to insist on discipline and rigour in the field as there was to urge historians to enter it; and by 1977 the body of work in the history of American society, especially that of the colonial period, had begun to generate a critical literature of its own. See Edward N. Saveth, ed., *American History and the Social Sciences* (New York, 1964); Samuel P. Hays, "A Systematic Social History," in *American History: Retrospect and Prospect*, edited by G. Grob and G. Billias (New York, 1971), 315–66; and Richard Beeman, "The New Social History and the Search for 'Community' in Colonial America," *American Quarterly* XXIX, 4 (Fall 1977): 422–43. Canadian historians, urged in 1965 to give attention to the history of society and more especially the class component in it, took up the task with a steadily growing enthusiasm. For S.R. Mealing's suggestion that this approach would be a profitable one, see his "The Concept of Social Class and the Interpretation of Canadian History," *CHR*, XLVI 3 (Sept. 1965): 201–18. For a survey of the work produced, see Carl Berger, "Social and Intellectual History," in *Canada Since 1867: A Bibliographical Guide*, edited by J.L. Granatstein and Paul Stevens (Toronto, 1974), 75–86; Michael Cross, "Canadian History," in *Literary History of Canada*, edited by C.F. Klinck et al. (Toronto, 1976), III: 63–83; and H.L. Hanham, "Canadian History in the 1970s," *CHR* LVIII, 1 (March 1977): 2–22.

74. H.K. Ralston, "Patterns of Trade and Investment on the Pacific Coast, 1867–1892: The Case of the British Columbia Salmon Canning Industry," *BC Studies*, 1 (Winter 1968–69): 37–45; Patricia E. Roy, "Direct Management From Abroad: The Formative Years of the British Columbia Electric Railway," in *Enterprise and National Development: Essays in Canadian Business and Economic History*, edited by Glen Porter and Robert D. Cuff (Toronto, 1973), 101–21.

75. J.M.S. Careless, "The Lowe Brothers, 1852–1870: A Study in Business Relations on the North Pacific Coast," *BC Studies*, 2 (Summer 1969): 1–18; the same author's "The Business Community in the Early Development of Victoria, British Columbia," in *Canadian Business History: Selected Studies, 1497–1971*, edited by David S. Macmillan (Toronto, 1972), 104–23; Norbert MacDonald, "Seattle, Vancouver, and the Klondike," *CHR* XLIX, 3 (Sept. 1968): 234–46; and the same author's "Population Growth and Change in Seattle and Vancouver, 1880–1960," *Pacific Historical Review* XXXIX, 3 (Oct. 1970): 297–321.

76. Begg, for example, saw the triumph of white civilization, however unfortunate for the Indians themselves, as at once inevitable and a sign of progress; Scholefield thought them "lawless savages" kept in hand by the "paternal solicitude" of the Hudson's Bay Company; and Coats and Gosnell found them an "inferior" and "docile" people who had lived no more than a "barren existence." See Begg, "The Native Tribes and Civilization," 115–19; Scholefield, "Part One," in Scholefield and Gosnell, *A History of British Columbia*, 57, 85; and Coats and Gosnell, *Sir James Douglas*, 80. The one important exception to this general rule was the treatment given the Indians by Father A.G. Morice, whose anthropological interests coupled with his sojourn among the Indians allowed him to develop a degree of sympathy with their culture, value, and institutions. See A.G. Morice, *The History of the Northern Interior of British Columbia, 1660–1880* (Toronto, 1904).

77. By 1928 Howay could concede that "the Indian had his own standards of morality," and by 1942 he found it possible to note "the finely balanced economic and social fabric" of tribal life. See Howay, *British Columbia: The Making of a Province*, 9; Howay, Sage, and Angus, *British Columbia and the United States*, 13.

78. Ormsby's general history gave them scant attention, and her 1960 appeal for new work made no reference to them at all. Ormsby, *British Columbia*, and the same author's "Neglected Aspects."

79. See, for example, Forrest LaViolette's *The Struggle for Survival: Indian Cultures and the Protestant Ethic in British Columbia* (Toronto, 1961, 1973), which makes the point that Indian concern to preserve the potlatch did not grow out of heathenish perversity but was the consequence of a desire to preserve a key element in a functioning social system, and Wilson Duff's *The Indian History of British Columbia*. Volume I. *The Impact of the White Man* (Victoria, 1965), which argues that Indian culture was capacious and elastic enough to absorb, at least for a time, innovations in technology, social organization, and culture introduced by the whites.

80. Jean Usher, "Duncan of Metlakatla: the Victorian Origins of a Model Indian Community," in *The Shield of Achilles: Aspects of Canada in the Victorian Age*, edited by W.L. Morton (Toronto, 1968), 286–310; *William Duncan of Metlakatla: A Victorian Missionary in British Columbia* (Ottawa, 1974).

81. Robin Fisher, *Contact and Conflict: Indian-European Relations in British Columbia 1774-1890* (Vancouver, 1977), xi, xiv.

82. Coats and Gosnell dealt with them in unflattering terms with a clear emphasis on steps taken to restrict Asian entry, while as late as 1928 Howay could refer to the Japanese as "wily little yellow men." See Coats and Gosnell, *Sir James Douglas*, 336-37; Howay, *British Columbia*, 265.

83. "All intelligent people," he wrote, "are willing to admit that Canada, the United States, Australia, and New Zealand have a perfect right to keep their country [*sic*] as white as possible; but it is highly desirable that they should always consider the honour and dignity of the Oriental nations, so that in excluding the orientals they will not create racial hatred and racial conflict in the future." Tien-fang Cheng, *Oriental Immigration in Canada* (Shanghai, 1931), 267.

84. A.R.M. Lower, *Canada and the Far East* (New York, 1940), Charles J. Woodsworth, *Canada and the Orient: A Study in International Relations* (Toronto, 1941).

85. "Conclusion," in Charles H. Young and Helen R.Y. Reid, *The Japanese Canadians* (Toronto, 1938), 171-93.

86. Forrest LaViolette, *The Canadian Japanese and World War II: A Sociological and Psychological Account* (Toronto, 1948), 283.

87. "All," Durkheim wrote in *The Rules of Sociological Method* (trans. Sarah A. Solovay and John H. Mueller (Chicago, 1938), 41), "that [sociology] asks is that the principle of causality be applied to social phenomena." Cited in H. Stuart Hughes, *Consciousness and Society: The Reconstruction of European Social Thought 1890-1930* (New York, 1958), 281.

88. Ken Adachi, *The Enemy That Never Was: A History of the Japanese Canadians* (Toronto, 1976).

89. Barry Broadfoot, *Years of Sorrow, Years of Shame: The Story of the Japanese Canadians in World War Two* (Toronto, 1977).

90. See, on the first point, her review of Adachi's book in *CHR* LIX, 2 (June 1978): 255-57. Her own understanding of the issue can be found in Patricia E. Roy, "The Oriental 'Menace' in British Columbia," in *The Twenties in Western Canada*, edited by S.M. Trofimenkoff (Ottawa, 1972), 243-58; "Introduction," Hilda Glynn-Ward, *The Writing on the Wall* (Toronto, 1974), vi-xxxi; and "The Soldiers Canada Didn't Want: Her Chinese and Japanese Citizens," *CHR* LIX, 3 (Sept. 1978): 341-57.

91. W.P. Ward, *White Canada Forever: Popular Attitudes and Public Policy Towards Orientals in British Columbia* (Montreal, 1978), 92-93.

92. Sage, "Five Canadas," 34.

93. "The distinctly new feature in Vancouver's make-up [in the post-war period]," he insisted, "was the great increase in persons of European origin." (MacDonald, "Population Growth and Change in Seattle and Vancouver, 1880-1960," 316.)

94. Dorothy Blakey Smith, *Ethnic Groups in British Columbia: A Selected Bibliography* . . . (Victoria, 1957).

95. John Norris, *Strangers Entertained: A History of the Ethnic Groups of British Columbia* (Vancouver, 1971).

96. George Woodcock and Ivan Avakumovic, *The Doukhobors* (Toronto and New York, 1968).

97. Coats and Gosnell, *Sir James Douglas*, 338, 342.

98. Edith Dobie, "Party History in British Columbia 1903-1933," *Pacific Northwest Quarterly* (hereafter *PNQ*) XXVII, 2 (April 1936): 154.

99. What he wrote of the period 1897 to 1904, indeed, summarized his sense of the politics of the preceding thirty years: ". . . the [political] events referred to appear highly kaleidoscopic in their rapidity of succession and changing complexities and combinations. . . .Conditions were in a state of ferment, of unrest, and the process of clarification which ensued [the formation of parties] might be compared to a casual admixture of highly reactive chemical elements." (Gosnell, "Part Two," in Scholefield and Gosnell, *A History of British Columbia*, 149.)

100. Neil Robinson, "The Struggle for Responsible Government," in *Builders of the West: A Book of Heroes*, edited by F.W. Howay (Toronto, 1928), 232-36.

101. F.W. Howay, *British Columbia: The Making of a Province* (Toronto, 1928), 241; W.N. Sage, "British Columbia," in *The Story of Canada*, 348.

102. The introduction of party lines in 1903, suggested Edith Dobie, had been made partly as the result of a desire on the part of the province's elites to avoid political division based solely on opposition between socialists and non-socialists, since, in their view, such a division could only augment the strength of the

socialists, and partly to ensure much-needed stability in the interest of getting particular programs approved. Edith Dobie, "Some Aspects of Party History in British Columbia, 1871–1903," *Pacific Historical Review* I, 2 (June, 1932): 247, 250. The major change introduced into the province's political life by the CCF's assumption of the status of official opposition, she wrote in a second article, produced "what seems a new and genuine party alignment on the question of the fundamental structure of society" and so pointed to the existence of a clear relationship between economic interest and political behaviour. Edith Dobie, "Party History in British Columbia 1903–1933," *PNR* XXVII, 2 (April, 1936): 165.

103.   W.N. Sage, "Federal Parties and Provincial Political Groups in British Columbia, 1871–1903," *British Columbia Historical Quarterly* (hereafter *BCHQ*) XII, 2 (April 1948): 152.

104.   John Tupper Saywell, "Labour and Socialism in British Columbia: A Survey of Historical Development Before 1903," *BCHQ* XV, 3–4 (July-Oct. 1951): 129–50.

105.   Margaret A. Ormsby, "The United Farmers of British Columbia: An Abortive Third-Party Movement," *BCHQ* XVII, 1-2 (Jan.-June 1953): 53–73.

106.   Donald Creighton, "Sir John Macdonald and Canadian Historians," *CHR* XXIX, 1 (March 1948): 7.

107.   In undertaking to investigate a regionally or provincially based political formation in terms of the social, economic and geographical factors that brought it into being, each of these scholars demonstrated a far surer grasp of the nature and complexity of the links between these two sets of phenomena than anything which had up to that time been produced by students of the British Columbia experience. See W.L. Morton, *The Progressive Party in Canada* (Toronto, 1950); Seymour Martin Lipset, *Agrarian Socialism: The Cooperative Commonwealth Federation in Saskatchewan. A Study in Political Sociology* (Berkeley, 1950); C.B. Macpherson, *Democracy in Alberta: Social Credit and the Party System* (Toronto, 1953); L.G. Thomas, *The Liberal Party in Alberta: A History of Politics in the Province of Alberta 1905–1921* (Toronto, 1959).

108.   Margaret Ormsby, "Neglected Aspects of British Columbia's History," *British Columbia Library Quarterly* XXIII, 4 (April 1960): 10.

109.   Coats and Gosnell, *Sir James Douglas*, 335.

110.   Stuart Jamieson, "Regional Factors in Industrial Conflict: The Case of British Columbia," *Canadian Journal of Economics and Political Science* XXVIII, 3 (Aug. 1962): 405–16.

111.   Paul Phillips, *No Power Greater: A Century of Labour in British Columbia* (Vancouver, 1967), 160–62.

112.   Ibid., 162-64.

113.   See Martin Robin, "The Social Bases of Party Politics in British Columbia," *Queen's Quarterly* LXXII, 4 (1965–66): 675–90; his "British Columbia: The Politics of Class Conflict," in *Canadian Provincial Politics: The Party Systems of the Ten Provinces*, edited by Martin Robin (Toronto, 1972), 27–68; his *The Rush for Spoils: The Company Province 1871–1933* (Toronto, 1972); and his *Pillars of Profit: The Company Province 1934–1972* (Toronto, 1973). For a sharply critical comment on Robin's work, see Alan C. Cairns, "The Study of the Provinces: A Review Article," *BC Studies* XIV (Summer 1972): 73–82; for Robin's reply and a further comment by Cairns, see *BC Studies* XVI (Winter 1972-73): 77–82.

114.   Sage's insistence, in opposition to the Laurentianism that was emerging in the 1930s as an important organizing principle in the study of Canadian history, that the regions of Canada should provide the main focus of the historian's study, found a parallel on the prairies in the form of W.L. Morton's 1946 plea for a Canadian history that would take due account of the experience, and point of view, of the parts which composed it. Not, however, until the late 1960s, when shifts in the distribution of national power had persuaded some eastern-based historians that a centralist view of the country's history was no longer tenable, did the regional approach find a following in their part of the country. See Sage, "Five Canadas"; W.L. Morton, "Clio in Canada: The Interpretation of Canadian History," *University of Toronto Quarterly* XV, 3 (April 1946): 227–34; J.M.S. Careless, " 'Limited Identities' in Canada," *CHR* L, 1 (March 1969): 1–10; Paul G. Cornell, et al., *Canada: Unity in Diversity* (Toronto, 1967); Mason Wade, ed., *Regionalism in the Canadian Community, 1867-1967: Canadian Historical Association Centennial Seminars* (Toronto, 1969).

115.   For a recent example of this kind of cosmopolitan regionalism, see A.D. Scott, "Introduction: Notes on a Western Viewpoint," *BC Studies* XIII (Spring 1972): 3–15.

SECTION 2
SOCIAL HISTORY

SOCIAL HISTORY IN CANADA: A REPORT ON THE "STATE OF THE ART"†

DAVID GAGAN AND H. E. TURNER

It is impossible to do justice to the recent historiography of Canadian social history if one accepts as "social" history everything that, whether for convenience or through misrepresentation, is claimed to be social history. Consequently, this review is highly selective in two ways. It embraces only scholarship which falls within parameters of a rather arbitrary definition of social history. Within this context, subsequently, our review attempts to identify the central thrust of that scholarship within the last ten years. If, in so doing, our intent has been to scale down the task assigned to us, it has also been to cut away the overburden of "history with the politics left out" in order to reveal the richest veins of *societal* history which lie beneath.

Several historians have developed extended, and fruitful, definitions of social history.[1] We will not rehearse their arguments or those of their critics here. For our purposes, social history is the study of the historical processes which prompted change and continuity in those social relationships that, taken altogether, describe and explain a whole way of life. Social history, in short, is the stuff of societal history if, by societal history, we mean the total human order in a given era, age or epoch.[2] Finally, by "social history" we mean also history that treats society not as a museum of artifacts to be described, but as a constantly changing archive of public and private experience awaiting both empirical investigation and theoretical speculation aimed at delineating the historical meaning of social reality.

Internationally, in the last decade or so social history has interested itself in a broadly defined catalogue of "groups": women, children, adolescents, the elderly; family and household; voluntary associations, political factions, professional and vocational groups, "crowds" and "movements"; social classes; local populations and civilizations. At the centre of all these inquiries, however, there appear to be three related themes or issues common, and crucial, to societal history — the timing, the sources, and the effects of social discontinuity. Similarly, recent social history has been organized, generally, around a fairly narrow range of investigative approaches and theoretical perceptions such as demography, material life, mentalities (collective consciousness or cultural cohesiveness), prosopography (collective biography stressing interest group dynamics), and social structure analysis. The life-cycle and social transformation ("reformation" might be a better word) have provided the essential reference points for much recent social history.[3] The conceptual frameworks are narrower still. Industrialization, urbanization, "modernization" and, in a variety of formulations, economic determinism, have provided the theoretical anchors for most current analyses of social discontinuity.

†*Archivaria* 14 (Summer 1982): 27–52.

English-Canadian Historiography

In the last decade or so Canadian historians have been no less preoccupied with social history than have their counterparts in Britain, Europe and the United States. The annual registers of dissertations in progress swell with entries under social, economic, and cultural history; a learned journal devoted exclusively to social history is a thriving enterprise; at least two series provide outlets for major contributions to the field; and the Social Sciences and Humanities Research Council of Canada now specifically encourages mission-oriented research in three areas of interest to social historians — population aging, the family and the socialization of children, and women in the labour force. In short, social history as a field for both teaching and research has become a major industry among Canadian historians. But after a decade of production it is nevertheless an industry with a very limited inventory. English-Canadian social history in particular has been preoccupied with three subjects: women, the working class, and social reformation.

Indeed, it is easy enough to conclude that movements of social reform are in fact the singular focus of historians of English-Canadian society, because so many other areas of research can be subsumed under this heading. Women's history is a case in point. In spite of the rapid advancement, and growing diversification, of this field, and in spite of the appearance of some truly seminal exceptions to the rule, women's history remains for the moment essentially the history of the "woman question" as it was debated by both sexes in late Victorian and Edwardian Canada. More generally, women's history is the history of women's public experience, singly or in groups, as the promoters of "social" or "maternal" feminism, alternately object and agent of the social reform movement in Canada, 1890–1930. Some of the best writing in this vein conveniently appears in a single volume, *A Not Unreasonable Claim: Women and Reform in Canada 1880s–1920s.*[4] The central theme of this historiography is the failure of the "first generation of women's activists in Canadian history" to trade on their moral and social responsibility for the quality of domestic life — the seed bed of social transformation — for a "package deal leading to extended social responsibilities and rights" in the public sphere.[5] Perhaps the most remarkable aspect of this historiography is the stridency of the judgments which attend the evidence of failure among these early "feminists." Their inability to rise above, or to develop an adequate critique of the "cult of domesticity" which kept them in thraldom and thwarted the advent of a feminist revolution, is evidently a source of deep consternation to modern women's historians. But like the "cult of youth" which promoted the denigration of old age in the era of "young Canada" and again in this century, the cult of true womanhood 1880–1920 was an idea whose time, in the popular imagination, had come. The early feminists' failure to run against the tide of society's collective consciousness is only disappointing in the harsh light of ideological imperatives as foreign to their value systems as courtly love is to ours.

To the extent that this activism was motivated by the changing experience of women in education and employment during the two or three decades preceding the advent of the "woman question," women's history has necessarily turned as well to the problems of women in the workplace, women in the professions, and the education of women. Happily, the recent work of academic historians in these aspects of women's history has been, on balance, less phlegmatic and more solidly rooted in historical evidence than, for example, some of the superficial essays that appeared in *Women at Work, Ontario, 1850–1930*.[6] Nevertheless, research and writing in this area have tended to be rather narrowly focussed on the effects of industrialization on the life-cycle experiences of girls and women newly freed from "homework" as their single preoccupation by the opportunity, or the necessity, of participating in the workforce. Here, women's history rubs shoulders with working-class history, labour history, historical demography, and the history of education, since the propensity, after mid-century, to educate girls for careers other than marriage, the nature of vocational opportunities available to educated and uneducated women, the conditions of work, and the effects of working outside the home on the family and on life-cycle patterns (age at marriage, childbearing, mortality) are all intimately interconnected. Extant research has scarcely probed the enormous complexity of these interrelated themes, leaving us, for the moment, with an incomplete landscape. At one extreme it is populated primarily by professional women whose experience in the marketplace made them the spokeswomen and torchbearers for the early feminist movement. At the other extreme, the experience of poor working women has been brought into sharper relief as the history of a docile, exploited, insecure pool of cheap labour caught between the competing disciplines of home and factory. In this respect, two noteworthy recent studies attempt to recreate the whole way of life of a particular group of "working" women, those who participated in the Canadian fur trade.[7] Here, the whole woman — wife, mother, labourer, diplomat, chattel, entrepreneur — is revealed within the context of the complex social and economic infrastructures of fur-trade society in which working women, unlike their counterparts in the era of industrialization, achieved a status coincident with their contribution to the fur-trade economy.

Modern Canadian society, on the other hand, has clung to the belief, well into this century, that women derived their status from the domestic imperatives associated with the cult of true womanhood. Thus, even when Canada's war effort from 1939–1945 required the mobilization of women for industrial employment, it was regarded by the authorities as very irregular, the fulfilment by women of a patriotic obligation not to be condoned as a "right" when the emergency passed and women were expected to return to their normal regimes.[8] Given the duration of this attitude, and the existence of compelling evidence that elsewhere the "emancipation" of women from unrelieved domesticity took place first *within* the confines of the family in the form of birth control, of the redefinition of marital relationships, of the discovery of the pleasures of sorority and of intellectual "networking,"[9] it is rather surprising that more women's historians have not attempted to probe the experience of Canadian women in marriage and within the family. Such Canadian evidence as there is on the subject (most of it derived from the work of historical demographers) suggests that new patterns of family formation and marital fertility which foreshortened periods of child rearing, higher rates of school attendance among children, and new residency patterns among adolescents, the advent of knowledge about methods of family limitation, the widespread availability of domestic help, greater longevity and, with the spread of urbanization, the gradual segregation of the home from the workplace,[10] conspired, in the last third of the nineteenth century, to create a new domestic regime common to more and more women. Amid these conditions, women might have expected to undergo, in increasing numbers, a "normal" (i.e., "modern") life-cycle pattern which at least created the potential for a feminist revolution, albeit a quiet one, within the so-called "proper sphere," the family. Until we know more about women's experience in this private sphere, at any rate, the reasons for the success or failure of their cause in the public arena of sexual politics will continue to evade us.

The history of the family is another of those areas of English-Canadian social history which seems to proceed along two parallel lines of inquiry. One is firmly rooted, as the foregoing discussion suggests, in the literature of social reform. The other reflects the more recent discovery, by social historians, of the family as the lowest common denominator of demographic and social structural analysis, in effect a laboratory for the study of the sources, the timing and the effects of social discontinuity in larger populations. Research on the side of family-centred reform is inseparable from two other areas of social history research, childhood and education, more generally the socialization of children. In fact, it is probably correct to say that interest in the family as a subject of historical study in English-Canadian historiography arose out of the more broadly based enquiries of educational historians into the history of school reform in Canadian society. Consequently, much of the family-centred historical research now in print, including such major studies as Michael Katz's *The People of Hamilton*, reflects at least an initial interest in the social processes which promoted state intervention through public school systems and compulsory education legislation and in the family's traditional responsibilities for the education and socialization of children.[11] The burden of this research leans toward the thesis that families generally resisted this intrusion into their customary sphere of authority. The greatest resistance came from those families (the poorest and least skilled) whose children might have benefitted most from compulsory formal schooling, albeit schooling with a hidden agenda (social control and the creation of a more skilled labour force in an era of rapid industrialization).

The socialization of children is, similarly, the thrust of family-centred research associated with the movements of social reform at the end of the nineteenth century. Here, concern lies with the reformers' perception of children as the agents of social transformation, tender seedlings whose place in and contribution to a socially progressive, morally upright and politically just society seemed to depend on the quality of the social and domestic environments in which they were raised. Much of the literature on "maternal feminism" cited above[12] bears directly on this question as does the recent, but limited, research in such areas as public health, social welfare policy, and crime.[13] The consensus seems to be that, if the forces of social change "made a new sort of growing up inevitable, they did not prescribe its shape and form. What the reform movement did . . . was to draw the plans for and rough in many of the dimensions of a transformed childhood"[14] through programs of social regeneration directed at the quality of family life and, more fundamentally, at the role of women in the family. What does not emerge from this family-centred research, however, is a very clear picture of the material conditions of life among the families and their children who were the objects of these reform movements. Katz's book is a singular exception for the mid-nineteenth century. Another is Joy Parr's *Labouring Children: British Immigrant Apprentices to Canada, 1869–1924* (London, 1980). Another subject closely related to family history suffers from the same bias to an even greater degree. Adolescence and youth is a subject virtually neglected in all of its aspects by Canadian social historians.[15] At least a partial remedy for this tendency to visualize women, children, adolescents, and the family only through the eyes, and with the perceptions, of social reformers is to be found in that other stream of family-centred societal analysis, demographic and social structural history, in which the realities of individual social experience at various stages in the cycle of life are exposed to light.

Research on this side of the history of the family tends to be less well-developed among English-Canadian historians than it is among their European, British, and American counterparts or their colleagues in Quebec. In part this is a problem of sources insofar as effective research depends upon the existence of long runs of family-centred records—usually parish registers, census returns, birth, death and marriage registers, assessment and other property records largely generated by churches and local government whose archival services have only recently begun to develop. It also depends on the mastery of the techniques of historical demography (family reconstitution in particular) and, depending on the size of the population under study, more or less familiarity with quantitative methods and even the application of computers to historical research.[16] For all of these reasons, family-centred demographic and social structural research in English Canada has been limited in two ways. Problems of sources have confined the research to mid-Victorian Ontario, for the most part, while the development of evidence on a broadly-based, comparative level awaits the maturation of a younger generation of scholars trained in the theory and methods of quantitative analysis, subjects relatively new to graduate study in history in Canada.

Nevertheless, the few historians who have been active in the field have generated a complex picture of the effects of social change on the structure, function, and culture of family life, of the adaptative strategies employed, historically, by Canadian families to promote continuity in the face of change, of the cycle of family life and of life styles within the family. Moreover, sufficient work has been done now to expose the startling variety of familial experience that abounded in the past. Rural/urban differences, social structural variants, ethnic variations and patterns which differ between new and old areas of agricultural settlement, and between commercial and industrial cities, have been discovered in the timing of family formation, in rates of reproduction within marriage, in the size and composition of households, in relationships between parents and children, and in familiar economic strategies related to the making of livings (especially the widespread phenomenon of geographical mobility as the panacea for social immobility).[17] Indeed, the central concern of these studies is the larger framework of local, regional, and national economics which determined the nature of economic opportunity in the past and, therefore, the sources and the timing of social discontinuity which is revealed, at the microcosmic level of family life, as a process of adaptation to quantum shifts in the material bases of life.[18]

To borrow a phrase from the French social historian Fernand Braudel, capitalism (commercial, industrial, agrarian) and material life form the elementary nexus of
this historiography in which the historical face of social inequality in Canada is
associated with the unequal distribution of economic opportunity and its rewards.
In sum, family-centred social structural analysis attempts, however imperfectly,
to understand the dimensions of social "class" in Canadian society. By sorting
among a variety of individual characteristics — sex, ethnicity, occupation, stage
of life, literacy, and religious affiliation — in relation to the distribution of wealth,
it is possible to identify both the boundaries of social rank and the common
attributes of the personnel of each rank.[19] This is an enormously fruitful and
vastly underworked field of historical endeavour. In spite of the pitfalls inherent
in the tendency to generalize on the basis of rather limited evidence and, at least
so far, chronologically restricted frames of reference, it is the only history of
social classes which takes the nature of relationships between (or among) classes
as a subject of empirical investigation rather than as *a priori* assumptions. This is
not the case with the great bulk of the historiography of social classes in English-
Canadian society. In baseball parlance, the infield is shaded to the left, there's a
vast hole down the right field line, and no one in the dugout is likely to pull one
to the right side. In other words, working-class history dominates the field, its
spokespersons are committed to the recovery and celebration of the long-neglected
cultural alternative to the way of life of the entrepreneurial classes who dominated the Laurentian economy, and there seems to be little interest among Canadian historians in elite prosopography in spite of the fact that what we know
about the shared attributes of Canada's upper classes in in fact slim and dated.[20]

The result, at any rate, has been an outpouring, in the last decade, of published
research on the history of the labouring classes in English-Canadian society. With it
has come a sometimes bitter debate between the so-called "new" social historians who claim to have redefined "labour history" as the history of "working-
class culture," and the "old" guard who resent the implication that their history
("a category of political economy, a canon of saintly working-class leaders, a
chronicle of union locals or a chronology of militant strike actions"[21]) is now
irrelevant. One of their number has in turn accused the "new" boys of wilfully
misrepresenting the labour movement and its leadership as the products and
defenders of "an Archie Bunker-charivari culture" which may not, in fact, have
existed, and in any case not as autonomously as its modern proponents contend.[22] The "cultural conflict" school dismisses these criticisms as the product of
political, not intellectual positions, yet claims to have distanced itself from both
the romanticism of the old left and the pragmatism of the neutral school of
labour history precisely by virtue of its superior ideological purity.[23] And so the
debate goes on, while both sides continue to add measurably to our knowledge
of labour and/or working-class history.

For the social historian, however, the historiography (on both sides) which
deals with the social condition of the working class from time to time is inevitably more attractive, not because of its ideological persuasiveness but because it
establishes reference points for the study of social structural relationships and the
comparative study of social classes. By definition, much of the "cultural conflict" literature focusses on the era of industrialization when the advent of new

modes of production forced workers to adapt their traditional way of life to the processes of social discontinuity and, in the end, to defend their "culture" against the alternative posed by the triumph of industrialism. A few scholars continue to be interested in the pre-industrial worker, the farm labourer and the tramping artisan;[24] but there is considerable room still for analyses, particularly prosopographical studies, of the labouring classes "before the fall," especially with reference to the much touted openness of Canadian society in the first half of the nineteenth century. Perhaps more to the point, the devastation wrought by industrial capitalism on working-class culture is comprehensible only in the light of evidence about the "traditional" character of working-class culture in pre-industrial society.

For the time being, however, the burden of working-class history has fallen upon those who toil in the shadows of the dark satanic mills. Their object, generally, is to illuminate a whole way of life, to identify and to explain the existence of an autonomous culture set apart from the main currents of social development in Canada by the special attributes of working-class life and the mentality or consciousness they sustained. Two major treatments of working-class culture in crisis in the age of industrialization are in print.[25] They illustrate both the strengths and weaknesses of the genre. The reader is introduced not only to the concepts of working-class "culture" and "consciousness" in their theoretical ramifications, but is exposed to the complex and subtle ways in which consciousness and culture were reinforced by working experience in the workplace, in community and neighbourhood, in leisure activity, in the labour temples, and in the political backrooms. In this respect the research is thorough, imaginative, and challenging. On the other hand, this scholarship is preoccupied with the fate of the aristocracy of labour rather than with the masses of working poor; it dwells excessively on the activities of the great white hope of the skilled artisans, the Knights of Labour; and it has produced little in the way of theoretical inventiveness or methodological improvements which might have added new dimensions to our perception of Canada's Victorian working-class society. This may be too hasty a judgment on an area of relatively recent activity; but even a cursory review of the table of contents of the field's journal, *Labour/Le Travail*, suggests that working-class history is, for the moment at least, rooted firmly in the empirical investigation of strikes, worker control in the workplace, labour in politics, and worker ideology. Theory, methods and *problématique* are scare commodities.

It will come as no surprise, then, that most of the best article-length reporting on working-class matters falls into the same mould.[26] However, at one remove from the "cultural" school of working-class history stands the work of a small but growing band of scholars who have taken up the question of the quality of working-class life with particular reference to the material condition of the labouring poor. It is useful to read them in conjunction with the "cultural" historians because of the light they shed on the relative "autonomy" of working-class culture. Here the emphasis is on incomes, housing standards, public health, welfare and, in the end, the painful poverty which pricked the conscience of middle-class Christian social activists and compelled them to act.[27]

The record of their activities in the temperance and prohibition movements, in the field of public health and welfare, in child and youth-centred programs, in woman and family-centred reforms, in urban politics, planning and beautification, and in the cleansing of the human spirit with the new light of a social "gospel" accounts for a high percentage of the last decade's output of the history of English-Canadian society.[28] Surprisingly, no scholar has attempted a synthesis in spite of the fact that both the now well-developed historiography and the interests of Canadian social history cry out for a comprehensive treatment of social reform in which these disparate elements are bonded together by a central, organizing thesis. This idea in no way diminishes the seminal contribution of Richard Allen's *The Social Passion: Religion and Social Reform in Canada 1914–28* (Toronto, 1973) and its insistence on the thesis that the successes and failures of the reform movement can only be assessed when the movement is seen as a religious manifestation, as a social gospel concerned with the quality of earthly human relations. But the jury is still out on the extent to which the reforming impulse was also, for example, a "controlling" impulse with motives more attuned to the realities of secular social relationships forged in the mounting heat of class confrontation, and to a "total way of life" increasingly buffetted by winds of dissent as the processes of social discontinuity accelerated their pace and as the map of social transformation was rapidly enlarged.

In the last analysis, what strikes the reviewer about the historiography of English-Canadian social history is the narrowness of its focus, its methodological conservatism, and the relative absence of theoretical and conceptual creativity. English-Canadian social history in the last decade has been solidly entrenched in the period 1850–1914; much of the activity has centred on developments in central Canada and, within that context, on a handful of related subjects. The 1920s and the 1940s have been steadfastly ignored. Studies of rural society are out of fashion. Private experience remains closetted; and the rich are still Canadian history's least visible minority. Quantitative history has gained few converts, social science methodology remains suspect, and theory — begged, borrowed or invented — is steadfastly ignored in the interests of narration untrammelled by either speculation about or commitment to a systematic theory of social discontinuity.[29] For all of these reasons, English-Canadian social history, alive and vigorous as it is, is still a long way from maturity. With a bit of luck, Canadian historians will not rediscover political history while social history still requires their continued suport and ministrations.

French-Canadian Historiography

The methods and approaches of social historians have had a considerable impact upon the writing of the history of Quebec. In the last twenty years or so, scores of books and articles have been produced there that reflect the theoretical and methodological apparatus of social history. There are many reasons for that. One of the most obvious concerns sources. Quebec historians have access to a very rich mine of material, particularly demographic and legal records, well-suited to quantitative exploitation. Another reason arises from a coincidence: just as the perspectives and tools of social history were being developed in Europe, French

Canadians were becoming dissatisfied with the image of the society as it was presented through the works of the clerico-nationalist historians.[30] The history of Quebec, that is to say, would have been rewritten in any event. The availability and success of the new approaches made it inevitable that they would be used.

On the other hand, it is clear also that they have been used unevenly, with some areas of historical studies receiving far more attention than others. Historical demography, for example, is highly developed in Quebec. Considerable work has been also done on class and ideology. But women's studies remain largely unexploited, especially by francophone historians. Similarly, and perhaps surprisingly, not very much social history has been written involving the Roman Catholic Church. Most of the effort of Quebec historians has been concentrated on investigating the years before 1900. Since that is the case, and also for reasons of space, this survey will concentrate upon those years, and have very little to say about the twentieth century.[31]

Demographic studies are basic to social history as it is written everywhere: "l'histoire d'un peuple, c'est d'abord la triomphe de la vie sur la mort, des naissances sur les décès."[32] In Quebec, however, they have been given even more importance because of the nature of the development of the francophone population. By the early 1970s, historians had revealed the main characteristics of its demographic behaviour. There was a stable population base in the St. Lawrence valley which had been growing rapidly since the early seventeenth century and which in the nineteenth and twentieth centuries was affected by two major factors — emigration to the United States and movement from rural to urban milieus.[33] But neither of these phenomena was significant before about 1850 and, therefore, in the population pool that existed before that time demographers had what one of them has called a "magnifique laboratoire" in which to work.[34] In the last few years they have begun to take full advantage of the resource.

French Canadians, of course, have long displayed a keen interest in genealogy and in the general area of population studies. In fact, some recent work has been based upon information gathered by earlier researchers. There is, for example, a study of the characteristics — origins, family connections, age at the time of marriage, number of children — of a sample of the *voyageurs* extracted from the mass of genealogical data collected by Archange Godbout and published in the 1950s.[35] More important, however, is the work completed and in progress using archival sources as its raw material. Among the many publications of Marcel Trudel there are two of pure demography that must be mentioned. There is, first, his astonishingly detailed cross-section of New France in 1663 which contains information on every individual who is recorded as being in the colony at that time.[36] Also there is his report of the high degree of population mobility in the first half of the seventeenth century. Although he offered no general explanation for it, Trudel revealed an unexpected propensity by the early settlers to move from holding to holding.[37] More ambitious is Louise Dechêne's *Habitants et Marchands de Montréal au XVIIe siècle*. This book, which is surely social history at its best — a carefully constructed picture of a whole society in motion built largely from quantified data upon a strong base of demographic information — contains many illuminating insights about the early population of New France. Her findings go far beyond demography, and among the most interesting of them is her contention that there were in effect two economies in the St. Lawrence valley — the family-centred *habitant* agricultural economy and the urban mercantile economy—with few connections existing between them.[38] In this connection and parenthetically, one might draw attention to some other works on New France of a generally non-demographic nature. There are the studies of merchants and commerce: Christopher Moore on the cod economy of Île Royale; Louis Michel on the enterprises of a rural merchant; and J.F. Bosher on the French Protestant families trading with the colony.[39] Peter Moogk's interesting attempt to investigate social ranking in New France deserves mention as well as G.A. Dickenson's revisionist look at the reality of seigneurial justice.[40] Finally, there are two attempts to get at the very difficult area of *mentalités*. Contrary to what Jules Michelet found in France, François Rousseau, through an examination of the Hôtel-Dieu in Quebec, discovered no particular fear of hospitals in the society of New France.[41] And André Lachance has drawn some interesting conclusions about social values from an analysis of insults which led to court action by the victims.[42]

But to return to the subject of population studies, it seems unlikely that future research will seriously challenge all the demographic conclusions arrived at by Trudel, Dechêne and the other researchers into the seventeenth century.[43] But there seems no doubt that there will be some changes and that all work done up to now will be modified — even if only by a changing perspective. This is because, whereas demographic studies up to the mid-1970s were done, so to speak, "by hand," since then demographers in Quebec have turned to the computer. The strength of the expectations awakened by the new technology can be seen in Hubert Charbonneau's prediction that his book on the population of New France, which was published in 1975, would be the last one utilizing traditional techniques.[44] Charbonneau is well-qualified to speak, heading, as he does in tandem with Jacques Légaré, the ambitious project taken on by the Département de démographie of the Université de Montréal. This Programme de Recherche en Démographie Historique (PRDH) has as its objective the reconstruction of the whole population of Quebec from 1608 to 1850. Relying primarily upon parish registers and upon what nominal census data is available, the Montreal team hopes eventually to be able to produce a biographical dossier on every individual "qui ont mis le pied sur la térritoire québécois" up to mid-nineteenth century.[45]

Equally impressive is the task undertaken by Gérard Bouchard and his associates in the Société de Recherche sur les Populations (SOREP) of the Université de Québec at Chicoutimi. Since 1972 this team of demographers has been engaged in building a comprehensive data bank of the population of the Saguenay-Lake St. John area from 1838 until at least 1931.[46] The relative geographical isolation of the area as well as the abundance of documentation make the Saguenay region another excellent laboratory for demographic investigation. Moreover, the nature of the regional economy — a colonization area in which employment in the timber-lumber industry was possible in conjunction with agriculture — gave it added importance. Because so many French Canadians have divided their energies between agriculture and another economic activity, it seems at least plausible that significant findings by the SOREP team could be applied to other areas and other times.

Both Bouchard and Charbonneau bubble with optimism over the prospects of their respective projects.[47] In the long term, Bouchard tells us, perhaps there will be the possibility of an *"histoire globale"* achieved through the use of computers; at the very least we can expect to learn a great deal about the precise configurations and operations of social structures.[48] But none of that will be possible, and both groups realized it from the beginning, without impeccable methodology. A great deal of effort, therefore, has been expended in the last few years in solving procedural problems. Much preliminary work has been done, for example, in checking the reliability of the documentary base, the parish registers of baptisms, marriages, and deaths, the various nominal censuses of New France as well as those of 1851, 1861, and 1871.[49] Moreover, since township and parish boundaries change over time, a method had to be developed to assure that the same geographical area was considered in successive nominal censuses. Otherwise, an observed population movement might not really have occurred but would be an illusion traceable simply to variations in the size of the basic census unit.[50] Finally, there is the problem of changes in the way individual names were recorded in the documents and the desirability of eliminating errors resulting from orthographic and other similar variations.[51]

These problems seem to have been dealt with—a test conducted by the Saguenay group has traced 97.5 percent of the married couples mentioned in a sample of baptism, marriage, and death records—and some preliminary results have begun to appear.[52] The population of the Saguenay region, for example, was characterized by high growth rates, a surplus of men over women, and a high proportion of young people.[53] There was, moreover, so much population movement that the research group claims to have destroyed the myth of "l'immobilisme des Canadiens français."[54] Between 1851 and 1871 more than 60 percent of the population of the area moved, and of these transients about one-half left the region completely while the remainder relocated within it.[55] Although the team is not yet ready with a complete and tested hypothesis, they appear to explain this mobility in the same way as was done in the Peel County project. That involves succession practices for agricultural land which maintain the integrity of the family farm at the price of forcing most of the children to move elsewhere.[56]

There are two other final points to be made. First, it seems clear that the rate of transience in the Saguenay region, while high, was nevertheless considerably lower than that found by David Gagan in Peel County, Ontario.[57] It may be that the two areas are not comparable, although at least one observer thinks they are.[58] It may also be that the disparity is not real but is the result of a methodological difference.[59] It is a small problem but it does invite resolution.

The other point is more important, with large implications for the socioeconomic history of Quebec. In a book published in 1977 on the *agro-forestière* economy of the Saguenay area,[60] Norman Séguin treated the region as a hinterland of the Quebec-Montreal metropolitan centre and argued that the timber-lumber industry, controlled from outside, and agriculture, did not exist in a complementary relationship but were in basic conflict. Séguin contended, in fact, that the demands of the timber-lumber component were directly responsible for keeping agriculture in an undeveloped state and for retarding the urbanization of the region. Gérard Bouchard has disagreed with Séguin's analysis. Bouchard concedes that Séguin's argument may have some relevance on the question of urbanization. But he claims that the undeveloped agriculture of the area was a result, primarily, of its isolation from urban markets. The inhabitants of the region, led by their traditional elites, clamoured for connection with the outside world. The forest industry, however, could exist using only natural means of transportation, and it may bear some responsibility for the long delay in joining the Saguenay by road and rail to Quebec and Montreal. But, Bouchard says, that was the extent of its responsibility.[61]

The debate, however, does not appear to be over.[62] The same conflictual relationship has been found in another socio-economic area. Allan Greer has just published his study of the *voyageurs* from the Sorel area, and has argued that employment in the fur trade also resulted in underdeveloped agriculture.[63] In their recent synthesis of the history of post-confederation Quebec, moreover, Linteau, Robert and Durocher seem slightly to favour Séguin's position.[64] If the analysis carries the day in those two places and activities, then work on similar structures in other places will have to be reconsidered and the world of the *colon* may be viewed quite differently.

Many social historians in Quebec have concentrated their efforts upon investigating one large question and its many ramifications: What was the nature of the society that existed in Quebec from the Conquest until the end of the nineteenth century, how was it formed, and how did it change? Involved in that basic question are considerations concerning the economic base, social groups and social classes and their interrelationships, religion, ideology, and so on. To begin discussing some features of its current state, one starts with the work of Jean Hamelin and Fernand Ouellet. Hamelin's description, based largely upon quantitative analysis and published about twenty years ago, of the dependent nature of the economy and of the mercantile community of New France is well known.[65] Taking up where Hamelin left off, using a Laurentian model of geographic-economic space and the familiar approach and devices of the *Annales* school, Fernand Ouellet spent the last twenty years attempting to write the *histoire globale* of almost the whole of the succeeding century.[66] It is simply impossible here to do anything like justice to the results. All that can be done is to draw attention, in summary form, to some of his more important findings:

(a)   the central position of wheat farming and the commercialization of agriculture as explanatory factors accounting for social change in Lower Canada;

(b)   the agricultural crisis, beginning around the turn of the nineteenth century, which was a consequence of rapid population growth, a shortage of arable land, and poor agricultural techniques;

(c)   the definition of and the interplay among the various social classes: the seigneurial aristocracy, the merchants of both languages, and particularly the emergent petite-bourgeoisie based, primarily, in the liberal professions;

(d)   the integration of class and ideology, especially the articulation of the concept of *la nation canadienne-française* by spokesmen for the petite-bourgeoisie around the turn of the century; and finally

(e) the way in which the interests of the *habitants* were subordinated to the class interests of the petite-bourgeoisie acting, ostensibly, in the name of the nation.

Ouellet's integrated portrait of Quebec society from 1760 to 1850 is unquestionably the outstanding historical work of recent years. Not only has it promoted interest in social history as a whole, but also, obviously, his somewhat iconoclastic perspective has stimulated further research into the history of the early nineteenth century. And not all of the results confirm his findings. There is, for example, the reassessment of Quebec agriculture offered by John McCallum.[67] By comparing the development of French-Canadian agriculture to that of other regions of North America, McCallum is able to argue that the decline of wheat farming in the St. Lawrence valley was owing more to its marginal competitive position than to the deficient agricultural techniques of the *habitant* farmer.[68] Then there is the extensive production of Gilles Paquet and Jean-Pierre Wallot. Much of their work is too theoretical and abstract to be dealt with in detail here,[69] but one or two points can be made. Drawing extensively upon concepts developed in the social sciences, Paquet and Wallot would see Lower Canada as part of a broad Atlantic community in which social change (modernization) was impelled by the exigencies of a developing capitalist market economy.[70] To Jean-Pierre Wallot, the petite-bourgeoisie of Lower Canada seem to be a much more progressive force than Ouellet is willing to concede.[71]

The suggestions made and points raised by Paquet and Wallot may yet force reconsideration and revision of Ouellet's presentation. But at the moment their more concrete and specific historical studies of aspects of the early nineteenth century deserve attention. First there is the early work in which they urge the overwhelming importance of the division of patronage in the social and political struggles of the period.[72] But of more importance to the question of the nature and mechanics of society in early nineteenth-century Quebec is the challenge Paquet and Wallot have offered to Fernand Ouellet's *crise agricole* of the years after 1802.[73] The debate over the timing, extent, even the existence of the crisis, seems to have subsided but may not yet be over.

Several studies on other specific matters which can be classed as part of the social history of early nineteenth-century Quebec have appeared over the past few years.[74] What must be mentioned separately, however, is P.A. Linteau's and J.-C. Robert's research on Montreal in the 1820s. Fernand Ouellet has shown that, unwilling or unable to adjust to technological and organizational change, French-Canadian merchants dropped out of the fur trade toward the end of the eighteenth century.[75] In their place and in place of the seigneurial group, leadership of the French-Canadian community then passed to the petite-bourgeoisie. Linteau and Robert set out to determine if there was a material basis which allowed this emergent group to maintain its ascendency in francophone society even though the large economic concerns were controlled by English-Canadians. In Montreal in 1825 the answer they found was ownership of real estate, something that Paquet and Wallot suggest may have begun as early as 1800 and which Linteau's own work on Maisonneuve extends on to the twentieth century.[76]

Late in the nineteenth century J.D. Borthwick published his *History and Biographical Gazeteer of Montreal to the Year 1892* which contains information on hundreds of "notables" of the city. J.-C. Robert has analyzed this data and concluded that, among the men included, there was a high proportion of immigrants from Great Britain, and that the French-Canadian middle-class component was very small.[77] Not long ago the latter finding would have been accepted without question. But recent research indicates that it is probably a distortion traceable to Borthwick's method of selection, because it seems increasingly likely that there was an economically active French-Canadian bourgeoisie in nineteenth-century Montreal. There is, for example, the well-documented case of E.-R. Fabre who owned and operated a very successful *librairie* for many years in the first half of the century.[78] G. Tulchinsky has also demonstrated French-Canadian participation in mid-nineteenth-century commercial life—La Compagnie du Richelieu, a small water-transport concern operated by a group of francophones of Montreal, was successful in a highly competitive area.[79] Similarly, Paul-André Linteau has argued forcefully for a significant French-Canadian presence in the middle ranks of commerce and business between 1850 and 1914.[80] Subsequently, he suggests, for economic rather than cultural reasons, French-Canadian businessmen like Alphonse Desjardins were "marginalized" in the period of consolidation after World War I.

These attempts to delineate the French-Canadian bourgeoisie are promising. But given the aim of comprehending the social whole, it is evident that much more research has yet to be done, not only in the urban centres but also in the towns and villages. And it might also be said, parenthetically, that the same is true of the English-Canadian middle class who, despite some exceptions, remains an undifferentiated, nameless, and faceless group in so much of the writing about Quebec.

Laymen of the lower middle class shared social leadership of francophone Quebec through much of the nineteenth century with the men and women of the Roman Catholic Church. Given the massive importance of the Church as an institution, and the numbers, variety, and clarity of definition of the clergy, it is somewhat disappointing that they have not been the subject of much more research by social historians.[81] The traditional picture of the Church, first defined by the priest-historians of the mid-nineteenth century and refined and perpetuated by clerico-nationalists since then, has, of course, been recognized as inadequate for at least twenty-five years. And historians have gone some distance in providing a new overview. Its outlines can be seen through the periodization adopted by the most recent summary — it was a Church that was successively "naissante" (1608–1760), "soumise" (1760–1838), "de plus en plus romaine" (1840–1896), "thriomphliste" (1896–1940) and "incertaine" (1940–1970).[82]

But much remains to be done, as the material for a more extensive treatment is accumulating so slowly. For the very early period there are important sections on the Church and religious life in the work of Marcel Trudel and Louise Dechêne. Trudel provides us with probably all the demographic information that will ever be available for the 37 men and 41 women of the Church who were in New France in 1663.[83] As to Dechêne, the conclusion of her carefully considered chapter on the subject is that the Church in New France was orthodox, slightly Jansenist, and that the religious atmosphere was not particularly *devôt* but was "très ordinaire."[84] On this subject also, one might mention the attempt by Marie-André Cliche to determine the degree of religiosity of the people of New France by statistical analysis of the contents of some 800 *clauses testamentaires*.[85] M.-A. Bedard, similarly, has looked at the French Protestants who came to New France, while Jean Blain's survey of the literature on the question of the morality of the colony is very useful.[86]

For the post-Conquest years, there are, of course, the findings of Fernand Ouellet on the position of the Church in society.[87] In a recent study Ouellet has tried to establish some approximation of the standard of living of the *curés* of the early nineteenth century compared to the members of their parishes.[88] The subject of the financial position of one diocese has also been examined by Réal Boucher.[89] In addition, two other works need mention. One is Jean-Pierre Wallot's account of the very delicate legal and political position of the Church in the early nineteenth century and the sometimes unruly behaviour of the French-Canadian congregations of the time.[90] The other is Richard Chabot's fascinating exploration of the positions taken by local *curés* vis-à-vis lay elites on the contentious issues of the pre-rebellion years.[91]

Pertaining to the middle part of the century there is a noteworthy essay by Serge Gagnon which analyzes religious life in the Diocese of Montreal from a series of pastoral reports produced between 1853 and 1868.[92] But more important is Gagnon's extensive analysis of the way in which the history of New France was written in the nineteenth century. Treating written history as an ideological weapon, Gagnon illustrates how conceptions of the past and volumes of hagiography were used to buttress the ultramontane claims for predominance in Quebec made by so many nineteenth-century churchmen.[93] There are, in addition, many other studies of ideologies, particularly ultramontanism, for the years after 1850.[94] And, in a different vein, is Jean Ray's statistical analysis of "le clergé nicolétain."[95]

Finally, there exist some studies of the Church's exposure to industrial capitalism in the late nineteenth century. William Ryan's investigation of the attitude of the clery to industry in *La Mauricie* is an older work that is still useful.[96] Among the newer productions Gérard Bouchard's examination of priests, capitalists, and workers at Chicoutimi is outstanding. Bouchard argues that the morality taught to workers by the priests and the modes of behaviour approved by them were the same as those necessary for employment in industry. Rather than conflicts, that is, Bouchard found "une étoite alliance de classes entre clercs et industriels" in the Saguenay area.[97]

Bouchard's essay serves to introduce the area of working-class history.[98] The broad lines of development of the group are well-enough known — there was a movement over time from a society characterized by a miniscule non-agricultural work force with manufacturing in the hands of artisans and apprentices to a recognizably modern proletarianized society. Generally speaking, the development of the working class in Quebec fits that pattern. The implied exception are the *voyageurs*, part of the work force of the fur trade and semi-proletariat of the early years of Canadian history. There has been some research on the *voyageurs* recently. Hubert Charbonneau's previously mentioned article on their geographic distribution and demographic behaviour is one piece.[99] There is also information on the *voyageurs* integrated into Fernand Ouellet's synthesis.[100] And finally, there is the revisionist study published by Allen Greer which was previously mentioned.[101] As to the world of the artisans and apprentices, there is an older study by Peter Moogk as well as two more recent efforts — Marise Thivierge on the Quebec leather workers (1660–1760) and the work on the apprentice artisans (1660–1815) by Jean-Pierre Hardy and David-Thierry Ruddel.[102]

While the creation of a large urban proletariat waited upon the process of industrialization that began in earnest in the 1880s,[103] there was a work force living in the cities long before that. This *"classe ouvrière"* in Montreal in the years from 1790 to 1820 is the subject of an excellent piece recently published by Robert Tremblay. Working from a sample of *actes d'engagements* and *conventions de marché*, and utilizing quantitative methodology, Tremblay has uncovered a great deal of information on the makeup, organization, division of labour, and remuneration of this pre-industrial working class.[104] By the early nineteenth century, it is clear that the artisanal system was rapidly disintegrating. That is the conclusion arrived at also by Joanne Burgess. Her investigation of the boot and shoe industry in Montreal reveals large organizational changes taking place long before the advent of mechanization. The increasing demands of the market led to a division of labour as early as the 1820s which was simply accelerated when machinery began to be used extensively after 1850. By the 1860s the boot and shoe industry was organized in factories with unskilled or semi-skilled labour operating steam-driven machines. In the same decade the Knights of St. Crispin called the first strike.[105]

But the end of the *artisanat*, if it came slowly in some occupations, could also come with dramatic suddenness in others. That is the burden of Margaret Heap's study of the strike of the Montreal *charretiers*. She argues that since they owned their own means of production, their horses and carriages, these men were in the same position as artisans. Their continued independence was at issue in the strike of 1864, and when they were defeated — basically by the Grand Trunk Railway — they were reduced immediately to proletarian status.[106]

Another group that has recently received attention is the railway construction workers. Because of their transient nature, information about these men is particularly scanty. But some of them happened to be working in the Sherbrooke area just as the census of 1851 was being conducted, and Jean-Paul Kesteman's article is based on the information gathered from a sample of about 1,600 names. His findings about the national origins (few French-Canadians and many Roman Catholic Irish) are not surprising. What is new is his conclusion that most of them were married and lived with their families in the shanties, the single men being integrated into the various households as boarders.[107]

By the 1880s there was a large and growing urban working class, especially in Montreal. Indeed, if John McCallum is right, these underpaid proletarians were the major asset which allowed Montreal industrialists to compete, particularly in the Ontario market.[108] In any case, this was the group to which the Knights of Labour made its appeal in the years after 1882. Fernand Harvey's fine study of that organization reveals that, for reasons which he explains, it was more successful in Quebec than anyplace else in North America. And that was despite the fact that the Knights' incursion into the province was met by the intransigent hostility of the local elites, especially the clergy. Conscious of class, reformist and utopian, the Knights of Labour provided a preliminary focus for the social discontent accompanying industrialization. Its eventual demise cleared the way for the continentalist business unionism of the American Federation of Labor and the nationalist confessional unions of the Roman Catholic Church.[109]

While not much of a concrete nature is known about working-class culture during the late nineteenth century, there is some information accumulating on the material conditions of the lives of the workers. Fernand Harvey has concluded from his examination of the testimony before the Royal Commission on the Relations of Labour and Capital (1887) that the world of the artisan was by that time only a fading memory and that the social problems of *"capitalisme sauvage"* had already begun to appear.[110] J. De Bonville has also contributed through his examination of the writings of Jean-Baptiste Gagnepetit. That was the pen-name of Jules Helbronner, one of the reformist members of the royal commission of 1887 and a journalist whose observations of the social conditions of the Montreal working class were published in *La Presse* from 1884 to 1894.[111] Finally, because of its familiarity, only mention need be made of Terry Copp's *Anatomy of Poverty*.[112]

For the years of Canadian history before the last half of the nineteenth century, very little has recently appeared in the area of women's studies.[113] There is Lilianne Plamondon's examination of the life of Marie-Anne Barbel, who upon her husband's death inherited his business and ran it successfully through the mid-eighteenth century. Other women like her, the author tells us, were not uncommon.[114] Then there is Sylvia Van Kirk's study of the marriages between fur traders and Indian and *Métis* women which, she argues, generations of scandalized references notwithstanding, were crucial to the establishment of early western society.[115] But, with only a few exceptions, the field remains untouched. Consider, for example, the female religious communities. A few years ago Micheline Dumont-Johnson pointed out how important the *religieuses* had been in Quebec society since 1640.[116] But with the exception of Sr. Marguerite Jean's book[117] nothing seems to have resulted for the period before 1850. Perhaps we will have to wait until the results of the demographic studies currently underway have stimulated interest, before more research is done.

The last half of the nineteenth century is only a little better served. Suzanne Cross's older study of the distribution of working women in Montreal and their employment opportunities (domestic service then industry on the whole) deserves mention.[118] So also does Bettina Bradbury's later examination of "the family economy."[119] Susan Mann Trofimenkoff has pillaged the testimony of the witnesses before the royal commission of 1887 in an attempt to define the perceptions of female labour of the time.[120] And finally, Micheline Dumont-Johnson's examination of day-care facilities provided in Montreal and elsewhere by the Grey Nuns deserves attention. First established around 1860, their institutions cared for thousands of children of working-class mothers between that time and the end of the century. One can echo the author's conclusion: that they were needed and used is clear evidence of the disintegration of the family unit which accompanied industrialization.[121]

Conclusion

That social history is a vigorous, diversified, and increasingly high-powered branch plant of Canadian historiography in the 1980s is an inescapable fact. Its vigour arises not only from the zeal of the youngest generation of Canadian historians who wield the cutting edge of recent scholarship, but equally from a general weaning of the historical profession away from more traditional concerns into areas of investigation once considered intellectually inferior to the cut and thrust of national politics.

The diversity of the enterprise is, perhaps, less astonishing, and in any case may be more apparent than real. Working-class history, movements of social reform, and women's history continue to preoccupy anglophone social historians; demography, the history of the family, social structural history and, to a lesser extent, working-class history, francophone historians. It is probably the case as well that among anglophone historians urban society has proved to be a more attractive milieu than rural society has been for their colleagues in Quebec. But these qualifications do not detract from the fact that within each of these areas of investigation the research is multi-faceted and increasingly inventive.

It is nevertheless clear that if, by inventiveness, we mean the bringing together of theory, method, and evidence in a convincing evocation of the historical imagination, francophone historians have been somewhat more successful than their English-Canadian counterparts. Whatever other reasons may be cited for this disparity, the central fact is the nature of social history itself. Social history is, by definition, an exercise in comparative history. Civilizations emerge, as Fernand Brandel has pointed out, from the historical experiences of many limited populations resolving, in common ways, common problems associated with the material regularities of life. For social history to succeed as an informative intellectual exercise, it is necessary that social historians, each working in his or her own little world of historical experience, ask common questions about common phenomena, employing similar hypotheses and data in order to comprehend the nature of social reality in this limited sphere. Only in this way will the universality of certain themes in our past, and the uniqueness of others, especially the sources and the consequences of social discontinuity, become comprehensible. Francophone historians seem to be much more solidly rooted in this internationally comparative context than the social historians of English Canada who have much to gain from paying more attention to the work of their counterparts in Europe, Britain, and the United States.

Meanwhile, Canadian social history is alive and well, its practitioners are engaged in a variety of heated but healthy debates, and some subjects have been developed to the point where they now await an ambitious synthesizer. Others — medicine and public health, adolescence, the professions, elite prosopography — await the attention they richly deserve.

Notes

1. See, for example, E.J. Hobsbawn, "From Social History to the History of Society," in *Essays in Social History*, edited by M.W. Flinn and T.C. Smout (Oxford, 1974), 1–23; H.J. Perkin, "Social History," in *Approaches to History*, edited by H. Finberg (London, 1961), 51–82; R. Mandrou, "Primat de l'histoire sociale: Propos sans paradoxes," *Histoire sociale/Social History* (hereafter *HS/SH*) (April 1968): 7-15; Michiel Horn and Ronald Sabourin, *Studies in Canadian Social History* (Toronto, 1974), 7–17.

2. This is Hobsbawm's point; and see also Raymond Williams, *Culture and Society* (New York, 1960), xviii.

3. Hobsbawn, "From Social History to the History of Society," organizes social historical inquiry around demography and kinship, urban studies, social classes, mentalities, social transformation, and movements of social protest. Perkin, "Social History," employs the concepts of the ecology, anatomy (social structure), physiology (material life), pathology (social problems) and psychology of societies.

4. Linda Kealey, ed., *A Not Unreasonable Claim: Women and Reform in Canada, 1880s–1920s* (Toronto, 1979). See especially Wayne Roberts, " 'Rocking the Cradle for the World': The New Woman and Maternal Feminism, Toronto 1877–1914," 15–46; Wendy Mitchinson, "The W.C.T.U.: 'For God, Home and Native Land': A Study in Nineteenth Century Feminism," 151–168; and Veronica Strong-Boag, "Canada's Women Doctors: Feminism Constrained," 109–130. Other important contributions to this literature include: Veronica Strong-Boag, *The Parliament of Women: the National Council of Women in Canada* (Ottawa, 1976); Terry Morrison, "Their Proper Spheres': Feminism, the Family, and Child-Centred Social Reform, 1875–1900," *Ontario History* (hereafter *OH*) LXVIII (1976): 45–64; Carol Bacchi, "Race Regeneration and Social Purity: A Study of the Social Attitudes of Canada's English-Speaking Suffragists," *HS/SH* XI (1970): 460–74. See also Ramsay Cook and Wendy Mitchinson, eds., *The Proper Sphere: Women's Place in Canadian Society* (Toronto, 1976).

5. Wayne Roberts, " 'Rocking the Cradle,' " 45.

6. See Alison Prentice, "The Feminization of Teaching in British America and Canada, 1845–1875," *HS/SH* VIII (1975): 5–19; D. Suzanne Cross, "The Neglected Majority: The Changing Role of Women in 19th Century Montreal," *HS/SH* IV (1973): 202–23; Bettina Bradbury, "The Family Economy and Work in an Industrializing City: Montreal in the 1870s," *Historical Papers* (hereafter *HP*) 1979: 71–96; Gail Cuthbert Brandt, " 'Weaving It Together': Life Cycle and the Experience of Female Cotton Workers in Quebec, 1910-1950," *Labour/Le Travailleur* (hereafter *L/LT*) VII (1981): 113–26; Joan Sangster, "The 1907 Bell Telephone Strike: Organizing Women Workers," *L/LT* III (1978); Ian Davey, "Trends in Female School Attendance in Mid-Nineteenth Century Ontario," *HS/SH* VIII (1975) 238–54; and see *Women at Work, Ontario, 1850–1930* (Toronto, 1974).

7. Jennifer S.H. Brown, *Strangers in Blood: Fur Trade Company Families in Indian Country* (Vancouver, 1980); and Sylvia Van Kirk, *"Many Tender Ties": Women in Fur Trade Society, 1670–1870* (Winnipeg, 1980).

8. Ruth Pierson, "Women's Emancipation and the Recruitment of Women into the Canadian Labour Force in World War II," *HP* (1976): 141–73.

9. Carl N. Degler, *At Odds: Women and the Family in America from the Revolutionary War to the Present* (New York, 1980).

10. See note 17 below.

11. Michael B. Katz, *The People of Hamilton, Canada West: Family and Class in a Mid-Nineteenth-Century City* (Cambridge, Mass., 1975); and see Alison Prentice, *The School Promoters: Education and Social Class in Mid-Nineteenth-Century Upper Canada* (Toronto, 1977); Frank Denton and Peter George, "Socio-Economic Influences on School Attendance: A Study of a Canadian County in 1871," *History of Education Quarterly* (hereafter *HEQ*) XIII (1974): 223–32; Ian Davey, "The Rhythm of Work and the Rhythm of School," in *Egerton Ryerson and His Times*, edited by Neil McDonald and Alf Chaiton (Toronto, 1978), 221–53; Alison Prentice, "Education and the Metaphor of the Family: The Upper Canadian Example," *HEQ* XII (1972): 281–303. More generally, see the articles in the special issue of the *HEQ* XII (1972), devoted to educational reform in Canada.

12. Note 4, above, especially Terry Morrison, " 'Their Proper Sphere': Feminism, the Family and Child-Centred Social Reform in Ontario, 1876–1900," *OH* (1976): 45–64 and 65–74.

13. See Susan E. Houston, "Victorian Origins of Juvenile Delinquency: A Canadian Experience," *HEQ* XII (1972): 254–80; Andrew Jones and Leonard Rutman, *In the Children's Aid: J.J. Kelso and Child Welfare in Ontario* (Toronto, 1981); Suzann Buckley, "Ladies or Midwives? Efforts to Reduce Infant and Maternal Mortality," in *A Not Unreasonable Claim*, 131-50; Paul Bator, "The Struggle to Raise the Lower Classes: Public Health Reform and the Problem of Poverty in Toronto, 1910–1921," *Journal of Canadian Studies* (hereafter *JCS*) XIV (1979): 43–49; Dianne L. Matters, "Public Welfare Vancouver Style, 1910–1920," *JCS* XIV (1979): 3–12.

14. Neil Sutherland, *Children in English-Canadian Society: Framing the Twentieth Century Consensus* (Toronto, 1976), 241; and see the introduction to Michael Katz and Paul Mattingly, eds., *Education and Social Change: Themes From Ontario's Past* (New York, 1975); also Neil Semple, " 'The Nurture and Admonition of the Lord': Nineteenth-Century Canadian Methodism's Response to 'Childhood'," *HS/SH* XIV (1981): 157–75.

15. See Michael Bliss, " 'Pure Books on Avoided Subjects': Pre-Freudian Sexual Ideas in Canada," *HP* (1970): 89-108; and David MacLeod, "A Live Vaccine: The YMCA and Male Adolescence in the United States and Canada, 1870–1920," *HS/SH* XI (1978): 5–25.

16. See E. Shorter, *The Historian and the Computer: A Practical Guide* (New York, 1975); Charles M. Dollar and Richard Jensen, *Historian's Guide to Statistics: Quantitative Analysis and Historical Research* (New York, 1971); Roderick Floud, *An Introduction to Quantitative Methods for Historians* (London, 1973); E.A. Wrigley, ed., *An Introduction to English Historical Demography* (New York, 1966). A scholarly journal, *Historical Methods Newsletter*, provides a continuing forum for discussion of theoretical and methodological problems.

17. Katz, *The People of Hamilton, Canada West*; David Gagan, *Hopeful Travellers: Families, Land and Social Change in Mid-Victorian Peel County, Canada West* (Toronto, 1981); Chad M. Gaffield, "Canadian Families in Cultural Context: Hypotheses from the Mid-Nineteenth Century," *HP* (1979): 48–70; Herbert J. Mays, " 'A Place to Stand': Families, Land and Permanence in Toronto Gore Township, 1820–1890," *HP* (1980): 185–211; Darrell A. Norris, "Household and Transiency in a Loyalist Township: The People of Adolphustown, 1784–1822," *HS/SH* XIII (1980): 399–415; Lorne Tepperman, "Ethnic Variations in Marriage and Fertility: Canada, 1871," *Canadian Review of Sociology and Anthropology* (hereafter *CRSA*) II (1974): 324–43; Marvin McInnis, "Child Bearing and Land Availability: Some Evidence from Individual Household Data," in *Population Patterns in the Past*, edited by R.D. Lee (New York, 1977), 201–27; Frank T. Denton and Peter George, "The Influence of Socio-Economic Variables on Family Size in Wentworth County, Ontario, 1871," *CRSA* X (1973): 334-45; Bradbury, "The Family Economy"; Richard Houston, *Numbering the Survivors: The Standish Family of Ireland, Ontario, and Alberta* (Agincourt, 1979).

18. See John McCallum, *Unequal Beginnings: Agriculture and Economic Development in Quebec and Ontario Until 1870* (Toronto, 1980); John Isbister, "Agriculture, Balanced Growth, and Social Change in Central Canada since 1850: An Interpretation," *Economic Development and Cultural Change* 25 (1977): 673–97; D.A. Lawr, "The Development of Farming in Ontario, 1870–1914: Patterns of Growth and Change," *OH* LXIV (1972): 240–51; James M. Gilmour, *Spatial Evolution of Manufacturing, Southern Ontario, 1851–1891* (Toronto, 1972); Douglas McCalla, *The Upper Canada Trade 1834-1872: A Study of the Buchanan's Business* (Toronto, 1979).

19. See note 17, above, and also A. Gordon Darroch and Michael Ornstein, "Ethnicity and Occupational Structure in Canada in 1871: The Vertical Mosaic in Historical Perspective," *Canadian Historical Review* (hereafter *CHR*) LXI (1980): 305–33; Kevin Burley, "Occupational Structure and Ethnicity in London, Ontario, 1871," *HS/SH* XI (1978): 390–410; Harvey J. Graff, *The Literacy Myth: Literacy and Social Structure in the Nineteenth-Century City* (New York, 1979); Herbert J. Mays and Helmut Manzl, "Literacy and Social Structure in Nineteenth-Century Ontario: An Exercise in Historical Methodology," *HS/SH* VII (1974).

20. Three recent exceptions are McCalla, *The Upper Canada Trade*; Gerald Tulchinsky, *The River Barons: Montreal Businessmen and the Growth of Industry and Transportation 1837–53* (Toronto, 1977); and Patrick A. Dunae, *Gentlemen Emigrants: From the British Public Schools to the Canadian Frontier* (Vancouver, 1981). Canadian historians have produced nothing comparable to, for example, Edward Pessen's *Riches, Class and Power Before the Civil War* (Lexington, Mass., 1973), although Michael Bliss, *A Living Profit: Studies in the Social History of Canadian Business, 1883–1911* (Toronto, 1974) provides an excellent analysis of the collective social assumptions of the entrepreneurial class in late Victorian Canada.

21. Gregory Kealey and Peter Warrian, eds., *Essays in Canadian Working Class History* (Toronto, 1976), 7-8.

22. Kenneth McNaught, "E.P. Thompson vs. Harold Logan: Writing About Labour and the Left in the 1970s," *CHR* LXI (1981): 141-68, and reprinted in this volume.

23. Gregory S. Kealey, "Labour and Working-Class History in Canada: Prospects in the 1980s," *L/LT* 7 (1981): 67-98; and David Bercuson, "Through the Looking Glass of Culture: An Essay on the New Labour History and Working-Class Culture in Recent Canadian Historical Writing," *L/LT* 7 (1981): 96-112. Both articles are reprinted in David Bercuson, ed., *Canadian Labour History: Selected Readings* (Toronto: Copp Clark Pitman, 1987). The Bercuson, Kealey and McNaught articles cited here offer an admirable summary of both the debate and the historiography. They should be required reading for anyone interested in labour history.

24. Michael S. Cross, "The Shiners' War: Social Violence in the Ottawa Valley in the 1830s," *CHR* LIV (1973): 1-26; Judith Fingard, "The Winter's Tale: Contours of Pre-industrial Poverty in British America, 1815-1860," *HP* (1974): 65-94; Rainer Baehre, "Pauper Emigration to Upper Canada in the 1830s," *HS/SH* XIV (1981): 339-68; Leo A. Johnson, "Land Policy, Population Growth and Social Structure in the Home District, 1793-1851," *OH* LXIII (1971): 41-60; John Herd Thompson, "Bringing in the Sheaves: The Harvest Excursionists, 1890-1929," *CHR* LIX (1978): 467-89; *Hopeful Travellers*, esp. Chap. 5; Michael Katz, *The People of Hamilton*, esp. Chap. 3; Patricia E. Malcolmson, "The Poor in Kingston, 1815-1850" in *To Preserve and Defend: Essays on Kingston in the Nineteenth Century*, edited by Gerald Tulchinsky (Montreal, 1976), 281-98; and especially Steven Langdon, "The Emergence of the Canadian Working-Class Movement, 1845-1875," *JCS* VIII (1973): 3-13.

25. Bryan D. Palmer, *A Culture in Conflict: Skilled Workers and Industrial Capitalism in Hamilton, Ontario, 1880-1914* (Montreal, 1979); Gregory S. Kealey, *Toronto Workers Respond to Industrial Capitalism, 1867-1892* (Toronto, 1980).

26. For example, Peter Warrian, " 'Sons of Toil': The Impact of Industrialization on Craft Workers in Late 19th Century Ontario" in *Industrial Development in Southern Ontario*, edited by David Walker and James Bater (Waterloo, 1974), 71-98; Craig Heron and Bryan D. Palmer, "Through the Prism of the Strike: Industrial Conflict in Southern Ontario, 1901-1914." *CHR* LVIII (1977): 423-58; Gregory Kealey, "Artisans Respond to Industrialism: Shoemakers, Shoe Factories and the Knights of St. Crispin in Toronto," *HP* 137-157; Gregory S. Kealey and Bryan D. Palmer, "The Bonds of Unity: The Knights of Labour in Ontario, 1880-1900," *HS/SH* XIV (1981): 369-411; Wayne Roberts, "The Last Artisans: Toronto Printers, 1896-1914," in *Essays in Canadian Working Class History*, 125-42; Russell Hann, "Brainworkers and the Knights of Labour: E.E. Shepherd, Phillips Thompson, and the *Toronto News*, 1883-1887," in *Essays in Canadian Working Class History*, 35-59. And see, for comparative purposes, Donald Avery, *"Dangerous Foreigners": European Immigrant Workers and Labour Radicalism in Canada, 1896-1932* (Toronto, 1979).

27. Terry Copp, *The Anatomy of Poverty: The Condition of the Working Class in Montreal, 1897-1929* (Toronto, 1974); Michael J. Piva, *The Condition of the Working Class in Toronto, 1900-1921* (Ottawa, 1979); Bradbury, "The Family Economy and Work in an Industrializing City: Montreal in the 1870s"; and see Gregory S. Kealey, ed. *Canada Investigates Industrialism* (Toronto, 1973).

28. In addition to works previously cited see: Richard Allen, "The Social Gospel and the Reform Tradition in Canada, 1890-1930," *CHR* XLIX (1968): 381-99; J.M. Bliss, "The Methodist Church and World War I," *CHR* XLIX (1968): 213-33; Paul Rutherford, ed., *Saving the Canadian City: The First Phase, 1880-1920* (Toronto, 1974); Paul Rutherford, "Tomorrow's Metropolis: The Urban Reform Movement in Canada, 1890-1920," *The Canadian City: Essays in Urban History*, edited by G.A. Stelter and A.F.J. Artibise (Toronto, 1979); Walter Van Nus, "The Fate of City Beautiful Thought in Canada, 1893-1930," *HP* (1975): 191-210; James D. Anderson, "The Municipal Government Reform Movement in Western Canada, 1880-1920" in *The Usable Urban Past: Planning and Politics in the Modern Canadian City*, edited by A.F.J. Artibise and Gilbert A. Stelter (Toronto, 1979), 73-111; Graeme Decarie, "Something Old, Something New . . . Aspects of Prohibitionism in Ontario in the 1890s" in *Oliver Mowat's Ontario*, edited by Donald Swainson (Toronto, 1972), 154-73; Gerald Hallowell, *Prohibition in Ontario* (Ottawa, 1976); Wendy Mitchinson, "The YWCA and Reform in the Nineteenth Century," *HS/SH* XII (1979): 368-84; Angus McLaren, "Birth Control and Abortion in Canada, 1870-1920," *CHR* LIX (1978): 319-40; Christopher Armstrong and H.V. Nelles, *The Revenge of the Methodist Bicycle Company* (Toronto, 1976); E.R. Forbes, "Prohibition and the Social Gospel in Nova Scotia," *Acadiensis* 1 (1971): 11-36; John H.

Thompson," 'The Beginning of Our Regeneration': The Great War and Western Canadian Reform Movements," *HP* (1972): 227–46. This list is intended to be representative, not exhaustive.

29. See, for example, Robert Nisbet, *Social Change and History: Aspects of the Western Theory of Development* (New York, 1969); Peter Laslett, *The World We Have Lost* (London, 1965); G. Leff, *History and Social Theory* (London, 1969); Hayden V. White, "The Burden of History," *History of Theory* 5 (1966): 111–34; Philip Abrams, "The Sense of the Past and the Origins of Sociology," *Past and Present* 55 (1972): 18–32; Robert F. Berkhofer, Jr., *A Behavioral Approach to Historical Analysis* (New York, 1969); T.C. Cochran, "The Social Sciences and the Problem of Historical Synthesis," *The Social Sciences in Historical Study* (New York, 1964), 157–71.

30. For discussions of recent historical writing in Quebec, see Jean Blain, "Économie et société en Nouvelle France . . . ," *Revue d'histoire de l'Amérique française* (hereafter *RHAF*) (June 1972): 3–30, (Sept. 1974): 163–86, and (Dec. 1976): 323–62; Alfred Dubuc, "L'influence de l'école des *Annales* au Québec," ibid. (Dec. 1979), 357–86; G. Paquet and J.-P. Wallot, "Pour un meso-histoire du XIXe siècle canadien," ibid., 387–425; F. Ouellet, "La formation d'une société dans la vallée du Saint-Laurent . . . ," *CHR* (Dec. 1981) 407–50.

31. We have also made no attempt to be comprehensive.

32. Jacques Henripin, in Hubert Charbonneau, *Vie et mort des nos ancêtres: étude démographique* (Montreal: Les Presses de l'Université de Montréal, 1975), 13.

33. For a discussion and a sampling of earlier population studies see Hubert Charbonneau, *La population du Québec: études rétrospectives* (Montreal: Boréal Express, 1973).

34. Ibid., 13.

35. H. Charbonneau, B. Desjardins, and P. Beauchap, "Le comportement démographique des voyageurs sous le regimé français," *HS/SH* (May 1978): 120–33. Charbonneau, *Vie et mort . . .* is based in part on the same data.

36. M. Trudel, *La population du Canada en 1663* (Montreal: Fides, 1973).

37. M. Trudel, "L'instabilité des censitaires du temps des Cent-Associés," *HS/SH* (April 1974): 98–109.

38. L. Dechêne, *Habitants et marchands de Montréal au XVIIe siècle* (Paris: Plon, 1974).

39. C. Moore "The Other Louisbourg: Trade and Merchant Enterprise in Île Royale 1713–1758," *HS/SH* (May 1979); L. Michel, "Un marchand rural en Nouvelle-France: François-Augustin Bailly de Messain, 1709-1771," *RHAF* (Sept. 1979): 215–62; J.F. Bosher, "French Protestant Families in Canadian Trade, 1740-1760," *HS/SH* (Nov. 1974); and "A Quebec Merchant's Trading Circles in France and Canada: Jean-André Lamaletie before 1763," ibid. (May 1977): 24–44. See also, J. Igartua, "The Merchants of Montreal at the Conquest: Socio-Economic Profile," *HS/SH* (Nov. 1975): 275–93.

40. P.N. Moogk, "Rank in New France: Reconstructing a Society from Notarial Documents," *HS/SH* (May 1975); J.A. Dickenson, "La justice seigneuriale en Nouvelle-France: le cas de Notre-Dame des Anges," *RHAF* (Dec. 1974): 323–46.

41. F. Rousseau, "Hôpital et société en Nouvelle-France: l'Hôtel-Dieu du Québec à la fin du XVIIe siècle," *RHAF* (June 1977): 29–47.

42. A. La Chance, "Une Étude de mentalité: les injures verbales en Canada au XVIIIe siècle (1712-1748)," *RHAF* (Sept. 1977): 229–38.

43. For some other work that is in whole or in part demographic, see L. Dechêne, "La croissance de Montréal au XVIIe siècle," *RHAF* (Sept. 1973): 163-79; C. Pouyez, "La population de l'Île Royale en 1752," *HS/SH* (Nov. 1973): 147–75; G. Proulx, "Soldat à Québec, 1748-1757," *RHAF* (March 1979): 535–63; Yves Landry, "Mortalité, nuptialité et canadianisation des troupes françaises de la guerre de Sept ans," *HS/SH* (Nov. 1979); J.E. Igartua, "Le comportement démographique des marchands de Montréal vers 1760," *RHAF* (Dec. 1979): 427–45; J. Mathieu et al., "Les alliances matrimoniales exogames dans le gouvernement de Québec, 1700-1760," *RHAF* (June 1981): 3–32.

44. Charbonneau, *Vie et mort*, 8.

45. Y. Landry, ed., *Programme de Recherche en Démographie Historique: Rapport de l'année 1980-1981* (Montreal: Université de Montréal, 1981), 1. The annual reports give the best idea of the massive scope of PRDH. But see also J. Légaré, A. La Rose, and R. Roy, "Reconstitution de la population canadienne au XVIIe siècle: méthodes et bilan d'une recherche," *Recherches sociographiques* (hereafter *RS*) (Sept.-Dec. 1973): 383-400, and P. Beauchamp, H. Charbonneau, B. Desjardins, and J. Légaré, "La reconstitution

automatique des familles: un fait acquis," *Population* (Sept. 1977): 375–99. For some preliminary results—
G. Olivier-Lacamp and J. Légaré, "Quelques characteristiques des ménages de la ville de Québec entre 1666
et 1716," *HS/SH* (May 1979): 66–78.

46.   G. Bouchard, *Société de Recherche sur les Populations: Rapport Annuel 1980–81* (Chicoutimi: Université
de Québec, 1981). The development of the project can be followed in G. Bouchard's articles "L'histoire
démographique et le problème des migrations. L'example de Laterrière," *HS/SH* (May 1975): 21-33,
"L'histoire de la population et l'étude de la société saguenayenne aux XIXe et XXe siècle," *RHAF* (June
1977): 3–27, and "Family Structures and Geographic Mobility at Laterrière, 1851, 1935," *Journal of Family
History* (Winter 1977): 350–69.

47.   Charbonneau, *Vie et mort*, 22; G. Bouchard, C. Pouyez, and R. Roy, "L'Avenir des fichiers de
population dans les sciences humaines: le projet de fichier-réseau de la population saguenayenne," *Études
Canadiennes/Canadian Studies* (Dec. 1980): 38 ff.

48.   Ibid., 40–41.

49.   The following is a sample of articles dealing with source criticism: H. Charbonneau, et al., "La
population du Canada aux recensements de 1666 et 1667," *Population* (1967): 1051–54, "Recensements et
registres paroissaux du Canada durant le période 1665-1668," ibid. (1970): 97–124; "Le recensement
nominatif du Canada en 1681," *HS/SH* (April 1971): 77–98; D.P. Gagan, "Enumerator's Instructions for
the Census of Canada in 1852 and 1861," *HS/SH* (Nov. 1974); L. Lavellée, "Les archives notariales et
l'histoire sociale de la Nouvelle-France," *RHAF* (Dec. 1974): 385–403; G. Landry, "Étude critique du
recensement du Canada de 1765," *RHAF* (Dec. 1975): 323–51; Gerard Bouchard et André La Rose, "La
réglementation du contenu des actes de baptême, marriage, sepulture au Québec des origines à nos jours,"
RHAF (June 1976): 67–84; R. Roy and H. Charbonneau, "Le contenu des registres paroissiaux canadiens
du XVIIe siècle," *RHAF* (June 1976): 85–97; G. Allaire, "Les engagements pour la traite des fourrures:
évaluation de la documentation," *RHAF* (June 1980): 3–26; G. Morin, "La représentativité de l'inventaire
après décès—l'étude d'un cas: Québec an début du XIXe siècle," *RHAF* (March 1981): 515–34; P. Dufour,
"La construction navale à Québec 1760-1825: sources inexplorées et nouvelles perspectives de recherces,"
RHAF (Sept. 1981): 253–62; R.M. McInnis, "Some Pitfalls in the 1851–1852 Census of Agriculture in
Lower Canada," *HS/SH* (May 1981): 219–31.

50.   C. Pouyez and M. Bergson, "L'étude des migrations au Saguenay (1842–1931): problèmes de
methode," *HS/SH* (May 1978).

51.   R. Roy, et al., "Le jumelage des données nominatives dans les recensements: problèmes et
méthodes," *HS/SH* (May 1980).

52.   G. Bouchard and P. Brard, "La programme de reconstitution automatique des familles
saguenayennes: données de base et résultats provisoires," *HS/SH* (May 1979): 170–85.

53.   R. Roy, et al., "Le jumelage . . . ."; C. Pouyez, et al., "La mobilité géographique en milieu rural: le
Saguenay, 1852-1861," *HS/SH* (May 1981): 123–55.

54.   Ibid.

55.   Ibid.

56.   Ibid.

57.   Ibid.

58.   Ian Winchester, "Review of Peel County History Project and the Saguenay Project," *HS/SH*
(May 1980): 195–205.

59.   R. Roy, et al., "Le jumelage . . . ".

60.   N. Séguin, *La conquête du sol au XIXe siècle* (Trois Rivières: Boréal Express, 1977).

61.   G. Bouchard, "Introduction à l'étude de la société saguenayenne aux XIXe et XXe siècles," *RHAF*
(June 1977): 3–77; See also the review of Séguin's book by F. Ouellet, *HS/SH* (Nov. 1977): 439–47.

62.   G. Gaudreau, "Le rapport agriculture-forêt au Québec: note historiographique," *RHAF* (June
1979): 6778.

63.   Allan Greer, "Fur Trade Labour and Lower Canadian Agrarian Structures," *Canadian Historical
Association Annual Reports* (hereafter *CHAR*) (1981): 197–214.

64.   P.-A. Linteau, R. Durocher, J.-C. Robert, *Histoire du Québec Contemporain (1867-1929)* (Montreal:
Boréal Express, 1979), 127–31.

65.   J. Hamelin, *Économie et société en Nouvelle-France* (Quebec: Les Presses de l'Université Laval, 1960).

66. F. Ouellet, *Histoire économique et sociale du Québec, 1760-1850: Structures et conjoncture* (Montreal: Fides, 1966); *Lower Canada (1791-1840), Social Change and Nationalism* (Toronto: McClelland and Stewart, 1980), trans. and adapted by P. Claxton; *Elements d'histoire sociale du Bas-Canada, 1760-1850* (Montreal, 1972); "Dualité économique et changement technologique au Québec (1760-1790)," *HS/SH* (Nov. 1976); "Officiers de milice et structure sociale au Québec (1660-1815)," *HS/SH* (May 1979); "Libéré ou Exploité! Le paysan québécois d'avant 1850," *HS/SH* (Nov. 1980); "La formation d'une société dans la vallée du Saint-Laurent. . . ." *CHR* (Dec. 1981); "Histoire et sociologie: le point de vue d'un historien," *CHAR* (1966).

67. J. McCallum, *Unequal Beginnings: Agriculture and Economic Development in Ontario and Quebec until 1870* (Toronto: University of Toronto Press, 1980).

68. Ibid., Chaps. 1-3.

69. For example, J. Paquet et J.-P. Wallot, "Pour une mesohistoire du XIXe siècle canadien," *RHAF* (Dec. 1979): 387-425, "Groupes Sociaux et pouvoir: le cas Canadien au tournant du XIXe siècle," *RHAF*, (March 1974): 509-564.

70. J. Paquet and J.-P. Wallot, "International Circumstances of Lower Canada, 1786-1810: Prolegomenon," *CHR* (Dec. 1972).

71. J.-P. Wallot, *Un Québec qui bougeait—trame socio-politique du Québec au tournant du XIXe siècle* (Montreal: Boréal Express, 1973).

72. J. Paquet and J.-P. Wallot, *Patronage et pouvoir dans le bas Canada (1794-1812)—Un essai d'économie historique* (Montreal: Les Presses de l'Université de Québec, 1973).

73. G. Paquet and J.-P. Wallot, "Crise agricole et tensions socio-éthniques dans le Bas-Canada, 1802-1812: éléments pour un ré-interpretation," *RHAF* (Sept. 1972); "The Agriculture Crisis in Lower Canada, 1802-1813: *mise au point.* A Response to T.J.A. LeGoff"; T.J.A. LeGoff, "The Agriculture Crisis in Lower Canada, 1802-1812: A Review of a Controversy," *CHR* (March 1974); "A Reply," *CHR* (June 1975); F. Ouellet, "Le myth de l'habitant sensible au marché! Commentaires sur la controverse LeGoff—Wallot et Paquet," *RS* (Jan.-April 1976).

74. John Hare, "L'Assemblée legislative du Bas-Canada, 1792-1814: députation et polarisation politique," *RHAF* (Dec. 1973): 361-397, and "La population de la ville de Québec, 1795-1805," *HS/SH* (May 1974); R.G. Bouliane, "The French Canadians and the Schools of the Royal Institution for the Advancement of Learning," *HS/SH* (Nov. 1972): 144-64; J. Bernier, "La construction domiciliaire à Québec, 1810-1820," *RHAF* (March 1978): 542-61; B.C. Elliott, "The Famous Township of Hull: Image and Aspirations of ? Pioneer Quebec Community," *HS/SH* (Nov. 1979); J. Bernier, "François Blanchet et le mouvement réformiste en médecine au début du XIXe siècle," *RHAF* (Sept. 1980): 223-44; J.I. Little, "Colonisation and Municipal Reform in Canada East," *HS/SH* (May 1981): 93-121; E. Kolish, "Le Conseil legislatif et les bureaux d'enregistement (1836)," *RHAF* (Sept. 1981): 217-30; B. Tunis, "Medical Education and Medical Licensing in Lower Canada: Demographic Factors, Conflict and Social Change," *HS/SH* (May 1981): 67-91. For the middle part of the century, see also J. Lamonde, "Inventaire des études et des sources pour l'étude des associations 'littéraires' québécoises francophones au 19e siècle (1840-1900)," *RS* 2 (1975); "Les associations au Bas-Canada: de nouveaux marchés aux idées, 1840-1867," *HS/SH* (Nov. 1975): 361-69; R.A. Farrell, "The Rise and Decline of Science at Quebec, 1824-1844," *HS/SH* (May 1977): 77-91; A. Metcalf, "The Evolution of Organized Physical Education in Montreal, 1840-1895," *HS/SH* (May 1978): 144-66; G. Bernatchez, "La société littéraire et historique de Québec (The Literary and Historical Society of Quebec), 1824-1890," *RHAF* (Sept. 1981): 179-92.

75. F. Ouellet, "Dualité économique."

76. P.-A. Linteau and J.-C. Robert, "Propriété foncière et société à Montréal: une hypothèse," *RHAF* (June 1974): 45-65; J.-P. Bernard, P.-A. Linteau, and J.-C. Robert, "La structure professionelle de Montréal en 1825," *RHAF* (Dec. 1976): 383-415; G. Paquet and J.-P. Wallot, "Les inventaires après décès à Montréal au tournant du XIXe siècle," *RHAF* (Sept. 1976): 163-221; P.-A. Linteau, R. Durocher, and J.-C. Robert, *Histoire du Québec contemporaine,* 464. See also L. Dechêne, "La rente du faubourg Saint-Roch à Québec — 1750-1850," *RHAF* (March 1981): 569-96.

77. J.-C. Robert, "Les notables de Montréal au XIXe siècle," *HS/SH* (May 1975). Robert is fully aware of the limitations of the sample.

78. J.-L. Roy, "Livres et société bas-Canadienne: croissance et expansion de la libraire Fabre, 1816–1855," *HS/SH* (Nov. 1972): 117–43.

79. G. Tulchinsky, "Une enterprise maritime canadienne-française: La Compagnie du Richelieu, 1845–1854," *RHAF* (March 1973): 559–82.

80. P.-A. Linteau, "Quelques réflexions autour de la bourgeoisie québécoise, 1850–1914," *RHAF* (June 1976): 55–66. The process of "marginalization" is pursued in the relevant sections of P.-A. Linteau, J.-C. Robert, and R. Durocher, *Histoire du Québec contemporaine*.

81. There is, of course, an enormous bulk of material about the Church in Quebec that was written in the past. And historians working in a traditional manner continue to add to it.

82. N. Voisine, *Histoire de l'Élise catholique au Québec (1608–1970)* (Montreal: Fides, 1971).

83. Trudel, *Le Population*, 120, 260–2, 289, 319–20.

84. Dechêne, *Habitants*, 450–76.

85. Marie-Aimée Cliche, "Les attitudes devant la mort d'après les clauses testamentaires dans le gouvernement de Québec sous le régime français," *RHAF* (June 1978): 57–94.

86. M.-A. Bédard, "La présence protestante en Nouvelle-France," *RHAF* (Dec. 1977): 325–49; J. Blain, "La mortalité en Nouvelle-France: les phases de la thèse et de l'anti-thèse," *RHAF* (Dec. 1973): 408–16.

87. References are scattered through his works, but see especially *Social Change and Nationalism*.

88. F. Ouellet, "Libéré ou exploité," 349–55.

89. R. Boucher, "L'Endettement de l'évêché de Saint-Hyacinthe au XIXe siècle: le rôle décisif de Charles La Roque dans l'extinction de cette dette," *RHAF* (March 1980): 557–74.

90. J.-P. Wallot, "Religion and French Canadian Mores in the Early Nineteenth Century," *CHR* (March 1971).

91. R. Chabot, *Le curé de campagne et la contestation locale en Québec (de 1791 aux troubles de 1837–1838)* (Montreal: Hurtubise, 1975).

92. S. Gagnon, "Le diocèse de Montréal durant les années 1860," in P. Hurtobise, et al., *Le laic dans l'Église canadienne-française de 1830 à nos jours* (Montreal: Fides, 1972).

93. S. Gagnon, *Le Québec et ses historiens de 1840 à 1920: La Nouvelle-France de Garneau à Groulx* (Quebec: Les Presses de l'Université Laval, 1978).

94. There has been a great deal of work done on ideology in nineteenth-century Quebec which cannot begin to be included here. Some overviews and representative selections are: F. Dumont, et al., *Idéologies au Canada français (1850–1900)* (Quebec: Les Presses de l'Université Laval, 1971); Nadia Fahmy-Eid, "Ultramontanisme, idéologie et classes sociales," *RHAF* (June 1975): 49–68, "Éducation et classes sociales: analyse d'idéologie conservatrice — cléricale et petite bourgeoise — au Québec au milieu du 19e siècle," *RHAF* (Sept. 1978), and *Le clergé et le pouvoir politique au Québec: Une analyse de l'idéologie ultramontaine au milieu du XIXe siècle* (Montreal: Hurtubise, 1978); S. Gagnon, "L'histoire des idéologies québécoises: quinze ans de réalisations," *HS/SH* (May 1976): 17–20; D. Monière, *La developpement des idéologies au Québec des origines à nos jours* (Montreal: Les Éditions Québec Amérique, 1977); C. Morissoneau, *La terre promis: le mythe du Nord québécois* (Montreal: Hurtubise, 1978).

95. J. Roy, "Le clergé nicolétain 1885–1904: aspects sociographiques," *RHAF* (Dec. 1981): 383–96.

96. W.F. Ryan, *The Clergy and Economic Growth in Quebec, 1896–1914* (Quebec: Les Presses de l'Université Laval, 1966). Also J.I. Little, "The Parish and French Canadian Migrants to Compton County, Quebec, 1851–1891," *HS/SH* (May 1978).

97. G. Bouchard, "Les prêtres, les capitalistes et les ouvrières à Chicoutimi (1846–1930)," *Mouvement social* (July-Sept. 1980): 5–23.

98. This survey does not attempt to move past 1900. For the working class in the twentieth century see: F. Harvey, ed., *Le mouvement ouvrier au Quebéc* (Montreal: Boréal Express, 1980) and especially the editor's excellent historiographical introduction; F. Harvey, ed., *Aspects historiques du mouvement ouvrier au Québec* (Montreal: Boréal Express, 1973); G. Hamelin et F. Harvey, eds., *Les travailleurs québécois, 1941–1971* (Quebec: Université de Laval, 1976).

99. See note 6.

100. Especially, F. Ouellet, "Dualité économique et changement technologique au Québec (1760–1790)," *HS/SH* (Nov. 1976): 256–96.

101. See note 34.

102. M. Thivierge, "Les artisans du cuir à Québec (1660–1760)," *RHAF* (Dec. 1980): 341–56; Jean-Pierre Hardy et David-Thierry Ruddel, *Les apprentis artisans à Québec, 1660–1815* (Montreal: Les Presses de l'Université du Québec, 1977).

103. For an overview of the last half of the nineteenth century, there is the older but still very useful Jean Hamelin, ed., *Les travailleurs québécois, 1851–1896* (Montreal: Les Presses de l'Université du Québec, 1973). And also, H.C. Pentland, "The Development of a Capitalist Labour Market in Canada," *Canadian Journal of Economics and Political Science* (Nov. 1959): 450–61.

104. R. Tremblay, "La formation matérielle de la classe ouvrière à Montréal entre 1790 et 1830," *RHAF* (June 1979): 39–50.

105. J. Burgess, "L'industrie de la chaussure à Montréal: 1840–1870 — le passage de l'artisanat à la fabrique," *RHAF* (Sept. 1977): 187–210.

106. M. Heap, "La grève des charretiers à Montréal, 1864," *RHAF* (Dec. 1977): 371–95.

107. J.-P. Kesteman, "Les travailleurs à la construction du chemin de fer dans la région de Sherbrooke (1851–1853)," *RHAF* (March 1978): 525–45.

108. McCallum, *Unequal Beginnings*, Chap. 7.

109. F. Harvey, "Les Chevaliers du Travail, les États-Unis et la société québécoise, 1882–1902" in *Le mouvement ouvrière*, 69–130.

110. F. Harvey, *Révolution industrielle et travailleurs* (Montreal: Boréal Express, 1978).

111. J. De Bonville, *Jean-Baptiste Gagnepetit: Les travailleurs Montréalais à la fin du XIXe siècle* (Montreal: L'Aurore, 1975).

112. T. Copp, *The Anatomy of Poverty: The Condition of the Working Class in Montreal, 1897–1929* (Toronto: McClelland and Stewart, 1974).

113. As in the case of working-class studies, there is some (but not much) material for the twentieth century which this essay does not deal with. See R. Pierson and B. Light, "Women in the Teaching and Writing of Canadian History," *The History and Social Science Teacher* (Winter 1982): 83–96.

114. L. Plamondon, "Une femme d'affaires en Nouvelle-France: Marie-Anne Barbel, veuve Fornel," *RHAF* (Sept. 1972): 165–85. (For an English version of Plamondon's article, see Veronica Strong-Boag and Anita Clair Fellman, eds., *Rethinking Canada: The Promise of Women's History* (Toronto: Copp Clark Pitman, 1986).)

115. S. Van Kirk, *"Many Tender Ties": Women in Fur Trade Society in Western Canada, 1700–1850* (Winnipeg: Watson and Dwyer, 1980).

116. M. Dumont-Johnson, "Les communautés religieuses et la condition féminine," *RS* (Jan.-April 1978): 79–102.

117. Sr. M. Jean, *Évolution des communautés religieuses de femmes du Canada de 1639 à nos jours* (Montreal: Fides, 1977).

118. D.S. Cross, "The Neglected Majority: The Changing Role of Women in Nineteenth-Century Montreal," *HS/SH* (Nov. 1973): 202–23.

119. B. Bradbury, "The Family Economy and Work in an Industrializing City: Montreal in the 1870's," *CHAR* (1979): 71–96.

120. S.M. Trofimenkoff, "One Hundred and Two Muffled Voices: Canada's Industrial Women in the 1880's," *Atlantis* (Fall 1977): 66–82.

121. M. Dumont-Johnson, "Des garderies au XIXe siècle: les salles d'asile des Soeurs Grises à Montréal," *RHAF* (June 1980): 27–55.

HISTORICAL WRITING ON NATIVE PEOPLE IN CANADA†

ROBIN FISHER

Historical writing on Canada's native people, like many aspects of Canadian history, has burgeoned in the last ten years. The growth of native history is undoubtedly related to the flourishing of social history, but it has also been stimulated by contemporary developments in Canadian society, particularly the increased assertiveness of the native people and the growing awareness of their needs and problems by other Canadians. Within Canadian historiography, as in Canadian society, the indigenous people have stepped out of the background to become major players. Consequently, while there are still many important gaps, there is now a considerable body of historical literature and, in some areas, a lively and stimulating scholarly debate.

At the beginning of the decade James Walker, in his essay "The Indian in Canadian Historical Writing,"[1] quite correctly pointed out that the native peoples of Canada had either been ignored by historians or dealt with in terms of negative stereotypes. There were the works of a few hardy pioneers like A. G. Bailey,[2] but those moving into the area in the early 1970s were virtually starting from scratch. So little work on native peoples had been done by Canadian historians that, in the introduction to *The Chippewa and their Neighbors*,[3] Harold Hickerson could announce the use of primary documents to reveal past developments in an Indian culture, that is to say the historical method, as a grand new discovery. Such a pronouncement could only be made in the absence of a vigorous historical literature and as a result of lack of communication between the disciplines.

Since 1970 conversations between academic disciplines have become more frequent and fruitful. Historians working on indigenous peoples have been influenced by the work of historical geographers and especially by anthropologists. A combination of history and ethnography had produced the hybrid sub-discipline of ethnohistory. Although ethnohistory appears to be somewhat difficult to define in any way that makes it distinct from history, there is no doubt that those who call themselves ethnohistorians have made major advances in the study of native peoples. A notable example is Charles A. Bishop, *The Northern Ojibwa and the Fur Trade*.[4] Bishop successfully combines the techniques of field observation and documentary research to describe cultural change among the Ojibwa during the fur trading period. Historians may, however, be a bit disconcerted by the fact that he starts with the present and then works back in time, a procedure that is evidently known as "upstreaming." As the Indians appreciated, paddling

†*History and Social Science Teacher* 17, 2 (Winter 1982): 65–72.

against the current can be arduous. The most successful exponent of ethnohistory in Canada is undoubtedly Bruce Trigger. His superb, two-volume *The Children of Aataentsic*[5] is surely the model for others to follow. Trigger uses archaeological and ethnographic sources to describe the traditional culture of the Huron, and adds historical material to show the changes that occurred from the time of European contact to the destruction of Huronia in the middle of the seventeenth century. Those who are daunted by these magisterial volumes may find his earlier little book, *The Huron*,[6] a more manageable way of gaining access to Trigger's work, but with that introduction the reader should move on to the *The Children of Aataentsic*. The perspective of the geographer Conrad Heidenreich has also been brought to bear on the same area. *Huronia: A History and Geography of the Huron Indians 1600–1650*[7] is an effort to reconstruct the physical and human geography of Huronia, and it concentrates on the period of relative cultural stability prior to the disruptions beginning in the late 1630s. Moving to another region of Canada, volume one of Wilson Duff's *The Indian History of British Columbia*[8] is not so much an ethnohistory as a history written by an anthropologist. This brief account is still a good introduction to the history of the Indians of the northwest coast, even though others have subsequently dealt with aspects of that history in more detail.

For historians, because there are severe limitations on our ability to elucidate the pre-contact cultures in any detail, the history of native peoples really begins with the arrival of Europeans. This is not to suggest that we should ignore the indigenous cultures, but rather that contact is the baseline from which we can adequately describe these cultures and, more importantly, analyse change over time. From the coming of the Europeans to the present day, the history of Canada's native peoples falls into two broad phases; the first, the period of early contact and the fur trade, and the second following the establishment of European settlement. Naturally the length of each period and the point of change from one to the other varied greatly from region to region.

Work done by Canadian historians on native peoples during the fur trading period is much more substantial and sophisticated than that which has been done on the period of settlement. Indeed the history of the fur trade is perhaps the only area of historical writing where the literature on Canada is superior to that on the United States.

Writing on the fur trade in Canada began with Harold Innis. His classic work, *The Fur Trade in Canada*[9] (first published in 1930), laid considerable emphasis on the Indians' role in fur trade economics. But, while not ignoring the Indians, Innis's primary interest was to describe the European side of the story, and so he tended to see the Indians in terms of their reactions to European initiatives rather than acting according to their own cultural norms. Recently Innis's research and conclusions have come under attack. In "A Belated Review of Harold Adams Innis, *The Fur Trade in Canada*,"[10] W.J. Eccles has drawn our attention to the need for a critical examination of the book. In the process, however, Eccles has confirmed, rather than denied, the creative contribution that Innis has made to fur trade history. Not, apparently, noticing what has been going on over the last ten years, Eccles begins his article by asserting that "A reappraisal of the Canadian fur trade is long overdue." In fact, a reappraisal of the fur trade has been underway on several fronts. The economics of the trade, the nature of fur trade society, and the impact that it had on the indigenous cultures have all been the subject of scrutiny and reevaluation.

The nature of the economic relationship between Indian and European fur traders has been closely examined in the work of Arthur Ray. *Indians in the Fur Trade*[11] is a fairly general discussion of the role of the Cree and Assiniboine in which Ray argues that, although the trade brought changes to these Indian cultures, it constituted a partnership that required the co-operation of Indian and European. The idea that the fur trade was a reciprocal relationship between the two races has also been developed by other authors, including Robin Fisher in his discussion of both the maritime and the land-based fur trade on the northwest coast in *Contact and Conflict*.[12] Ray's more recent book *"Give Us Good Measure": An Economic Analysis of Relations Between the Indians and the Hudson's Bay Company Before 1763*, co-authored with Donald B. Freeman,[13] concentrates on the economic interaction during the early years of contact between the Hudson's Bay Company and the Indians around Hudson's Bay. At the heart of this work is a computer analysis of statistical data taken from the company's account books. In pressing this economic analysis, Ray is reacting against interpretations that hold that the Indians did not behave according to economic norms as we would understand them. The first to make this point was E.E. Rich in an important article on "Trade Habits and Economic Motivation among the Indians of North America,"[14] but it has been elaborated more recently by A. Rotstein who argues that the Indians saw the fur trade in terms of such non-economic factors as traditional politics and institutionalized gift exchange. Unfortunately Rotstein's work is less accessible than Ray's two books. Rotstein's major statement is in his doctoral dissertation,[15] but his argument can be sampled in his article "Trade and Politics: An Institutional Approach."[16] The relative importance of economic and non-economic factors in the Indians' involvement in the fur trade has yet to be conclusively determined, and it may well be that the distinction is somewhat artificial. As usual in human history, motives were probably mixed.

Also mixed was the racial make-up of fur trade society, and this unique social order is being closely examined by historians. Particular attention has been paid to the role of women in the fur trade. In a series of articles, Sylvia Van Kirk has shown that Indian and mixed-blood women made a crucial contribution to the functioning of the fur trade. In " 'The Custom of the Country': An Examination of Fur Trade Marriage Practices"[17] she argues that the relationships between the fur traders and their women tended to be lasting ones, and in " 'Women in Between': Indian Women in Fur Trade Society in Western Canada"[18] she shows that these marriage alliances facilitated the development of the trading relationship between Indian and European. Jennifer S.H. Brown, in the recent book *Strangers in Blood: Fur Trade Company Families in Indian Country*,[19] looks at kinship and social relations on a broader front. She is particularly concerned to examine the contrasting patterns of the Hudson's Bay and North West Companies. In doing so Brown comes to a different conclusion from Van Kirk, at least in the case of the North West Company. Brown argues that the mobility of the Northwesters meant that their domestic relations were more casual than those of the Hudson's Bay Company employees. Having made this distinction, she goes on to draw out its implications for fur trade families. The more traditional interest in the distinctive society that developed at Red River continues to occupy historians. John E. Foster has looked at a group that later formed a segment of Red River society in "The Origins of the Mixed Bloods in the Canadian West,"[20] and Frits Pannekoek has made a "Probe into the Demographic Structure of Nineteenth-Century Red River."[21]

As these studies of fur trade society show, the trade involved the contact of two cultures and the development of a relationship that brought change to both. Historians differ, however, in their assessments of the nature of the impact of the fur trade on the Indians. One of the most stimulating, and perhaps controversial, excursions into this area has been made by Calvin Martin. In *Keepers of the Game: Indian-Animal Relationships and the Fur Trade*[22] Martin has argued that the traditional mutual relationship between the Indians and the animal world was broken by the combined influence of the fur trade, the missionaries, and European disease. This particular thesis is placed in the context of the more general contention that the fur trade was a disaster for the Indians who were involved in it. While Martin presents a strongly argued case supported by a certain amount of evidence, he is quite mistaken when he claims that all fur trade scholars are in "uniform agreement" with his general position. As already suggested, one of the problems with maintaining that, once the European arrived, it was down hill all the way for the Indians, is that there are too many unanswered, and perhaps unanswerable, questions about the pre-contact way of life. But, even starting at the point of contact, much recent fur trade scholarship indicates that the fur trade may have been a mixed blessing, but was not an unmitigated disaster, for the Indians. This interpretation is implicit in Arthur Ray's two books and is made quite explicit in his essay on "Fur Trade History as an Aspect of Native History."[23] In this essay Ray exhorts us to pay more attention to the creative role of the Indian in the fur trade. A similar case is made in more detail for the Indians west of the Rockies by Fisher in *Contact and Conflict*.

Having outlined some of its salient features, the best introduction to the range and diversity of fur trade scholarship is to be found in Carol M. Judd and Arthur J. Ray, *Old Trails and New Directions*.[24] Virtually all of the authors mentioned above are either included or referred to in this volume. Perhaps they follow more old trails than new directions, but that very much depends on how new is new in the fast-moving world of fur trade scholarship in the 1970s.

However one interprets the fur trade period, there is no question that with the arrival of settlers the native people of Canada faced more difficult circumstances. The onset of European settlement certainly increased the pace of change in the indigenous cultures, but its impact on the native people does not seem to have quickened the interest of Canada's historians to the same extent as the fur trade has done. One should not, of course, leave the impression that the distinction between the fur trading and settlement frontiers was always an absolute one. New France, for example, was a settlement colony in which the fur trade played an integral part. A study that focusses on explorers, missionaries, and government officials, but does not ignore the fur traders, is by Cornelius J. Jaenen, *Friend and Foe*.[25] In this book, Jaenen describes French attitudes towards the

Indians: attitudes that were a product of their European intellectual background and the nature of the North American contact experience. Studies of European ideas about indigenous people rely on the records left by the literate and it is, therefore, worth pointing out that Jaenen has also attempted the much more difficult task of describing "Amerindian Views of French Culture in the Seventeenth Century".[26]

In those areas of the country where there was a sharper division between fur trade and settlement, there are studies that straddle both eras. In *Contact and Conflict*, Fisher sees a very clear distinction between the mutual relationship that existed between Indian and European during the fur trading period and the destructive impact of the settlement frontier on the indigenous cultures of British Columbia. On Canada's east coast there was, according to L.F.S. Upton, a more subtle distinction between the two phases of Indian-European contact. *Micmacs and Colonists: Indian-White Relations in the Maritimes, 1713–1867*[27] is a history of the first group of North Americans to come into contact with Europeans. During this period of early French contact and the subsequent contest for the control of the maritimes by the French, British, and Americans, the Micmac experienced definite cultural change but still had room to manoeuvre as they played one side off against another. With the establishment of firm British control in 1783, however, their freedom of choice was severely curtailed and, in the three colonies of Nova Scotia, New Brunswick, and Prince Edward Island, government policies were characterized by ignorance and neglect. The consequent dispossession and decline of the Micmacs is typical of the fate of many of Canada's native peoples faced with the influx of settlers, but the process in other regions has not been described in monographs comparable to those by Fisher and Upton.

We could do, for instance, with a volume dealing with the impact of prairie settlement on the Indians. In this area the Indians have probably suffered somewhat as a result of historians' long-standing interest in the Métis. This is not to say that the prairie Indians have been ignored altogether, although one is tempted to conclude that more interest has been shown in the Indians who came north to Canada from the United States after the Battle of the Little Big Horn. Among others, Gary Pennanen in "Sitting Bull: Indian Without a Country"[28] and, on a more popular level, C. Frank Turner in *Across the Medicine Line*[29] have dealt with this subject. There has been a certain amount of work on land policy and its effects on the indigenous Canadians of the prairies. *Native Rights in Canada*, edited by Peter A. Cumming and Neil H. Mickenberg,[30] discusses the historical development of the legal position of native people, particularly in relation to land, and contains sections dealing with the prairies. There are a number of articles dealing with aspects of the land question in specific areas. One example is "Indian Land Surrenders in Southern Saskatchewan," by Stewart Raby.[31] There have been biographical studies of prominent Indian leaders of which Hugh A. Dempsey's *Crowfoot: Chief of the Blackfeet*[32] is probably the best. *One Century Later*, edited by Ian A.L. Getty and Donald B. Smith[33] contains several articles dealing with the Indians of western Canada since the signing of Treaty Seven in 1877. Interestingly, however, the longest, and also the least innovative, of these papers is on "Displaced Red Men: The Sioux in Canada." One can list a number of specific works, but it is time they were all brought together and used as the basis for a general synthesis of the impact of settlement on the prairie Indians.

In his pioneering work *The Birth of Western Canada*[34] (first published in 1936), George F.G. Stanley included chapters on the Indians and argued that they were an example of a primitive culture facing disaster as a result of the encroachment of a superior civilization. Today historians would no longer use the words "primitive" and "civilized," nor would they accept the dichotomy that they suggest, and yet the basic interpretation of the impact of settlement on the Indians has not changed much. It is generally held that the Indians were left with very little room to move and that, while some would argue that they played a creative role during the fur trade, most see settlement as an essentially destructive force for Canada's native peoples. Perhaps it is time to consider the extent to which the Indians might have continued to take the initiative, even after the fur trade, and the degree to which their cultures have survived, even if in a modified form. One author who has taken this line is Rolf Knight in *Indians at Work*.[35] In contrast to others who have argued that the Indians of British Columbia played a marginal role on the settlement frontier, Knight claims that they provided an important source of labour for the development of the resource economy. Unfortunately, this is a swashbuckling work in which the author flails about at all and sundry and yet has a cavalier attitude both to evidence and to the use of the English language. It is certainly to be hoped that others will take up this theme and give it the attention it deserves.

The missionaries were one group of Europeans who consciously attempted to eliminate many aspects of native culture. Perhaps because they were often such aggressive agents of culture change, and because some missionaries were unattactive personalities, they have not received much attention from historians of the 1970s. Jaenen and others have looked at the role of Roman Catholic missionaries working among the Indians during the French regime, but the only full-length scholarly study of a Protestant missionary is *William Duncan of Metlakatla*[36] by Jean Usher. Duncan was a fascinating individual and Usher has written a well-researched and well-argued account of his missionary career before he moved his mission to Alaska in the mid-1880s. There are many other missionaries who warrant similar attention. While the missionaries were adamant advocates of cultural change, they were not always successful in the long run, and it is also time for an investigation of the extent to which native groups either resisted missionary teaching or moulded it to serve their own ends.

There are a number of other major gaps in the historical literature on Canada's native peoples. For instance, there are very few Indian histories written by Indians. Books that have been written by Indians, perhaps not unreasonably, have often been polemical in tone and more concerned with current politics than with past history. The best known of these is Harold Cardinal's *The Unjust Society*,[37] which was written in response to the federal government's white paper on Indian affairs. Cardinal is not unmindful of the past, but none of his major concerns, nor his approach, is historical. *These Mountains Are Our Sacred Places*,[38] by Chief John Snow is based on a particular sense of dissatisfaction about the treatment of Indians in Canada but also on a fair amount of documentary research. More books like this one would facilitate our understanding of how the past is viewed by native people.

Another real need is for a good general history of Canada's indigenous people. Earlier in the decade E. Palmer Patterson II tackled this task when he wrote *The Canadian Indian*.[39] The attempt was premature since there were not enough good monographs to provide the basis for such a work. The time seems ripe for another general history.

There is also room for comparative history. Canada contains many diverse groups of native peoples who had different historical experiences, and yet it is also true that common patterns and themes can be seen across the country. Comparison of these similarities and differences would be a stimulating exercise. One small step in this direction was taken by L.F.S. Upton, who compared "Contact and Conflict on the Atlantic and Pacific Coasts of Canada."[40] Although he was comparing Canada's farthest extremities, Upton suggested that the contact experiences of the Indians of the east and west coasts had more in common with each other than with those of the inland Indians. Given a solid basis of new work on Canada, we could also make comparative forays across the international boundary. Now that we have more detail on Canada's native peoples, we can reexamine, and if necessary revise, earlier, and possibly facile, comparisons with the United States.

But let us not conclude negatively. While there are some areas that still require attention, it is more important to emphasize the positive point that a great deal of good writing on Canada's native peoples has been published over recent years. Ten years ago it was astounding how little most Canadians knew about the cultures and history of the country's indigenous people. That situation has now changed considerably. If it is true that there is now a greater knowledge and understanding of native people, then the schools have played an important part in reducing the level of ignorance. At long last, teachers are being assisted by historians who are providing the materials to continue this educational process and, hopefully, to foster the further development of inter-racial understanding.

Notes

1. James W. St. G. Walker, "The Indian in Canadian Historical Writing," Canadian Historical Association, *Historical Papers* (1971): 21–47.

2. Alfred Goldsworthy Bailey, *The Conflict of European and Eastern Algonkian Cultures, 1504–1700: A Study in Canadian Civilisation* (Saint John: New Brunswick Museum, 1937).

3. Harold Hickerson, *The Chippewa and Their Neighbors: A Study in Ethnohistory* (New York: Holt, Rinehart & Winston, 1970).

4. Charles A. Bishop, *The Northern Ojibwa and the Fur Trade: An Historical and Ecological Study* (Toronto and Montreal: Holt, Rinehart & Winston, 1974).

5. Bruce G. Trigger, *The Children of Aataentsic: A History of the Huron People to 1660* (Montreal and London: McGill-Queen's University Press, 1976).

6. Bruce G. Trigger, *The Huron: Farmers of the North* (New York: Holt, Rinehart & Winston, 1969).

7. Conrad Heidenreich, *Huronia: A History and Geography of the Huron Indians 1600–1650* (Toronto: McClelland and Stewart, 1971).

8. Wilson Duff, *The Indian History of British Columbia*. Vol. 1. *The Impact of the White Man*. Anthropology in British Columbia Memoir no. 5 (Victoria: Provincial Museum, 1964).

9. Harold A. Innis, *The Fur Trade in Canada: An Introduction to Canadian Economic History* (Toronto: University of Toronto Press, 1956).

10. W.J. Eccles, "A Belated Review of Harold Adams Innis, *The Fur Trade in Canada*," *Canadian Historical Review* (hereafter *CHR*) LX, 4 (1972): 419–41.

11. Arthur J. Ray, *Indians in the Fur Trade: Their Role as Trappers, Hunters, and Middlemen in the Lands Southwest of Hudson Bay, 1660–1870* (Toronto: University of Toronto Press, 1974).

12. Robin Fisher, *Contact and Conflict: Indian-European Relations in British Columbia, 1774–1890* (Vancouver: University of British Columbia Press, 1977).

13. Arthur J. Ray and Donald B. Freeman, *"Give Us Good Measure": An Economic Analysis of Relations Between the Indians and the Hudson's Bay Company Before 1763* (Toronto: University of Toronto Press, 1978).

14. E.E. Rich, "Trade Habits and Economic Motivation Among the Indians of North America," *Canadian Journal of Economics and Political Science* XXVI, 1 (1960): 35–53.

15. A. Rotstein, "Fur Trade and Empire: An Institutional Analysis" (Ph.D. dissertation, University of Toronto, 1967).

16. A. Rotstein, "Trade and Politics: An Institutional Approach," *Western Canadian Journal of Anthropology* III, 1 (1972): 1–28.

17. Sylvia Van Kirk, " 'The Custom of the Country': An Examination of Fur Trade Marriage Practices," in *Essays in Western History*, edited by Lewis H. Thomas (Edmonton: University of Alberta Press, 1976).

18. Sylvia Van Kirk, " 'Women in Between': Indian Women in Fur Trade Society in Western Canada," Canadian Historical Association, *Historical Papers* (1977): 30–46.

19. Jennifer S.H. Brown, *Strangers in Blood: Fur Trade Company Families in Indian Country* (Vancouver: University of British Columbia Press, 1980).

20. John E. Foster, "The Origins of the Mixed Bloods in the Canadian West" in *Essays in Western History*, edited by Lewis H. Thomas.

21. Frits Pannekoek, "A Probe into the Demographic Structure of Nineteenth-Century Red River," in *Essays in Western History*.

22. Calvin Martin, *Keepers of the Game: Indian-Animal Relationships and the Fur Trade* (Berkeley and Los Angeles: University of California Press, 1978).

23. Arthur Ray, "Fur Trade History as an Aspect of Native History" in *One Century Later: Western Canadian Reserve Indians Since Treaty 7*, edited by Ian A.L. Getty and Donald B. Smith (Vancouver: University of British Columbia Press, 1978).

24. Carol M. Judd and Arthur J. Ray, eds., *Old Trails and New Directions: Papers of the Third North American Fur Trade Conference* (Toronto: University of Toronto Press, 1980).

25. Cornelius J. Jaenen, *Friend and Foe: Aspects of French-Amerindian Cultural Contact in the Sixteenth and Seventeenth Centuries* (Toronto: McClelland and Stewart, 1976).

26. Cornelius J. Jaenen, "Amerindian Views of French Culture in the Seventeenth Century," *CHR* LV, 3 (1974): 261–91.

27. L.F.S. Upton, *Micmacs and Colonists: Indian-White Relations in the Maritimes, 1713–1867* (Vancouver: University of British Columbia Press, 1979).

28. Gary Pennanen, "Sitting Bull: Indian Without a Country," *CHR* LI, 2 (1970): 123–40.

29. C. Frank Turner, *Across the Medicine Line* (Toronto: McClelland and Stewart, 1973).

30. Peter A. Cumming and Neil H. Mickenberg, eds., *Native Rights in Canada*, 2nd ed. (Toronto: Indian-Eskimo Association of Canada, 1979).

31. Stewart Raby, "Indian Land Surrenders in Southern Saskatchewan," *Canadian Geographer* XVII, 1 (1973): 36–52.

32. Hugh A. Dempsey, *Crowfoot: Chief of the Blackfeet* (Edmonton: Hurtig, 1972).

33. Getty and Smith, eds., *One Century Later: Western Canadian Reserve Indians Since Treaty 7*.

34. George F.G. Stanley, *The Birth of Western Canada: A History of the Riel Rebellions* (Toronto: University of Toronto Press, 1960).

35. Rolf Knight, *Indians at Work: An Informal History of Native Indian Labour in British Columbia, 1858–1930* (Vancouver: New Star Books, 1978).

36. Jean Usher, *William Duncan of Metlakatla: A Victorian Missionary in British Columbia* (Ottawa: National Museum of Man, 1974).

37. Harold Cardinal, *The Unjust Society: The Tragedy of Canadian Indians* (Edmonton: Hurtig, 1969).

38. Chief John Shaw, *These Mountains Are Our Sacred Places: The Story of the Stoney Indians* (Toronto and Sarasota: Samuel Stevens, 1977).

39. E. Palmer Patterson II, *The Canadian Indian: A History Since 1500* (Don Mills: Collier-Macmillan, 1972).

40. L.F.S. Upton, "Contact and Conflict on the Atlantic and Pacific Coasts of Canada," *BC Studies* 45 (Spring 1980): 103–15. Also in *Acadiensis* IX, 2 (1980): 3–13.

WORKING-CLASS CANADA: RECENT HISTORICAL WRITING†

BRYAN D. PALMER

Unlike its predecessors . . . ,[1] this essay makes no effort to cover the literature of its field comprehensively. For those who seek broad discussions of writing in Canadian working-class history there already exists a substantial body of work, and more is promised.[2] What follows, then, is a critical commentary that remains highly selective (and arbitrarily so), an eclectic, at times overtly personal, examination of some recent scholarly writing that aims to illuminate *differences* of approach, method and conception. English Canada will be the central concern, and French-Canadian labour historians, many associated with the Regroupement de Chercheurs en Histoire des Travailleurs Québécois, will find no place in the following pages.[3] Finally, while some historians seem convinced that "working-class studies in the next few years will help transform qualitatively our view of the Canadian past,"[4] this essay reflects a more pessimistic assessment of the Canadian historical profession's willingness to listen. Historians in this country have seldom embraced class as an analytical category,[5] *never* treated Marxism (and some of the recent writing in Canadian working-class history is "tainted" with this most pernicious of influences) as anything more than a vulgar, dogmatic doctrine,[6] and only rarely, if ever, allowed themselves the latitude of qualitative transformation.[7]

Until quite recently the Canadian labour historian has been a rare animal. Working-class history, when it was written, was often the product of labour economists, trade union advocates or political scientists. At times it emerged as a by-product, evolving out of other interests and concerns. Nevertheless, distinct approaches to labour's past did develop. While Canada never cultivated a sophisticated institutional school of trade union history similar to that established at the University of Wisconsin by John R. Commons and his associates,[8] this orientation attracted some early advocates. Harold Logan first introduced the need for such work in the late 1920s, and stimulated some fascinating local research while teaching at the University of Western Ontario.[9] These preliminary efforts have been enriched substantially by Eugene Forsey's diligent research. In a series of important articles, written over the course of the last three decades, and in his now completed history of the trade union movement in Canada during the period 1812–1902 [*Trade Unions in Canada 1812–1902* (Toronto: University of Toronto Press, 1982)], Forsey provides those interested in labour history with much-needed reference works.[10] This early body of literature was complemented by pioneering efforts to go beyond workers' organizations, as urban historian J.I. Cooper examined Montreal's social structure in the 1850s and tranquillity and

†*Queen's Quarterly* 86 (Winter 1979): 594–616.

turbulence among French and Irish ship labourers in Quebec.[11] Cooper's studies, however, seemed strangely out of step in the 1950s, and that decade's view of labour history was coloured by two monographs. Canada's major moment of labour upsurge, the Winnipeg General Strike of 1919, received its first detailed treatment in 1950 by historian D. C. Masters, and nine years later Kenneth McNaught explored the career of a major figure in that upheaval, and future leader of the CCF, J. S. Woodsworth. These two approaches, focussing upon labour's institutional history and involvement in movements of political protest, dominated developments in the field for many years, and were the subject of important, if flawed, studies by Charles Lipton, Martin Robin, Paul Phillips, and Gad Horowitz.[12]

These works, and others, set the stage for Canada's first generation of labour historians, who would continue to probe working-class radicalism, politics, and institutions, largely in the context of the twentieth century. Premier among this group has been David Jay Bercuson, whose analysis of the background and development of the Winnipeg General Strike stresses the continuity of labour-capital strife in a boom town on the urban industrial frontier, as well as "the futility and tragedy of massive confrontation combined with hysteria and intransigence." Bercuson has followed this first book with a suggestive, if tentative, discussion of labour radicalism and the western industrial frontier, and an account of the rise and fall of Canada's radical House of Labour — the One Big Union, institutional expression of the workers' revolt against capitalism and narrow craft unionism in the years 1919–1927. As competent, detailed narratives of the major incidents in western labour radicalism, Bercuson's work lays the foundations for future studies. But in the interpretative realm historians will find many a bone to pick at. In his discussion of the Winnipeg General Strike, for instance, Bercuson breaks no new ground, and essentially reiterates that the strike was merely a struggle for collective bargaining rights gone wrong. This piece of conventional wisdom has had a long life, first given scholarly credentials in Masters' early study. More recently, Bercuson's efforts to explore the origins of labour radicalism lay stress upon working conditions and the "unique fermentation" of immigrant groups in the Canadian west. Perhaps such factors can explain the peculiarities of Canadian labour radicalism, but one wonders about the One Big Union's successes south of the border, which Bercuson documents in a fine chapter on the invasion of the United States. One senses, as well, that Bercuson's impatience with doctrinal questions and theoretical debates on the left ill-suit him to explore the role and impact of such groups as the Socialist Party, which certainly get short shrift in his arguments. It is odd, indeed, that an historian so blatantly anti-Marxist should adopt an approach to labour radicalism that smells suspiciously of economic determinism, proclaiming in the opening chapter of his history of the OBU that the emergence of the western labour movement was "natural and inevitable." This is undeniably true, as far as it goes, but as William A. Pritchard, prominent in the workers' revolt, noted in 1919: "Only fools try to make revolutions, wise men conform to them." It is the human dimension of that effort to *make* revolution, as well as the act of conforming to dramatic change on the industrial frontier, that Bercuson's analyses seem to miss.[13]

Pursuing similar themes, A. Ross McCormack, in a stimulating discussion of Canadian radicalism, isolates three strands in the western Canadian labour movement prior to the rise of the OBU. McCormack's dissection of labour radicalism also posits the primacy of harsh conditions in the industrial west in stimulating opposition and breeding discontent, but unlike Bercuson he is at home among the personalities and sects of the western radical movement: he knows intimately the labour politicians like Arthur Puttee and the theoreticians of revolt like E. T. Kingsley. He travels from the "impossibilism" of British Columbia's Socialist Party through the Wobblies' bitter alienation to the city of Winnipeg, where independent labour party advocates seemed dominant. These experiences produced McCormack's western Canadian radical movement, composed of three discernible elements. First, and ultimately victorious in the struggle for hegemony in the radical west, were the labourite reformers. Primarily of English or Scots origin and rooted in the urban-based trade unions, these dissidents sought change via the ballot, working to establish the equivalent of the British Labour Party in the Canadian west. Second were the militant syndicalist rebels, industrial unionists committed to combat against the narrow, economistic union, the unscrupulous employer and the antagonistic state. Drawn from the isolated lumber camp or the dramatically exploited migratory working class, these rebels favoured workplace resistance, avoiding all political struggle. Finally, there were the revolutionary Marxists. Cultivating ties among coal miners and immigrants, although themselves often city-dwellers of Anglo-Saxon origin, these dedicated, if doctrinaire, socialists were cognizant of capitalism's resiliency in the face of anything but the most uncompromising blend of political and economic action. Weak on the origins of radicalism, perhaps a little too neat and tidy to do justice to the awkward complexities of the radical west, and definitely confusing in its efforts to direct the various radical streams towards their ultimate conclusion in 1919, McCormack's *Reformers, Rebels and Revolutionaries* — is, nonetheless, the best discussion of Canadian radicalism to date.[14]

Expanding upon one aspect of McCormack's work (although not consciously developed in this vein) is Donald Avery's *"Dangerous Foreigners,"* an effort to probe the immigrant experience in mining, lumbering, harvesting, and railroad construction. Viciously exploited at the work site, locked out of the dominant culture, shunned or patronized by traditional Canadian institutions, the "alien" worker turned to revolutionary groups, writing an important chapter in the history of labour radicalism between 1896 and 1932. In a tightly argued account Avery provides us with a thorough treatment of Canadian nativism, documenting the immigrants' important place in the Canadian economy as well as the society's refusal to admit them to its ranks, resorting to periodic "red scares," first in the well-known hysteria of the World War I years, and then in a 1931-32 attack on the Communist Party, which harboured significant numbers of foreign workers, particularly Finns and Ukrainians. This book promises to establish the importance of ethnicity in the Canadian working-class experience, and opens up an area neglected for far too long.[15]

As one moves outside of the Canadian west, radicalism recedes into obscure corners seldom explored by this generation of labour historians. International unionism captivates attention. Robert Babcock addresses the American penetration of the Canadian labour movement in his study of "continentalism" before the First World War. As a balanced assessment of the positive and negative consequences of the presence of the American Federation of Labor in Canada, Babcock's study provides a thorough account of the post-1896 organizing drive, labour politics, and the struggle to determine the character and nature of the Canadian labour movement. Detailing the Trades and Labour Congress' failure to pose an effective alternative to the superior resources, prestige and power of the American international craft unions, Babcock concludes on a predictably nationalistic note. In "a country wracked if not yet wrecked by regionalism," he argues, "the loss of a truly national labour institution was doubtless unfortunate." This was certainly the view of Patrick M. Draper, an early Canadian nationalist and trade-union leader, but he, like Gompers, was one of labour's lieutenants, albeit a minor one. Despite the merits of this fine study, the rest of the army of labour — the rank-and-file workers — remains well in the background. Its reactions to the American takeover of the Canadian labour movement remain unexplored.[16]

Similar strengths and weaknesses characterize Irving M. Abella's *Nationalism, Communism and Canadian Labour*. Here we enter the world of Canadian labour leaders in the period of the Great Depression, World War II and the Cold War. Abella explores the arrival of the CIO in Canada, the resulting unsuccessful struggle for an autonomous Canadian labour movement, and the eventual expulsions and mergers which led to the creation of the Canadian Labour Congress in 1956. Along the way Abella provides us with a fascinating but grisly story of the unholy alliances, crass opportunism, and unprincipled machinations that social democratic forces within the labour movement resorted to in their relentless efforts to rid their ranks of Communist influence. We view the events, again, from the eyes of Charles Millard and Aaron Mosher, central figures in the events of the period, and catch only a fleeting glimpse of the hundreds of thousands of unorganized and largely unskilled workers enrolled in the ranks of Canadian trade unionism in these years.[17] Since the publication of this book, Abella has edited two useful volumes, both of which attempt to address more centrally the experience of ordinary workers. The first, a collection of essays on six twentieth-century strikes, puts some flesh on the bones of industrial conflict, originally sketched in Stuart Marshall Jamieson's survey of strike activity from 1900 to 1966. Some might quibble with Abella's choice of strikes, but all of the essays illuminate a central historical process: the role of the Canadian government, or state, in suppressing conflict.[18] In collaboration with David Millar, Abella has also compiled a documentary collection on the Canadian worker, a companion to a similar source book edited by Michael S. Cross on the workingman in the nineteenth century. Although undoubtedly a useful collection of documents, this edited volume suffers from introductions which often seem to contradict the sources which follow.[19]

This is all solid stuff. Both the quality and the quantity of work (much of which is passed by here) produced by this first generation is partly responsible for recent talk of the last ten years as "a golden age of Canadian historical writing," a period that has witnessed "a remarkable renaissance in working-class studies."[20]

Of course, all of these historians would resent my casual lumping of them together in an undifferentiated mass: each scholar noted above would express criticism of others' work, and all might legitimately make a claim for the distinctiveness of their own approach. Nevertheless, in terms of training, approach, and concerns this group shares certain characteristics, both intellectual and sociological. In the pages that follow, these historians will be considered as a collectivity, although I am well aware that they lack cohesiveness; I adopt this procedure only to highlight certain *tendencies* in historical writing.

All of this first generation, it seems, has taken to heart J. M. S. Careless's 1969 call for attention to region, ethnicity, and class.[21] And this has been both the success and the failure of these historians. For in probing certain "limited identities" of Canada's past they have begun the long-awaited examination of working-class life, but they have done so in predictably *limited* ways. Their histories of aspects of the working-class past have followed directly in the footsteps of what we might call the Canadian historiographical tradition. It is the "large" issues that have preoccupied this generation, the main events and the political and institutional questions, and they have painted their studies on national or regional canvasses, necessarily glossing over many problematic issues, missing a subtle or complex development here, simplifying a nuance there.

The result is an impressive body of literature that still raises countless questions. Was the Winnipeg General Strike, for instance, merely a mundane fight for collective bargaining rights, elevated to prominence by employer and government intransigence? Or was the strike an exemplary moment in the history of Canadian radicalism, its leaders representative of, in W.A. Pritchard's words, "the fighting section of the trade union movement"? Bercuson and Masters have given us one answer, the participants another.[22] Was the strike *just* "a crushing defeat to the labour movement," a senseless upheaval that ruined lives, "a raw, dirty deal"? Or does memory of the event linger somewhere deeper in the collective consciousness of the Canadian working class?[23] Can we possibly understand labour radicalism in the west *only* as a *reflection* — natural, inevitable, instinctive, almost commonplace — of the peculiarities of the Canadian industrial frontier, a superstructural derivation of the economic basis of society? Or might we profit from a discussion of human agency, of class values and antagonisms?[24] How fruitful is the imposition of virtually Weberian, ideal-type categories upon the history of western radicalism, dichotomizing (as McCormack does) the experiences of reformer, rebel, and revolutionary? Was the victory of reformism actually a function of "the nation's orderly and moderate political culture"?[25] Did radicalism ever extend, in any significant way, beyond the west? Recent work suggests the possibility of this, especially in Nova Scotia, among the miners, and perhaps in central Canada, among the machinists, but more research is essential.[26] Were immigrant workers the bulwark of bolshevism, or, rather, the reserves of reaction, sojourners with few attachments to Canada, and few reasons to rebel against the opportunities of their new land? Was the disciplined persistent socialism of the Finnish community at all comparable to the spontaneous eruption of the peasant village, which manifested itself in violent ethnic clashes at the Lakehead involving Greeks and Italians, and sporadic outbreaks on railway construction sites, often led by immigrant workers marching under a makeshift red flag — demonstrations of the ethnic community on strike?[27] Must we regard the rise of the American Federation of Labor in Canada as conspiratorial *and* damaging?[28] And is it necessary to project this "continentalist" approach into the 1930s with the emergence of the CIO, and argue that "for the Canadian workingman old traditions die hard." As reviews of Abella's book have suggested, this "psychological" truism has little explanatory force. At least part of international unionism's success in the Depression and World War II years began with what Abella has failed to consider: first, rank-and-file militancy and innovation; second, the particular Canadian experience and policies of the Communist Party, especially the impact of the Workers' Unity League; and, third, perhaps, the legislative lag separating the United States government's mandate to organize, granted in 1935 with the Wagner Act, from the Ontario Collective Bargaining Act of 1943.[29] Simplistic answers to many of these questions are, of course, easily provided, but they merely lead into even more difficult interpretive areas which have been little explored.

To pose such questions is to walk in the shadows of institutions, to rub shoulders with the upper echelons of the labour leadership, to engage in dialogues of an explicitly political nature, and to peer down at "dangerous foreigners" from the lofty heights of immigration commissions. Canadian historians have always felt comfortable in these surroundings and activities, which is not to say that work emanating from such quarters is without merit. This first generation of labour historians broke new ground decisively in their studies of the working-class experience, but they accomplished their tasks (and defined them) in the old ways. These were the men their mentors *wanted* to produce. Only rarely (although recently with more frequency) did they seem concerned with the international literature in the field, seldom with theory.[30] Untouched by radical sentiment, much of this generation reflected a hard-nosed, tough-minded approach to their subject. "The average union member," explained Abella while writing that individual out of his study, "plays an unimportant role in the affairs of his union."[31] Even when experimenting with relatively innovative techniques, such as oral history, these historians turned to traditional concerns: key personages, central events, major developments.[32] There was none of the hankering after "a more authentic description and analysis of ordinary everyday life and the material regularities that shape group existence" that Carl Berger has associated with the "unfocussed, rhetorical and occasionally indiscriminate" enthusiasm for social history visible in the pages of the work of this first generation of labour historians.[33] Like Dickens's Gradgrind, they sought only "the facts." Their commitment, their engagement, was and is in the service of *professional* historical writing. It is no surprise to see such historians drift away from the working class into other areas of inquiry, or attain a measure of power and authority in the discipline. If their works often seem uninspired, their prose slightly arid, they regard themselves differently. Their work, they would argue, tackles the important questions, and does so without undue dramatizations. They are the "realists."

For all of their strengths, however, these "realists" face certain problems. Briefly stated, they often appear as prisoners of their sources, incarcerated by the period which they study. Twentieth-century evidence is top-heavy with royal commissions, "official" union correspondence, prime ministers' papers, RCMP files, and justice department collections. Small wonder that such data yield histories of an essentially institutional/political character, and zero in on the labour movement and the working-class experience from a particular vantage point. So total is this generation's immersion in these sources and this context that they occasionally seem incapable of looking back to a time when national institutions and leaders, traditional political activity, and central events were not the only questions to address; when the east was not necessarily conservative, and the radical west had not yet emerged. Irving Abella reveals a naïve innocence of the class experience, for instance, when writing that, "Labour's trauma started at Winnipeg in 1919. Until then its horizons seemed unclouded and propitious."[34] This, of course, writes out of the historical record the *entire* nineteenth-century experience, as well as violent years of employer opposition to unionism in the pre-war period and countless struggles of the war years. As one moves back into the dark years of the nineteenth century, it appears that the experiences of workers (as well as the sources available to historians) were markedly different from what was to come. To liberate working-class history from its institutional/political focus, to effect a jailbreak out of the confines of twentieth-century sources, questions and dilemmas, was thus on the agenda. Enter the second generation.

The second generation, like the first, is a diverse lot, but its members, too, share a certain intellectual and sociological space. Compared to the first generation they are less firmly entrenched in the profession, more likely to have been trained in the United States and thus more comfortable with the broad range of questions the international literature in working-class history confronts. Internationalism rather than nationalism characterizes their stance on many questions, and separates them from many radical scholars operating within the political economy tradition. Marxism exerts a forceful influence upon their work, although few could agree as to what *kind* of Marxism is best employed in the service of working-class history; what passes for Marxism in one quarter is often regarded as distinctly *un*Marxist in another. The sympathies, engagement, and commitment of this group are generally to the subjects they study, rather than to the profession, opening their work to the usual charges of distortion and ideological bias, as if *certain* historical writing is above all of this. Their honesty and openness have served them poorly.[35] From the English Marxists (E.P. Thompson, E.J. Hobsbawm, and Raymond Williams) this group has learned of the importance of culture, of conflict as a way of life, and of the value of exploring class as a relationship with its own dynamics, internal and external, rather than as a static category acted upon and molded by impersonal forces and hegemonic groups.[36] A reading of David Montgomery and Harry Braverman has impressed upon them the importance of studying workplace relations, of examining the impact of technological change and managerial innovations.[37] Finally, with the rich work of Herbert G. Gutman, this second generation came to appreciate the significance of the local setting in the nineteenth century, where the texture of working-class life often seemed strikingly different from what historians concerned with national issues had suggested.[38]

This second generation was not entirely without Canadian precedent. Indeed, it followed paths of historical inquiry first opened by perhaps the most significant, if unappreciated, commentators on the nineteenth-century working-class experience. The Marxist economic historian, H. Clare Pentland, published stimulating discussions of the emergence of a capitalistic labour market and the Lachine canal strike of 1843 that were but part of a larger assessment of labour and the development of industrial capitalism in Canada.[39] Frank William Watt, a literary critic, made a brilliant effort to rescue nineteenth-century labour reformers from oblivion, arguing that the cultural dimensions of the National Policy were vigorously opposed by an important contingent of working-class radicals and dissident intellectuals.[40] These works, however, exercised little immediate impact, and among professional historians the institutional/political questions, reflected in the works of Bernard Ostry and Donald Creighton, still appeared to dominate discussion.[41] Steven Langdon, in a bold but naïve attempt to outline the emergence of the Canadian working-class movement in the years 1845–1875, struggled to go beyond this framework, but remained trapped within it. His premature effort to cover a large and difficult topic led him to overgeneralize and misconstrue the degree of class consciousness present as early as 1872, when the struggle for the nine-hour day erupted across south-central Canada. His major source, the newspaper clippings of the Canadian Labour Congress files on labour history, structured his narrative around questions of trade-union growth, conflict and political action, and forced him to avoid local contexts and cultural life.[42]

Gregory S. Kealey's and Peter Warrian's 1976 collection, *Essays in Canadian Working Class History*, signalled the arrival of the second generation. Most of the assembled studies evolved out of a concern with the pre-World War I experience that the first generation had largely avoided, detailed local developments (almost exclusively in Ontario) and attempted to explore specific conflict situations, cultural processes, and trade or ethnic groupings. Evidence, on the whole, came from newspapers, local records, and quantifiable data; few prime ministers' papers were cited here.

The finest essay in the book, Russell Hann's analysis of labour reformer Phillips Thompson and his relationship to the popular journalism of the 1880s, is consciously structured around concerns first elaborated by Frank Watt. A difficult and complex piece, it flows out of Hann's intimate knowledge of the radical working-class press. The essay's significance lies in its insights into the strengths of the brainworkers of the 1880s, their commitment to popular education and elevation of public opinion, their ultimate vision of a more humane social order. Through an examination of the reform and popular press, Hann is able to illuminate long neglected cultural corners of the 1880s, and in the process he reveals that the dramatic gulf separating "high" and "low" culture in our own day was far from inevitable. During the 1880s, in fact, vital minds could find fulfillment speaking to and writing for the masses. The failure of that experience of the 1880s has, of course, had important repercussions in the twentieth century, not the least of which is our own difficulty in understanding men like Phillips Thompson and his milieu.[43] Gregory S. Kealey's examination of the Orange Lodge in Toronto introduces us to another easily misunderstood aspect of working-class culture. For many years the Orange Order has been viewed as but an appendage of the Tory party, a mere tool in the hands of political partisans whose bigotry and penchant for violence is well entrenched in Canadian historiography. In the lead essay in the Kealey and Warrian volume, however, we are introduced to a different body, as this innovatively revisionist treatment establishes the working-class character of the Orange Lodge in Toronto. It is refreshing to be given this detailed picture of the labouring man's significant place in Toronto's lodges, although Kealey's efforts to establish the Orange Order as a source of strength for the emerging labour movement are open to challenge. At best the Orange experience was an ambivalent one. My own contribution to the collection, a rather crudely stated exploration of the social and cultural background of working-class organization in London, Ontario, and the culmination of that process in a classic street railway confrontation in 1898-99, seems, upon reflection, to suffer from similar shortcomings. Its strength lies in presenting a depiction of some components of working-class associational life and linking them to a major moment of confrontation; but the weaknesses are pronounced: the failure to explore skilled-unskilled relations; the avoidance of the political; and the excessively optimistic, if unintended, depiction of efforts to secure workers' control as a form of class consciousness.

Two other essays also explore specific conflict situations. David Frank's thorough history of the 1922 Cape Breton coal strike provides a sophisticated look at one of the most significant labour-capital battles in the twentieth century. Bound together by common Scots background and traditions, the miners of Cape Breton opposed the externally owned coal companies, and Frank's account illustrates how a grasp of a region's economic history can provide the ground upon which to build a history of workers' struggles. Less successful, but nonetheless stimulating, is Jean Morrison's account of freight handlers at the Lakehead, and their involvement in six strikes between 1902 and 1912. Structuring her argument around a consideration of ethnicity and violence, Morrison examines the different response of British, Greek, and Italian labourers to the confrontation tactics of the railway managers. Among these unskilled labourers, Greeks and Italians waged violent "revolts" against the railways, while the British pursued a more orderly opposition, organizing trade unions. Morrison seems to imply that the different response of "alien" workers was a consequence of their status as "first generation" industrial workers, not yet fully adapted to the rules of the capitalistic labour market, while the "second generation" British workers had experienced sufficient exposure to industrial society to ensure lawful behaviour. If one reads between the lines, and gazes into the future while doing it, it is all too easy to see labour-capital conflict vanish as soon as everyone has been "modernized." But that would not explain the continuities in labour-capital confrontation, just as Morrison's essay cannot satisfactorily explain why the same British workers who were orderly at the Lakehead were patently disorderly in the west, or why the "revolts" of Greek and Italian workers were often replaced by docility, acquiescence, and fearful retreat.

Finally, three contributions explore aspects of working-class culture in laboratories relatively undisturbed by strife and struggle. Two students of Michael B. Katz present findings on workers' housing and literacy, employing quantitative techniques to recover dimensions of the working-class experience lost to historians dependent upon conventional sources. Both essays are difficult going, even ponderous, but are important as statements on new ways of looking at labouring people. Michael Doucet's discussion of working-class housing is by far the most significant, demonstrating that in Hamilton between 1852 and 1881 the gap separating rich and poor widened: the relative value of the homes occupied by the working class declined; differences in home ownership levels for the rich and the poor increased; and working-class housing, once scattered throughout the "pre-industrial" city, became concentrated in the least attractive areas of Hamilton. The distance between classes, in these years of industrial capitalist consolidation, had widened, and that process attained a physical presence in the history of Hamilton's houses. Harvey J. Graff's examination of literacy among workers at the Hawkesbury Lumber Company seems to demonstrate the obvious: that among unskilled lumber workers literacy did not significantly relate to individual rewards, apparently exercising little impact on productivity. Had Graff examined printers, a highly literate group immersed in a distinctive craft culture, he would have had a different story to tell. Wayne Roberts takes this as his theme, contributing an article on Toronto's printers at the turn of the century. In this depiction of an important trade grouping we are introduced to a highly skilled, organized sector of the working class that exhibited a remarkable ability to protect its workplace autonomy and artisanal traditions. It is to Roberts' credit that he can both appreciate the printers on their own terms, recognizing their achievement in maintaining a "manly independence" in the face of capitalism's many incursions, and stand back and see them for what they were: something of an antique in a working-class world that shared few of their experiences, and little of their commitment.

While many have recognized the significance of this first effort, criticizing the book's many and varied weaknesses but also praising its strengths,[44] the rumblings of discontent among the first generation have been audible.[45] Among the second generation, as well, these early essays have produced an occasional posture of reaction.[46] Michael J. Piva thought the turn to culture premature, arguing that "we must attempt to ground the discussion [of the working-class record] in as complete an understanding as possible of the structure of the work force and the material conditions of daily life." Piva, explicitly Marxist in his convictions and orientation, thus addressed a theme originally pursued by Terry Copp. Were the early twentieth-century years, traditionally viewed as a time of intensive economic growth and domestic prosperity, actually beneficial for the Canadian working class? Did workers' living standards — their real wages, housing and working conditions, and life situations — actually improve during the prosperity apparently produced by rapid industrialization? Copp argued the contrary case, attempting to demonstrate that in Montreal, between 1897 and 1929, working-class standards of living deteriorated; and Piva has developed a study of Toronto workers between 1900 and 1921 around a similar argument.[47] This work is stimulating and much needed. Some historians will be persuaded by the argument, but the statistical ambiguities, flowing out of deficiencies in the evidence, are sufficiently great to ensure that many will remain unconvinced.

Piva's exhortation to avoid the social, cultural, and political realms of the class experience until we know more about the structural makeup of the workforce and the material conditions of everyday life appear sound enough advice. The only catch is that it is offered by an historian who has worked through the kind of twentieth-century sources upon which such an argument can be based. But as one reaches back into the nineteenth century these sources disappear, dry up or become distressingly problematic. It is difficult indeed to reconstruct a precise picture of material conditions from the surviving nineteenth-century evidence, and discussions of poverty in this period usually lack the statistical grounding and, to many, force of conviction, of work set in a later period, when published documentation of a more suitable, "solid" type is available. Often, in fact, studies of working-class life address questions of the poor *through* the cultural experience, and probe deteriorating standards by examining opposition to such impersonal forces as mechanization, technological innovation and skill dilution, or changing work regulations and conditions. They are not necessarily weaker for their lack of "hard data."[48] Much of this difficulty can be overcome through sophisticated use of quantification, a costly, elaborate but potentially fruitful technique that depends largely on accessibility to manuscript census material.[49] The census, however, has only recently been cleared for use up to 1881, meaning that the entire experience of the 1880s and 1890s, if not the 1870s, is inaccessible. Prior to 1851, when the census was inaugurated, the problem is exacerbated by a complete lack of such data. The mid-century, then, is the only period during the nineteenth century when *precise* reconstruction of the structural makeup of the workforce is possible, and uncovering the nature of material conditions of existence remains a difficult task. Finally, Piva's study, for all of its virtues, may well present *too* bleak a picture of working-class life. Were there no mechanisms of "getting by" that may well have eased the strain of many harsh realities? Were there no victories at the workplace? Were militants always without power? To be sure, these were difficult years, but it is possible to read the sources differently, and to see moments, however transitory, of working-class resistance that did not end in crushing defeat.[50]

As one examines the nineteenth-century experience these moments become more clearly defined, appear with some regularity and seem sharply impressed on the historical record. Gregory S. Kealey's examination of certain skilled trades in Toronto between 1860 and 1892 and my own work on Hamilton craft workers in the pre-World War I years strongly suggest that at the workplace a significant degree of control over their lives was exercised by nineteenth-century workingmen.[51] In the cultural sphere, too, as we begin to "decode" ritualistic forms of behaviour like the charivari, whitecapping and mumming, it appears that the lower classes may well have cultivated a limited autonomy, defining their own conception of right and wrong in opposition to the legal conventions of an emerging bourgeois society, taking the organization of such activities as the family fishery into their own hands.[52] Their view of women workers, long dominated by suggestions of women's passivity and resignation, a consequence of a crippling femininity and women's internalization of society's imposed domestic ideals,[53] seems about to be revised by attention to the workplace ecology of female workers and the difficulties that this structural situation posed for effective organization and resistance.[54] This emerging literature, then, premises itself on the need to examine negotiation, reciprocity, and adaptation within the class experience, rather than rely on tired clichés and conventional widsoms, especially those positing working-class powerlessness and acquiescence. Anthropological concerns and insights have enriched many presentations, as has a regard for mediation, or what we might describe as processes of intercession and reconciliation between class adversaries.[55] All of this work, of course, is suggestive rather than definitive, and understandably and necessarily takes interpretative chances.

The venturesome nature of the second generation, their willingness to pose these difficult questions and to argue in this vein, has drawn attack from some quarters. *Labour/Le Travailleur* [now *Labour/Le Travail*], annual publication of the Committee on Canadian Labour History, has been the intellectual medium through which much of the second generation's work has been presented to the Canadian academic community. It has recently been caricatured in the pages of this quarterly in a transparently paranoid attack upon what Terry Morley rather indiscriminately labels the "romantic left."[56] Morley's polemic deserves a blunt reply. It also tempts me to develop a defence of romanticism.[57] But here it is only possible to lay bare his argument. "The romantic leftists," claims Morley, "are never more eloquent — one is tempted to say poetic — than when talking of the workers." After admitting the merit in many of the articles published in *Labour*, Morley moves quickly to his main complaints: "much of the writing necessarily denigrates the role played by social democrats in the formation of the industrial trade union movement in Canada, and unnecessarily glorifies both the Communist Party and an idealized working man."

This is a confused and confusing account, primarily because Morley appears to want to attack both the first and the second generation, attributing the sins (in his view) of one generation promiscuously to another. Does Professor Morley really believe that A. R. McCormack, David J. Bercuson and Irving M. Abella (all of whom sit on the editorial board of *Labour/Le Travailleur* and publish in its pages) are romantic leftists who, with poetry and passion, idealize the ordinary workingman? Yet these *are* the historians who have written about the subjects Morley concentrates upon: the twentieth-century record of radicalism, trade-union growth, and Communist Party and CCF-NDP activity. Can Morley honestly argue that Gregory S. Kealey, Wayne Roberts, Russell Hann, and myself (who perhaps *are* of the left, and some of whom *do* write with passion) denigrate the role played by social democrats, glorify the Communist Party and harbour contempt for trade union leaders when our own (essentially nineteenth-century) work rarely touches on these topics of the second and third quarter of the twentieth century? The answers to these questions, in addition to many more, are so obvious that one wonders how Morley's delusions could actually have found their way on to the printed page. His attack on *Labour* has little to do with an accurate assessment of the work of labour historians, and nothing to do with an understanding of that work. It comes from the pen of an academic of social democratic leanings who does not like what labour historians have been doing. Unable to meet the first generation on the twentieth-century ground that defines his own interests, incapable of accepting the particular engagement and commitment of the second generation, which flies in the face of his own engagement, and largely unaware of the peculiarities of the nineteenth-century past — which knows few communists and few social democrats — about which they write, Morley resorts to a slander of views and motives that reflects only his own historical naïveté.

Labour/Le Travailleur provides an appropriate note on which to conclude this discussion for it has, on one level, brought first and second generation together. The four issues of the journal published to date have expressed a wide range of concerns and approaches to the working-class experience of the nineteenth and twentieth centuries. One senses that it has not been a particularly peaceful co-existence. Questions of engagement and sympathy, approach and style, continue to divide, an inevitable consequence of differences in political convictions and individual temperaments. But it should be clear to all that twentieth-century work must address the nature and texture of workplace and community life,[58] while those probing the nineteenth century cannot continue to avoid the "large" institutional and political questions.[59] Equally important is the necessity of pushing the chronological boundaries of working-class studies both forward, into the 1940s and 1950s,[60] and backward, into the pre-Confederation period about which we know so little.[61] Changes in technology and management strategy, and the resulting impact on working-class life, demand further work,[62] as do relations among classes in the formative years of industrialization.[63] Ethnicity must be examined by those who can reach into specific immigrant communities through foreign-language sources, dealing with them on their own terms and as part of the larger Canadian society.[64] The working-class family still awaits its student.[65] Given the rich nature of the sources, it is surprising that the Knights of Labor are virtually unstudied.[66]

These and countless other topics may be explored in the future by the first and second generations of labour historians, and we can expect many disagreements. This is as it should be. Perhaps even a third generation will confront them, if it is not stillborn, killed by the lack of employment opportunities or silenced by a hostile profession. But whoever chooses to engage in such investigations must grapple with an essential historical reality: the past is a different country, and people are likely to do things differently there. Calvin Martin, in recent studies of Indian life and culture, has suggested that if historians are to understand the aboriginal experience in North America they must first recognize that there was a time, long ago, when Indians talked to animals.[67] Working men and women, although not so far removed from ourselves culturally and chronologically, may well have acted in ways equally foreign to our twentieth-century preconceptions of acceptable behaviour, especially in those dark recesses of the nineteenth century. The historian unprepared to explore such behaviour sensitively, even sympathetically, will pass over much of importance.

Notes

1. See W. Peter Ward, "Western Canada: Recent Historical Writing," *Queen's Quarterly* 85 (1978): 271–88; John Weaver, "Urban Canada: Recent Historical Writing," *Queen's Quarterly* 86 (1979): 75–97.

2. On approaching the Canadian working-class past see Russell G. Hann, et al., *Primary Sources in Canadian Working Class History, 1860–1930* (Kitchener: Dumont, 1973): 9–12; Russell G. Hann and Gregory S. Kealey, "Documenting Working Class History: North American Traditions and New Approaches," *Archivaria* 4 (1979): 92–114. Michael S. Cross, "To the Dartmouth Station: A Worker's Eyeview of Labour History," *Labour/Le Travailleur* (hereafter *L/LT*) 1 (1976): 193–208, presents an

assessment of the scholarly literature in a jocular vein, while Kealey, "The Working Class in Recent Historical Writing," *Acadiensis* 8 (1978): 116–35, examines more obscure, popular and partisan works, especially the publications of small, radical presses. Kealey and Peter Warrian, eds., *Essays in Canadian Working Class History* (Toronto: McClelland & Stewart, 1976), contains a useful bibliography. Kealey has also examined the treatment of class in Canada prior to 1950 in an unpublished essay, "Looking Backward: Reflections on the Study of Class in Canada" (Dalhousie University, 1979), while Kenneth McNaught is preparing an essay on "Labour and the Left" for the *Canadian Historical Review* (hereafter *CHR*). [See "E.P. Thompson vs. Harold Logan: Writing About Labour and the Left in the 1970s" in *CHR* LXII, 2 (1981): 141–68, and reprinted in this volume.]

3. For a sampling of this work see André Le Blanc and James Thwaites, *Le Monde Ouvrier au Québec: bibliographie retrospective* (Montreal: Presses de l'Université du Québec, 1973); Jacques Rouillard, *Les Travailleurs du Coton au Québec, 1900–1915* (Montreal: Presses de l'Université du Québec, 1974); Jean-Pierre Hardy and David-Thierry Ruddel, *Les Apprentis Artisans à Québec, 1660–1815* (Montreal: Presses de l'Université du Québec, 1977).

4. Kealey, "Working Class in Recent Historical Writing," 135.

5. See Stanley Mealing, "The Concept of Social Class and the Interpretation of Canadian History," *CHR* 46 (1965): 201–218; H.J. Hanham, "Canadian History in the 1970s," *CHR* 58 (1977): 2–22.

6. Stanley Ryerson's work, especially *Unequal Union: Roots of Crisis in the Canadas, 1815–1874* (Toronto: Progress, 1968), has been shamefully abused. For all of its flaws, the corner into which it has been shoved by professional historians is undeserved. Cf., Ryerson, "Marxism and the Writing of Canadian History," *Marxist Review* 4 (1947): 46–51; Ryerson, " 'Race,' 'Nationality,' and the Anglo-Canadian Historians," *Canadian Jewish Outlook* 11 (1973): 3–4, 12. Leo Johnson, whose *History of the County of Ontario, 1615–1873* (Whitby: Corporation of the County of Ontario, 1974) and articles on land settlement stand as significant efforts to present a Marxist perspective on the social structure of early Ontario, has fared only slightly better. Perhaps Canada's most distinguished international scholar (a rival for Harold Innis?) was E.H. Norman, a Japanese specialist of decidedly socialist humanist leanings, described by E.J. Hobsbawm as a "brilliant historian." Finding the professional milieu of academia stifling, he became a diplomat, and committed suicide in Cairo in 1957 while under attack by the United States Senate Subcommittee on Internal Security. Found "guilty" of associating with Communists during his days at Columbia, Norman was, of course, falsely "convicted": innuendo rather than evidence prevailed. Despite a well-established reputation as a leading authority on early Japan, Norman's works remain unknown and unappreciated in Canada. Canadian historians bore no responsibility for this tragic death, but as one Tokyo correspondent implied, they can be held partly accountable for condemning Norman's work to obscurity, a legacy of the 1950s and 1960s, when the fashion prevailed of dismissing Norman as a Marxist, writing out of the past, a man whose vocabulary contained such outmoded terms as "oppressor," "the ruling class" and "feudal remnants." On Norman see Cyril Powers, "E.H. Norman as a Historian: A Canadian Perspective," *Pacific Affairs* 50 (1977–78): 660–67; Charles Taylor, *Six Journeys: A Canadian Pattern* (Toronto: Anansi, 1977), 105–52; E.J. Hobsbawm, "Vulnerable Japan," *New York Review of Books* (17 July 1975); Andrew Horvat, "McCarthyism and the Death of a Canadian Diplomat," *Canadian Review* 4 (1977): 14–17. While they were ignoring Norman, Canadian historians were also quick to pigeonhole any Canadian work that did not fall easily within conventional boundaries. Note Roger Graham's response to Henry Ferns and Bernard Ostry, *The Age of Mackenzie King: The Rise of the Leader* (London: Heinemann, 1955), in the (Regina) *Leader-Post*, entitled "Cast in a Marxist Mould: Mr King and the Class Struggle," a clipping in Arthur Meighen Papers, Series 6, General Correspondence, Public Archives of Canada, MG 26 1, v. 226, 148929. This kind of Cold War posture suggests the need for a critical evaluation of the "politics of professionalism" on the order of Jesse Lemisch, *On Active Service in War and Peace: Politics and Ideology in the American Historical Profession* (Toronto: New Hogtown, 1975). A beginning has been made in Thomas Schofield's introduction to Lemisch's study (esp. 11–24), where the anti-Marxism of a number of noted Canadian historians is discussed.

7. This reflects my reading of Carl Berger, *The Writing of Canadian History: Aspects of English-Canadian Historical Writing: 1900 to 1970* (Toronto: Oxford University Press, 1976).

8. See John R. Commons, *Myself* (Madison: University of Wisconsin Press, 1963); Richard T. Ely, *Ground Under Our Feet: An Autobiography* (New York: Macmillan, 1938); Mary O. Furner, *Advocacy and Objectivity: A Crisis in the Professionalization of American Social Science, 1865–1905* (Lexington: University of Kentucky Press, 1975).

9. Harold Logan, *History of Trade Union Organization in Canada* (Chicago: University of Chicago Press, 1928); *Trade Unions in Canada* (Toronto: Macmillan, 1948); W.L. Davis, "A History of the Early Labour Movement in London, Ontario" (MA thesis, University of Western Ontario, 1930).

10. See, for a sampling of Forsey's writing, "The Telegraphers' Strike of 1883," *Transactions of the Royal Society of Canada*, series 4, 9 (1971): 245–60; "Some Notes on the Early History of Unions in P.E.I.," *CHR* 46 (1965): 346–51; "Insights into Labour History in Canada," *Relations Industrielles* 20 (1965): 445–65; "A Note on the Dominion Factory Bills of the 1880s," *Canadian Journal of Economics and Political Science* (hereafter *CJEPS*) 13 (1947): 580–83; *The Canadian Labour Movement, 1812–1902* (Ottawa: Canadian Historical Association Booklet No. 27, 1974). Forsey's major work can be consulted in unpublished form. See "History of Canadian Trade Unionism," typescript, forthcoming, University of Toronto Press, public Archives of Canada, Reel M-2214.

11. J.I. Cooper, "The Social Structure of Montreal in the 1850s," Canadian Historical Association *Papers* (1956): 63–73; "The Quebec Ship Labourers' Benevolent Society," *CHR* 30 (1949): 336–43.

12. D.C. Masters, *The Winnipeg General Strike* (Toronto: University of Toronto Press, 1950); Kenneth McNaught, *A Prophet in Politics: A Biography of J.S. Woodsworth* (Toronto: University of Toronto Press, 1959); Charles Lipton, *The Trade Union Movement of Canada, 1827–1959* (Montreal: Canadian Social Publications, 1968); Martin Robin, *Radical Politics and Canadian Labour, 1880–1930* (Kingston: Industrial Relations Centre, 1968); Gad Horowitz, *Canadian Labour in Politics* (Toronto: University of Toronto Press, 1968); Paul Phillips, *No Power Greater: A Century of Labour in British Columbia* (Vancouver: B.C. Federation of Labour, 1967).

13. David Jay Bercuson, *Confrontation at Winnipeg: Labour, Industrial Relations, and the General Strike* (Montreal: McGill-Queen's University Press, 1974), esp. 175; Bercuson and Kenneth McNaught, *The Winnipeg General Strike: 1919* (Toronto: Longman, 1974); "Labour Radicalism and the Western Industrial Frontier: 1897–1919" *CHR* 58 (1977): 154–75; *Fools and Wise Men: The Rise and Fall of the One Big Union* (Toronto: McGraw-Hill Ryerson, 1978).

14. McCormack, *Reformers, Rebels, and Revolutionaries: The Western Canadian Radical Movement, 1899–1919* (Toronto: University of Toronto Press, 1977).

15. Donald Avery, *"Dangerous Foreigners": European Immigrant Workers and Labour Radicalism in Canada, 1896–1932* (Toronto: McClelland & Stewart, 1979). Cf., Avery, "Continental European Immigrant Workers in Canada, 1896–1919: From 'Stalwart Peasants' to Radical Proletariat," *Canadian Review of Sociology and Anthropology* 12 (1975): 53–63.

16. Robert Babcock, *Gompers in Canada: A Study in American Continentalism Before the First World War* (Toronto: University of Toronto Press, 1974). An earlier version of this study was subtitled "A study in American labor imperialism."

17. Irving Martin Abella, *Nationalism, Communism and Canadian Labour: The CIO, the Communist Party, and the Canadian Congress of Labour, 1935–1956* (Toronto: University of Toronto Press, 1973).

18. *On Strike: Six Key Labour Struggles in Canada, 1919–1949* (Toronto: James Lewis & Samuel, 1974); Jamieson, *Times of Trouble: Labour Unrest and Industrial Conflict in Canada, 1900–1966* (Ottawa: Task Force on Labour Relations, 1968).

19. Irving Abella and David Millar, eds., *The Canadian Worker in the Twentieth Century* (Toronto: Oxford University Press, 1978); Cross, ed., *The Workingman in the Nineteenth Century* (Toronto: Oxford Univesity Press, 1974).

20. See Ramsay Cook, "The Golden Age of Canadian Historical Writing," *Historical Reflections* 4 (1977): 137–49; Hann and Kealey, "Documenting Working Class History," 92.

21. Careless, " 'Limited Identities' in Canada," *CHR* 50 (1969): 1–10.

22. Norman Penner, ed., *Winnipeg 1919: The Strikers' Own History* (Toronto: James Lewis & Samuel, 1975); W.A. Pritchard letter, *Canadian Forum* (July 1974), 31.

23. Bercuson, *Confrontation at Winnipeg*, 194–95; Bercuson, "Recent Publications in Canadian Labour History," *History and Social Science Teacher* 14 (1979): 181; Gerry Kopelow, "The Winnipeg General Strike," *Weekend Magazine*, 12 May 1979; J.E. Rae, "The Politics of Class: Winnipeg City Council, 1919–1945," in *The West and the Nation: Essays in Honour of W.L. Morton*, edited by Carl Berger and Ramsay Cook (Toronto: McClelland & Stewart, 1976), 232–49.

24. Bercuson, "Labour Radicalism and the Western Frontier," *Fools and Wise Men*; Peter Warrian, "The

Challenge of the One Big Union Movement in Canada, 1919–1921" (MA thesis, University of Waterloo, 1971).

25. McCormack, *Reformers, Rebels, Revolutionaries*, 171. Cf., Abella and Millar, *Canadian Worker*, esp. 3–6.

26. "A Rebel Voice: Fred Thompson Remembers Halifax, 1919–1920," *This Magazine* 12 (1978): 7–11; E.R. Forbes, *The Maritime Rights Movement, 1919–1927: A Study in Canadian Regionalism* (Montreal: McGill-Queen's University Press, 1979), 41–43; David Frank, "Class Conflict in the Coal Industry: Cape Breton, 1922," in *Essays*, edited by Kealey and Warrian, 161–84; Dawn Fraser, *Echoes From Labor's Wars: Industrial Cape Breton in the 1920s* (Toronto: New Hogtown, 1976); Nolan Reilly, "The Origins of the Amherst General Strike, 1890–1919" (paper presented to the Canadian Historical Association, June 1977); Michael Bliss, *A Canadian Millionaire: The Life and Business Times of Sir Joseph Flavelle, Bart. 1858–1939* (Toronto: Macmillan, 1978), 265–66, 271, 281–83; Myer Siemiatycki, "Munitions and Labour Militancy: The 1916 Hamilton Machinists' Strike," *L/LT* 3 (1978): 131–51. For a sceptical view of machinists' radicalism see Craig Heron, "The Crisis of the Artisan: Hamilton's Metal Workers, 1896–1930" (paper presented to the Third Conference on Blue Collar Workers, Windsor, 4–6 May 1979).

27. Varpu Lindstrom-Best, "The Socialist Party of Canada and the Finnish Connection, 1905–1911" (paper presented to the Canadian Ethnic Studies Conference, October 1979); Jean Morrison, "Ethnicity and Violence: The Lakehead Freight Handlers Before World War I," in *Essays*, edited by Kealey and Warrian, 143–60; A.B. Woywitka, "The Drumheller Strike of 1919," *Alberta Historical Review* 21 (1973): 1–7. Cf., Victor Greene, *The Slavic Community on Strike* (Notre Dame: University of Notre Dame Press, 1968); John Bodnar, *Immigrants and Industrialization: Ethnicity in an American Mill Town, 1870–1940* (Pittsburgh: University of Pittsburgh Press, 1977).

28. Babcock, *Gompers in Canada*, 89.

29. Abella, *Nationalism, Communism, Canadian Labour*, esp. 218. See the reviews by Kealey, *Labor History* 15 (1974): 130–34; and Gary Teeple, *Queen's Quarterly* 81 (1974): 452–55; as well as John A. Willes, *The Ontario Labour Court, 1943–44* (Kingston: Industrial Relations Centre, 1979); Laurel Sefton McDowell, "The Formation of the Canadian Industrial Relations System During World War II," *L/LT* 3 (1978): 175–96.

30. Avery's *"Dangerous Foreigners"* necessarily deals with the international literature, and is refreshingly interested in theoretical questions, but note how cavalierly he considers E.P. Thompson and Neil Smelser, fierce antagonists, to reflect complementary approaches to the study of collective protest (47–48). Bercuson's recent history of the OBU touches the international literature, but only selectively. McCormack's work seems better grounded in the international writing.

31. Abella, *Nationalism, Communism, Canadian Labour*, v.

32. See Abella, "Oral History and the Canadian Labour Movement," *Archivaria* 4 (1977): 115–21. Contrast this with the statements in Russell Hann, "Introduction," in *The Great War and Canadian Society: An Oral History*, edited by Daphne Read (Toronto: New Hogtown, 1978), 9–38; Peter Friedlander, *The Emergence of a UAW Local, 1936–39: A Study in Class and Culture* (Pittsburgh: University of Pittsburgh Press, 1975).

33. Berger, *Writing of Canadian History*, 264.

34. Abella, *On Strike*, xii.

35. A refreshing exception to this tendency is Michael S. Cross, "Recent Writings in Social History," *History and Social Science Teacher* 14 (1979), esp. 156–57, which attempts to briefly evaluate some of this work on its own terms. Cf., Cross, "To the Dartmouth Station," which, although critical of much recent work, is also fair-minded. Cross, in fact, seems to straddle first and second generations.

36. The literature here is now immense. An introduction to the subject is provided in a special issue of the *Radical History Review* 19 (1978–79), which explores the contribution of British Marxism in essays on Thompson, Williams, and Hobsbawm.

37. See David Montgomery, "The 'New Unionism' and the Transformation of Workers' Consciousness, 1909–1922," *Journal of Social History* 7 (1974): 509–29; "Workers' Control of Machine Production in the Nineteenth Century," *Labor History* 17 (1976): 485–509; Harry Braverman, *Labor and Monopoly Capital: The Degradation of Work in the Twentieth Century* (New York: Monthly Review Press, 1974). Cf., Bryan D. Palmer, "Class, Conception, and Conflict: The Thrust for Efficiency, Managerial Views of Labor, and

Working-Class Rebellion, 1903–1922," *Review of Radical Political Economics* 7 (1975): 31–49; Bruno Ramirez, *When Workers Fight: The Politics of Industrial Relations in the Progressive Era, 1898–1916* (Westport, Conn.: Greenwood, 1978).

38. Herbert G. Gutman, *Work, Culture, and Society in Industrializing America: Essays in Working-Class and Social History* (New York: Knopf, 1976); Montgomery, "Gutman's Nineteenth Century America," *Labor History* 19 (1978): 416–29.

39. H. Clare Pentland, "Labour and the Development of Industrial Capitalism in Canada" (PhD dissertation, University of Toronto, 1960); "The Lachine Strike of 1843," *CHR* 29 (1949): 255–77; "The Development of a Capitalistic Labour Market in Canada," *CJEPS* 25 (1959): 450–61. Cf., Gregory S. Kealey, "H.C. Pentland and Working Class Studies," *Canadian Journal of Political and Social Theory* 3 (1979).

40. Frank William Watt, "Radicalism and English-Canadian Literature Since Confederation" (PhD dissertation, University of Toronto, 1957); "The National Policy, the Workingman and Proletarian Ideas in Victorian Canada," *CHR* 40 (1959): 1–26.

41. Bernard Ostry, "Conservatives, Liberals and Labour in the 1870s," *CHR* (1960): 93–127; "Conservatives, Liberals and Labour in the 1880s," *CJEPS* 27 (1961): 141–61; D.G. Creighton, "George Brown, Sir John Macdonald, and the 'Workingman'," *CHR* 24 (1943): 362–76. Local studies undertaken in these years fell into a surprising silence. Note Richard Rice, "A History of Organized Labour in Saint John, New Brunswick, 1813–1890" (MA thesis, University of New Brunswick, 1968).

42. Steven Langdon, *The Emergence of the Canadian Working-Class Movement, 1845–1875* (Toronto: New Hogtown, 1975), previously appearing in a two-part article in 1973 issues of the *Journal of Canadian Studies*.

43. See also Russell G. Hann, "An Early Canadian Labour Theorist," *Bulletin of the Committee on Canadian Labour History* 4 (1977): 38–43; T. Phillips Thompson, *The Politics of Labor* (New York, 1887; Toronto: University of Toronto Press, 1975).

44. Note the reviews in *Queen's Quarterly* 85 (1978): 130–31 (Terry Copp); *CHR* 59 (1978): 95–96 (H.C. Pentland); *American Historical Review* 82 (1977): 776–77 (A.R. McCormack).

45. Bercuson, "Recent Publications in Labour History," 180. Cf., Michael B. Katz, Michael J. Doucet, and Mark Stern, "Migration and the Social Order in Erie County, New York, 1855," *Journal of Interdisciplinary History* 7 (1978): 700. Katz, Doucet and Stern attack the use of "British models." Bercuson seemed unduly upset by the book's introduction, and flailed away at "preachiness," "sermonizing" and "self-proclaimed ideological mission." He erred in asserting that each essay started with "due obeisance to E.P. Thompson, the guru of modern 'working class historians'," and suggested that contributors were "determined to shoehorn their subjects into a Thompsonian mould regardless of any violence done to history in the process." In fact, a number of the essays make no mention of Thompson in notes or text, while the majority of the articles, even when citing Thompson, are relatively uninfluenced by his work. On the whole, this hardly constitutes "due obeisance" or "shoehorning." What Bercuson's caustic assessment reveals is the strength of resentment against an *engaged* history of a particular sort. Thompson's work, long associated with a tradition of socialist humanism, elicits an almost irrational response from historians whose commitment is to the *status quo*. Bercuson is simply one more body on the bandwagon of anti-Thompsonians, and his tirade against "preachiness" is itself preachy, a sermon from the mount. I have explored aspects of Thompson's politics and work in "E.P. Thompson: Marxism, Humanism, and History" (paper presented to the New York State Association of European Historians, 28th Annual Meeting, 6–7 October 1978). Cf., Alan Dawley, "E.P. Thompson and the Peculiarities of the Americans," *Radical History Review* 19 (1978–79): 33–60; Richard Johnson, "Thompson, Genovese and Socialist-Humanist History," *History Workshop* 6 (1978): 79–100.

46. See the preface in Gene Howard Homel, "James Simpson and the Origins of Canadian Social Democracy" (PhD dissertation, University of Toronto, 1978).

47. Terry Copp, *The Condition of the Working Class in Montreal, 1897–1929* (Toronto: McClelland & Stewart, 1974); Michael J. Piva, *The Condition of the Working Class in Toronto, 1900–1921* (Ottawa: University of Ottawa Press, 1979), esp. x.

48. See Kealey, *Working Class Toronto at the Turn of the Century* (Toronto: New Hogtown, 1973); Kealey,

ed., *Canada Investigates Industrialism: The Royal Commission on the Relations of Labour and Capital, 1889* (Toronto: University of Toronto Press, 1973); "Artisans Respond to Industrialism: Shoemakers, Shoe Factories, and the Knights of St Crispin in Toronto," Canadian Historical Association, *Papers* (1973): 137–57; Judith Fingard, "The Winter's Tale: The Seasonal Contours of Pre-Industrial Poverty in British North America," ibid. (1974): 65–94; "The Decline of the Sailor as a Ship Labourer in 19th Century Timber Ports," *L/LT* 2 (1977): 35–53; "Masters and Friends, Crimps and Abstainers: Aspects of Control in 19th Century Sailortown," *Acadiensis* 8 (1978): 22–46; Kenneth Duncan, "Irish Famine Immigration and the Social Structure of Canada West," *Canadian Review of Sociology and Anthropology* 2 (1965): 19–41. Useful material on the standard of living in Canada in the 1870s can be gleaned from Edward Young, *Labor in Europe and America: A Special Report on the rate of wages, the cost of subsistence, and the condition of the working classes, in Great Britain, France, Belgium, Germany and other countries of Europe, also in the United States and British America* (Philadelphia: S.A. George, 1875); J.G. Snell, "The Cost of Living in Canada, 1870," *Histoire sociale/Social History* (hereafter *HS/SH*) 12 (1979): 186–91.

49. See Michael B. Katz, *The People of Hamilton, Canada West: Family and Class in a Mid-Nineteenth-Century City* (Cambridge: Harvard University Press, 1975), esp. 44–93.

50. Compare Piva, *Condition of Working Class in Toronto*, 143–70, with Craig Heron and Bryan D. Palmer, "Through the Prism of the Strike: Industrial Conflict in Southern Ontario, 1901–1914," *CHR* 58 (1977): 423–58.

51. Gregory S. Kealey, " 'The Honest Workingman' and Workers' Control: The Experience of Toronto Skilled Workers, 1860–1892," *L/LT* 1 (1976): 32–68; Palmer, *A Culture in Conflict: Skilled Workers and Industrial Capitalism in Hamilton, Ontario, 1860–1914* (Montreal: McGill-Queen's University Press, 1979). Cf., Wayne Roberts, "Artisans, Aristocrats, and Handymen: Politics and Unionism among Toronto Skilled Building Trades Workers, 1896–1914," *L/LT* 1 (1976): 92–121.

52. Palmer, "Discordant Music: Charivaris and Whitecapping in Nineteenth Century North America," *L/LT* 3 (1978): 5–62; Gerald M. Sider, "Christmas Mumming and the New Year in Outport Newfoundland," *Past & Present* 71 (1976): 102–25.

53. Note the argument in the majority of articles in *Women at Work: Ontario, 1850–1930* (Toronto: Women's Press, 1974).

54. Wayne Roberts, *Honest Womanhood: Feminism, Feminity, and Class Consciousness Among Toronto Working Women, 1893–1916* (Toronto: New Hogtown, 1976); Alice Klein and Wayne Roberts, "Besieged Innocence: The 'Problem' and the Problems of Working Women—Toronto, 1896–1914," in *Women at Work*, 211–60. Cf., Joan Sangster, "The 1907 Bell Telephone Strike: Organizing Women Workers," *L/LT* 3 (1978): 109–30; D. Suzanne Cross, "The Neglected Majority: The Changing Role of Women in 19th Century Montreal," *HS/SH* 6 (1973): 202–23; Susan Mann Trofimenkoff, "One Hundred and Two Muffled Voices: Canada's Industrial Women in the 1880s," *Atlantis* 3 (1977): 67–82.

55. Bryan D. Palmer, "Most Uncommon Common Men: Craft and Culture in Historical Perspective," *L/LT* 1 (1976): 5–31; Gerald M. Sider, "The Ties That Bind: Culture and Agriculture, Propriety and Property in the Newfoundland Village Fishery" (paper presented to the Canadian Historical Association, June 1978); Ian McKay, "Capital and Labour in the Halifax Baking and Confectionery Industry During the Last Half of the Nineteenth Century," *L/LT* 3 (1978): 63–108; Michael J. Piva, "The Aristocracy of the English Working Class: Help for an Historical Debate in Difficulties," *HS/SH* 7 (1974): 270–92.

56. Terry Morley, "Canada and the Romantic Left," *Queen's Quarterly* 86 (1979), esp. 114–15. Morley was reviewing four books which had little to do with working-class history, and nothing at all to do with *Labour/Le Travailleur*. The assault is all the more disturbing for being patently gratuitous.

57. See, for instance, E.P. Thompson, *William Morris: Romantic to Revolutionary* (New York: Pantheon, 1977), esp. 763–816; "Romanticism, Utopianism and Moralism: the Case of William Morris," *New Left Review* 99 (1976): 83–111.

58. See, for instance, Patricia V. Schulz, *The East York Workers' Association: A Response to the Great Depression* (Toronto: New Hogtown, 1975); Bruce Scott, " 'A Place in the Sun': the Industrial Council at Massey-Harris, 1919–1929," *L/LT* 1 (1976): 158–92; Tom Traves, *The State and Enterprise: Canadian Manufacturers and the Federal Government, 1917–1931* (Toronto: University of Toronto Press, 1979), 86–94.

59.   The publication of Gregory S. Kealey's *The Working Class Response to Industrial Capitalism in Toronto, 1867–1892* (Toronto: University of Toronto Press, 1980) should establish that the second generation is not without concern for political issues.

60.   McDowell, "Formation of Industrial Relations System"; Terry Copp, ed., *Industrial Unionism in Kitchener, 1937–41* (Kitchener: Cumnock, 1976).

61.   Bryan D. Palmer, "Kingston Mechanics and the Rise of the Penitentiary, 1833–1836" (paper presented to the Ontario Historical Society, June 1978); Michael S. Cross, "The Shiner's War: Social Violence in the Ottawa Valley in the 1830s," *CHR* 54 (1973): 1–25; Catharine Vance, "Early Trade Unionism in Quebec, 1833–34: The Carpenters' and Joiners' General Strike in Montreal," *Marxist Quarterly* 3 (1962): 26–42. The rebellions of 1837–38 have been particularly ill served. See Beverley D. Boissery and F. Murray Greenwood, "New Sources for Convict History: The Canadian Patriotes in Exile," *Historical Studies* 18 (1978): 277–87; George Rudé, *Protest and Punishment: the Story of the Social and Political Protesters Transported to Australia, 1788–1868* (Oxford: Oxford University Press, 1978).

62.   James W. Rinehart, *The Tyranny of Work* (Toronto: Longman, 1975).

63.   P.F. Neary, " 'Traditional' and 'Modern' elements in the Social and Economic History of Bell Island and Conception Bay," Canadian Historical Association *Papers* (1973): 105–36. Note, too, the exciting American work: Anthony F.W. Wallace, *Rockdale: The Growth of an American Village in the Early Industrial Revolution* (New York: Knopf, 1978); Joseph E. Walker, *Hopewell Village: The Dynamics of a Nineteenth Century Iron-Making Community* (Philadelphia: University of Pennsylvania Press, 1966).

64.   Robert F. Harney and his work with the multicultural history society promises much. See, for instance, Harney, "Montreal's King of Italian Labour: A Case Study of Padronism," *L/LT* 4 (1979).

65.   American studies have begun to explore the role of the working-class family in transmitting values, and in easing the process of adaptation to change, especially to changes resulting from the new rigours and disciplines of capitalist society. The importance of the family economy in sustaining workers in the midst of economic crisis, and the place of the family in securing jobs for its members has also been examined. See Herbert G. Gutman, *The Black Family in Slavery and Freedom, 1750–1925* (New York: Pantheon, 1976); Daniel J. Walkowitz, *Worker City, Company Town: Iron and Cotton-Worker Protest in Troy and Cohoes, New York, 1855–84* (Urbana: University of Illinois Press, 1978); Tamara K. Hareven and Ralph Langenbach, *Amoskeag: Life and Work in an American Factory City* (New York: Pantheon, 1978); Hareven, "Women's Time, Family Time, and Industrial Time: The Interaction between Immigrant Families and Industrial Life, Manchester, New Hampshire, 1900–1940," *Journal of Urban History* 1 (1975): 365–89; Hareven, "The Laborers of Manchester, New Hampshire, 1912–1922," *Labor History* 16 (1975): 99–116.

66.   Gregory S. Kealey, Russell Hann and myself are in the final stages of preparing a book on the Order in Ontario, 1880–1900. Previous work has been crude and is now dated by the availability of new sources. See Douglas R. Kennedy, *The Knights of Labour in Canada* (London: University of Western Ontario, 1956); Victor Oscar Chan, "Canadian Knights of Labour with special reference to the 1880s" (MA thesis, McGill University, 1949).

67.   Calvin Martin, *Keepers of the Game: Indian-Animal Relationships and the Fur Trade* (Berkeley: University of California Press, 1978). Cf. other statements by Martin: "The Four Lives of a Micmac Copper Pot," *Ethnohistory* 22 (1975): 111–33; "Ethnohistory: A Better Way to Write Indian History," *Western Historical Quarterly* 9 (1978): 41–56.

E.P. THOMPSON VS. HAROLD LOGAN: WRITING ABOUT LABOUR AND THE LEFT IN THE 1970s †

KENNETH McNAUGHT

Over the past ten years or so, many younger historians have cast critical eyes on the rather slender accumulation of writing on Canadian labour organization, strikes, and "industrial relations" which they were asked to consult as graduate students. They were not favourably impressed. The existing literature, they observed, concerned itself almost entirely with endeavours to organize labour, and the evolution of governmental and business responses to such efforts. Moreover, most of the literature expressed an establishment point of view; it was "élitist," ignoring the real experience of the working class and minimizing the "aberrant" manifestations of proletarian radicalism. The Young Turks deplored equally the meliorist mentality which permeated discussion of political action on the left. In the social-economic sphere, formal mainstream unionism and collective bargaining had received the lion's share of attention. Conventional wisdom endorsed either social democracy or liberal reformism as the most legitimate and promising political expressions of labour's interests. In short, the received version was myopic, biased, and managerial. H. A. Logan's classic, if mind-numbing, account of trade unions in Canada exhibited starkly the bias both in subject matter and in the social-political preconceptions which lurked behind a liberal objectivity. Deeply disturbing was his appraisal of the role of the communists: "All in all the effort of the Communists, for all their idealistic sacrifices, seems to have brought mainly loss to progressive trade unionism in Canada when viewed through other than Marxian eyes . . . ."[1]

In their critical assessment of all this, many graduate students in the 1960s and early 1970s were attracted by one or more expressions of that diaphanous phenomenon, the New Left. They read and took to heart the critics of liberal corporate capitalism. They found particularly congenial those who concluded that the *dirigiste* and repressive nature of the system had achieved such a degree of sophisticated social manipulation and "hegemony" that direct action was required. The complicity of Canadian élites in support of American-dominated western capitalism led the young rebels to contemplate means of obstructing and even reversing the course of events as they perceived them. Unhappy, also, with the expansive, prosperous complacency of Canada's sixties they identified themselves, not infrequently, with foreign movements of protest and revolution — with the campaigns for nuclear disarmament, with left-wing nationalist movements in the beleaguered regions of European and American imperial power, with volatile American movements for racial equality, participatory democracy, and ending

†*Canadian Historical Review* LXII, 2 (1981): 141–168.

the intervention in Vietnam. Nor was their excitement merely vicarious. Particularly in protesting against the Vietnam war and the lack of student participation in the governance of universities they took part in "confronting" and sometimes disrupting university administration, conducting "occupations," teach-ins, and guerilla theatre, and achieving some changes in the atmosphere and structure of universities.

The writing of the past decade has been influenced not only by the political-social ambience of the sixties but also by a shift of emphasis within the historical fraternities of western Europe, Britain, and the United States. A marked stress on social history worked together with Marxist and other egalitarian critiques of advanced capitalism and imperialism to define new questions to be asked of Canadian history. The trends from abroad brought with them implicit guidelines— both for those attracted to the left and those who wished primarily to flesh out the somewhat skeletal academic version of our past.[2] A general stimulus came from the French *Annales* school, from the work of Antonio Gramsci and from the German neo-Marxists, which stressed the cultural underpinnings of capitalism and employed modern, complex conceptions of the state. More direct influences were those of "empirical" Marxism evident in British historical analysis. E. P. Thompson, E. J. Hobsbawm, Raymond Williams, G. Stedman Jones, and others, produced a torrent of writing which suggested new approaches, new questions to be asked about Canadian society and labour. Particularly appealing was the British effort to rediscover the positive characteristics of working-class life, apart from trade unionism, and to apply a neo-Marxist, fluid concept of class and the evolution of class consciousness. Students fed on the notion of a nearly inevitable *embourgeoisement* of the lower orders in Canada found exciting the British depiction of a working-class culture underlying the changing expression of class consciousness and buttressing resistance to the discipline of industrial capitalism. Congenial also was the British stress on locality and lost causes. When applied to Canadian labour history, these analytical thrusts led to a positive interaction with the more general trend to study the roles of regionalism, urbanization, and "limited identities."

The British influence was strong also in the United States where it was reflected in the work of labour historians such as David Montgomery, Herbert Gutman, and Melvin Dubofsky. In America the critique of traditional labour history merged with the general assault on "consensus" history which had evolved in the 1950s. With a heady mix of populism and Marxism the new American radical history produced by people as diverse as W. A. Williams, Gabriel Kolko, James Weinstein, and Stephan Thernstrom analysed problems of a newer industrial society, more familiar methods of social control or class "hegemony," in an environment more similar in some ways to that of Canada than was the British. Of special interest to young Canadian scholars was the founding in 1960 of *Labor History*. This journal began with a sense that the AFL-CIO merger in 1955 had heralded a reinvigoration of the American labour movement. Throughout the 1960s, however, its articles reflected a growing disillusionment with a hard-hat business unionism whose consumerism seemed to confirm the orthodox interpretations of labour-capitalist relationships which had been presented by historians such as

Commons, Ely, Perlman, and Taft. Studies of labour leadership and union history, while not disappearing, began to be overshadowed by efforts "to show that labor history is more than the rise and fall or failures and successes of organizations — that it also consists of elucidating the role of the workers."[3]

Determined to launch a similar drive in Canada, a number of young historians brought to their task not only extensive reading of the literature from abroad and direct involvement in radical student activities at home, but also personal contacts with the people who were spearheading the new approaches — at labour history sessions of American and Canadian historical associations, at labour history conferences, the most notable of which was held at Rutgers University in 1973, and occasionally by pursuing senior degrees in the United States.[4] Specifically Marxist analysis of the structural imperatives of American capitalism, of the crucially unhelpful role of middle-class progressivism, and of the resistance potential of the provinces of the American informal empire gained a moral boost when Gabriel Kolko moved from Buffalo to Toronto in 1970.

One of the most impressive results of this intellectual ferment of the sixties has been a diligent searching for sources as well as warm differences of opinion about the utility of non-traditional source material. Discussion in the early seventies led to formation of a Committee on Canadian Labour History (CCLH), a newsletter, a bulletin, and a journal. Composition of the committee, as well as of the editorial and advisory boards it created, reflected a broad range of views — a good deal broader than one might gather from a recent article which implies that the committee and its publications are mere creatures of "the romantic leftists."[5] Various brands of Marxism, as of more traditional labour history, have been represented by the people who directed or contributed to the work of the committee — as it is suggested by their union, university, archival, and civil service affiliations. Issues of the semi-annual *Bulletin* and the annual journal, *Labour/Le Travailleur* [now *Labour/Le Travail*], since 1976[6] have published a range of articles, reviews, project reports, archival notes, and documents which has established the committee's publications as the focal point of contemporary work in Canadian labour history. While the committee has given emphasis to the social-cultural aspects of working-class history, and to varieties of Marxist interpretation, it has also given appropriate attention to the continuing and important work in institutional labour history. The editorial board's original statement of purpose has been generally followed: " . . . Canadian history lacks a sufficient understanding of the lives of the workers. Productive human energy has played a vital role in the development of Canadian society. Our common life has also been richly endowed with the cultural contributions of generations of working men and women. It will be the constant endeavour of *Labour/Le Travailleur* to rectify an all too general Canadian ignorance of these legacies."

Despite an apparent breadth of interest and the importance of its work in stimulating bibliographical and source-finding projects[7] the committee's efforts have unquestionably been influenced by a desire to establish the centrality of class culture and class conflict in the evolution of Canadian capitalist society. In this they were probably encouraged by an upsurge of industrial unrest and strikes in the mid-sixties and also by the work of the Task Force on Labour Relations, of which Stuart Jamieson's *Times of Trouble* was the best known publication and is still the best general account of labour relations in the twentieth century.[8] Like the radical critics of consensus in the United States, the leading spirits of the committee seemed often to seize upon each evidence of conflict, violence, or tension in Canadian history with a view to completing an ideological jig-saw puzzle whose missing pieces had been either deliberately or unconsciously ignored by bourgeois historians. While the more traditional history had recorded plenty of incidences of violence in strikes, religious confrontations, elections, and "cultural conflicts" such as the two *affaires Riel* or the Quebec conscription riots, such occurrences have been viewed either as aberrations or as too complex to be ascribed to the inexorable unfolding of class conflict.[9] Many of the CCLH group, reviewing such events, strove not only to enrich our knowledge of the common people but also to find evidence of a popular culture and even a revolutionary potential. In so doing they have frequently drawn upon concurrent writing in political economy by Marxist scholars such as Leo Panitch, Gary Teeple, Wallace Clement, and Tom Naylor[10] for a supporting analysis of the nature and develop- ment of Canadian capitalism. Indeed, the interconnections have been sufficiently numerous to lead Norman Penner to record his belief that "a small but growing section of the intellectuals are turning to Marxism not just as an academic exercise, but with the aim of influencing the direction of socialist thought along revolu- tionary lines."[11] Yet, within the CCLH cluster there has been no agreement on the relative weighting to be assigned to such "forces" as culture, economic struc- ture, class consciousness, leadership, political-constitutional forms, imperial-colonial relationships, ethnicity, or nationalism — or even on the extent to which history should be politically didactic. Thus there appears a healthy tension between the Marxists in the CCLH group and the more traditional historians both inside and outside the group.

Beyond the occasionally acerbic differences, however, two characteristics are shared by nearly all who have contributed recently to the field: an interest in social history and class attitudes, and particularly in regional and local experience. And despite the significance I have imputed to the neo-Marxist brigade as a stimulant, the most substantial writing on labour and the left draws lightly, if at all, on Marxist theory or on the methodology of the new social history. A survey of the recent writing leaves one with the strong apprehension that the more concerned authors are with description and narrative, the more implicit their analysis, and the less obtrusive their ideological imperatives, the more effective is the result.

Impelled by the desire, whether ideological or not, to discover and depict the conditions of life and labour in the Canadian past, a stream of books and articles grappled with the thorny problem of sources. Not surprisingly, given the predeter- mined dearth of private papers, the main sources have been newspapers, the records of labour organizations, and a wide array of governmental publications, with personal papers and business records in a supportive role. That lack of interest, not of sources, has been the reason why most previous historical writing virtually ignored the life of the common people, as industrialism took root, was proclaimed by Gregory Kealey when he published in 1973 an edited version of the report of the Royal Commission on the Relations of Capital and Labour — which, at the end of the 1880s, had amassed superlative evidence on working conditions inside and outside the country's rapidly multiplying factories.[12] Kealey made plain his belief that as further facts were accumulated we would come to know intimately the interaction between the evolution of Canadian capitalism and the ever-growing workforce required by the system. As he and others of the CCLH group pursued their research they described various dynamics which were of a much different order than those merely of competing merchant and industrial capitalists and basically accommodating trade union leaders. The new picture was both simpler and more complex: simpler in its assertion of continuous class conflict, more complex in its attempt to delineate a Thompsonian evolutionary "process" of working-class consciousness.

In 1976 Kealey and Peter Warrian edited a collection of essays[13] which examined a generous range of working-class experience and culture. The authors stressed the survival of an artisanal tradition, workers' efforts to retain control of their conditions of work, to exploit such institutions as the Orange Order, to promote their welfare, and to cope with a relative decline in the quality and quantity of their housing. The essayists discussed also the workers' relationship to reform-minded "brainworkers," their readiness to meet force with force, and the catalytic function of ethnic diversity in potentially violent situations. They expressed differing views on the question of where to find the well-spring of working-class attitudes and actions: in a residual culture, in day-to-day experience, or in the interaction of these with socialist intellectuals such as Phillips Thompson and pragmatic politicians and labour leaders. Nevertheless, the editors' introduction is accurate in ascribing to the book a consensus and, because that consensus also comprehends the writing of a majority of the CCLH group, both concurrent and subsequent, it is worth quoting several key statements:

> Canadian historical writing has left little room for the inclusion of ordinary working people . . . . Yet working people belong at the centre of the picture, not on the edges where they are now placed.
> The major contribution of the "new" history has been to redefine "labour history" as "working class history." Thus, labour history ceases to be simply . . . a problem of industrial relations, a canon of saintly working class leaders, a chronicle of union locals or a chronology of militant strike actions . . . . Moreover, the working class is a variegated grouping. Class must be understood as both a "vertical" or economic relationship and as a "horizontal" or cultural relationship. In the vertical sense class involves the relationship of exploitation that exists between capitalist and wage labourer. In the horizontal sense class concerns the beliefs, values, ideas and traditions that people carry with them in their lives and work. These two categories are separated only in analysis; in reality they are dialectically intertwined. Class is a completely historical concept. It does not exist as a "thing," as Edward Thompson has frequently pointed out.
> The new social history is not concerned with filling in the interstices of the old Canadian historiographic traditions with odd facts and events . . . . Instead, when completed, it will constitute a new, distinctive synthesis of Canadian history.

Hoisting the flag to the mast is always fun, particularly if the flag is red, and more especially if a mariner's guide (even an imported one) is ready to hand. Moreover, if the navigational pointers on the largely British-made guide were generally clear enough, there was excitement to be had exploring a largely uncharted sea with its very particular local, regional, and ethnic currents. Yet it is the endeavour to enrich our knowledge of these cross-currents, rather than the often tortuous application of the chart's theoretical propositions, that has been of most permanent value.

What Kealey and Warrian point out about their pioneer collection of essays is true also of most of the other work of the CCLH group: "A similarity they share, however, is that all deal with single cities, towns or regional communities. This immersion in local materials allows each to capture the historical experience of these workers with real sensitivity to local variation." Beyond this, there are beliefs shared by a majority of the group: that class conflict is the basic force in our history, that between 1850 and 1925 "the pre-industrial society of independent commodity producers, both farmers and artisans, was transformed into an industrial society," and that what most needs examining is the way in which workers responded to such change together with the nature of the resulting working-class consciousness. Differences of interpretation emerge: how far was the workers' defence against new forms of industrial discipline derived from a pre-industrial artisanal culture, and how far from a forward-looking readiness to evolve new devices such as across-trade unions? Despite a willingness to search out and describe the varieties of the workers' experience and responses, however, two rather marked tendencies modify the intra-group differences. The first is to descry much sharper conflict and much simpler explanations of such conflict than the evidence seems to warrant.[14] The second proclivity is to accept an essentially revolutionary goal as the inner purpose of historical research and writing: "If nothing else, it should be clear that the 'problem' is not the worker but rather the continued existence of industrial capitalist society. Those of us who write working-class history should, as E.J. Hobsbawm has recently reminded us, always remember that our history, like all social science, is concerned with changing the world as well as interpreting it . . . . This is not an injunction to romanticize the past, for that will not help working-class people achieve their aim and ours — the ability to make their own lives and history."[15]

Most overt amongst the celebrants of "the rich and vibrant culture of the artisan" has been Bryan Palmer in several articles and his published thesis.[16] Minimizing the importance of unions as such, Palmer has sought to picture an evolutionary, "autonomous" working-class culture which was "a central component of the matrix of control mechanisms" in the developing industrial capitalism. Despite a turgid neo-Marxist theoretical framework and a good deal of information about the experience of Hamilton's workers, the Knights of Labour, and other organizations, Palmer's structure is almost anecdotal. In a sense it fills in some of the interstices and provides a more detailed background than was previously available for understanding our social history, rather than providing any convincing new interpretation of the role of the working class and its spokesmen.[17] Further emphasis on the efforts of artisans to use their "residual culture" (customs?) to retain "control" of the workplace has been given by other writers of the CCLH group, especially Wayne Roberts, Craig Heron, Gregory Kealey, James Rinehart, Edward McKenna and, to some extent, Stephen Langdon.[18]

The major venture of synthesizing the work of discovering previously neglected patterns of working-class experience is Gregory Kealey's *Toronto Workers Respond to Industrial Capitalism, 1867–1892* (Toronto, 1980). Kealey chose Toronto "because of its economic importance and its key role in the development of the early labour movement." Toronto workers, he writes, "were amongst the first to experience the industrial revolution, to join international unions, to create a city labour centre, and to initiate a province-wide, and later a national labour organization." "The 'making' of the Toronto working class," he tells us, "lay in industrialization and in the workers' response to that process." Concentrating on specific groups and organizations, Kealey discusses also the political role of the workers, emphasizing their relationships with major parties as well as the beginning of a socialist critique. He differs sharply from those Marxists, such as Tom Naylor, who argue that Canadian capitalists' mercantile preoccupation retarded industrial growth, and accepts the position of those such as H. C. Pentland, Stanley Ryerson, and L.R. Macdonald who maintain that "industrial capitalist development in central Canada in the period under study displays no such weaknesses." Spanning the interests and purposes of the CCLH group, Kealey concludes his well-documented survey (which a non-Marxist reader might assume would lead in a different direction) with the assessment that "the transitional nature of the 1870's and 1880's bred a labour reform movement which simultaneously looked forward and backward. Much of the movement's strength lay in the workers' knowledge of a past that was totally different from their present. They knew that industrial capitalism was a social system with a history; it was neither natural nor pre-ordained . . . . The precision of the socialist critique was a major gain for the Toronto working class, but the declining number of those whose vision transcended the established system was a major loss. Class conflict, of course, continued."[19]

Not all of the recent writing proceeds from some version of formal Marxism; indeed, much of the best work takes a sceptical view of the scantily defined notions of class, culture, control, or, even, conflict. Virtually all, however, has responded to the need to fill glaring gaps in our previous "from the top down" historical writing. In this broader spectrum the sharpest differences crop up when the respective writers assign priority, usually implicitly, to the roles of leadership or grass roots, to region, locality, or nation. Amongst those who have sought to extend, without overt ideological commitment, our knowledge of labour history, David Bercuson has been particularly active. With increasing stress upon regional contexts he has given special attention to the impact of industrialism on the West. His analysis of industrial relations in Winnipeg provides not only the best account of the 1919 general strike in that city, it also presents a sophisticated analysis of the social-economic development of Winnipeg with a balanced description of the interaction between employers and workers, the role of organizations, the experience of comparative isolation, and refreshing attention to personalities.[20] Similarly, in his account of the One Big Union,[21] Bercuson seeks to explain the origins and course of Canadian syndicalism, the varying purposes of OBU leaders, and the nature of the effective repression implemented by employers, governments, and the international unions. While class conflict looms large, the players are not merely automata. Bercuson illustrates vividly the conditions in the mines, forests, and factories, and the differences are documented. If his conclusions are less at variance with the more traditional interpretation than are those of the Marxist galaxy, and contain no call to further the revolution, they also rest upon a more comprehensive use of sources. Despite our deepened comprehension of the radical political purpose of some labour leaders, there has emerged no reason to doubt that the main impulses to labour organization and action have come from the perceived need of union recognition and improvement both of wages and working conditions rather than from cultural imperatives or revolutionary intent.

An approach to western labour history similar to Bercuson's is taken by A. Ross McCormack in several articles and an important monograph on western radicalism.[22] McCormack stresses the particular circumstances of primary and secondary industrial activity in the West and effectively distinguishes the three main streams of the western labour movement. The conclusions of his analysis are of particular interest. He writes that "massive state repression of the last industrial union crusade engraved into the collective memory of the working class a residual solidarity, a tradition labourites used to legitimize their every action." Yet, he observes, the quiescence which followed the "bad beating" taken by the workers in the strikes of 1918–19 "was a function of improved social conditions." The attitude of the reformers rather than the revolutionaries came to be "shared by men and women across the country" and led to a new social democratic movement by the end of the twenties. Although clearly sympathetic to the western militants, McCormack comments with subdued realism that "labourism's tactics and ideology (after 1919) were not incompatible with the nation's orderly and moderate political culture." If there is a "dark and bloody ground" in labour historiography at the moment, this is it.

A more ambivalent, yet critically important, contribution to the interpretative controversy has been made by Irving Abella in his monograph dealing with the struggles which surrounded the establishment of the CIO in Canada.[23] Abella's carefully researched account of the resurgence of industrial unionism in the thirties argues that the most effective organizers were communists and that they made good use of a groundswell of nationalism in the working class. The take-off of an independent Canadian industrial union organization was frustrated principally by the CCFers who, claims Abella, were motivated mainly by an urgent political need to deny a union base to the communists and, conversely, to acquire such a base for themselves. Perhaps Abella's work is closest to the eye of the storm. By neo-Marxist class culture enthusiasts he is castigated for short-changing social history and over-emphasizing the leadership component, yet they can scarcely be totally unappreciative of the hefty pat on the back he gives the communists for such thrusts as that of the Workers Unity League. Those with a social democratic penchant who tend to stress the institutional approach to working-class history bridle at Abella's description of the CCFers as "ruthless" in their largely successful machinations to oust communists from influential union posts. They also question sharply his assumption that Canadian workers were ready, by the end of the thirties, for a completely independent union structure. Bercuson, for example, writes that "No alliance of Catholic unions from Quebec, Communist-led unions in the Workers Unity League and national Canadian unions led by extreme anti-Communists such as Aaron Mosher in the All-Canadian Congress of Labour, was ever likely."[24] — Controversy over Abella's analysis raises profound questions which, in view of their historiographical significance, it is surprising that most Canadian labour historians do not confront explicitly. Those questions, I think, may be boiled down thus: what are the root causes of the usually disadvantaged position of the working class? In recognizing and defining such disadvantage and what might be done to correct or modify it, what are the initiating and most effective agencies, and what is the relationship between individual leadership on the one hand, and spontaneous class action on the other? What is the significance of the social-political tradition of Canada in shaping the methods and determining the results of workers' collective action? Of course there are many implicit answers given to some or all of these questions in much of the writing which is the subject of this discussion. But by and large the answers are, in fact, *a priori* assumptions rather than clearly defined responses. At one end of the spectrum the Marxists proclaim that the exigencies of a developing capitalist system, no matter how interestingly affected by local and regional variables, or even by leadership personality, necessarily produce class conflict whose eventual outcome must be overthrow (or undermining) of the system. Despite the claim that their conceptualization illumines their researches, in fact the totality of the concept tends, as often as not, to impart an antiquarian aspect to their work. At the other end of the spectrum, those who continue to flesh out the history of unions, strikes, and political action vary in the importance they attribute to the role of leaders, ideologies, political and social traditions, and rank-and-file spontaneity. Rejecting the element of determinism in the Marxist analyses, they seem shy of publicly dissecting their own preconceptions. Most, of course, heatedly reject allegations from the left that they are simply blinkered liberals who cannot discern their own ideology and thus end up as meliorist lackeys of a very purposeful corporate capitalism.[25]

The work of detailing the institutional evolution of Canadian labour, of recovering the story of forgotten strike and other action on the economic front, of piecing together the workers' approaches to politics and parties has, meanwhile, gone forward — often benefiting from the trendy concern with culture and locality. The best "straight" survey remains Jamieson's *Times of Trouble* and a useful supplement to this is a collection of essays edited by Abella.[26] Together with Jamieson's book, David Kwavnick's close examination of the efforts of the Canadian Labour Congress to influence governmental policy provided material essential to understanding the unique Canadian format of labour's relationship to the party system.

While much of the writing about strikes has focussed upon particular struggles, most also carries implications for a larger canvas. A landmark was the translation and republication, edited by Pierre Elliott Trudeau, of the superb account of the 1949 asbestos strike in Quebec.[27] First published in 1956, this collection of ten essays with the editor's wide-ranging introduction is by far the best account in

English not only of the explosion at Asbestos but also of the particularity of the Quebec labour movement and the background of the Quiet Revolution. Antedating the impact in Canada of the "new social history," as well as of neo-Marxism, *The Asbestos Strike* nevertheless exhibits methods and insights in its depiction of workers within a total cultural-economic milieu that might well be a cause of some envy amongst more doctrinaire neophytes; there is, of course, a somewhat nostalgic resonance to the editor's intimation that, politically, the CCF best represents (1956) the aspirations of Quebeckers.

A number of articles and short monographs have also examined strikes and labour relations experiments. Brian Hogan produced an analysis of the 1919 Cobalt strike with careful attention to the local and provincial contexts, while Laurel MacDowell's study of the Kirkland Lake gold strike of 1941–42 shows how institutional labour history can be enriched by depicting interaction amongst local social structures, personal perceptions and interests, and federal-provincial political relations.[28] Examining a victorious railway strike of 1876–77, Desmond Morton also takes full account of the local community while describing the disingenuous role of the federal government in conveying "military aid to the civil power."[29] Yet, in emphasizing parliamentary refusal to make it easy for anyone to summon military aid, Morton calls sharply into question the traditional Marxist view of the industrial state. Implicit in this and other pieces by Morton is the proposition that working-class responses to industrial capitalism are inextricably intertwined with local and broader social-political attitudes and that class consciousness is not often a uniform phenomenon. In 1877, for example, the Tories broke ranks in response to Blake's Breaches of Contract bill and "the remnants of Canada's union movement" supported the bill, while much of the reason for the strikers' success was "the hostility to the Grand Trunk which pervaded all levels of society in most of the towns along its line and which neutralized the normal responses of mayors and aldermen."

A good deal of the recent writing, with or without an interpretative slant, examines living and working conditions in localities and regions with a total result that tempts one to predict that we are within sight of a broad synthesis. Terry Copp has provided a thorough description of working-class life in Montreal (1897–1929) which is at once scholarly and deeply moving, as well as articles on other aspects of life and labour in Ontario and Quebec.[30] Michael Piva's analysis of the conditions of Toronto's working class (1900–21) provides a useful counterpart to Copp's book and, despite contentious conclusions about an absolute decline in the standard of living and the inutility of reform endeavours, is rich in detail.[31] Copious illustration of life during the 1930s and of other aspects of deprivation have been provided in formats varying from strictly academic to non-professional recollection.[32]

Together with recent research on the working class in general, some of the writing on the position of women in Canadian history has paid special attention to women in the work force. Joan Sangster's article on the 1907 strike against Bell is particularly revealing in describing how a struggle in which the 400 operators got no wage increase, no union, and no improvement in the threatening conditions of work yet displayed "a militancy and solidarity which contradicted the contemporary dictums." As in most of his involvement with labour, Mackenzie King during the operators' strike pushed for labour peace rather than a just settlement, while even more distressingly the TLC and most male unionists seemed unsympathetic, disapproving of women in industry and fearing "petticoat rule."[33]

The role of the immigrant within the working class has been, along with that of women, one of the most neglected aspects of labour history. While nearly all of the writing on strikes, unionization, and working-class culture touches on the question, few deal with it specifically; Don Avery has made a very useful beginning.[34] On the reverse theme of native people within the work force an excellent monograph by Rolph Knight reaches some interesting conclusions about the experience of Canadian Indians: almost everywhere they have been involved with varieties of wage labour, skilled and unskilled, for over a century; social and cultural practices of particular Indian groups "could be and were retained along with wage work"; and "despite a variety of contractions and booms which affected Indian labour in the past, the semi-permanent unemployment and reserve dependence which affects increasing numbers of Indian people today is a relatively recent phenomenon . . . . It is a product of more or less contemporary political and economic forces."[35]

On a crucially important component in the organizational mix of Canadian labour, Robert Babcock's study of the so easily achieved American domination of the TLC and its affiliates prior to 1914 was a major contribution to formal union history.[36] Babcock, in effect, documents exactly what Pentland had outlined, that in 1902 "A.F.L. unions took control of the T.L.C., kicked everybody else out, made the T.L.C. a pensioner of the A.F.L. (at $500 a year) and retained this domination thereafter."[37] The chief effects of American labour's parallel imperialism, according to Babcock, were the empowering of the internationals to subvert Canadian moves toward industrial unionism, to drain off substantial amounts from Canadian coffers, and to entrench a business union resistance to independent political party action by Canadian unionists. That the majority of Canadian union leaders approved the international connections, and worked to strengthen them, is underplayed by Babcock. Yet the incubus of Sam Gompers did lie heavily upon Canadian labour; his substantial contribution to the defeat of industrial unionism in 1919 was only one incident in an uninterrupted policy of thwarting all efforts at across-craft organization and of organizing the unskilled. In Babcock's view, this legacy, together with steady financial leakage southward, also impeded efforts of the TLC to act as an effective pressure group.

The Gompersite influence in Canada, so profoundly opposed to union flirtation with socialism or affiliation with a political party, has led much recent analysis of the politics of the left to focus on the need and possibility of a political process quite different from that which seems to constrict labour and the left in the United States. By the end of the sixties the uncomely ideological shadow of Louis Hartz had stretched northward; its penumbra could be seen in Gad Horowitz's study of labour and politics and more tentatively in Walter Young's history of the CCF.[38] Here, the determinism of North American liberal notions was seen as explaining the impediments in the path of Canadian socialism and, especially, the difficulty in persuading organized labour to commit itself to effective third party action. Horowitz's "Tory touch," resulting from a delayed "point of congealment" in the ideology of the Canadian new nation, explained the limited success of socialism and thus the difference between Canada and the United States in this respect.[39] The endeavour to adapt American consensus interpretations to explain a non-existent Canadian two-party system and "the failure of Canadian socialism" met heavy weather in the seventies.[40]

Norman Penner, surveying the history of the "Canadian Left,"[41] argued for far more than Horowitz's "Tory touch." The National Policy, according to Penner, expressed a common political culture which had evolved out of the merger of the remnants of New France's clerical absolutism with the rigid authoritarianism of post–1760 British Toryism. This very unLockean ascendancy successfully suppressed the pre-industrial rebellions, and it was only with the re-emergence of "sectional, group, class and national differences" at the end of World War I that "liberal reformism" became the dominant attitude of Canadian society. By that time, too, "the socialist idea" had become a part of the Canadian ideological spectrum — imported mainly by British working-class immigrants. According to Penner, Canadian socialism (which he equates with the Left) had become "predominantly Marxist in character" by 1903. Also, it was essentially proletarian with "a complete absence of any intellectuals in the socialist ranks." With this somewhat astigmatic perception, Penner then delineates twentieth-century socialism in terms of the scholastic debates in the Communist Party about when and when not to co-operate with other progressive movements inside and beyond the labour unions. His penultimate conclusion is that the party erred in following the vacillating ukases of the Comintern and not learning quickly enough from Woodsworth's CCFers the correct way to domesticate socialism. Democratic socialist intellectuals are excluded from Penner's discussion, presumably on the ground that they were really liberal reformists, and he takes no account of CCF-NDP achievements either in opposition or in office. Penner's litany, however, ends on an up-beat, noting "the spectacular growth" of the Waffle, deploring the dispersal of that "organized caucus," and applauding a resurgence of Marxism in academe.

There has been a good deal of publication and republication of Marxist political recollections and contemporary analyses over the past few years.[42] The 1970 FLQ crisis, the rise of the Parti Québécois,[43] and the 1980 Quebec referendum further illuminated the Marxist concept of "the national question" in Canada. As with the Waffle's proclamation that socialism could only be achieved in a Canada that is politically and economically independent of the United States, so Marxists saw in Quebec a similarly crucial conjuncture. Moreover, Quebec nationalism, being racially based and more assiduously honed, seemed an especially promising tool with which to undermine the capitalist order maintained by anglophone Canadian and American manipulation of the provincial and federal states. A flood of serial and monographic publication suggested not only francophone Marxist acceptance of this formula for revolutionary change but also widespread support from anglophone Marxists inside and beyond Quebec. Progressive journals such as *Canadian Forum*, *This Magazine*, and *Canadian Dimension* complemented Montreal's *This Generation* and *Last Post* in demanding Quebec's "right of self-determination." Use of historical analysis was as important in left-wing separatism as it had always been across the spectrum of Quebec nationalism. Sociologists and other *Péquiste* and Marxist scholars employed the new ideologies of colonial liberation and terrorism, adjusting them to the Papineau-*Patriote* mythology which saw in pre-industrial rebellion the expression of a people's nationalism and protest. But the important research of Fernand Ouellet, together with disillusionment with the outcome of the Lévesque-Morin-Laurin approach to sovereignty-association, raised questions for Marxists — about parliamentarism, PQ accommodation of anglophone capitalism, and the historicist use of the Papineau legend.[44]

A certain sinuosity characterized the Marxist view of nationalism. While Canada must break free from American economic imperialism by using the power of the state to roll back the US takeover, so too must Quebec break free from, and thus constrict, the overweening power of that same federal state. Yet the Marxist analysis drew support from many anglophone liberal and social democratic intellectuals who endorsed the recital of "English" Canada's transgressions. Some sixty-two such anglophones joined in "A Plea to English Canada" two weeks prior to the 1980 referendum. The plea pronounced that in order to redress past grievances and to demonstrate their belief in the right of national self-determination (that poignant principle of Lenin and Wilson), "English Canadians" must accept, in advance of secession, Lévesque's proposed "association." Endorsing the dismantling of the Canadian federal state, and thus rejecting use of that state to strike blows at American imperial power, the neo-Marxist left revised the position taken by its predecessors of the 1920s and 1930s who had been far more interested in capturing Ottawa than in seizing the provincial capitals where the power of American investors was seen as total.

Academic Marxist analysis of the Canadian state and of the recently accelerated devolution of power is, of course, more complex than that shown at the level of quotidian propaganda. Marxists are by no means in total agreement about such matters as the extent of and reasons for "deindustrialization," or even the degree of independence enjoyed by the high command of Canadian business.[45] As a result, the dividing line between the doctrinaire and the pragmatic left is frequently indistinct. One evidence of slippage from orthodoxy was the publication by James and Robert Laxer of a critical analysis of the sins of Canadian liberalism.[46] Because the Laxers' central argument is that the anti-nationalist, anti-collectivist liberalism of which Mr Trudeau is both legatee and expediter is responsible for our continental drift and, thus, all our other economic woes, their book earned an appreciative endorsement from George Grant—thus obligingly boxing the political compass and implying that Horowitz's celebrated red Tory is alive and well, if headed for the Dartmouth Station.[47] The Laxers' depiction of the Liberal sell-out and the consequent inability of Ottawa to grapple with balance-of-payments deficits, energy resources, deindustrialization, and other economic problems is complemented by a more dubious contention: that it is only the Liberals who have failed to give adequate attention to sub-national collectivities: "Operating within the assumptions of the Canadian Liberal system, English Canadians have conceived of democracy in individual terms, with no notion of the rights of national communities. Allied to this perspective has been the notion that in a liberal system, the essential shape of the economy is determined by private corporate forces even if the most important ones are foreign-based. The results of these two basic and shaping ideas are now upon us: the first idea has driven the Québécois to elect a government determined to seek political independence from Canada; the second has allowed the Canadian economy to become a truncated dependency of the American economy with increasingly bleak prospects. The two results are mutually reinforcing."

Such reasoning is agreeable to a broad section of the articulate left, from Edward Broadbent to the Revolutionary Marxist Group. But in their cautious approach to prescription the Laxers stop far short of fanning the embers of class struggle or, indeed, of any positive assault on Confederation. Like the NDP itself they seem unsure whether the road to social salvation lies through Ottawa, Quebec City, or Regina.[48] Nevertheless, *The Liberal Idea of Canada* is at odds with Penner's frivolous estimate of the centrality of Marxism.[49] The political left in Canada remains far closer to the centre than either Penner or the utopian revolutionaries would have us believe.

Much recent writing, and some important reprinting, points to complexity rather than to any emerging simplicity in our methods of change and our basic attachment to continuity. The intermingling of ideas about change and continuity, together with a lively sense of the efficacy of parliamentary and common law precedents, have been brilliantly illustrated in two collections of essays by Frank Scott and Eugene Forsey.[50] Both Scott and Forsey collaborated in the work of the League for Social Reconstruction and the writing of *Social Planning for Canada*, both have given critically important support to labour unionism and a social democratic party, and both have been vigilant not only in the protection of civil and parliamentary freedom but also in clarifying and extending our notions of how best to use such freedom in the service of ordinary Canadians. Such men, with dashes both of Bloomsbury and religious conviction, should confound those who hanker after the purities of class conflict and deny a role to middle-class concern in the evolution of the left in Canada. These men, and others like them, blur doctrinal categories in Canada as elsewhere; certainly they cannot be taken as proving that the "real" left is confined either to orthodox Marxists or to the culture of the inarticulate.

The more we come to know about the complexity of the reform process in Canada the clearer it becomes that a tolerance of diverse analyses and prescriptions lies close to the heart of the matter. Somewhat different from the consensual compulsion discerned in the United States by scholars as different as Louis Hartz and C. Vann Woodward,[51] this basic tolerance is, of course, doubted by many civil libertarians, *nationalistes*, and direct-action enthusiasts. Yet it explains the survival of democratic socialism, political communism, and a willingness to debate openly whether the country should continue to exist. The question of how far this distinctive indulgence stems from a kind of Tory self-confidence, the opportunities to influence legislation offered by the parliamentary system, a deep strain of protestant and utilitarian liberalism, or a curious combination of all three is moot. Its effect, nevertheless, has been to render the pragmatic left, both in unionism and politics, of greater influence than the dogmatic left. The exotic role of the Marxist left, no matter how effective its practical contribution to militant industrial union organizing, is made evident in Ivan Avakumovic's somewhat uneven study of the Communist Party, which stresses even more strongly than does Penner the obedience of that disciplined organism to the kaleidoscopic instructions of the International.[52]

Because of blurring at the political edges, one man's socialist is another's bourgeois dupe. Jimmy Simpson, Toronto's "first socialist mayor," is described by Penner as a Marxist, while Gene Homel's major study of Simpson portrays him as motivated by a mixture of religious concern, working-class experience, and British Labour thinking.[53] Homel's work, partly because it is based on personal papers as well as newspapers and public records, presents a more convincing picture of class relationships, mediating social-political organizations, craft culture and social mobility than do the cliometricians and neo-Marxists—for whom the word "leader" is usually repugnant and the need to categorize imperative. In describing the roots of democratic socialism in central Canada, Homel corrects a previous tendency to discover such origins principally amongst the more militant workers and schismatic clergy of the west.

The variety of the left, as well as its east-west interconnections, was further emphasized in Richard Allen's sympathetic treatment of the social gospel movement.[54] By drawing the attention of many congregations to the requirement of "working for the kingdom here and now," social gospel ministers had a secularizing influence on the Protestant churches. By supporting the union movement, organizing and preaching in "labour churches," writing for labour and farmers' papers, and going directly into politics they were an essential component of Canadian social democracy. Allen's important book does not discuss an interesting comparison with the American movement: the more pronounced tendency of the Canadian social gospellers to be active in the formation of a political party and the influence they exercised in keeping the CCF distinct from the communists.[55] The importance for the left of a democratic and an undogmatic image was examined by Gerald Caplan in a study of the Ontario CCF.[56] While Caplan discusses the morale problem of the rise and decline of democratic socialist political strength, he minimized the cyclical aspect of that phenomenon and the consequent socialist survival in Canada as opposed to the fate of the Socialist Party of America. If the Ontario CCF between 1943 and 1945 moved from the euphoria of official opposition to the trauma of sharp electoral reverses, the Saskatchewan CCF at the same time was able to form North America's first socialist government.

Farmer-labour co-operation, as well as the social gospel, were central in the life of William Irvine, whose biography was written by Anthony Mardiros.[57] In his admiration for his subject, Mardiros tends to over-simplify the heady, sometimes contradictory, mixture of social gospel, populism, guild socialism, social credit, anti-militarism, "old country" roots, and farmer-labour enthusiasms that made Irvine such an excellent symbol of the Canadian left.

A different yet equally important expression of the complexity of the left was the amalgam of Fabianism and progressivism which found a focus in the League for Social Reconstruction and the *Canadian Forum*. Michiel Horn's study of the LSR describes carefully the role of intellectuals in the evolution of Canadian socialism, and the interplay of idealism and pragmatism that underpinned the

CCF.[58] Use of parliamentary and party methods to build effective co-operation amongst workers, farmers, and those broad service sections of the population which remain resistant to Marxist docketing has been stressed by Desmond Morton and Walter Young.[59] And retrieving primary material on a wide range of social history and reform thought was the extremely useful series of reprints edited by Michael Bliss and now by H.V. Nelles. *The Social History of Canada* series[60] is now indispensable to any student of labour and the left who is not *parti pris*.

If any dialectic has been at work in all this scholarly activity, its third stage is by no means in view. The heat has not subsided,[61] but neither has there emerged a clear antithesis, let alone a synthesis. The cannonading from the left has served principally to achieve those goals which the captains of artillery most vigorously rejected at the beginning of the campaign. The class-conscious researchers have filled in some serious gaps in our social history and they have also tempted others to concern themselves profitably with the regional and local contexts of labour history. Nevertheless, while our knowledge of the conditions of life and labour has been noticeably extended, no thesis has emerged with a convincing new explanation of our labour structure, of governmental labour policy, nor of the nature and role of the political left. On the contrary, most of the recent writing strengthens older notions: that the most effective workers' response to an ever tightening industrial discipline was unionization; that the slow evolution of effective unionization reflected differences of region, culture, and industrial context; that, while gross inequalities and exploitation produced the fears and goals of the workers, the forms and policies of unionization were determined by leaders — a great many of whom became "collaborators"; that violence has been provoked and employed more often by the state than by the workers; that despite clear evidence of various perceptions of class membership and class conflict, the dominant expressions of such perceptions have been the non-revolutionary strike and efforts to influence governmental policy through pressuring the major parties and/or supporting a democratic socialist party. Efforts to depict, or simply to assert, a free-standing working-class culture in the past (let alone the present) have failed to provide a credible new principle of historical interpretation, while the picture of a complex society in which progressivism, unionism, socialism, and political capitalism have been consistently interactive has been more definitely etched.

The lines along which future research might seek further explanation of this non-revolutionary tale should include detailed examination of the relationship between, on the one hand, real standards of living, social security, and collective bargaining rights, and, on the other, the growth and policies both of the unions and the CCF-NDP. While this blindingly innovative recommendation may come as small surprise, its acceptance would nevertheless contribute to a realistic assessment of the roles of leadership, militancy on the economic front, parliamentarism, and extra-parliamentarism. Those young researchers who have been lovingly adapting E.P. Thompson to the mines, production lines, and even the countryside of Canada's past might well recall the emphasis Clare Pentland placed upon educated leadership when he was discussing the struggles and gains of the 1930s and 1940s: "The outcome was that, again, the competence gap between employers (managers) and workers had narrowed very dangerously, inviting conflict between self-confident workers and defensive, unimaginative employers. The union leadership created in this period—which for many years employers said was too smart for them — remained in office almost to the present day."[62] That smart union leadership was not the product of any autonomous working-class culture. It grew out of an increasing sophistication and education. And its goal was not to defend an Archie Bunker-charivari culture but, rather, to liberate those who had been entrapped by the economic-cultural constraints imposed by political capitalists.

Notes

1. H.A. Logan, *Trade Unions in Canada* (Toronto, 1948), 344. Some other titles representative of the institutional, social democratic, or reformist view of labour history are E.A. Forsey, "History of the Labour Movement in Canada" in *Canada Year Book* (Ottawa, 1967); Douglas Kennedy, *The Knights of Labor in Canada* (London, Ont., 1956); John Crispo, *The Role of International Unionism in Canada* (Toronto, 1967); Stuart Jamieson, *Times of Trouble: Labour Unrest and Industrial Conflict in Canada, 1900–66* (Ottawa, 1968); G. Horowitz, *Canadian Labour in Politics* (Toronto, 1968); Martin Robin, *Radical Politics and Canadian Labour* (Toronto, 1968); D.C. Masters, *The Winnipeg General Strike* (Toronto, 1950); Kenneth McNaught, *A Prophet in Politics: a Biography of J.S. Woodsworth* (Toronto, 1959); Walter Young, *The Anatomy of a Party: the National CCF, 1932–61* (Toronto, 1969); William Rodney, *Soldiers of the International: a History of the Communist Party of Canada, 1919–29* (Toronto, 1968).

2. A perceptive article on recent trends in social history is Laurence Stone, "The Revival of Narrative: Reflections on a New Old History," *Past and Present* 85 (1979). A very critical treatment of sociological history, particularly interesting because it touches on recurring tension between Marxist and social history and on the appearance of such tension in much writing about what might be called the common woman, is Tony Judt, "A Clown in Regal Purple: Social History and the Historians," *History Workshop* (Spring 1979).

3. For an excellent review of these developments in the United States see Robert H. Zieger, "Workers and Scholars: Recent Trends in American Labour Historiography," *Labor History* (Spring 1972).

4. For example, Gregory Kealey with Herbert Gutman at Rochester; Bryan Palmer with Melvin Dubofsky at Binghamton; Russell Hann at Harvard.

5. Terry Morley, "Canada and the Romantic Left," *Queen's Quarterly* (Spring 1979). Amongst those closely associated with the work of the Canadian Committee on Labour History were Irving Abella, Gregory Kealey, David Bercuson, Ross McCormack, Terry Copp, John Battye, Russell Hann, Michael Cross, Jacques Rouillard, James Thwaites, Nancy Stunden, Edward Seymour, and Ed Finn. The advisory board was equally broad in its professional connections and points of view, including at various times Royden Harrison, David Montgomery, Stuart Jamieson, Kenneth McNaught, Clare Pentland, Stanley Ryerson, Fernand Ouellett, Jean Hamelin, and Gérard Dion.

6. *Bulletin of the Committee on Canadian Labour History* 1 (Spring 1976) to 8 (Autumn 1979); *Labour/Le Travailleur* (hereafter *L/LT*) I–IV (1976–79). Beginning with volume V in 1980, the journal absorbed the bulletin and began semi-annual publication.

7. Although not officially publications of the committee, the following were produced by people closely associated with it: Russell Hann, Gregory Kealey, and Peter Warrian, eds., *Primary Sources in Canadian Working Class History, 1860–1930* (Kitchener, 1973); Wayne Roberts, ed. *The Hamilton Working Class, 1820–1977* (Hamilton, 1978). Bibliographic essays are included in Gregory Kealey and Peter Warrian, eds., *Essays in Canadian Working Class History* (Toronto, 1976); Daphne Read, ed., *The Great War and Canadian Society* (Toronto, 1978); Russell Hann and Gregory Kealey, "Documenting Working Class History," *Archivaria* 4 (1977). In 1980 the Canadian Committee on Labour History published *The Labour Companion: a Bibliography of Canadian Labour History Based on Materials Printed from 1950 to 1975*, compiled by G. Douglas Vaisey (Halifax, 1980), especially useful for references on French-Canadian developments.

8. The federal task force produced twenty-three special reports. See Jamieson, *Times of Trouble*.

9. Interest in collective violence was stimulated by the international spate of writing on the subject. In Canada the theme was dealt with specifically in my "Collective Violence and the Canadian Political Tradition," in *Courts and Trials*, edited by M. Friedland (Toronto, 1975); Michael Cross, "The Shiners' War: Social Violence in the Ottawa Valley in the 1830's," *Canadian Historical Review* (hereafter *CHR*) LIV (1973), and "Stony Monday, 1849: the Rebellion Losses Bill in Bytown," *Ontario History* (Summer 1971); Jean Morrison, "Ethnicity and Violence: the Lakehead Freight Handlers before World War I," in *Essays*, edited by Kealey and Warian. It was also touched upon in studies undertaken by the Centre of Criminology, University of Toronto, and at Carleton University. See Robert Jackson, M.J. Kelly, and T.H. Mitchell, *Collective Conflict, Violence and the Media in Canada, 1976*; Centre of Criminology, University of Toronto, *Report: Workshop on Violence in Canadian Society* (Toronto, 1975). An important analysis of social relationships in the context of military intervention during strikes is Desmond Morton, "Aid to the Civil Power: the Canadian Militia in Support of Social Order," *CHR* LI (1970). See also Don MacGillivray, "Military Aid to the Civil Power: the Cape Breton Experience in the 1920's," *Acadiensis* (Spring 1973).

10. Leo Panitch, *The Canadian State* (Toronto, 1977); Gary Teeple, ed., *Capitalism and the National Question in Canada* (Toronto, 1972); Wallace Clement, *Continental Corporate Power: Economic Linkages between Canada and the United States* (Toronto, 1977), and *The Canadian Corporate Elite: an Analysis of Economic Power* (Toronto, 1975); Tom Naylor, *The History of Canadian Wealth* (Toronto, 1976).

11. *The Canadian Left: a Critical Analysis* (Toronto, 1977).

12. *Canada Investigates Industrialism* (Toronto, 1973).

13. *Essays in Canadian Working Class History* (Toronto, 1976). In addition to Kealey, the essayists were Russell Hann, Harvey Graff, Michael Doucet, Bryan Palmer, Wayne Roberts, Jean Morrison, and David Frank.

14. Ibid., e.g., 9: "This was the period [from the 1890s to the 1920s] in which capitalists decided that they must take minute control over the work process which they had previously left largely to the purview of the skilled workers. They named the new technique 'scientific management.' But this attempt engendered a working-class response, the 'new unionism,' an overtly syndicalist and militant response that led in Canada to the events of 1919 in Winnipeg and later to the events in Cape Breton between 1922 and 1925." This cannot be faulted except for its over-simplification, especially in excluding such variables as regional and industrial characteristics, ethnicity, and leadership. Such non-class factors are, of course, given much attention by other recent studies, including some by people associated with the CCLH, but the emphasis seems to vary inversely to the degree of Marxist commitment.

15. Ibid., 12. Hann's essay on Phillips Thompson is a perceptive discussion of a "brain worker" and labour journalist committed to such goals.

16. "Most Uncommon Common Men: Craft and Culture in Historical Perspective," *L/LT* (1976); "Class Conceptions and Class Conflict . . . 1903–22," *Review of Radical Political Economics* VII (1975); "Discordant Music: Charivaris and Whitecapping in Nineteenth Century North America," *L/LT* (1978); *A Culture in Conflict: Skilled Workers and Industrial Capitalism in Hamilton, Ontario, 1860–1914* (Montreal, 1979).

17. Palmer, like most Canadian labour historians, has not been seduced by cliometrics, seeking rather, "to probe traditional sources." The principal exercise in quantitative analysis of class and social mobility is Michael Katz, *The People of Hamilton, Canada West: Family and Class in a Mid-Nineteenth Century City* (Cambridge, Mass., 1975).

18. Gregory Kealey, "Artisans Respond to Industrialism: Shoemakers, Shoe Factories and the Knights of St. Crispin in Toronto," Canadian Historical Association (hereafter CHA) *Report* (1973), and *Toronto Workers Respond to Industrial Capitalism, 1867–1892* (Toronto, 1980); Craig Heron and Bryan Palmer, "Through the Prism of the Strike: Industrial Conflict in Southern Ontario, 1901–1914," *CHR* LVIII (1977); Edward McKenna, "Unorganized Labour against Management: the Strike at the Chaudière Lumber Mills, 1891," *Histoire sociale/Social History* (Nov. 1972); Wayne Roberts, "Artisans, Aristocrats and Handymen: Politics and Unionism among Toronto Building Trade Workers, 1896–1914," *L/LT* (1976); and "Labour and Reform in Toronto, 1896–1914" (PhD thesis, University of Toronto, 1978); Steven Langdon, *The Emergence of the Canadian Working Class Movement, 1847–75* (Toronto, 1975); James Rinehart, *The Tyranny of Work* (Toronto, 1975). Related to different aspects of the control problem are the following: Bruce Scott, "A Place in the Sun: the Industrial Council at Massey-Harris, 1919–29," *L/LT* (1976); Ian McKay, "Capital and Labour in the Halifax Baking and Confectionery Industry during the last Half of the Nineteenth Century," *L/LT* (1978); John H. Thompson and Allen Seager, "Workers, Growers

and Monopolists: the 'Labour Problem' in the Alberta Beet Sugar Industry during the 1930's," *L/LT* (1978); Sally Zerker, "George Brown and the Printers' Union," *Journal of Canadian Studies* (Feb. 1975); J.H. Tuck, "Union Authority, Corporate Obstinacy and the Grand Trunk Strike of 1910," CHA *Report* (1976); Douglas Baldwin, "A Study in Social Control: the Life of the Silver Miner in Northern Ontario," *L/LT* (1977); John Battye, "The Nine Hour Pioneers: the Genesis of the Canadian Labour Movement," *L/LT* (1979); Leo Johnson, *History of the County of Ontario* (Toronto, 1974); Wallace Clement, "The Subordination of Labour in Canadian Mining," *L/LT* (Spring 1980); Allen Seager, "Minto, New Brunswick: A Study in Canadian Class Relations Between the Wars," *L/LT* (Spring 1980).

19. Kealey leaves no doubt about his Marxist analytical framework, giving specific commendation to Pentland's "The Role of Capital in Canadian Economic Development before 1875," *Canadian Journal of Economics and Political Science* (hereafter *CJEPS*) (1950): 457–74; "Development of a Capitalist Labour Market in Canada," *CJEPS* (1959): 450–61; and "Labour and the Development of Industrial Capitalism in Canada" (PhD thesis, University of Toronto, 1960); and to Ryerson's *Unequal Union* (Toronto, 1968). Perhaps the most original essay published in *Labour/Le Travailleur* to date (1979 issue) is "The Canadian Industrial Relations System: Some Formative Factors," in which the late Professor Pentland summarized the analysis he prepared for the Woods task force on industrial relations. See also Kealey's "H.C. Pentland and Working Class Studies," *Canadian Journal of Political and Social Theory* III (1979).

20. David Jay Bercuson, *Confrontation at Winnipeg: Labour, Industrial Relations and the General Strike* (Montreal, 1974). A briefer recent account of the strike is Kenneth McNaught and David Bercuson, *The Winnipeg Strike: 1919* (Toronto, 1974). The same event as seen day by day in the workers' newspaper is present in Norman Penner, ed., *Winnipeg 1919: the Strikers' Own History of the Winnipeg General Strike* (Toronto, 1975). Two articles on the strike's aftermath are H.C. Pentland, "Fifty Years After," *Canadian Dimension* (July 1969) and J.E. Rae, "The Politics of Conscience: Winnipeg after the Strike," CHA *Report* (1971).

21. *Fools and Wise Men: The Rise and Fall of the One Big Union* (Toronto, 1978). Bercuson discussed other aspects of unionism in "Organized Labour and the Imperial Munitions Board," *Industrial Relations/Relations industrielles* XXVIII, 3 (1973), and "Tragedy at Bellevue: Anatomy of a Mine Disaster," *L/LT* (1978).

22. *Reformers, Rebels and Revolutionaries: the Western Canadian Radical Movement, 1899–1919* (Toronto, 1977); "Arthur Puttee and the Liberal Party," *CHR* LI (1970). A very perceptive article by Gerald Friesen examines the role of the Socialist Party of Canada, arguing that the 1919 strikes "marked the failure, not the victory of the SPC." "Yours in Revolt: the Socialist Party of Canada and the Western Canadian Labour Movement," *L/LT* (1976).

23. *Nationalism, Communism, and Canadian Labour* (Toronto, 1973).

24. "Recent Publications in Canadian Labour History," *History and Social Science Teacher* XIV, 3 (1979).

25. There are exceptions to the reluctance to define and discuss, within the context of labour history, questions which are central to all history. One such occurred at a session of the first North American Labour History Conference at Wayne State University in October 1979. Two papers, one by Terry Copp, "Anti-Communism in a Cold Climate: the I.U.E. in Canada," and other by Irving Abella, "Communism and the Canadian Labour Movement," brought into focus the roles of ideology, pragmatically conceived class interest, national and regional traditions, and leadership.

26. Irving Abella, ed., *On Strike: Six Key Labour Struggles in Canada, 1919–49* (Toronto, 1974). David Kwavnick cast a critical eye on union leaders in *Organized Labour and Pressure Politics: the C.L.C., 1955–68* (Montreal, 1972). A number of articles focussed on particular strikes: Stanley Scott, "A Profusion of Issues: Immigrant Labour, the World War and the Cominco Strike of 1917," *L/LT* (1977); Myer Siemiatycki, "Munitions and Labour Militancy: the 1916 Machinists' Strike," *L/LT* (1978); Alan Seager, "The Pass Strike of 1932," *Alberta History* (Winter 1977); Duart Snow, "The Holmes Foundry Strike in Sarnia, 1937," *Ontario History* (March 1977); Anne B. Woywitka, "The Drumheller Strike of 1919," *Alberta Historical Review* (Winter 1973). Paul McEwan's *Miners and Steelworkers: Labour in Cape Breton* (Toronto, 1976), discusses the strikes of 1909–11. In 1975 the *Labour Gazette* published its seventy-fifth anniversary issue, and remained the best continuing source for organizational developments, current strikes, and government policy — until its untimely demise in 1978.

27. P.E. Trudeau, ed., *The Asbestos Strike* (Toronto, 1974). Most other French-language studies of Quebec labour have not been translated. See, e.g., F. Harvey, ed., *Aspects historiques du mouvement ouvrier au Québec* (Montreal, 1973); Jean Hamelin, ed., *Répertoire des grèves dans la province de Québec au XIXe siècle* (Montreal,

1970); Jacques Rouillard, *Les travailleurs du cotton, 1900–15* (Quebec, 1974), and "Le Québec et le congrès de Berlin, 1902," *L/LT* (1976); Marie Lavigne and Jennifer Stoddart, "Les travailleuses Montréalaises entre les deux guerres," *L/LT* (1977); Alfred Charpentier, "La conscience syndicale lors des grèves du textile en 1937 et de l'amiante en 1949," *L/LT* (1978).

28. Brian Hogan, *Cobalt: Year of the Strike, 1919* (Cobalt, 1978); Laurel MacDowell, "Remember Kirkland Lake: the Effects of the Kirkland Lake Gold Miners' Strike, 1941–42" (PhD thesis, University of Toronto, 1979), and "The Formation of the Canadian Industrial Relations System during World War II," *L/LT* (1978). MacDowell concludes that "because of their wartime experiences, the C.C.L. industrial unions formed a relatively permanent alliance with the C.C.F.," but that "perhaps the most important achievement of this period was in making unions an integral part of the labour relations process at every organized plant," while the grievance procedures made permanent changes in "the status of employees on the shop floor."

29. "Taking on The Grand Trunk: the Locomotive Engineers' Strike of 1876–7," *L/LT* (1977). While fully recognizing the occasions on which a class has acted with inner unity, Morton is equally concerned with other areas of tension which to Marxists tend simply to deflect the maturation of class consciousness. In a presidential address to the Canadian Historical Association he criticized a different class interpretation, that of the late Donald Creighton, observing that: "I was not born in Calgary nor raised in Regina and Winnipeg to worship at the shrine of the C.P.R. For working people, their role in the 'National Dream' was to labour diligently, accept lower wages than south of the border, and rejoice in the Trade Unions Act of 1872 which was, quite literally, a nullity." ("History and Nationality in Canada: Variation on an old Theme," CHA *Historical Papers*, 1979). Some interesting studies of particular phases of the organizing problem are Glen Makahonuk, "Trade Unions in the Saskatchewan Coal Industry, 1907–45," *Saskatchewan History* (Spring 1978); Richard McCandless, "Vancouver's Red Menace of 1935: the Waterfront Situation," *BC Studies* (Summer 1974); Judith Fingard, "The Decline of the Sailor as a Ship Labourer in the Nineteenth Century Timber Ports," *L/LT* (1977); Anthony Thomson, "The Large and Generous View: the Debate on Labour Affiliation in the Canadian Civil Service, 1918–28," *L/LT* (1977); R.A. Miller and Fraser Miller, eds., *Canadian Labour in Transition* (Toronto, 1971); Victor Levant, *Capital and Labour: Partners?* (Toronto, 1971), which discusses the role of company unions; Jacques Rouillard, *Les syndicats nationaux au Québec de 1900 à 1930* (Quebec, 1979), which gives a careful account of the growth and frustration of Quebec "national" unions, and the interaction amongst church-led unions, corporatism, and collective bargaining; Sally Zerker, "A History of the Toronto Typographical Union, 1832–1925" (PhD thesis, University of Toronto, 1972); Rosemary Speirs, "Technological Change and the Railway Unions, 1945–72" (PhD thesis, University of Toronto, 1974); André LeBlanc and James Thwaites, *Le monde ouvrier au Québec: bibliographie retrospective* (Quebec, 1973). The best general account of the context of contemporary unionism is H.D. Woods, Sylvia Ostry, and Mahmood Zaidi, *Labour Policy and Labour Economics in Canada* (Toronto, 1973).

30. *The Anatomy of Poverty: the Condition of the Working Class in Montreal, 1897–1929* (Toronto, 1974) and, as editor, *Industrial Unionism in Kitchener, 1937–47* (Kitchener, 1976); "The Experience of Industrial Unionism in Four Ontario Towns, 1937–47," (CHA paper, 1978).

31. *The Condition of the Working Class in Toronto, 1900–21* (Ottawa, 1979).

32. See, e.g., L.M. Grayson and M. Bliss, eds., *The Wretched of Canada: Letters to R.B. Bennett, 1930–35* (Toronto, 1971); Evelyn Dumas, *The Bitter Thirties in Quebec* (Montreal, 1975); Irving Abella and David Millar, eds., *The Canadian Worker in the Twentieth Century* (Toronto, 1978); Michael Cross, *The Workingman in the Nineteenth Century* (Toronto, 1974); E. Bradwin, *The Bunkhouse Man*, edited by Jean Burnet (Toronto, 1972); ILWU Local 500 Pensioners, *Man Along the Shore* (Vancouver, 1975); Morden Lazarus, *Years of Hard Labour* (Toronto, 1974); Andy Macdonald, *Bread and Molasses* (Toronto, 1976); Tom McEwan, *The Forge Glows Red: from Blacksmith to Revolutionary* (Toronto, 1974); Rolph Knight, *A Very Ordinary Life* (Vancouver, 1974); Christine Kouhi, "Labour and Finnish Immigration to Thunder Bay, 1876–1914," *Lakehead University Review* (Feb., 1976); Alan Seager, "Class Consciousness, Class Anarchy: Three Alberta Coal Towns during the Great Depression," (CHA paper, 1979); John H. Thompson, "Bringing in the Sheaves; the Harvest Excursionists, 1896–1929," *CHR* LIX (1978); Victor Hoar, ed., *Recollections of the On-to-Ottawa Trek by Ronald Liversedge* (Toronto, 1973); Michiel Horn, ed., *The Dirty Thirties: Canadians in the Great Depression* (Toronto, 1972).

33. Joan Sangster, "The 1907 Bell Telephone Strike: Organizing Women Workers," *L/LT* (1978). See also, Veronica Strong-Boag, "The Girl of the New Day: Canadian Working Women in the 1920's," *L/LT*

(1979), which concludes that "For women, inequality in the workplace did not disappear, it merely modernized its forms." Evidence of the continuity of this problem is also in S.M. Trofimenkoff's "One Hundred and Two Muffled Voices: Canada's Industrial Women in 1880's," *Atlantis* (Fall 1977) and reprinted in *Rethinking Canada*, edited by Veronica Strong-Boag and Anita Clair Fellman (Toronto, 1986), and Janice Acton, Penny Goldsmith, and Bonnie Shepherd, eds., *Women at Work: Ontario, 1850–1930* (Toronto, 1974).

34. "Canadian Immigration Policy and the Alien Question, 1896–1919" (PhD thesis, University of Western Ontario, 1973); "Canadian Immigration Policy and the Foreign 'Navvy'," CHA *Historical Papers*, 1972; "Continental European Immigrant Workers in Canada: from Stalwart Peasants to Radical Proletariat," *Canadian Review of Sociology and Anthropology* XII, 1 (1975); *"Dangerous Foreigners": European Immigrant Workers and Labour Radicalism in Canada, 1896–1932* (Toronto, 1979). The Multicultural History Society of Ontario has devoted considerable attention to the question, but usually within the general social history of immigration. See R.F. Harney, "Montreal's King of Italian Labour: a Case Study of Padronism," *L/LT* (1979). See also D.S. Shea, "The Irish Immigrant Adjustment to Toronto, 1840–60," *Canadian Catholic Historical Review* XXXIX (1972).

35. *Indians at Work: an Informal History of Native Indian Labour in British Columbia, 1856–1930* (Vancouver, 1978). Knight includes a very thorough bibliography and a helpful appendix on the "Historical Background to Indian Labour."

36. *Gompers in Canada: a Study in Continentalism before the First World War* (Toronto, 1974).

37. See note 19.

38. Horowitz, *Canadian Labour in Politics*; Young, *Anatomy of a Party*.

39. Supplementing the emphasis on liberal ideology were the sociological interpretations of the Clark-Zakuta category, stressing frontier-metropolis conflict and the personal therapy of membership in "lost cause" groups. See, e.g., Leo Zakuta, *A Protest Movement Becalmed: a Study of Change in the C.C.F.* (Toronto, 1964); S.D. Clark, J.P. Grayson, and Linda Grayson, eds., *Prophesy and Protest: Social Movements in Twentieth Century Canada* (Toronto, 1975); Roger O'Toole, *The Precipitous Path* (Toronto, 1977), which examines the "pathology" of four Toronto political sects.

40. Much of the criticism of the inevitability-of-liberalism determinant was implicit; for specific comment see my "Comment on the *Liberal Tradition in America*" in *Failure of a Dream*, edited by J. Laslett and M. Lipset (New York, 1974), and "The Multi-party System in Canada," in *Essays on the Left*, edited by L. Lapierre et al. (Toronto, 1971). Both *Essays on the Left* and T.O. Lloyd, ed., *Agenda '70* (Toronto, 1968) contain essays on the past and present of democratic socialism.

41. *The Canadian Left: a Critical Analysis* (Toronto, 1977).

42. See, e.g., Mary Jordan's memoir of Bob Russell, *Survival* (Toronto, 1975); Phyllis Clark and William Beeching, eds., *Yours in the Struggle: Reminiscences of Tim Buck* (Toronto, 1977); Oscar Ryan, *Tim Buck: a Conscience for Canada* (Toronto, 1975); Peter H. Weinrich, *A Select Bibliography of Tim Buck* (Toronto, 1974); Tim Buck, *Lenin and Canada* (Toronto, 1970).

43. The best non-Marxist accounts of this turbulent passage are J.T. Saywell, *Quebec '70* (Toronto, 1972), and *The Rise of the Parti Québécois* (Toronto, 1977).

44. For the ideology of the FLQ see Pierre Vallières, *White Niggers of America* (Toronto, 1971). On Péquisite sociology and purposes, see Marcel Rioux, *Quebec in Question* (Toronto, 1971) and René Lévesque, *My Quebec* (Montreal, 1979). A compendium from *This Generation* is Dimitri Roussopoulos, *Quebec and Radical Social Change* (Montreal, 1974). See also, S. Milner and H. Milner, *The Decolonization of Quebec* (Toronto, 1973). For continuing Marxist analysis see publications of Black Rose Press, Montreal, and New Hogtown Press and Progress Books, Toronto. Fernand Ouellet's brilliant portrayal of the social-economic evolution of pre-Confederation Quebec, and especially of the *patriotes*, robbed Papineau of much of his populist clothing and carried the implication that Lévesque nationalism might be something of a replay. See *Le Bas Canada, 1791–1840* (Montreal, 1976); *Histoire économique et sociale du Québec, 1760–1850* (Montreal, 1966); *Social Change and Nationalism*, trans. Patricia Clark (Toronto, 1980). The best Quebec labour bibliography is André Leblanc and James Thwaites, *Le monde ouvrier au Québec: bibliographie retrospective* (Montreal, 1973).

45. In addition to citations in note 10, see Craig Heron, ed., *Imperialism, Nationalism, and Canada* (Toronto, 1977). The best recent book on the nature of a major party from the scholarly left is Reginald Whitaker, *The Government Party* (Toronto, 1977); the most penetrating analysis to date of the relationships

amongst the interests of big business, other class or group interests, and government is Tom Traves, *The State and Enterprise: Canadian Manufacturers and the Federal Government 1917–1931* (Toronto, 1979).

46.   James Laxer and Robert Laxer, *The Liberal Idea of Canada: Pierre Trudeau and the Question of Canada's Survival* (Toronto, 1977).

47.   See Michael Cross, "To the Dartmouth Station: a Worker's Eye View of Labour History," *L/LT* (1976), in which Cross gives a sprightly, if expurgated version of the view of the historical establishment entertained by the Marxist conclave in Dalhousie's history department: "Historians are usually too bloody gutless to let you know what they really think." Professor Grant recently decided to move to Dalhousie from McMaster in protest against the triumph of American academic mores in Hamilton.

48.   The pragmatic left, like the class-culture Marxists, has cast a tolerant eye on its own regional vagaries — as the NDP premier of Saskatchewan called for caution in the general war against Ottawa while *Le Devoir* rejoiced to report that the NDP leader in Quebec would vote "oui" in the referendum. Ironically, the classic 1935 socialist argument for central authority was republished as provincialism was peaking: *Social Planning for Canada* (Toronto, 1975).

49.   I have used the term "Marxism" as if it were fairly well understood, although it is seldom defined by those who denominate themselves by it. I assume that while democratic socialists attribute importance to class consciousness and the essentially inequitable relationships in industrial society, they do not consider class struggle to be the mainspring of history, the total overthrow of existing institutions as either possible or desirable, or parliamentarism as a merely subsidiary tool.

50.   Eugene Forsey, *Freedom and Order: Collected Essays* (Toronto, 1974); F.R. Scott, *Essays on the Constitution*, (Toronto, 1977).

51.   Louis Hartz, *The Liberal Tradition in America* (New York, 1955); C. Vann Woodward, Introduction to *A Comparative Approach to American History* (New York, 1968).

52.   *The Communist Party of Canada: a History* (Toronto, 1975). Avakoumovic's *Socialism in Canada: A Study of the CCF-NDP in Federal Politics* (Toronto, 1978) is extremely impressionistic.

53.   "James Simpson and the Origins of Canadian Social Democracy" (PhD thesis, University of Toronto, 1978). See also Homel's "Fading Beams of the Nineteenth Century: Radicalism and Early Socialism in Canada's 1890's," *L/LT* (Spring 1980), and Allen Mills, "Single Tax, Socialism and the Independent Labour Party of Manitoba: the Political Ideas of F.J. Dixon and S.J. Farmer," *L/LT* (Spring 1980).

54.   *The Social Passion: Religion and Social Reform in Canada, 1914–28* (Toronto, 1971).

55.   I suggest this comparison in "Norman Thomas and the American Consensus," *Canadian Forum* (June-July 1978).

56.   *The Dilemma of Canadian Socialism: the CCF in Ontario* (Toronto, 1973). Even more sceptical is Michael Cross, *The Decline and Fall of a Good Idea: CCF-NDP Manifestoes, 1932–69* (Toronto, 1974).

57.   *William Irvine: The Life of a Prairie Radical* (Toronto, 1979).

58.   *The League for Social Reconstruction: Intellectual Origins of the Democratic Left in Canada, 1930–42* (Toronto, 1980). Diversity and fine political shadings are suggested also in Ramsay Cook, "Henry George and the Poverty of Canadian Progress," CHA *Historical Papers* (1976). Jack Granatstein edited a selection of *Canadian Forum* writings, 1920–70, in *Forum* (Toronto, 1970).

59.   Desmond Morton, *NDP: The Dream of Power* (Toronto, 1974), a brief history suggestive of new research areas; Walter Young, "M.J. Coldwell: the Making of a Social Democrat," *Journal of Canadian Studies* (April 1974). See also Doris French Shackleton, *Tommy Douglas* (Toronto, 1975), and Nelson Wiseman, "A Political History of the Manitoba CCF-NDP" (PhD thesis, University of Toronto, 1975).

60.   Social History of Canada, University of Toronto Press, 1973–; Bliss was succeeded as series editor in 1978 by H.V. Nelles, and new monographs are now being considered alongside edited reprints.

61.   See, e.g., Bryan Palmer's article in reply to Terry Morley, "Working Class Canada: Recent Historical Writing," *Queen's Quarterly* (Winter 1979–80).

62.   *L/LT* (1979), 23. It is possible that if the disciples of Thompson recognized, with the master, the significance of such books as the Bible and *Pilgrim's Progress* in the making of the working class, we would all be much further ahead. It is also conceivable that Thorstein Veblen's North American perceptions might be more helpful in understanding our class relationships than the notes by Gramsci in his Italian prison.

A SENSE OF TIME AND PLACE: THE HISTORIAN'S APPROACH TO CANADA'S URBAN PAST†

GILBERT A. STELTER

"Urban history," according to H.J. Dyos, "is the most newly discovered continent and into the scramble for it goes every kind of explorer."[1] In this sense, anyone who studies the urban past is an urban historian, but this is not to suggest that history as a discipline plays a central part with other disciplines assigned to the role of bit-players. The study of the city, past and present, requires an interdisciplinary approach based on a sound knowledge of what others in the field are doing. The aim of this paper is to outline the role of the historian (narrowly defined) in the study of the urban past in terms of subject matter, conceptualization and methodology. The question is: what can the historian contribute beyond a rather amateurish approach to the increasingly technical methodology employed today? In general, the contribution might be described as a special sense of time and place. In the context of other approaches, it falls somewhere between that of the social scientist interested in discovering general patterns and that of the local historian concerned only with the unique and particular. This rather nebulous middle ground perhaps is best defined by describing what historians think they are doing and by a selective look at what they have done.

The study of urban history in Canada and in Britain is still in its infancy, but interest in the field has grown rapidly in recent years.[2] Also growing is the use of American concepts, for the study of urban history is most highly developed in the United States, although it should be noted that the most significant approach to Canadian urban history — the metropolitan thesis — is essentially homegrown. Canadian historians of past decades could hardly be accused of having overemphasized the place of the city in Canadian history. In fact, as a group they were probably comparable to those Australian historians John McCarty describes, "who could be removed only forcibly from the Sydney bars they loved so well to the great outback about which they wrote so well."[3] Their neglect may be attributed to a general view that cities have not been a significant feature of Canadian development on the assumption that cities were relatively small and their populations constituted only a tiny proportion of the total Canadian population prior to the twentieth century.[4] But then how does one account for the slow growth of interest in the field in Britain, one of the most highly urbanized

†From Gilbert A. Stelter and Alan F.J. Artibise, eds., *The Canadian City: Essays on Urban History*, Carleton Library no. 109 (Toronto: McClelland and Stewart, 1977): 420–41. This paper is a slightly altered version of one presented at the fifty-second annual meeting of the Canadian Historical Association, Kingston, June 1973, and printed as "The Historian's Approach to Canada's Urban Past," *Histoire sociale/Social History* VII, 13 (May 1974): 5–22.

countries in the world by the late nineteenth century? It may have something to do with the fundamental question about what is the legitimate unit of historical inquiry. The positivist tradition — a denial of the possibility of studying anything but individuals, their actions, and relations — has been strong in Britain and Canada, theoretically undercutting the possibility of studying a social whole or collective such as a city. On the other hand, American historians were influenced by the great Chicago school of sociologists of the 1920s and seem to have been less suspicious of the social scientists' attempt to comprehend the human and physical scale of the city by the process of abstraction

One indication of the recent interest in urban history is the proliferation of newsletters in the field, reflecting in part the demand for up-to-date information about the work of like-minded souls elsewhere. The earliest and also the most successful of these newsletters is the *Urban History Newsletter* (University of Leicester), edited by H.V. Dyos. *The Urban History Group Newsletter* (University of Wisconsin, Milwaukee), superseded in 1975 by *Urbanism — Past and Present*, provides a useful bibliographic service, but the *Historical Methods Newsletter* is a better source for what is going on in the United States, especially among the quantitatively-oriented. A Canadian newsletter, the *Urban History Review* (National Museum of Man), edited by John Taylor and Del Muise (and since 1975 by Alan Artibise), has been published since early in 1972, specializing in brief articles about research projects, bibliographical surveys, and descriptions of source collections.

In the past decade, several conferences have been organized around urban history and are a type of barometer of the changing emphasis within the field. The published proceedings of the 1961 Conference on the City in History sponsored by Harvard and the Massachusetts Institute of Technology indicated an interest in theoretical speculation about where urban history should go; but most of the articles seem remarkably dated now. The results of a conference of the British History Group held in 1966 showed an emphasis on the physical and aesthetic, perhaps because urban history in Britain has developed in closer cooperation with geography than is the case in the United States where sociology has had the greater effect. An example of this is the 1968 Yale conference on nineteenth-century cities whose published report was interestingly subtitled *Essays in the New Urban History*. What was new in this "sociological history" was an emphasis on social structure and mobility studies, on quantifiable sources rather than the traditional archival sources, and a concern for the lower classes and minority groups.[5] An attempt at an interdisciplinary approach to the urban past brought geographers and historians together at the Historical Urbanization in North America Conference at York University early in 1973. The conference, if nothing else, seemed to illustrate the fact that geographers and historians have some common interests and methods, read some of the same material, and sometimes even understand each other (that is, they now use the same jargon).[6] Sessions on urban history at annual meetings of major historical associations have been another vehicle for presenting the results of recent research. For example, the Canadian Urban History Committee, a standing committee of the Canadian Historical Association, has been sponsoring sessions at the association's annual meetings since 1971.[7]

In spite of the interest and activity in the field of urban history, a succession of commentators have found little reason to rejoice. Many decry the lack of any apparent direction in the field for no generally accepted conceptual framework has emerged.[8] The assumption seems to be that such a framework is both possible and desirable. At any rate, most students who have suffered through an urban history course would agree with Sam Bass Warner that "except to the most imaginative reader, the usual shelf of urban history books looks like a line of disconnected local histories."[9] The situation, however, can hardly be attributed only to the perversity and stupidity of historians but is partly due to the nature of the historical discipline itself. Present in any branch of history are questions of description versus analysis, thematic versus wholistic approaches, or the extent to which models, concepts, and techniques should be borrowed from other disciplines. In addition, urban history presents some special questions. Perhaps the most vigorously debated issue recently is whether urban history should be concerned with the history of cities, as has generally been the case, or whether it should deal with the process of urbanization — the social processes that create cities. The case for the more traditional approach has been effectively argued by Oscar Handlin who has called for

> . . . fewer studies of the city in history than the history of cities. However useful a general theory of the city may be, only the detailed tracing of an immense range of variables, in context, will illuminate the dynamics of the processes. . . . We can readily enough associate such gross phenomena as the growth of population and the rise of the centralized state, as technological change and the development of modern industry, as the disruption of the traditional household and the decline of corporate life. But *how* these developments unfolded, what was the causal nexus among them, we shall only learn when we make out the interplay among them by focussing upon a city specifically in all its uniqueness.[10]

Eric Lampard has championed the cause of the macro-analytical approach by calling for historians to use two related paths to urban history; first, an emphasis on the process of urbanization as a phenomenon of population concentration resulting in an increase in the number and size of cities, and second, the comparative study of communities in a framework of human ecology, focussing on the changing structures and organization of communities in four specific and quantifiable references — population and environment mediated by technology and organization.[11] Lampard has not been without influence, yet many historians reject his proposals partly because they do not have the methodological capability of dealing with the processes he suggests and also because Lampard's approach is of only marginal value in dealing with the kinds of questions in which most historians are really interested — the nature of individual cities within special cultural contexts at specified times.[12]

Even if there were agreement on what should be studied, the problem remains of defining elusive terms such as "city" and "urban." So does the question of the role of the city in society. Is the city itself the source of social change as Arthur Schlesinger and others have argued in an attempt to replace the Turnerian frontier thesis with an urban interpretation of history? Or is the city only the result of larger forces in society?[13] A series of related questions concerns the purpose of studying urban history. Should the urban past be studied for its own sake or with a view to illuminating national history? Should the purpose of urban history be to help formulate historical social theory, that is, to shed light on the larger question of how society is put together and how it changes?[14] Or is the historical dimension studied in order to achieve a better understanding of the present? Sam Warner seems to think so. In the introduction to this study of suburbanization in Boston, Warner claims that "if the city is ever to become susceptible to rational planning there must be a common understanding of how the city is built."[15]

In retrospect, the apparent chaotic state of urban history is hardly surprising when one considers the complexity of the subject matter. Rather than decrying the fact that so many different approaches are being used, historians should instead regard this as a positive sign, for urban history has become one of the most exciting branches of the historical discipline with its practitioners in the vanguard of rethinking the nature of history as a field of study.

A discussion of the various approaches of urban historians, especially in the field of Canadian history, is best divided into two principal categories.[16] The first consists of those studies which deal with historical processes or events in an urban setting — anything that has happened in cities — without too much worry for what is "urban" in the subject. The second category includes work in which authors have concerned themselves with what is generically "urban" in their subject. The city is usually considered as a special kind of environment with unique patterns of social organization. These categories are somewhat similar to those Harvey Lithwick uses in distinguishing between problems *in* the city such as poverty, problems which are not necessarily unique to urban environments, and problems *of* the city such as scarce urban space, problems which are generated by the process of urbanization.[17]

The bulk of what is generally considered to be urban history in Canada (or elsewhere for that matter) fits into the first category, made up primarily of urban biographies and theme studies. The criticism which has been levelled at most of the work in this category is similar to recent criticisms of social history in general, of which urban history is often regarded as a spin-off.[18] Social history for too long has simply been that area of history that is left over, that is, the study of that which is neglected after the more traditional areas of history have staked out their claims. In the same sense, some historians have dealt with neglected events in history which happened to take place in cities and thus are urban historians. They do not, however, question what it is that is urban in their study.

The often maligned urban biography, however, sometimes has qualities which are missing in supposedly more sophisticated approaches to urban history. A distinguishing characteristic of good urban biography is an attempt to relate the complex facets of a modern city, and this concern for the totality of the urban experience is usually not present in thematic studies. Among the most successful American biographical examples are Blake McKelvey's Rochester, Bessie Pierce's Chicago, and Constance Green's Washington. In this same tradition, although much less detailed, is John Cooper's *Montreal* (1969), in which the relationship between various aspects of urban life are explored — transportation, municipal government, physical expansion, the nature of society, and social organization. A host of other biographies are less successful as urban history in that they tend to be narratives of virtually anything of interest that went on within a city's boundaries. Yet these often represent the tradition of local history at its best with carefully assembled masses of information about economic development, politics, and cultural activities.[19] Of the older biographies, several warrant mention in that they have become classics and have influenced all subsequent accounts. The chief of these is the seventeenth-century account by Dollier de Casson, *History of Montreal, 1640–1672*, and for early nineteenth-century Montreal, Newton Bosworth's *Hochelaga Depicta* (1839). For Toronto, Henry Scadding's *Toronto of Old* (1873) is still one of the most important sources on the early city.[20]

A second group of publications within the first category deals with a variety of themes — economic, social, political, and physical history in the context of cities. In the absence of any adequate theory of the modern city, it is hardly surprising that single-factor investigations would be the usual form of urban history.

The economic development of Canadian cities has received considerable attention with some of the best work emphasizing the role of the business élite in a city's commercial expansion. Conceptually, this is more than business history in an urban setting, valuable as that may be; in the research of J.M.S. Careless and his students, city growth is generally seen as the interaction of the decision-making of dynamic individuals or groups and technological and population change.[21] The rivalry between aspiring towns and cities for trade and transportation has not captured the imagination of Canadian historians to the degree that the subject has been examined in the United States, but studies of Montreal versus Toronto, Quebec versus Montreal, and Vancouver versus Seattle are examples of some of the most volatile rivalries.[22] The way in which cities promoted themselves, usually through a board of trade, in order to attract investment and immigration, has also been studied.[23] To a very great extent, Canadian urban development has been tied to the changing forms of transportation, from the sailing ships of the colonial period to the canals and railroads of the nineteenth century, but, surprisingly, the subject is only beginning to be examined thoroughly.[24] Another aspect of economic development — industrialization — has received only slight scrutiny; among the exceptions are a general analysis of manufacturing in late nineteenth-century central Canada and studies of shipbuilding in Saint John and Quebec.[25]

The study of urban society until recently was confined to an interest in the "impact" or "problems" approach to life in cities or to rather pedestrian accounts of cultural institutions such as the church or school. As in the United States, however, a systematic social history has become the rage, inspired by the publication of Stephan Thernstrom's *Poverty and Progress* (1964), and receiving a sort of *ex cathedra* status with the appearance of Thernstrom and Richard Sennett's *Nineteenth-Century Cities* (1969). Some critics of this new approach have pointed to the "over-reliance on unrefined demographic data, the tedium imposed by the jargon of much of this writing, and its characteristic failure to deal with the human side of society — with, in a word, *soul.*"[26] Also relevant is the criticism of

Sam Warner; in a recent review of *Nineteenth-Century Cities*, he pointed out: "These essays are the new *social* history. . . . Many are not urban history because the urban dimensions of the subjects investigated were not a major concern for their authors." By "urban dimension," Warner meant the inclusion of "the time, place and role of . . . cities and towns in the larger context of the shifting national network of cities."[27] On the other hand, it must be noted that this group has made a significant contribution to our understanding of urban society, even though much of their work is as yet preliminary. Then too, they have made a great effort to develop a common methodology and in particular to use common terms and a common manner of presentation to allow a systematic comparison of results from place to place.

The major Canadian example of this approach is the large-scale "Canadian Social History Project" directed by Michael Katz in which mid-nineteenth-century Hamilton is used as a case study.[28] A feature of this project is that information is coded on every individual rather than on merely a sampling. In Katz's view, the most significant early findings are that transiency and social inequality were present to a greater extent in mid-nineteenth-century cities than has been imagined. The project has received considerable attention because of the sophisticated quantitative methodology which has been developed. Equally important is the fact that the project is the first major historical examination of the class structure of Canadian society, a subject that has been largely ignored by Canadian historians.[29] The few previous studies, such as John Cooper's description of the social structure of Montreal in the 1850s, lack the methodological and conceptual rigor which characterizes the Hamilton study.[30] On the other hand, one misses Cooper's strong sense of time and place and humanistic concern for personality in Katz's analysis. Because of the understandable impact that the Hamilton study is making in Canadian urban history, it may be necessary to point out the danger of assuming that the findings for Hamilton typify the Canadian urban experience. It should be kept in mind that Hamilton was a very young and small city (only 14,000 in 1851), located on the western frontier, and hardly out of the frontier stage of development at a time when Montreal for example, had a population of over 50,000 and had been in existence for two hundred years.

The demographic tradition in the study of urban population based on Adna Weber's great *The Growth of Cities in the Nineteenth Century* (1899) has had few exponents among Canadian historians. For example, not one of the important general surveys of the size and composition of the Canadian urban population is by an historian.[31] Some of the studies of the population of individual cities warrant mention, however. Norbert MacDonald's comparison of the population of Vancouver and Seattle indicates, among other things, the effect of a national boundary on immigration policy and thus on the character of the population. Louise Dechêne's work on early Montreal has shown that Montreal was far smaller than census estimates have indicated and that it played a less significant role (in relation to Quebec City) in eighteenth-century French Canada than has usually been assumed.[32]

Other aspects of urban society which have been examined include topics we have traditionally associated with the field of social history. Among these are the "immigrant adjustment" studies, usually dealing with the post-famine Irish immigration,[33] the institutional reaction to poverty and other social problems, and the larger questions of reform and social welfare.[34] Surprisingly, there has been little historical research on the relations between French and English language groups in Canadian cities, even though the topic has elicited a good deal of interest at the national level.

In comparison with the literature available on other aspects of Canadian urban development, that on urban politics and government is relatively spare. The standard political science studies such as K.G. Crawford's *Canadian Municipal Government* (1954) usually have one chapter on historical development, but emphasize the formal powers and structure of municipal administration and not the question of who governs and why. The historical field is not entirely barren, however, with the role of the élite being a particular subject of interest. Guy Bourassa's study of the composition of the political élite in Montreal after 1840 shows how the basis of their power changed from that of wealth in business to support from either of the two major ethnic groups.[35] The struggle in early nineteenth-century Halifax between the old merchant oligarchy and an economically rising reform group has been examined by David Sutherland.[36] In early Calgary, according to Max Foran, the business and professional interests dominated the municipal government but apparently embodied the community's aspirations by enthusiastically promoting local development and defending the community's interests against outside forces.[37]

Canadian urban government appears to have escaped some of the worst excesses of their later nineteenth-century American counterparts. Why this should have been the case has intrigued a number of political scientists, chief among whom was Morley Wickett. Writing in 1906, Wickett argued that differences were due to the slower growth rate of Canadian cities, the relative homogeneity of the Canadian urban population (he wrote from Toronto), the simplicity of local government structures based on the British model, the greater respect for authority, non-partisan politics, and especially the relatively restricted municipal franchise.[38] On the other hand, another commentator, W.B. Munro, claimed that by 1929 Canadian cities were moving away from their English origins toward the American model in the form and spirit of the governments.[39] A recent study of the nonpartisan tradition in Canadian urban politics suggests that the tradition developed not as a matter of principle but because the relatively small scale and homogeneity of Canadian cities did not create a large enough area of disagreement over goals to maintain party interest.[40] Unfortunately, historians have not yet documented or refuted these generalizations.

A final theme which warrants some mention is that of the physical city. Several topics within this general theme, such as the history of architecture, town planning and housing, hold particular promise for the study of the urban past. Historians appear to agree that changing tastes in architectural building styles tell us a great deal about the character and aspirations of the people of a community. Generalizations in the field, however, must be regarded as tentative, for architectural historians are a notoriously individualistic lot, devastatingly critical of each other's judgements about individual buildings or the aesthetic qualities of certain architectural styles. What is "light, fanciful and imaginative" to one is "ostentatious and imitative" to another. Most reliable for the novice is the broad perspective of Alan Gowans. An example of his approach is his description of the changing building styles in nineteenth-century Toronto. He distinguishes between the early nineteenth-century Georgians who thought of architecture as the art of building well and the Victorians who subordinated simplicity and functional convenience to an architecture thought of as a kind of symbolic language with styles borrowed from other ages.[41]

The architectural history of individual Canadian cities is still in the pioneering stage, but studies such as Eric Arthur's delightful *Toronto, No Mean City* (1964) are useful commentaries on the changing physical qualities of a city. From the urban historian's point of view, however, most surveys of a city's architectural history read like the defensive briefs of architectural preservation committees. Even Eric Arthur tends to emphasize the monumental public buildings to the exclusion of the ordinary structures of a period. When homes are discussed, they are the mansions of the wealthy, not the great majority of middle and lower income homes which more truly characterized the city. Then, too, most of these studies deal with individual buildings and not with the streetscapes which gave a particularly urban flavor to the Georgian and Victorian periods of city development.[42]

The colonial nature of the nineteenth-century Canadian urban society (and probably much of twentieth-century society as well) is evident in the absence of indigenous building forms and in the continued reliance on architectural styles from the outside. The same situation apparently held true for the development of town planning, for the earliest layout and later planning of Canadian communities was determined by ideas from abroad. Several historians have suggested that the differences in original design of the towns reflected the particular character of the imperial power. In *Town Planning in Frontier America* (1969) John Reps describes the origins of the towns of Nouvelle-France as typically French, for the choice of site and the layout of the towns was left entirely to the individuals who had been granted trading or settlement rights. The result was actually the absence of planning, with Quebec developing as a compact non-linear town and Montreal as a linear town because of topography. He ignores Louisbourg, which more resembled the British garrison towns like Halifax and Toronto, which were set up with a gridiron plan directly on the orders of colonial authorities.[43] An explanation of why the British used the gridiron plan in particular is given by Peter Oberlander in his description of Col. Richard Moody's role as site selector and townplanner in British Columbia in the 1850s. Moody relentlessly used the gridiron despite the rough terrain partly because of his cultural baggage — regular and geometric patterns were fashionable in England — but also because it was easier to divide and sell land in this way and because the crudity of surveying at that time made schemes taking topography into account very difficult.[44]

In the early twentieth century, a town planning craze imported the "city beautiful" and "garden city" movements to Canada. The intellectual basis of this interest has been well described in an important article on the larger question of urban reform by Paul Rutherford.[45] The most important import during this period undoubtedly was the British planner Thomas Adams, who became the town planning advisor to the Commission of Conservation in Ottawa for seven years. Very little has been written about his role in Canadian planning except for Alan Armstrong's article outlining Adams' success in establishing a legal framework for planning in most of the provinces.[46] For an appreciation of his planning philosophy, which included the idea that urban and rural planning go hand in hand, one is forced to go back to his *Rural Planning and Development* (1917), *Outline of Town and City Planning* (1935), and his numerous articles and reports.[47]

The study of the physical city raises the question of sources, for most historians tend to rely on the written record to the virtual exclusion of visual records except for illustrative purposes. Canadian historians may find the geographer M.R.G. Conzen's guide to the use of town plans in urban history a bit esoteric (he uses British medieval town plans as an example),[48] but sources of this sort abound for the study of Canadian cities. For example, the National Map Collection of the Public Archives in Ottawa houses hundreds of historical maps and plans for each major city. Yet the demand for urban maps from this collection from interior decorators has probably exceeded that from historians.[49] Visual evidence such as drawings, prints, and photographs have been used even less often, although notable exceptions exist such as Gustave Lanctôt's beautiful "Images et figures de Montréal sous la France, 1642–1763" (1943).[50]

The literature discussed above dealt with cities or life in cities, but rarely with urban history as distinguished from social, economic, political or architectural history in the context of cities. A second group of publications provides a rough sort of second category in which the city is regarded as a special kind of social environment with unique internal and external patterns of organization. Two elements within this larger group merit attention, one of which emphasizes the metropolitan concept and the other the city building process. Both have been influenced by the tradition of the ecological sociologists and accept the necessity of studying the so-called "ecological complex" — the key variables of population, environment, technology, and organization — but both reject the determinism of the ecological school which omits elements of value. While the ecologists take the aggregate as their frame of reference, these historians emphasize the human and accidental, the contingencies of events and personalities.

The concept of metropolitanism has been popular in Canada presumably because the role of a few cities has been more apparent than in the United States where the frontier thesis of Frederick Jackson Turner held sway for such a long time. In a sense the framework for the use of the concept in Canada was laid by the Laurentian school of historians — Innis, Creighton, Lower, and others — although their emphasis was on staples, not cities. The direct intellectual basis for the concept, however, was the work of the Canada-born and educated economic historian, Norman S.B. Gras, who, in his *Introduction to Economic History* (1922), foreshadowed some of the main ideas of the ecologists. Gras emphasized the mutual dependence of the metropolis and hinterland and outlined four economic stages of metropolitan growth: a city began its growth as a marketing center, developed a manufacturing complex, became the hub of a communications network, and finally emerged as the focus of a financial system. The Gras model was rather rigidly applied by Donald C. Masters in his *The Rise of Toronto, 1850–1890* (1947), in which he traced the growth of Toronto's domination of Ontario and its competition with Montreal for hegemony over the broader Canadian hinterland. Not only was Masters' work a pioneering study in that a city's development was examined in the light of a major theoretical concept, but by attempting to relate social and cultural development ot the city's stages of economic development, he recognized an important principle — that economic changes in a city directly affect the nature of life in that city.[51]

The theoretical development of the metropolitan concept, especially the metropolis-hinterland relationship, is usually associated with J.M.S. Careless who first suggested the significance of the metropolitan interpretation for Canadian history in a seminal article in 1954.[52] Careless described the metropolitan relationship between cities as a feudal-like chain of vassalage, with Winnipeg, for example, tributary to Montreal but serving as the metropolis of a large region of its own in the prairie west. Montreal, in turn, was dependent on London, the major metropolis. This sort of interpretation, of course, is remarkably similar in outline to that of various theories about the way cities are connected to each other in a hierarchical system. The difference lies in what factors are emphasized in explaining the location and growth of cities. Historians like Careless have generally been critical of deterministic, mechanical doctrines of objective necessity, preferring instead a humanistic explanation in which the subjective traits of individuals or groups and the contingencies of time and place are not overlooked.

Careless has also considered the nature of the relationship between the metropolis and its hinterland. He has suggested that what is often described as regionalism could be better expressed in terms of metropolitanism, for "regions usually center on metropolitan communities, which largely organize them, focus their views and deal with outside metropolitan forces on their behalf."[53] This point has been illustrated in his description of the role of Saint John, Halifax, and St. John's in the development of Atlantic Canada in the latter half of the nineteenth century. While he shows how the metropolitan communities dominated their hinterlands, Careless argues that the two are mutually dependent. By implication at least, this raises the question of whether urban historians can legitimately study cities or life in cities without placing cities in their regional context or seeing them as part of a unit with their hinterland.

In addition to the work of Careless, the metropolitan concept has been applied to some cities and to some of the larger questions of Canadian history by a number of scholars. A good example of the former is Ruben Bellan's thesis on the rise of Winnipeg in which the author showed how objective factors such as strategic location and the development of western agriculture were combined with subjective factors such as the dynamic local leadership which secured the transcontinental railroad, won discriminatory freight rates, and saw to it that Winnipeg became the headquarters of the grain trade.[54] More generally, A.R.M. Lower recently has returned to the metropolitan theme which had been implied in his earlier works. In several rather poetic articles, he looks at some of the universal aspects of what he regards as two separate ways of life, that of the metropolitan and that of the provincial.[55] What Lower is suggesting is really something similar to the approach of the ecologist Robert Park who saw the city as a state of mind and a body of customs and traditions.[56]

The other significant approach in the second category is an emphasis upon the city-building process. In comparison with the influential metropolitan approach, the amount of work of this type done on Canadian cities is still slight but will probably increase substantially in the future. In general, this approach could be described as an attempt, in the tradition of Patrick Geddes and Lewis Mumford, to relate environmental and social change. The city is regarded as an artifact or physical container within which complex human and institutional relationships are established. In the work of one of the leading exponents of this approach, Sam Warner, a major concern has been to place social differentiation and its relationship to spatial distribution in the context of changing technology, especially improved mass public transportation: *Streetcar Suburbs* (1962); *The Private City* (1968).

One of the most important studies of a Canadian city in this tradition is Peter Goheen's *Victorian Toronto, 1850 to 1900; Pattern and Process of Growth* (1970). Goheen, an urban geographer, has attempted to apply some of the research techniques being used by students of contemporary cities to an historical subject. Goheen follows Warner's general thesis that the social geography of the city of 1860 was almost the reverse of the late nineteenth- and early twentieth-century city. Thus he finds that the social landscape of Toronto before the 1850s was a jumble of confusion. Commercial, industrial, and residential districts were tightly intermixed. Class distinctions were clearly drawn, but rich and poor lived in close proximity. All of this was changed after the 1860s in a period of rapid growth, industrialization, and improved public transportation. It was now possible to separate place of residence from place of work. Social differences slowly became translated into spatial segregation by economic rank.

While Goheen's work is valuable to the urban historian, some questions must be raised about his findings. It might well be that differentiation was more apparent in late nineteenth-century Toronto than in the early city. But what constitutes differentiation is surely a relative matter, depending on the size of the community and on attitudes. Obviously people cannot live as far apart in a small town, but they can still feel they are living apart. Whether attitudes about this sort of social segregation changed during the nineteenth century has not been examined. At any rate, some studies of the spatial arrangements of other Canadian cities suggest that differentiation by function and residentially by class and ethnicity existed long before the middle of the nineteenth century.[57]

The only detailed study of a Canadian city by an historian in which the Warner model is used is Alan Artibise's book on early Winnipeg.[58] Like other work in this tradition, this is not a definitive biography for many important events in Winnipeg's early history are not dealt with. But it is biographical in a specialized sense, for an attempt is made to relate the various factors that went into the process of creating Winnipeg's social and physical structure. As such, it is a useful complement to Bellan's work on Winnipeg's economic development. In general terms, Artibise's findings are similar to those Goheen describes for Toronto except that by 1914 Winnipeg was a more highly differentiated community — physically and socially — than Toronto where the population was relatively homogeneous.

The methodological differences apparent in the Goheen and Artibise studies are illustrative of the different emphasis of the disciplines of geography and history in their approach to the urban past. Goheen is primarily concerned with the population in aggregate terms in the ecological tradition. The result is a series of sophisticated tables and maps showing the changing location of various groupings based on occupations, religion, value of property, and so on. Artibise, by comparison, tends to stress the role of individual and group decisions, such as those of the commercial élite who controlled the municipal corporation, in determining the character of the city. The result is a more distinct image of a people and a city.

It would not be difficult to conclude this discussion of the nature and state of urban history — and of Canadian urban history in particular — on a negative note. There is, for instance, a marked absence of a conceptual framework or of comparative work. Many obvious topics have been ignored, while too many cities have yet to find their biographers. Still the growing activity in the field, the increased sophistication in methodology, and the genuine interest in interdisciplinary communication should lead instead to optimism about the place of the historical dimension in urban studies, and of the historian's role in studying the urban past.

Probably the approach which offers the greatest scope for the urban historian, in addition to theme studies and general analyses of the process of urbanization, is the study of the individual community. Based on the assumption that a community's life has meaning not discernible by a study of fragmentary portions only, this involves seeing a community as a whole and relating the parts to the larger context. This further necessitates combining local and universal interests. The urban historian, with feet in the twin camps of history and urban studies, is grounded in local history, seeing a community in its particularity and uniqueness and at the same time aware of the general and comparative aspects of the subject matter. Finally this involves an appreciation of the way in which human factors of personality and decision-making combine with large-scale, faceless social forces in the development of a community.

Notes

1. "Agenda for Urban Historians" in *The Study of Urban History*, edited by H.J. Dyos (London, 1968), 6.
2. Among the many excellent examples are essays by Dyos, Bédarida, and Checkland in *The Study of Urban History*; Eric Lampard, "American Historians and the Study of Urbanization," *American Historical*

Review 67 (1961): 49–61; Dwight W. Hoover, "The Divergent Paths of American Urban History," *American Quarterly* 20 (1968): 296–317; Charles Glaab, "The Historian and the American City: A Bibliographic Survey," *The Study of Urbanization*, edited by Philip M. Hau and Leo F. Schnore (New York, 1965).

3. "Australian Capital Cities in the Nineteenth Century," *Australian Economic History Review* 10 (1970): 107.

4. I have argued against the validity of the assumption in "From Colonial Outposts to Cities: Some General Characteristics of Canadian Urban History Before 1850" (paper presented at Historical Urbanization in North America Conference (hereafter HUNAC), York University, Jan. 1973).

5. Proceedings of the conferences were published as: Oscar Handlin and John Burchard, eds., *The Historian and the City* (Cambridge, 1963); Dyos, ed., *The Study of Urban History*; Stephen Thernstrom and Richard Sennet, eds., *Nineteenth-Century Cities, Essays in the New Urban History* (New Haven, 1969).

6. The proceedings of the conference, in the form of lengthy abstracts, will appear in the York University Discussion Paper Series.

7. The 1971 session at Memorial University was reported in the *Urban History Review* 1 (1972): 19–23; for a report of the 1972 session at McGill University, see the *Urban History Newsletter* (Leicester) 18 (1972): 13–15.

8. The most devastating critic has been Eric Lampard, especially in his "American Historians and the Study of Urbanization," but see also Roy Lubove, "The Urbanization Process: An Approach to Historical Research," reprinted in *American Urban History*, edited by Alexander Callow (New York, 1969).

9. "If All the World Were Philadelphia: A Scaffolding For Urban History, 1774–1930," *American Historical Review* 74 (1968): 27.

10. "The Modern City as a Field of Historical Study," 26.

11. For a more detailed explanation of this approach, see Lampard's "American Historians and the Study of Urbanization" and "The Dimensions of Urban History: A Footnote to the 'Urban Crisis'," *Pacific Historical Review* 39 (1970): 261–79.

12. See, for example, Michael Frisch, *Town Into City: Springfield, Massachusetts, and the Meaning of Community, 1840–1880* (Cambridge, 1972), 3–4.

13. Arthur M. Schlesinger, "The City in American Civilization" in *Paths to the Present* (New York, 1949); William Diamond, "On the Dangers of an Urban Interpretation of History," in *Historiography and Urbanization*, edited by Eric F. Goldman (Baltimore, 1941).

14. Samuel P. Hays, "Social Structure in the New Urban History" (paper presented at HUNAC, York University, 1973).

15. *Streetcar Suburbs, The Process of Growth in Boston, 1870–1900* (Cambridge, 1962), viii. The purpose of having the past illuminate the present is even more obvious in his recent *The Urban Wilderness: A History of the American City* (New York, 1972).

16. Bibliographical essays on the literature in Canadian urban history include two by Frederick H. Armstrong: "Urban History in Canada," *Urban History Group Newsletter* 28 (1969): 1–10; and "Urban History in Canada: Present State and Future Prospects," *Urban History Review* 1 (1972): 11–14. For Quebec see: Yves Martin, "Urban Studies in French Canada," in *French Canadian Society*, edited by Marcel Rioux and Yves Martin (Toronto, 1964); and Paul André Linteau, "L'histoire urbaine au Québec: bilan et tendances," *Urban History Review* 1 (1972): 7–10. For general bibliographies, see Gilbert A. Stelter, *Canadian Urban History: A Selected Bibliography* (Sudbury, 1972), and M.A. Lessard, "Bibliographie des villes du Québec," *Recherches sociographiques* 9 (Jan.–Aug. 1968): 143–209. Several bibliographies are now available listing the detailed material on individual cities. The best example is Paul-André Linteau, Jean Thivierge et al, *Montréal au 19ᵉ siècle, bibliographie* (Montreal, 1972).

17. *Urban Canada, Problems and Prospects* (Ottawa, 1970), 13–16.

18. Samuel P. Hays, "A Systematic Social History," in *American History, Retrospect and Prospect*, edited by G.A. Billias and G.N. Grob (New York, 1971).

19. In this category I would rank: G.P. de T. Glazebrook, *The Story of Toronto* (Toronto, 1971); Robert Rumilly, *Histoire de Montréal*, 3 vols. (Montreal, 1970–72); Kathleen Jenkins, *Montreal, Island City of the St. Lawrence* (New York, 1966); Marjorie Campbell, *A Mountain and a City, The Story of Hamilton* (Toronto, 1966); Lucien Brault, *Ottawa* (Ottawa, 1946). More popularly written but useful are: Thomas Raddall, *Halifax, Warden of the North* (London, 1950); J.A. Roy, *Kingston, The King's Town* (Toronto, 1966); Leslie

Roberts, *Montreal, From Mission City to World City* (Toronto, 1969); Wilfred Eggleston, *The Queen's Choice* (Ottawa, 1961).

20. Dollier de Casson, *History of Montreal, 1640–72*, translated by Ralph Flenley (New York, 1928); Newton Bosworth, *Hochelaga Depicta: The Early History and Present State of the City and Island of Montreal* (Montreal, 1839); Henry Scadding, *Toronto of Old*, abridged and edited by F.H. Armstrong (Toronto, 1966).

21. "The Business Community in the Early Development of Victoria, British Columbia," in *Canadian Business History: Selected Studies, 1497–1971*, edited by David S. Macmillan (Toronto, 1972); "The Development of the Winnipeg Business Community, 1870–1890," *Transactions of the Royal Society of Canada*, 4, 8 (1970): 239–54. See also Gerald Tulchinsky, "The Montreal Business Community, 1837–1863" in *Canadian Business History*; Frederick H. Armstrong, "George J. Goodhue, Pioneer Merchant of London, Upper Canada," *Ontario History* 63 (1971): 217–32; Henry C. Klassen, "L.H. Holton, Montreal Businessman and Politician, 1817–1867" (Ph.D. dissertation, University of Toronto, 1970); T.W. Acheson, "The Nature and Structure of York Commerce in the 1820's," *Canadian Historical Review* (hereafter *CHR*) 50 (1969): 406–28.

22. D.C. Masters, "Toronto vs. Montreal, The Struggle for Financial Hegemony," *CHR* 22 (June 1941): 133–46; Fernand Ouellet, "Papineau et la rivalité Québec-Montréal, 1820–1840," *Revue d'Histoire de l'Amérique française* 13 (Dec. 1959): 311–37; Norbert Macdonald, "Seattle, Vancouver and the Klondike," *CHR* 49 (1968): 234–46.

23. Fernand Ouellet, *Histoire de la Chambre de commerce de Québec* (Quebec, 1959); Alan Artibise, "Advertising Winnipeg: The Campaign for Immigrants and Industry, 1874–1914," *Manitoba Historical Society Transactions* 3, 27 (1970–71); Douglas McCalla, "The Commercial Politics of the Toronto Board of Trade, 1850–1860," *CHR* 50 (1969): 51–67.

24. A general evaluation of the role of transportation in the development of western cities is in J.M.S. Careless, "Aspects of Urban Life in the West, 1870–1914," in *Prairie Perspectives*, vol. 2, edited by A.W. Rasporich and H.C. Klassen (Toronto, 1972). Much of the material on individual cities is still in unpublished form. Examples are: Brian Young, "Railway Politics in Montreal 1869–1878" (paper presented at Canadian Historical Association annual meeting (hereafter CHA), McGill University, June 1972); Paul-André Linteau, "Le Développement du port de Montréal au début du XXe siècle" (paper presented at CHA, McGill University, June 1972); Patricia Roy, "Railways, Politicans and the Development of the City of Vancouver as a Metropolitan Center, 1886–1929" (M.A. thesis, University of Toronto, 1963).

25. E.J. Chambers and G.W. Bertram, "Urbanization and Manufacturing in Central Canada, 1870–1890," *Papers on Regional Statistical Studies*, edited by Sylvia Ostry and T.K. Rymes (Toronto, 1966); Richard Rice, "The Wrights of Saint John: A Study of Shipbuilding and Shipowning in the Maritimes, 1839–1855," in *Canadian Business History*; Albert Faucher, "The Decline of Shipbuilding at Quebec in the Nineteenth Century," *Canadian Journal of Economics and Political Science* 23 (1957): 195–215.

26. Dana F. White, "The Underdeveloped Discipline: Interdisciplinary Directions in American Urban History," *American Studies* (Spring 1971), 10.

27. *Journal of American History* 57 (1970): 737–38.

28. Michael B. Katz. *The People of Hamilton, Canada West: Family and Class in a Mid-Nineteenth Century City* (Cambridge, Mass., 1976) and in several articles including "Social Structure in Hamilton, Ontario," in *Nineteenth-Century Cities*, and "The People of a Canadian City, 1851–52," *CHR* 53 (1972): 402–26. For a more detailed view of this ongoing project, see the four interim reports published by OISE (1969–1973).

29. As an example, see S.R. Mealing. "The Concept of Social Class and the Interpretation of Canadian History," *CHR* 46 (1965): 201–18.

30. "The Social Structure of Montreal in the 1850's." *CHA Report* (1956): 63–73.

31. Leroy Stone, *Urban Development in Canada* (1961 Census monograph, Ottawa, 1967); Leo F. Schnore and G.B. Petersen, "Urban and Metropolitan Development in the United States and Canada," *Annals of the American Academy of Political and Social Sciences* 316 (Mar. 1958): 60–68; David Slater. "The Urbanization of People and Activities in Canada Including an Analysis of Components of the Growth of Urban Population" (unpublished essay, Dept. of Economics, Queen's University, 1960).

32. "Population Growth and Change in Seattle and Vancouver, 1880–1960," *Pacific Historical Review* 39 (1970): 297–321; "La croissance de Montréal au XVIIIe siècle," *Revue d'Histoire de l'Amérique française* 27 (1973): 163–179.

33. Derwyn S. Shea, "The Irish Immigrant Adjustment to Toronto, 1840–1860," *Canadian Catholic Historical Association Study Sessions* 39 (1972); G.R.C. Keep, "The Irish Adjustment in Montreal," *CHR* 31 (1950): 39–46; D.J. Cross, "The Irish in Montreal, 1867–1896" (M.A. Thesis, McGill University, 1969).

34. J.I. Cooper, "The Quebec Ship Labourer's Benevolent Society," *CHR* 30 (1949): 336–43; G.E. Hart, "The Halifax Poorman's Friend Society, 1820–27: An Early Social Experiment," *CHR* 34 (1953): 109–23; Tamara K. Hareven, "An Ambiguous Alliance: Some Aspects of American Influence on Canadian Social Welfare," *Histoire sociale/Social History* 3 (Apr. 1969): 82–98; Paul Rutherford, "Tomorrow's Metropolis: The Urban Reform Movement in Canada, 1880–1920," CHA, *Historical Papers* (1971): 203–24.

35. Guy Bourassa, "The Political Elite of Montreal: From Aristocracy to Democracy" in *Politics and Government of Urban Canada*, edited by L.D. Feldman and M.D. Goldrick (Toronto, 1969).

36. David Sutherland, "Gentlemen vs. Shopkeepers: Urban Reform in Early 19th Century Halifax" (paper presented at CHA, McGill University, June 1972).

37. M.L. Foran, "Calgary Town Council, 1884–1895" (M.A. thesis, University of Calgary, 1970) and his "Urban Calgary 1884–1895," *Histoire sociale/Social History* 5 (1972): 61–76.

38. *City Government in Canada* (Toronto, 1906).

39. *American Influences on Canadian Government* (Toronto, 1929).

40. James D. Anderson, "Nonpartisan Urban Politics in Canadian Cities" in *Politics in Urban Canada*, edited by Jack Masson and James Anderson (Toronto, 1972).

41. Gowans, "Introduction" to Ralph Greenhill, *The Face of Toronto* (Toronto, 1960), and especially *Building Canada, An Architectural History of Canadian Life* (Toronto, 1966). Another useful architectural history is Marion MacRae and Anthony Adamson, *The Ancestral Roof, Domestic Architecture of Upper Canada* (Toronto, 1963).

42. Among the best studies of individual cities are: Margaret Angus, *The Old Stones of Kingston* (Toronto, 1966), and A.J.H. Richardson, "The Old City of Quebec and Our Heritage in Architecture," *CHA Report* (1963): 31–41. Basically concerned with preservation, the following are nevertheless useful: A.G. Mckay, *Victorian Architecture in Hamilton* (Hamilton, 1967); Heritage Trust of Nova Scotia, *Founded Upon a Rock: Historical Buildings of Halifax and Vicinity Standing in 1967* (Halifax, 1967); L.B. Jensen, *Vanishing Halifax* (Halifax, 1968); John W. Graham, *A Guide to the Architecture of Greater Winnipeg, 1831–1960* (Winnipeg, 1960). For an excellent example of what can be done with the architectural and social history of a single building, see *St. Lawrence Hall* (Toronto, 1969), especially the chapters by Eric Arthur.

43. Michael Hugo-Brunt, "The Origins of Colonial Settlements in the Maritimes," *Plan Canada* 1 (1960): 78–114.

44. "The 'Patron Saint' of Town Planning in British Columbia" in *Planning the Canadian Environment*, edited by L.O. Gertler (Montreal, 1968).

45. "Tomorrow's Metropolis: The Urban Reform Movement in Canada," CHA, *Historical Papers* (1971): 208–10.

46. "Thomas Adams and the Commission of Conservation" in *Planning the Canadian Environment*. Adams was not the only well-known planner brought in. In the 1870s, for example, Frederick Law Olmstead planned Mount Royal park in Montreal. A.L. Murray, "Frederick Law Olmstead and the Design of Mount Royal Park, Montreal," *Journal of the Society of Architectural Historians* 26 (1967): 163–71.

47. In the magazine *Conservation of Life*, issued by the commission, and in annual *Proceedings of the National Conference on City Planning* (Boston, 1912–1914).

48. "The Use of Town Plans in Urban History," in Dyos, *The Study of Urban History*.

49. See the special issue of the *Urban History Review* 2 (1972), entitled "Resources for the Study of Urban History in the Public Archives of Canada." Included are the following brief articles: Edward Dahl, "The National Map Collection"; A.J. Birrell, "Photographic Resources"; M. Bell, "Paintings, Drawings and Prints Section."

50. *Transactions and Proceedings of the Royal Society of Canada* (1943): 53–78, with 22 plates.

51. The manner in which Masters applied the Gras model to Toronto has been questioned by Frederick H. Armstrong. In a reexamination of the validity of the concept for Toronto, Armstrong concluded that the date for the emergence of Toronto as an important economic centre should be pushed back from after the 1850s to the 1830s. "Metropolitanism and Toronto Re-examined, 1825–1850," *CHA Report* (1966): 29–40.

52. "Frontierism, Metropolitanism, and Canadian History," *CHR* 35 (1954): 1–21.

53. "Aspects of Metropolitanism in Atlantic Canada," in *Regionalism in the Canadian Community,*
1867–1967, edited by Mason Wade (Toronto, 1969), 117.

54. "The Rise of Winnipeg as a Metropolitan Centre" (Ph.D. dissertation, Columbia University, 1958).

55. "The Metropolitan and the Provincial," *Queen's Quarterly* 76 (Winter 1969): 577–90; "Townsman
and Countryman: Two Ways of Life," *Dalhousie Review* 50 (1970): 180–87; "Metropolis and Hinterland,"
South Atlantic Quarterly 70 (1971): 386–403.

56. "The City: Suggestions for the Investigation of Human Behaviour in the Urban Environment"
(1916), reprinted in Park, *Human Communities: The City and Human Ecology* (New York, 1952).

57. For example, see W.H. Parker, "The Towns of Lower Canada in the 1830's" in *Urbanization and its
Problems*, edited by R.P. Beckinsale and J.M. Houston (Oxford, 1968).

58. *Winnipeg: A Social History of Urban Growth, 1874–1914* (Montreal, 1975).

THE RE-BIRTH OF CANADA'S PAST: A DECADE OF WOMEN'S HISTORY†

MARGARET CONRAD

Ten years ago the Canadian Historical Association, at meetings in Kingston, Ontario, held its first session on the topic of women. Much has happened in the last decade to banish forever the silence surrounding women's culture and women's contribution to Canada's past. Drawing upon the methodologies of the new social history and fueled by the energies of multidisciplinary "area studies," Canadian women's history has emerged as an exciting new field of study, and supporting structures have quickly taken shape.[1] Although pioneer scholars in Canadian women's history often faced ridicule, hostility, or benign neglect, it is now generally recognized that women's history is an important area of study and that gender is a separate category of analysis which historians ignore only at the risk of rendering their work woefully inadequate.[2] As with other large categories such as class and ethnicity, the study of gender demands a whole new "angle of vision."[3] Historians who study women must consider new subjects of analysis such as reproduction and sexuality and be prepared to adopt novel notions of historical periodization. They must also devote more attention to the private sphere of human history, which has hitherto been considered appropriate for public consumption only when filtered through fictional accounts. By exposing the historical contradictions between public and private life, women's history promises to transform not only the way in which we view women in history but also how we assess the public sphere dominated by men and their institutions.

Ten years of hard work in the archives have netted significant results for Canadian women's history, nowhere more so than in the foundation of any field of study: bibliography. Since 1972 *The Canadian Newsletter of Research on Women* (now *Resources for Feminist Research*) has kept a running tally of national and international developments in women's studies, while in 1980 Beth Light and Veronica Strong-Boag published *True Daughters of the North* (Toronto: OISE Press, 1980), a 200-page, annotated bibliography of published primary and secondary sources on Canadian women's history. This indispensible research tool should permanently lay to rest any criticism based on the alleged paucity of sources for historical analysis. In Quebec Denise Lemieux and Lucie Mercier are supervising a massive bibliographic enterprise on women in Quebec for l'Institut Québécois de Recherche sur la Culture, which will be of immense value to historians.[4]

Collections of documents, like bibliographic aids, reveal the wealth of resources for women's history. In 1974 Michèle Jean contributed substantially to our understanding of Quebec women's recent history with her collection of documents

†*Acadiensis* XII (Spring 1983): 140-62. I would like to thank Wendy Mitchinson and Phillip Buckner for reading a draft of this review and offering valuable suggestions. As usual, Joy Cavazzi pitched in at the last minute to transform my tortuous handwriting into a typewritten manuscript. Without her help much of my writing would remain in the realm of "work in progress."

on *Québécoises du 20e siècle* (Montreal: Éditions du Jour, 1974). In English Canada, Ramsay Cook and Wendy Mitchinson followed the century-long debate over women's appropriate role in industrial society in *The Proper Sphere: Women's Place in Canadian Society* (Toronto: Oxford University Press, 1976); and The Canadian Women's Educational Press, a valuable ally in promoting women's studies, published *A Harvest Yet to Reap: A History of Prairie Women* (Toronto: Women's Press, 1976), a collective effort by feminist scholars to draw a regional profile of women's past experience.

Pioneer and Gentlewomen of British North America, 1713–1867 (Toronto: New Hogtown Press, 1980) is the first of a projected four-volume series of documents relating to women. Edited by Beth Light and Alison Prentice, *Pioneer and Gentlewomen* represents a new level of sophistication in documentary history. Its tightly written essays prefacing sections and chapters are easily the best secondary literature available on women in pre-Confederation English Canada. Further, the structure of the book, which groups documents according to stages in the "life-cycle" — now more appropriately called "life course" — suggests an important way of interpreting women's historical experience. Though many readers would prefer longer excerpts from the documents, the editors understandably decided to include a wider range of material. Light and Prentice are also to be congratulated for giving the Atlantic provinces "equal time" in this volume, though, in their quest for evidence, the editors were unfortunately exposed only to the most accessible documents, thereby missing some fascinating sources of women's history in Atlantic Canada during the "Golden Age." A more rigorous search of newspapers, legal records, and private papers would have yielded a richer harvest, especially in the public sphere of community and church activities.[5]

Prentice and Light have been criticized for not including more information on such matters as life expectancy, age of marriage, family size, literacy, years of schooling, and sex ratios of the population in British North America. This information is difficult to find, since demographers often omit gender as a category. Important exceptions to this generalization include Jacques Henripin, *Trends and Factors of Fertility in Canada* (Ottawa: Statistics Canada, 1972) and Hubert Charbonneau, *Vie et mort de nos ancêtres* (Montreal: Les Presses de l'Université de Montréal, 1975), as well as a growing list of articles. Despite pioneering work by Michael Katz and David Gagan, offering demographic evidence on women's lives,[6] we still continue to rely far too often on American statistics, never knowing if they apply to Canada or not. The intrepid scholar who offers an analysis of demographic factors as they apply to women will earn the undying gratitude of those trying to understand change over time in the lives of Canadian women.

As yet, monographs and textbooks in Canadian women's history are thin on the ground. Certainly we have nothing comparable to Carl Degler's *At Odds: Women and the Family in America from the Revolution to the Present*[7] which combines demographic and descriptive evidence in an ambitious and audacious interpretation of women's lives over a 200-year period. In Canada, only Québécois women can boast a survey history of their experience, a tribute to the advanced level of social science methodology and to the well-established tradition of collective scholarship in Quebec, as well as to the energy of the authors. Calling themselves "Le Collectif Clio," Marie Lavigne, Jennifer Stoddart, Micheline Dumont and Michèle

Jean have laboured for three years — or, as they prefer, 4 times 9 months — to produce *L'histoire des femmes au Québec depuis quatre siècles* (Montreal: Les Quinze, 1982). More than 500 pages in length, the book chronicles the changing conditions of work, reproduction, public policy, ideology, and material culture as they relate to women's lives. The authors reject the traditional periodization based on "political" events such as the Conquest and Confederation for categories they find more useful: 1617–1701, a period of "heroic" beginnings when women were relatively few and opportunities unusually numerous; 1701–1832 when women's productive lives were confined primarily to preindustrial rural homes; 1832–1900 when the male leaders of bourgeois society systematically and deliberately exorcised women from political and professional opportunities even as the collapse of the wheat economy and the rise of industry drastically transformed the productive role of women. More than half the book is concerned with the twentieth century, which the authors see as offering the most significant milestones in the history of women's collective consciousness and public status — the emergence of secular suffrage and reform organizations at the beginning of the century; the long overdue acquisition of the vote in 1940; the passing of Bill 16, giving women legal rights within marriage in 1964; and the beginning of the recent women's movement which the authors date from the autumn of 1969 when the Montreal Women's Liberation Movement was founded, the *Birth Control Handbook* published, and more than 200 women marched in the streets in protest against the prohibition of public demonstrations in Montreal.

It is impossible in a review such as this to fully discuss all the misconceptions exploded and conclusions reached in this important book. Those who have been following the literature in the history of women in Quebec will be familiar with much of the material — Sylvio Dumas's findings concerning the origins of the *filles du roi*; the work of Marta Danylewycz, Marguerite Jean, and Jacqueline Bouchard on female religious communities; the impressive body of literature available on women's paid labour in Quebec.[8] There is also a lucid account of the legal status of women in Quebec that will be welcomed by scholars. The authors confront directly Quebec's unfortunate record in granting women equal rights in voting privileges, education, work, and the law. The slow pace of secularization in education and social services, they argue, kept women in a clerically sanctioned position of subordination. Hence, the vanguard of secularly educated professional women who led the fight for women's rights in English Canada had a very weak counterpart in Catholic Quebec. Their schools and professional opportunities were constrained by structures often staffed by women but in the final analysis controlled by the male clerical hierarchy. The misogyny of male politicians, clerics, and bureaucrats is a familiar phenomenon to students of women's history but the examples of patriarchy cited here from the Quebec experience should make the most seasoned male chauvinist blanch.

By any standards *L'Histoire des femmes au Québec* is a landmark publication, its flaws dwarfed by the scale of the endeavour. Several problems, however, should be mentioned. Occasionally, the organization of the material results in unnecessary repetition, and authorities referred to in the text are not always cited in the bibliographies at the end of chapters and sections. Though the authors admit that the cutting edge of feminism in Quebec often emerges from non-francophone sectors, only sporadic references are made to minority women whose position in the conservative milieu of Quebec must have been exceedingly difficult. Moreover, while the authors must be commended for their innovative approach to periodization, 1760 is a starting date for a non-francophone presence in Quebec, not only of elité English ladies but also of the growing number of Irish and Scots women who, the authors tell us, comprised a significant proportion of the domestics and prostitutes in the nineteenth century. Clearly there is a chapter of women's history in Quebec behind such revelations. There is also a tendency throughout the book to see women purely as victims of patriarchal and capitalist oppression. It would be useful to have a fuller discussion of the private ways in which women exercised power and how they rationalized their second-class public status. Finally, the authors rely heavily on American monographs in their interpretations of such topics as housework and post-Second World War developments in Quebec. Given the fact that Québécois women so often marched to a different drummer in the nineteenth and twentieth centuries, more research on women's culture — that private sphere of women's lives which differs quite dramatically across ethnic, class, and occupational lines — is needed. This is merely to say that, like all good books, L'Histoire des femmes au Québec raises new questions. Given the productivity of feminist scholars in Quebec, we can assume that the answers will soon be delivered.

Quebec women are also well served by Susan Mann Trofimenkoff who in her Dream of Nation: A Social and Intellectual History of Quebec (Toronto: Macmillan of Canada, 1982) includes women's history in the general narrative. Such integration has been pitifully slow to develop in the historical scholarship of English Canada where the two solitudes based on "race" seem to have been replaced by solitudes based on gender. There is little excuse for this situation, since journal literature abounds, and several volumes of essays provide easily accessible evidence of the work accomplished in Canadian women's history. Two of these, Trofimenkoff and Alison Prentice, eds., The Neglected Majority (Toronto: McClelland and Stewart, 1977) and Marie Lavigne and Yolande Pinard, eds., Les femmes dans la société québécoise (Montreal: Boréal Éxpress, 1977) have been on the market since 1977. A more recent anthology, Barbara Latham and Kathy Kess, eds., In Her Own Right: Selected Essays on Women's History in British Columbia (Victoria: Camosun College, 1980), is the fruitful result of a student summer project based at Camosun College. As with most anthologies, the articles are uneven in quality, but they testify not only to the fine work being done by students in women's history but also to the massive amount of information available on "provincial" topics in unpublished papers and theses.

In their efforts to balance the record, scholars of women's history have managed to shed new light on that most Canadian of topics — the fur trade. Recent work by anthropologist Jennifer Brown, Strangers in Blood: Fur Trade Company Families in Indian Country (Vancouver: University of British Columbia Press, 1980), and historian Sylvia Van Kirk, "Many Tender Ties": Women in Fur Trade Society, 1670–1870 (Winnipeg: Watson & Dwyer, 1980), has revealed the role of Amerindian women as intermediaries in the fur trade alliances that were established between native tribes and European fur trading companies. From the native perspective, liaisons with the white intruders cemented special trading relations, while Europeans valued the productive skills, language ability and political power wielded by their "country wives." Without this quasi-family interaction, the course of the Canadian fur trade would have been profoundly altered and, so too, if we accept Harold Innis's interpretation of the central role of the fur trade, would the course of Canadian history.

By focussing on the interaction between the public and private sphere and between men and women, Brown and Van Kirk offer models for the way in which historical sources — most of them written by men — can be made to render up insights on the roles and motives of women in the past. Their findings shatter any illusions we may harbour about women being passive victims of their oppression. Amerindian women consciously chose to live with white fur traders in order to enhance their own power and to increase their share of the material wealth that resulted from the close association with European traders. It is possible as well that Indian women preferred the marriage conventions of European males to the polygamous relationships sanctioned by many tribes. That the rules of the fur game eventually changed to their disadvantage does not negate the fact that Amerindian women tried to carve out for themselves a privileged position in the economic system that dominated their lives. Brown and Van Kirk remind us that we should not treat all women, not even all Amerindian women, as an undifferentiated mass, since relationships varied over time and according to tribal and ethnic customs. It is this insight that points to future directions in the study of native women's history; for although we are truly privileged in having two monographs devoted to the experience of the "country wives," a danger exists that this relatively small group will be perceived as the only native women worthy of study. The vast majority of women who remained in their tribal relationships during the fur trade era require more attention. The tendency of early feminist scholars to look to Amerindian society for examples of a matriarchal "golden age" or a crucible for female oppression must gradually give way to an examination of the variety of conditions experienced by native women in the past.

In the United States much attention has been focussed on women in colonial society and the early years of the new republic. The same cannot be said of this period in Canadian women's history. Instead, scholars have leaped from the fur trade to industrial society. To some extent this focus is a result of the general interest in post-Confederation Canada in the 1970s. It is also prompted by the contemporary need to understand how we arrived at our present predicament. Despite, or perhaps because of, this present-mindedness, the debate surrounding women and industrialization is a vigorous one, informed by an impressive body of research. The tendency of women's history to shatter icons was inherent in the debate from the beginning. A paper delivered by D. Suzanne Cross at the CHA's first session on women in 1973 revealed that a significant percentage of Québécois women were in the paid industrial workforce in the nineteenth century and also that nuns provided day care services for working mothers.[9] These findings flew in the face of commonly held misconceptions about the homebound Québécois mother and the pious, secluded sisterhood. Cross's article was soon followed by *Women at Work: Ontario, 1850–1930* published by the Women's

Press in 1974. The authors outlined within a Marxist framework the occupational dimensions of women's subordination under capitalism, and underlined the importance of gender as well as class in analyzing such rarely researched topics as domestic work, prostitution, nursing, and women's organized resistance to exploitation in the workplace. Meanwhile, the contours of middle-class women's involvement in the public sphere in the late nineteenth century were drawn by Veronica Strong-Boag in *The Parliament of Women: The National Council of Women in Canada 1893–1929* (Ottawa: National Museum of Man, 1976). Strong-Boag concluded that the "separate sphere" of voluntary activity safely drew middle-class women into public life without directly threatening the power relationships in middle-class families or male ascendancy in war, politics, and business.

The subordination of working women in the hierarchical structures of business and unions, and the marginalization of middle-class housewives in voluntary organizations were important insights that prompted further research. Wayne Roberts in *Honest Womanhood: Feminism, Femininity, and Class Consciousness Among Toronto Working Women, 1893–1914* (Toronto: New Hogtown Press, 1976) attempted to explain the "failure" of women to attain equality in the industrial workforce by looking at the structure of women's work experience. Since the vast majority of women in the paid labour force were young and single, and married women often worked in small firms or at piece work in the home, their work experience, Roberts argued, was too fragmented to support sustained efforts to organize against discrimination. Moreover, women's primary responsibility for home and family caused them to concentrate their reform efforts on "evils" which threatened the home rather than those which exploited women in the paid labour force.

The preoccupation with domestic issues also shaped the women's movement as it emerged in the second half of the nineteenth century. This theme is explored in Linda Kealey, ed., *A Not Unreasonable Claim: Women and Reform in Canada* (Toronto: Women's Press, 1979). According to Kealey a "maternal feminist" ideology inspired the reform energies of most Canadian women between 1880 and 1930. In both the domestic and public spheres, she argues, middle-class women justified their increased power because of their roles as mothers of the next generation rather than as individuals demanding equal rights for themselves. The distinction between equal rights feminism and maternal feminism is a useful one, though it is not always clear that women one hundred years ago made such fine definitions. Evidence from the articles in the anthology suggests that women used whatever arguments were appropriate, drawing upon evangelical, liberal, and socialist rationales, as well as invoking maternal feminism. The latter, it could be argued, was the most effective approach, both in dealing with middle-class women who increasingly inhabited a child-oriented world, but especially in confronting men who had much to lose in both the public and private sphere if women challenged the canons of patriarchal power. Given the persuasiveness of the "separate spheres" doctrines in the late nineteenth century, it would be surprising if women, in attempting to enhance their status, did not try to parlay their assigned sphere into a base for exercising power. As Wendy Mitchinson argues in her article on the Woman's Christian Temperance Union, maternal feminism was more than a vehicle for maintaining the status quo: it often spurred women to take on public roles and to adopt ideas such as state-enforced prohibition which had distinctly radical implications for women and for society.

It is, of course, difficult to determine whether taking the line of least resistance was the best strategy for Canadian women at the turn of the century. Most of the authors of *A Not Unreasonable Claim* imply that such an approach was wrongheaded, and the evidence is clear that women achieved only partial victories: entry into the professions which imposed quotas on the number of women admitted to professional schools; bureaucratization of social services on the condition of surrender to male experts; a francophone women's movement turned inward by male-defined concepts of conservatism and nationalism; suffrage and prohibition laws which failed to usher in a brave new world of women's power over either their own sphere or in society generally. A collective sense of disappointment — and disapproval — emanates from *A Not Unreasonable Claim*. Only the maverick Flora Macdonald Denison, as described by Deborah Gorham, seems to rise above the image of the misguided society ladies who championed the cause of women and reform at the turn of the century.

The same image is offered of Canadian suffrage leaders by Carol Lee Bacchi, both in her article in *A Not Unreasonable Claim* and in her new book, *Liberation Deferred? The Ideas of the English-Canadian Suffragists, 1877–1918* (Toronto: University of Toronto Press, 1983). Bacchi concludes that the female suffragists failed to effect a social revolution for women because "the majority never had a revolution in mind." In proving this contention, Bacchi draws a profile of 156 suffrage leaders who flourished between 1877 and 1918. These women, she concludes, represented a small Anglo-Saxon, Protestant élite, urban-based, dominated by professionals (almost 60 percent held jobs) and wives of professionals who endorsed women's suffrage as part of a larger reform program devoted to race regeneration, social purity, and the family ideal. On the eve of the First World War, suffrage leaders still carried evangelical and temperance baggage which they dressed up in a progressive package calling for state-supported education, professionalization, and bureaucratization. Significantly, in 1914 the suffrage movement in Toronto split between a small Canadian Suffrage Association, the direct descendant of Emily Stowe's equal rights-oriented Toronto Women's Literary Society founded in 1877, and the much larger National Equal Franchise Union, committed to a multiplicity of reform causes of which suffrage was only one and not the most important. Farm and labour women, Bacchi argues, were never fully integrated into what were essentially urban, professional organizations. In short, feminist ideology did not inspire a broad national movement for female suffrage. Indeed, because of the conservatism of the majority of suffrage leaders, by 1914 the female franchise became desirable, not, as has been supposed, to reward women for their contribution to the war effort, but to bring more "right thinking" people to the polls in a wartime election and to garner support for provincial parties facing an electorate which had already embraced most of the reform package promoted by the suffragists. Having used maternal feminist arguments to justify the vote, women were left with an institutionalized double standard, a reform movement taken over by bureaucrats and professionals, and a world no longer inspired by idealism.

Bacchi's concise, lucidly written monograph supplements Cleverdon's earlier detailed treatment of the Canadian suffrage movement.[10] One wishes, however, that Bacchi had Cleverdon's sense of province and region. It may well be the case that the Toronto suffrage movement split in 1914. The same bifurcation did not always occur elsewhere. A study of the suffrage movement in New Brunswick by Mary Eileen Clarke[11] indicates that the same people led the suffrage movement throughout the period and that social (or maternal) feminists did not supplant equal rights feminists. On the contrary, the Saint John Association was nearly destroyed by its flirtation with socialist ideas at the turn of the century; its members consistently and publicly attacked "conservative" women's clubs that did not endorse suffrage; and it refused to support Borden's Union Government scheme for partial suffrage in 1917. Evidence offered by Bacchi suggests that suffrage organizations in the western provinces shared more with their Maritime counterparts than they did with their Toronto "headquarters." Bacchi has not one reference in her bibliography to Maritime sources and only a brief discussion on the evolution of the suffrage movement in western Canada. Such an observation is not just regional carping. The suffrage movement in Canada was constrained from the beginning by provincially defined conditions and timetables. The situation in Quebec amply demonstrates this fact. Moreover, the position of "farm" women on suffrage surely requires a more fundamental analysis than that they were tangential to urban-based suffrage organizations. The issue was, after all, larger than the specific clubs which promoted it and, as with all major "reforms," was supported for various reasons: to help the cause of farm families, to strengthen the prohibition fight, to secure healthier cities, and as an end in itself. Those busy and often much discriminated against professional women who dominated the ranks of the suffrage societies must have had more than maternal feminism in mind when they fought for political rights. No matter how they packaged it, at a very fundamental level female suffrage struck a blow at the patriarchal family — as anti-suffrage spokesmen, especially in French Canada, never tired of reminding listeners. In the final analysis, votes for women came too late. By 1917 it mattered little whether the suffrage movement was led by maternal feminists arguing for rights as women, or from equal rights feminists arguing for rights as human beings. The male-dominated structures of industrial society were already firmly in place.[12]

A problem shared by most of us writing women's history is that we sometimes argue from hindsight. Women's suffrage failed to usher in an era of equality, therefore the goals of the suffragists must have been unworthy. But one does not logically follow from the other. Indeed, it might equally be argued that if corporate capitalism, consumerism, flapperism, and the peace movement had not taken precedence over feminism and progressivism in the 1920s, the history of the suffrage movement would be treated differently. What we know of the later careers of the suffragists indicates a continuing interest in feminist activity, however misguided, which the "lost generation" of the 1920s and 1930s seems not to have embraced.[13] Perhaps the undermining of the intellectual justification for separate spheres — a story well told by Rosalind Rosenberg[14] — gave women few weapons with which to fight for equality from their grossly unequal starting position. Whatever the circumstances, it is the fate of women in the interwar years, not the goals of the suffragists, that historians must begin to study in order to understand the "failure" of suffrage.

As yet we have no monographic literature on women in the public sphere after the First World War. Articles by Strong-Boag, Lavigne, Stoddart and others indicate that the thrust of women's struggles for equality in the interwar years shifted as women strove to combine marriage and career, break into the professions now theoretically opened to them, influence bureaucratic structures which increasingly controlled their lives, resist discrimination in the job market and, in Quebec, struggle to attain the vote and reform of marriage laws.[15] These were not easy struggles, and victories were few. Nor did the Second World War bring anything more than temporary opportunities to break out of traditional patterns of subordination. Ruth Pierson's valuable articles point to a pernicious role on the part of the state in treating women as a reserve army of labour during the Second World War.[16] Evidence such as this and the tortuous reasoning behind the introduction of universal mothers' allowances in 1944 has prompted Veronica Strong-Boag to view state policy regarding women with a healthy feminist suspicion.[17]

Historical assessment of women after the Second World War is rare, though Joyce Hibbert's *War Brides* (Scarborough: Peter Martin Associates, 1978), is a compelling account through the use of oral interviews of 60 of more than 50,000 war brides who followed their husbands to Canada after the Second World War. Pat and Hugh Armstrong in *The Double Ghetto: Canadian Women and Their Segregated Work* (Toronto: McClelland and Stewart, 1978) examine workforce participation of women between 1941 and 1976, while Francine Barry does the same for Quebec in *Le travail de la femme au Québec: L'évolution de 1940 à 1970* (Montreal: Les Presses de l'Université du Québec, 1977). A lucid account, written by a participant in the women's movement since the 1960s, is Myrna Kostash, *Long Way From Home: The Story of the Sixties Generation in Canada* (Toronto: James Lorimer, 1980). Also of interest because it demonstrates the links between the "old" women's movement and the "new" is Cerise Morris's article on the movement for the Royal Commission on the Status of Women in Canada. Morris documents the importance of having a woman in the cabinet—Judy Lamarsh —to channel the pressure from the network of women's clubs whose post-suffrage history still awaits their historian.[18]

In women's history education is a favourite topic since it serves as a socializing agent as well as a sensitive indicator of prevailing attitudes toward women. The work of Alison Prentice and her colleagues at the Ontario Institute for Studies in Education has done much to disabuse us of the notion that teaching as a profession had been a uniform blessing or even a uniform experience for women.[19] Though women came to dominate the one-room schoolhouse in English-speaking areas of Canada in the late nineteenth century, they did so at salaries substantially lower than those of their male counterparts. When it came to collegiate and university education, women teachers were rare and female students were often hived off into exclusively female courses such as home economics and secretarial science.

The resistance of universities in Canada to the admission of women on an equal basis with men is another grim tale. If most "official" university historians have their way, the story will never be told. For this reason, the appearance of Margaret Gillett's *We Walked Very Warily: A History of Women at McGill* (Montreal: Eden Press, 1981) is an important landmark in the history of women in Canada. Although Stanley Frost was commissioned to produce a history of McGill, Gillett set out to write a parallel volume which would do justice to women's very separate experience at the institution. The history of the "Donaldas" — the name is derived from Donald Smith whose beneficence guaranteed separate education for women at Royal Victoria College rather than in co-educational facilities — is a fascinating one. Gillett devotes more than 200 pages to women's struggle to gain access to McGill; Frost allows only twelve, three of which consist of pictures. Critics have objected to Gillett's discursive style but she surely has many models in official university histories which "chronicle" the activities of every male benefactor and dean. Gillett points out that gaining admission to McGill did not mean equal access to all programs, credibility for female faculties such as food sciences and nursing, or equal treatment in extra-curricular activities. Historians tackling other institutions might do well to take a leaf out of Gillett's book in pursuing the fate of women beyond the date when they are admitted to the hallowed halls of academe.

In addition to exploring the history of women's public and working lives, Canadian scholars are now beginning to follow their British and American counterparts in focussing on the private world of women. It can be argued that because women have been relegated to a separate sphere, they do indeed have a separate culture — or, more accurately, separate cultures — which can be documented historically. The pursuit of women's culture is an exciting scholarly endeavour because whole new categories must be articulated for describing those aspects of women's lives which were separated from "malestream" culture. Since public documents rarely include direct evidence of women's lives, historians must turn to private chronicles — letters, diaries, autobiographies, and novels — as well as evidence from prescriptive literature and material culture in order to document women's experience.

Virtually all historical topics take on a different perspective when seen through women's eyes. This point is brought home upon a reading of Doug Owram's *Promise of Eden* (Toronto: University of Toronto Press, 1980) where one hears only men's voices and sees only a man's frontier. The work of Eliane Silverman and Susan Jackel offers a wholly alternative perspective on the "taming of the West." Silverman has collected oral interviews from women on the prairie frontier, and her approach is a good example of the kind of research now breaking new ground in women's history. Silverman contends that women have traditionally lived split lives, one in a male-dominated culture where they were subordinated by tradition, fear, loyalty and love, and a parallel one where their actions could range the full spectrum from intimacy to power.[20] Her probing questions elicit women's attitudes toward uniquely female rites of passage, friendship patterns, and mutual aid networks on the frontier.

In *A Flannel Shirt and Liberty* (Vancouver: University of British Columbia Press, 1982), Susan Jackel reveals that while men were acquiring and ruling the

West, unmarried middle-class British women were also spying out the land as a possible frontier of opportunity. Though Jackel admits that the number of "redundant" British women who came to "the last best West" is difficult to determine precisely, she argues that they formed the basis of a formidable network championing causes ranging from reform of the homestead laws to British imperial supremacy. This network was not confined only to the Canadian West. Organizations such as the Female Middle Class Emigration Society cultivated an enthusiastic readership for the books and articles which Jackel draws to our attention. One can imagine a similar study of the West through the eyes of women in eastern Canada, where enthusiasm for western horizons was also strong and organizational structures ranging from missionary societies to boards of education sponsored the feminine move westwards. Jackel has also edited two more reprints: Georgina Binnie-Clark's *Wheat and Woman* (Toronto: University of Toronto Press, 1979) and Elizabeth B. Mitchell's *In Western Canada Before the War* (Saskatoon: Western Producer Prairie Books, 1981), both of which are enriched by Jackel's solid introductions.[21]

Another valuable primary source are the youthful diaries of Elizabeth Smith edited by Veronica Strong-Boag as *A Woman With A Purpose: The Diaries of Elizabeth Smith, 1872–1884* (Toronto: University of Toronto Press, 1980). Known in later life as the wife of Adam Shortt and a volunteer activist par excellence, Elizabeth Smith trained as a medical doctor, one of the first Canadian women to do so. Her diaries chronicle her adolescent stint at teaching school and her subsequent medical training, both experiences constrained by the limited sphere to which women were confined in the late nineteenth century. Though she completed her medical degree, she retreated into marriage and volunteer work, never using her hard-won professional skills as a vehicle for material independence and feminist reforms. Smith's experience was not unusual for the first generation of professional women who were forced to choose between a career and marriage, but it is from diaries such as this that we see how youthful feminist idealism could be blunted by social conventions so deeply entrenched as to be virtually invisible.

Biographies of Canadian women of the calibre of Maria Tippett's *Emily Carr* (Toronto: Oxford University Press, 1979) are rare. However, scholars of women's history welcome a new edition of Elsie Gregory MacGill's *My Mother the Judge* (Toronto: Peter Martin Associates, 1981). Originally published in 1955, the biography of early feminist reformer Helen Gregory MacGill by her equally pioneering daughter has a spirited introduction by Naomi Black who situates the MacGill women in the context of Canadian feminism. Another noteworthy publication is Michael Hayden's collection of Hilda Neatby's writings, *So Much To Do, So Little Time* (Vancouver: University of British Columbia Press, 1983), a title taken from Neatby's speech on women to the Canadian Federation of University Women in 1952. Hilda Neatby (1904–1975) was the heir to the "victories" of the suffrage generation and faced her share of sexism as she pursued a career as a historian in the interwar years. Her triumphs were many. She rose to the headship of the History Department at the University of Saskatchewan, served on the Massey Royal Commission on the Arts, published a widely acclaimed critique of education, *So Little For the Mind* (1953), and in 1962 became the first woman president of the Canadian Historical Association. Hayden rightly concludes that

Neatby was an "old" feminist who spoke of duties rather than a "new" feminist who demanded rights, but she had a historical understanding of "feminism" and "the women's movement," terms which she herself used. This, along with her Presbyterian discipline and regional perspective, enabled her to withstand the chauvinist slights which often came her way.

Research in women's health and sexuality has revealed a continuing concern on the part of women for their treatment by men and offers compelling reasons why they should be thus preoccupied. Wendy Mitchinson, for instance, has discovered that at least some doctors at the turn of the century felt that women's mental states could be "improved" by gynecological operations.[22] Though Edward Shorter has recently tried to rescue the tarnished image of the medical profession in *A History of Women's Bodies* (New York: Basic Books, 1982), it is difficult to avoid the conclusion that doctors were not always as professional as they should have been and that a few more women doctors on the staff of hospitals might have averted more than a few knife-wielding experts. Obviously not all women knuckled under to the conspiratorial blandishments of doctors, lawyers, and clergymen. Angus McLaren in his article on birth control in Canada concludes that despite the law and public opinion women continued to try to limit the number of children they were forced to bear, and demographic trends in the twentieth century indicate that they were often successful.[23] We still await an analysis of women's perspective on the changing contours of the family, but those pursuing the elusive evidence of women's culture will almost certainly soon be in a position to give us the "inside" story.[24]

The difficulty for women of combining productive and reproductive roles in a world where the public and private spheres were becoming so sharply differentiated resulted in significant changes in the life courses of many women in the nineteenth century. In industrial settings women tended to marry later, and a larger number never married at all. Not until the Second World War did it become acceptable — though still not the norm — for married women to work outside the home unless they had to.[25] The conflict between "industrial time" and "family time" is a fruitful subject for examination. So too are the changing patterns of housework over the past 200 years. As yet we in Canada have nothing comparable to the work of Susan Strasser or Dolores Hayden.[26] We do, however, have Meg Luxton's *More Than A Labour of Love: Three Generations of Women's Work in the Home* (Toronto: Women's Press, 1980). Through oral interviews, participant observation, and documentary research, Luxton follows the changing circumstances of women's work in the home as it has been transformed by technology, municipal services, and human values in Flin Flon, Manitoba, since 1927. Pat and Hugh Armstrong devote a chapter to housework in their useful survey of the literature of women's work entitled appropriately *The Double Ghetto* but they only briefly mention the problem of the double day in *A Working Majority: What Women Must Do For Pay* (Ottawa: Canadian Advisory Council on the Status of Women, 1983). Bonnie Fox, ed., *Hidden in the Household: Women's Domestic Labour Under Capitalism* (Toronto: Women's Press, 1980) is an attempt by Marxist scholars to define "the peculiar nature" of domestic labour in capitalist society. These papers are a useful contribution to the domestic labour debate in Marxist circles, but unfortunately they offer little "grounded" historical analysis of the Canadian experience. Laura C. Johnson (with Robert E. Johnson) in *The Seam Allowance: Industrial Home Sewing in Canada* (Toronto: Women's Press, 1982) discuss the continued existence of women's piece work in the home and suggest a fruitful area for further historical research.

One area of study where women are only beginning to emerge from the grey mists of neglect is Atlantic Canada. Sadly, little has been published on women's history in the Atlantic region since Ruth Pierson reported on the state of the field in 1977. As Ernest Forbes implied in his historiographical article published in 1978, the lack of concrete information can lead to the most glaringly ridiculous generalizations when scholars attempt to include the region in their "national" studies. Only one article on a woman has appeared in *Acadiensis* since the journal began publication.[27] Other regional periodicals, such as *Them Days, Cape Breton's Magazine, The Island Magazine* and the *Nova Scotia Historical Quarterly* (now *Review*) have a better track record, while several unpublished honours and masters theses contribute substantially to our knowledge of women in the region.[28] Amateur historians have tackled the questions left begging by university-based scholars. John Edward Belliveau has offered us *The Splendid Life of Albert Smith and the Women He Left Behind* (Windsor: Lancelot Press, 1976) and James D. Davison has explored the contexts of female culture in the nineteenth-century Annapolis Valley in *Alice of Grand Pré* (Wolfville: Acadia University, 1981), and *Eliza of Pleasant Valley* (Wolfville: privately published, 1983).

An important monograph on women in Atlantic Canada has been written by folklorist Hilda Chaulk Murray who has used oral interviews to reconstruct the life course of women who comprise *More Than 50%* (St. John's: Breakwater Books, 1979) of the productive labour in the outport village of Elliston, Newfoundland. Murray describes in detail the various backbreaking tasks performed by women in the fish-based economy, and also traces kin and community networks which functioned in times of crisis. Particularly valuable is her treatment of customs surrounding such events as courtship, marriage, childbirth, and death. Rituals and rationales testify to women's participation in defining culture in the sense of assigning meaning and value to human actions. Unfortunately, Murray does not get a close look at men's culture. Before a final judgment is made on the status of outport women, a sensitive tape recorder should be placed in such exclusively male domains as the fishing boat and the Orange Lodge. Two other ground-breaking studies are Joyce Nevitt's *White Caps and Black Bands* (St. John's: Jesperson Printing Ltd., 1978) on the nursing profession in Newfoundland to 1934, and Linda Squiers Hansen's *Those Certain Women* (Fredericton: Associated Alumnae of UNB, 1982) on the alumnae society of the University of New Brunswick.

The literary heritage of Maritime women is rich, but until recently has been overshadowed by such obvious names as Lucy Maud Montgomery and Margaret Marshall Saunders. Montgomery and Saunders are certainly worthy of our interest. *My Dear Mr. M.: Letters to G.B. MacMillen from L.M. Montgomery*, edited by F.W.P. Bolger and Elizabeth R. Epperly (Toronto: McGraw-Hill Ryerson, 1980), is tremendously revealing of the "real" struggles of Montgomery as a writer and as a woman. A novel which deserves to be more widely distributed is Maria Amelia Fytche, *Kerchiefs to Hunt Souls* (Sackville: R.P. Bell Library, Mount Allison University, 1980), originally published in Boston in 1895. Carrie MacMillan's sensitive introduction locates Fytche's literary and feminist perspectives which are surprisingly "modern," reflecting a side to Maritime women that has scarcely been imagined.

The Atlantic region may be short on histories of women but the documentary evidence is abundant, particularly in the form of diaries and reminiscences, some of which are gradually finding their way into print.[29] Excerpts from Mary Bradley's experience in colonial New Brunswick have been published in *Atlantis*, as have the reminiscences of Loyalist matriarch Elizabeth Litchenstein Johnston.[30] A brief passage from the diary of Susan Woodman of Alberton, P.E.I., can be found in *The Island Magazine*, No. 3 (Fall-Winter 1977). Non-Entity Press has reproduced the diary of Loyalist Sarah Frost in a reprint of Walter Bates, *Kingston and the Loyalists of the "Spring-fleet" of 1783* (Woodstock, 1980) and "The Grandmother's Story" is appended to the reprint of Peter Fisher's *The First History of New Brunswick* (Woodstock, 1981). Mrs. Frances Beavan offers an imperial view of colonial life for men and women in *Life in the Backwoods of New Brunswick* (St. Stephen: Print'n Press Ltd., 1980), originally published in 1845. Charlotte Gourlay Robinson's *Pioneer Profiles of New Brunswick Settlers* (Belleville: Mika Publishing, 1980) draws upon material some of which has been lost since these sketches first appeared in the 1940s. Gourlay was New Brunswick's first woman pharmacist, and originally prepared these brief profiles of New Brunswick women for CBC radio. It would be useful to know more of Charlotte Gourlay Robinson as well as of the women whose lives she chronicled. Modern Maritime women have not been as enthusiastic as their "foremothers" in preserving their life stories, though there are noteworthy exceptions. Helen Creighton's *A Life in Folklore* (Toronto: McGraw-Hill Ryerson, 1975) is a valuable autobiography of a Nova Scotia "institution," and Carrie Best provides her perspective on growing up as a black girl in New Glasgow in *That Lonesome Road* (New Glasgow: Clarion Publishing Co. Ltd., 1977).

Newfoundland women have produced a virtual avalanche of life stories. Helen Porter's *Below the Bridge: A Memoir of Growing Up on the Southside* (St. John's: Breakwater Books, 1979) is a particularly perceptive chronicle. Eileen M. Williamson has published an opinionated view by someone "from away" who became editor of the first newspaper in the mining town of Springdale in *Outport: A Newfoundland Journal* (Scarborough: Medallion Books, 1980), while Jessie Mifflen provides revealing details of professional careers open to women in *Be You a Library Missionary Miss?* (St. John's: Harry Cuff Publications, 1981). Two accounts by "pioneers" demonstrate the opportunities offered to women in pre-Confederation Newfoundland and Labrador: Ilka D. Dickman, *Appointment to Newfoundland* (Manhattan, Kansas: Sunflower University Press, 1981) and Mina Hubbard, *A Woman's Way through Unknown Labrador* (St. John's: Breakwater Books, 1981). Dickman was a doctor who served as a district nurse (!) in Newfoundland in the early years of the Second World War. Her diary is a good primary source on gender roles, and the critical perspective of a professional outsider on everything from midwifery to communications is candidly refreshing.

Mina Hubbard, like Dickman, was not a Newfoundlander, but the indomitable spirit of this Ontario-born American woman inspired Pierre Berton to write a preface to this reprint of her 1908 account of her Labrador odyssey. Widow Hubbard crossed the Labrador peninsula in 1905 in order to vindicate her husband who died in the attempt the previous year. Hubbard has an eye for detail, and her story is a good example of the genre of adventure literature so popular in the early part of the century.

While English-speaking women in Atlantic Canada seem to have been prolific "scribblers," Acadian women were less likely to have kept written records. A fascinating exception was "Marichette," the pen-name of Emilie C. LeBlanc, whose letters to the editor of *L'Évangeline* have been published in Pierre Gérin and Pierre Marie Gérin, *Marichette, Lettres acadiennes — 1895–1898* (Sherbrooke: Les Éditions Naaman, 1982). Among other things, Marichette discussed women's suffrage and criticized the Acadian preoccupation with genealogy. Her refreshing perspective suggests a rich harvest to be reaped in the history of Acadian women. Unfortunately little research has yet been done. The recent anthology, Jean Daigle, ed., *Les Acadiens des Maritimes* (Moncton: Centre d'études acadiennes, 1980) offers only fleeting glances at Acadian women. Jean-Claude Dupont in *Histoire populaire de l'Acadie* (Quebec: Leméac, 1978) provides valuable information on the feminine material culture of Acadie while collective biographies — including Edith Commeau Tufts, *Acadiennes de Clare* (n.p., 1977) and Thérèse Lemieux and Gemma Caron, *Silhouettes Acadiennes* (Campbellton: Fédération des dames d'Acadie, 1981) — have kept the memory and experience of individual women alive. Prince Edward Island women have been similarly served by the Zonta Club of Charlottetown whose members have researched the biographies in *Outstanding Women of Prince Edward Island* (Charlottetown, 1981).

Native women in the Atlantic region are at last beginning to see the shape of their history. A study by Ellice B. Gonzalez, *Changing Economic Roles for Micmac Men and Women: an Ethnohistorical Analysis* has been published by the National Museum in its Mercury Series (Ottawa, 1981), while Ruth Holmes Whitehead's *Micmac Quillwork: Micmac Indian Techniques of Porcupine Quill Decoration, 1600–1950* (Halifax: Nova Scotia Museum, 1982), has raised the material culture of Micmac women to the level of high art. Finally, Johanna Brand's piece of investigative journalism on a Micmac woman who "went down the road" from Shubenacadie to Wounded Knee, brings the brutal facts of life of Amerindian women clearly into focus in *The Life and Death of Anna Mae Asquash* (Toronto: James Lorimer, 1978).

The foregoing survey indicates some of the ground covered by Canadian women's history over the past decade. New areas defined for study promise to keep scholars working for at least a century: women's cultures as they intersect with class, ethnicity, and region; women's protest and accommodation within male-dominated structures; men's attitudes toward women as they are shaped by doctrines of patriarchy and masculinity. And "old chestnuts" of Canadian history will also face sharp scrutiny in the near future.

The study of religion and the church in Canada will surely be among those topics transformed by women's history. Scholars have often noted that the churches in the vanguard of the social gospel movement also produced many of the early feminists. Yet the influence of women on the social gospel in Canada has not been fully examined, nor has the role of women in the emergence of the evangelical churches in the late eighteenth and early nineteenth centuries. In the realm of intellectual history the seemingly contradictory role of the churches as vehicles for the emancipation of women and as props to the status quo has not been explored in the Canadian context, nor has the impact on theosophical beliefs of the many feminists who embraced such doctrines at the turn of the century.[31]

Even political history — that bastion of male domination and preoccupation — will take on a different appearance under the influence of feminist re-vision. Barbara Roberts has already cleverly exposed Donald Creighton's masculine biases in his biography of John A. Macdonald,[32] and similar critiques could well be made of many other biographers who judge the private sphere only as it relates to the public career. Another area drawing the attention of researchers is the role of women in third party movements in Canada.[33] Is it just coincidence that once women received the vote the old two-party system became fragmented and that beginning in the 1920s Canadians were treated with parties and movements variously titled Progressive, Maritime Rights, CCF, Communist, Social Credit, Reconstruction, and Union Nationale? What part did women play not only in founding these movement-parties, but also in voting for them? How were women treated in the structures of parties, new and old? The answers to these questions promise to re-invigorate a field badly in need of revision.

We also need to understand the relationship of women to labour unions. Though it is still commonplace to claim that women are slow to organize and uniformly discriminated against by male-dominated unions, enough evidence exists of women's courage on the picket lines and participation in union executives to require a reassessment of the topic.[34] It is important to explore how women's segregated work affected their sense of power and how behaviour of women in the labour force differed across occupational and ethnic categories. Since the notion of equal pay for equal work was defined well before the First World War, we also need to look more closely at the methods used to marginalize women in unions and the ideology used — by both women and men — to justify it. No doubt a closer look at women's position in working-class households and the values shaping working-class culture will help us answer these important questions.

Family history, still in its infancy in Canada, bears few of the marks of women's history. Incredibly, the field has emerged without a sense of women's position in families and households.[35] It is within families that societal values are mediated, reshaped, and reproduced, and women's changing influence in this process needs to be better understood. Families, of course, change over time, and this change must be analyzed in relation to both women and men. Even the meaning of family life may differ according to gender. It can be argued, for instance, that under certain circumstances, men's families are nuclear while women's families are more extended, reaching out to incorporate distant blood relations. We have little information as yet about the experience of girls in the family context, a significant omission since the household has served so consistently as women's domain. Deborah Gorham has recently published *The Victorian Girl and the Feminine Ideal*,[36] which draws upon British sources, but we need a similar study for Canada where class and society for the same period were markedly different.

Families and households are also the settings where power relationships are established by means both peaceful and violent, legal and illegal. These power relations and their public manifestations must be studied historically; so, too, the concept of motherhood as it is defined in various cultures.[37]

Ethnic and migration studies will also benefit from a feminist perspective.[38] All too often, one looks in vain for a breakdown by gender in tables on immigration. Such information provides important clues to questions of culture and assimilation as well as motivation for uprooting. More important, women often experience migration differently from men, and their stories must also be told. Similarly, studies of rural outmigration frequently discuss only men on the move, though census figures suggest that it was often women who led the stampede to the cities where they could receive wages for the jobs they traditionally performed without pay at home.

It would be possible to go on indefinitely listing areas to be challenged by a feminist point of view. What is clear is that the hearty grasp of Canadian women's history in 1983 has far exceeded its tentative reach in 1973. Though a few purists may be dismayed by the mélange of activities and methodologies comprising the field, its eclectic quality is part of its strength in re-viewing a world too long controlled — and therefore defined — by half the human race.

Notes

1. The Women's Committee of the Canadian Historical Association was formed in 1975, and feminist historians were prominent in the founding of the Canadian Research Institute for the Advancement of Women (CRIAW), which since 1977 has served as an umbrella organization for multidisciplinary research. Historians were also well represented at the plenary sessions of the Canadian Women's Studies Association in 1981–82. Meanwhile, several Canadian-based women's studies publications have appeared — *The Canadian Newsletter of Research on Women* (1972) (since 1979 called *Resources for Feminist Research*), *Atlantis* (1975), *Canadian Women's Studies* (1978), and the *International Journal of Women's Studies* (1978). Journals such as *Histoire sociale/Social History, Labour/Le Travail, Ontario History*, and the *Revue d'histoire de l'Amérique française* have also served as outlets for articles on topics relating to women.

2. For a discussion of the developments in women's history during the 1970s in Canada, I am indebted to Alison Prentice, "Women's History in Canada: A Project in Process" (unpublished paper presented to the Colloquium on Social History, Carleton University, June 1982). See also Eliane Leslau Silverman, "Writing Canadian Women's History, 1970–82: An Historiographical Analysis," *Canadian Historical Review* (hereafter *CHR*) LXIII (Dec. 1982): 513–533; Veronica Strong-Boag, "The Fugitive Female: An Introduction to the Bibliography of Canadian Women's Studies," in *Bibliography for Canadian Studies: Past Trends and Future Needs*, edited by Anne B. Piternick (Toronto, 1982), 48–57.

3. Ruth Pierson and Alison Prentice, "Feminism and the Writing and Teaching of History," *Atlantis* 7 (Spring 1972), 41. See also Gerda Lerner, *The Majority Finds Its Past: Placing Women in History* (New York, 1979) and Elizabeth Fox-Genovese, "Placing Women's History in History," *New Left Review* 133 (May-June 1982): 14.

4. Also, Yolande Cohen recently identified 21 post-graduate theses on women's history out of some 423 completed theses on women in Quebec: see Yolande Cohen, "La Recherche universitaire sur les femmes au Québec, 1929–1980," *Resources for Feminist Research* X (Dec. 1981/Jan. 1982): 5–24.

5. In my search for sources on women's history in the mid-1970s, I was assisted by — in most cases — willing archivists and the *Union List of Manuscripts*, but was unable to determine what women's documents really contained. For instance, women's papers were judged by what information they provided on politics and economic developments, not by what they contributed to the understanding of women. Having read

many of the documents since my inventory was published ("Report on the Archival Resources of the Atlantic Provinces on the Subject of Women's History," *Canadian Newsletter of Research on Women* VII (July 1978): 103–11), it becomes clear that not only do women's documents need to be identified but that identified women's sources need to be re-evaluated in the light of developments in the field of women's studies. See also Veronica Strong-Boag, "Raising Clio's Consciousness: Women's History and Archives in Canada," *Archivaria* IV (Summer 1978): 70–82.

6. Michael Katz, *The People of Hamilton, Canada West* (Cambridge, 1975); David Gagan, *Hopeful Travellers: Families, Land, and Social Change in Mid-Victorian Peel County, Canada West* (Toronto, 1981). Readers of *Acadiensis* should be aware of the following sources pertaining to the Atlantic region: Douglas F. Campbell and David C. Neice, *Ties That Bind— Structure and Marriage in Nova Scotia* (Port Credit, 1979); Sheva Medjuck, "Family and Household Composition in the Nineteenth Century: The Case of Moncton, New Brunswick, 1851 to 1871," *Canadian Journal of Sociology* (hereafter *CJS*) 4 (Summer 1979): 275–86; and Medjuck's useful critique of Michael Katz's work, "The Importance of Boarding for the Structure of the Household in the Nineteenth Century: Moncton N.B. and Hamilton, C.W.," *Histoire sociale/Social History* (hereafter *HS/SH*) 25 (May 1980): 207–13; Lorne Tepperman, "Ethnic Variations in Marriage and Fertility: Canada 1871," *Canadian Review of Sociology and Anthropology* II (1974): 324–43; Patricia Thornton, "Some Preliminary Comments on the Extent and Consequences of Out-Migration from the Atlantic Region, 1870–1920," in *Merchant Shipping and Economic Development in Atlantic Canada*, edited by Lewis R. Fischer and Eric W. Sager (St. John's, 1982). Two articles published in *Acadiensis* also offer valuable clues to the patterns of women's lives: Gisa I. Hynes, "Some Aspects of the Demography of Port Royal, 1650–1755," *Acadiensis* III, 1 (Autumn 1973): 3–17, and Alan A. Brookes, "The Golden Age and the Exodus: the Case of Canning, Kings County," *Acadiensis* XI, 1 (Autumn 1981): 57–82.

7. (New York, 1980).

8. Sylvio Dumas, *Les Filles du Roi en Nouvelle-France* (Quebec, 1972); Marta Danylewycz, "Changing Relationships: Nuns and Feminism in Montreal, 1890–1925," *HS/SH* 28 (Nov. 1981): 213–34; Marguerite Jean, *Évolution des communautés réligieuses des femmes au Québec du 1639 à nos jours* (Montreal, 1977); Jacqueline Bouchard, "Facteurs de sortie des communautés réligieuses du Québec" (PhD dissertation, Université de Montréal, 1970).

9. *HS/SH* 6 (Nov. 1973): 202–23.

10. Catherine L. Cleverdon's *The Woman Suffrage Movement in Canada* (Toronto, 1950) was reprinted, with an introduction by Ramsay Cook, by the University of Toronto Press in 1974.

11. "The Saint John Women's Enfranchisement Association, 1894–1919" (MA thesis, University of New Brunswick, 1979).

12. For a revealing analysis of this process see Graham S. Lowe, "Women, Work, and the Office: The Feminization of Clerical Occupations in Canada, 1901–1931," *CJS* 5 (1980): 361–381.

13. Mary E. Hallett, "Nellie McClung and the Fight for the Ordination of Women in the United Church of Canada," *Atlantis* 4 (Spring 1979): 2–19; Veronica Strong-Boag, "Canadian Feminism in the 1920s: The Case of Nellie McClung," *Journal of Canadian Studies* 12 (Summer 1977): 58–68, Rudy C. Marchildon, "The 'Persons' Controversy: The Legal Aspects of the Fight for Women Senators," *Atlantis* 6 (Spring 1981): 99–113.

14. *Beyond Separate Spheres: Intellectual Roots of Modern Feminism* (New Haven, 1982).

15. Veronica Strong-Boag, "The Girl of the New Day: Canadian Working Women in the 1920s," *Labour/Le Travailleur* (hereafter *L/LT*) 4 (1979): 131–64; Marie Lavigne and Jennifer Stoddart, "Les travailleuses montréalaises entre les deux guerres," *L/LT* 2 (1977): 170–83; Jennifer Stoddart, "The Dorion Commission, 1926–1931: Quebec's Legal Elites Look at Women's Rights," in *Essays in The History of Canadian Law*, 1, edited by David Flaherty (Toronto, 1981), 323–57; Suzanne Buckley, "Efforts to Reduce Infant and Maternal Mortality in Canada Between the Two World Wars," *Atlantis* 2 (Spring 1977): 76–84.

16. At last count Ruth Roach Pierson had published six articles which, in the interest of her readers, should be put between the covers (preferably soft and cheap) of one book. At present they can be located in the following sources: "Women's Emancipation and the Recruitment of Women into the Canadian Labour Force in World War II," *Historical Papers* (1976): 141–73; " 'Home Aide': A Solution to Women's Unemployment After World War II," *Atlantis* 2 (Spring 1977): 85–97; " 'Jill Canuck': CWAC of All Trades, But No 'Pistol Packing Momma'," *Historical Papers* (1978): 106–133; "Ladies or Loose Women: The Canadian Women's Army Corps in World War II," *Atlantis* 4 (Spring 1979): 245–66; "The Double

Bind of the Double Standard: VD Control and the CWAC in World War II," *CHR* LXII (March 1981): 31–58; "Canadian Women and Canadian Mobilization During the Second World War," *Revue internationale d'histoire militaire* 51 (1982): 181–207.

17. Veronica Strong-Boag, "Working Women and the State: the Case of Canada, 1889–1945," *Atlantis* 6 (Spring 1981): 1–9; "Canada's Early Experiments with Income Supplements: the Introduction of Mothers' Allowances," *Atlantis* 4 (Spring 1979): 36–43; " 'Wages for Housework': Mothers' Allowances and the Beginnings of Social Security in Canada," *Journal of Canadian Studies* 14 (Spring 1979): 24–34.

18. Cerise Morris, " 'Determination and Thoroughness': The Movement for a Royal Commission on the Status of Women in Canada," *Atlantis* 5 (Spring 1980): 1–21.

19. Alison Prentice, "The Feminization of Teaching in British North America and Canada, 1845–1875," *HS/SH* 8 (May 1975): 5–20; "Towards a Feminist History of Women and Education" in *Approaches to Educational History*, edited by David Jones et al. (Winnipeg, 1981), 39–145; Marta Danylewycz, Beth Light, and Alison Prentice, "The Evolution of the Sexual Division of Labour in Teaching: A Nineteenth Century Ontario and Quebec Case Study" (unpublished paper presented to the Annual Meeting of the American Historical Association, Los Angeles, December 1981).

20. Eliane Leslau Silverman, "In Their Own Words: Mothers and Daughters in the Alberta Frontier, 1890–1929," *Frontiers* 2 (Summer 1977): 37–44, "Preliminaries to a Study of Women in Alberta, 1890–1929," Canadian Oral History Association *Journal* 3, 1 (1978): 22–26; "Women and the Victorian Work Ethic on the Alberta Frontier: Prescription and Description," in *The New Provinces: Alberta and Saskatchewan, 1905–1980*, edited by Howard Palmer and Donald Smith (Vancouver, 1980), 91–99.

21. Also useful are *A Pioneer Gentlewoman in British Columbia: The Recollections of Susan Allison*, edited by Margaret Ormsby (Vancouver: University of British Columbia Press, 1976) and *God's Galloping Girl: The Peace River Diaries of Monica Storrs, 1929–1931*, edited by W.L. Morton with Vera Fast (Vancouver: University of British Columbia, 1979). For other aspects of British female immigration see Suzanne Buckley, "British Female Immigration and Imperial Development: Experiments in Canada, 1885–1931," *Hecate: Women's Interdisciplinary Journal* 3 (January 1977): 26–40; Barbara Roberts, "A Work of Empire: Canadian Reformers and British Female Immigration" in *A Not Unreasonable Claim*, edited by Linda Kealey (Toronto, 1979), 185–201; "Sex, Politics and Religion: Controversies in Female Reform Work in Montreal, 1881–1919," *Atlantis* 6 (Fall 1980): 25–38; Marilyn Barber, "The Women Ontario Welcomed: Immigrant Domestics for Ontario Homes, 1870–1930," *Ontario History* LXXII (Sept. 1980): 148–172.

22. Wendy Mitchinson, "Historical Attitudes Toward Women and Childbirth," *Atlantis* 4 (Spring 1979): 13–34; "Gynecological Operations on the Insane," *Archivaria* X (1980): 105–14; "R.M. Bucke: A Victorian Asylum Superintendent," *Ontario History* LXII (Dec. 1981): 239–54; "Gynecological Operations on Insane Women: London, Ontario, 1895–1901," *Journal of Social History* 15 (Spring 1982): 467–484.

23. Angus McLaren, "Birth Control and Abortion in Canada, 1870–1920," *Canadian Historical Review* LVIX (Sept. 1978): 319–40.

24. For insights into nineteenth-century legal attitudes, see Constance Backhouse, "Shifting Patterns in Nineteenth Century Canadian Custody Law" in *Essays in the History of Canadian Law*, 1, edited by David Flaherty (Toronto: University of Toronto Press, 1981), "Nineteenth-Century Canadian Rape Law, 1800–92" in *Essays in the History of Canadian Law*, 2 (Toronto: University of Toronto Press, 1983).

25. On this topic see Gail Cuthbert Brandt, "Weaving it Together: Life Cycle and the Industrial Experience of Female Cotton Workers in Quebec, 1910–1950," *L/LT* 7 (Spring 1981): 113–26. See also Bettina Bradbury, "The Family Economy and Work in an Industrializing City: Montreal in the 1870s," *Historical Papers* (1979): 71–96 and Susan Trofimenkoff, "One Hundred and Two Muffled Voices: Canada's Industrial Women in the 1880s," *Atlantis* 3 (Fall 1977): 66–82.

26. Susan Strasser, *Never Done: History of American Housework* (New York, 1982); Dolores Hayden, *Grand Domestic Revolution* (Cambridge, 1981).

27. Ruth Pierson, "Women's History: The State of the Art in Atlantic Canada," *Acadiensis* VII, 1 (Autumn 1977): 121–31; E.R. Forbes, "In Search of a Post-Confederation Maritime Historiography, 1900–1967," *Acadiensis* VIII, 1 (Autumn 1978): 1–21, and reprinted in this volume; Lois D. Kernaghan, "A Man and His Mistress: J.F.W. DesBarres and Mary Cannon," *Acadiensis* XI, 1 (Autumn, 1981): 23–42.

28. Mary Eileen Clarke, "The Saint John Women's Enfranchisement Association, 1894–1919" (M.A. thesis, University of New Brunswick, 1979); Denise Hansen, "Sisters Unite: The United Baptist Women's Missionary Movement, 1867–1914" (B.A. honours essay, Acadia University, 1979); Peter D. Lambly,

"Towards a 'Living Wage': The Minimum-Wage Campaign for Women in Nova Scotia, 1920–1935" (Honours essay, Dalhousie University, 1977); Karen Sanders, "Margaret Marshall Saunders" (M.A. thesis, Dalhousie University, 1978).

29. A project to collect Maritime women's private chronicles is presently being undertaken by Toni Laidlaw (Dalhousie University), Donna Smyth (Acadia University) and myself. A report on that project has recently been published: Margaret Conrad, *Recording Angels: The Private Chronicles of Women from the Maritime Provinces of Canada, 1750–1950* (Ottawa: Canadian Research Institute for the Advancement of Women, 1983).

30. Bradley, *Atlantis* 7 (Fall 1981): 92–101; Johnston, *Atlantis* 4 (Spring 1979): 106–24 and 5 (Fall 1979): 154–82.

31. Michèle Lacombe, "Theosophy and the Canadian Idealist Tradition: A Preliminary Exploration," *Journal of Canadian Studies* 17 (Summer 1982): 100–18. See also, Christopher Headon, "Women and Organized Religion in Mid and Late Nineteenth Century Canada," *Journal of the Canadian Church Historical Society* 20 (March-June 1978): 3–15; Wendy Mitchinson, "Canadian Women and Church Missionary Societies in the Nineteenth Century: A Step Towards Independence," *Atlantis* 2 (Spring 1977): 57–75. For influential American work, see Ann Douglas, *The Feminization of American Culture* (New York, 1977); Barbara Berg, *The Remembered Gate: Origins of American Feminism, The Woman and the City 1800–1860* (New York, 1978); Barbara Leslie Epstein, *The Politics of Domesticity: Women, Evangelism, and Temperance in Nineteenth Century America* (Middletown, Conn., 1981).

32. Barbara Roberts, " 'They Drove Him to Drink' . . . Donald Creighton's Macdonald and His Wives," *Canada: An Historical Magazine* (Dec. 1975): 50–64.

33. John Manley, "Women and the Left in the 1930s, The Case of The Toronto CCF Women's Joint Committee," *Atlantis* 5 (Spring 1980): 100–19; Angus McLaren, " 'What Has This Got to Do with Working Class Women?' Birth Control and the Canadian Left, 1900–1939," *HS/SH* 28 (Nov. 1981): 435–54; Deen Beeby, "Women in the Ontario C.C.F., 1940–1950," *Ontario History* LXXIV (Dec. 1982): 258–83. On women in politics see M. Janine Brodie and Jill McCalla Vickers, *Canadian Women in Politics: an Overview* (Ottawa, 1982); Sylvia B. Bashevkin, "Social Change and Political Partnership: The Development of Women's Attitudes in Quebec," *Comparative Political Studies* 16, 2 (1983): 147–72.

34. Michelle Lapointe, "Le syndicat catholique des allumetières de Hull, 1919–1924," *Revue d'histoire de l'Amérique française* 32 (March 1979): 603–28; Joan Sangster, "The 1907 Bell Telephone Strike: Organizing Women Workers," *L/LT* 3 (1978): 109–30; Star Rosenthal, "Union Maids: Organized Women Workers in Vancouver, 1900–1915," *BC Studies* XLI (1979): 36–55; Eileen Suffrin, *The Eaton Drive: The Campaign to Organize Canada's Largest Department Store, 1948 to 1952* (Toronto, 1982).

35. Rayna Rapp, Ellen Ross, and Renate Bridenthal, "Examining Family History," *Feminist Studies* 5 (Spring 1979): 174–99; Emily M. Nett, "Canadian Families in Socio-historical Perspective," *CJS* (Summer 1980): 239–60.

36. (Bloomington, Indiana, 1982).

37. Canadian scholars wondering how family history and women's history interact would do well to turn to two British monographs: Jane Lewis, *The Politics of Motherhood: Child and Maternal Welfare in England, 1900–1939* (Montreal, 1980) and Diana Gittins, *Fair Sex: Social Change and Family Structure: Women, Work and the Decline of Family Size, 1900–1939* (London, 1982).

38. See a special issue of *Ethnic Studies* XIII, 1 (1981) devoted to ethnicity and femininity, and edited by Danielle Juteau-Lee and Barbara Roberts.

CLIO AS AN ETHNIC: THE THIRD FORCE IN CANADIAN HISTORIOGRAPHY†

ROBERTO PERIN

Acknowledging the importance of ethnicity has become a convention in North America. Although the phenomenon has existed at least since the turn of the century, it only attracted serious attention with the eruption in the United States of the civil rights movement and in Canada of an increasingly assertive Quebec nationalism during the Quiet Revolution. Is it mere coincidence that ethnic groups began to be "discovered" at a time when both states faced serious threats to their integrity? Since that time, writers have marvelled at the persistence of ethnicity even though they were not quite sure what was persisting. Indeed, scholars have been singularly hard-pressed to define the phenomenon. Some see it in purely subjective terms: individuals feel themselves to be ethnics because they identify with aspects of their ancestral culture. Others maintain that "ethnicity concerns privilege, not primarily culture . . . ."[1] It becomes in this way an instrument to promote social mobility either for the individual or the group. But describing a concept's use still does not indicate what it is. Undaunted by such theoretical niceties, some scholars proclaimed ethnicity as significant a social category as class itself.[2]

From this, it is not difficult to see why ethnic revivalists in recent years have increased their demands. Ethnic culture, they insist, must pass from the private to the public sphere. Olga must come out of the closet and be as free to be herself in Wonderland as Anglo Alice is.[3] Some maintain that languages other than English and French must have official status.[4] Others call for the creation of ethnic social movements to force a re-allocation of power in favour of the "third force."[5] This discussion has taken place in apparent ignorance of the last twenty years of Quebec history, which might have provided ethnic revivalists with a sense of perspective, if not realism.

Historical writing inevitably mirrors the concerns of the present. In the ethnic euphoria of the sixties, historians began to view the immigrant experience not as an abrupt break with the past, but rather as continuity. Ethnic culture did not stand as a powerful barrier between newcomers and their land of adoption because this old culture lived on, transplanted to the new soil and nurtured by the warm atmosphere of the ethnic neighbourhood.[6] Sociologists provided a theoretical dimension to this view with the concept of institutional completeness[7] in which development and increasing diversification of ethnic institutions allowed an individual to live a culturally self-contained existence in his or her community without reference to the receiving society. That this said more about the geographical, social, or cultural isolation of the individual than about the institutions' vitality

†*Canadian Historical Review* LXIV, 4 (1983): 441–67.

was not immediately apparent to these theorists. Writing ethnic history, therefore, meant keeping a record of those many institutions and customs which were brought over intact from the mother country and which flourished in the New World. Historians were to approach the study of ethnic communities in the same way they wrote about French or English Canadians with their distinct and complete cultures. This view complemented the belief in cultural pluralism and tolerance which became official dogma in both the United States and Canada.

There were major flaws, however, in this ethnic triumphalism. Community intellectuals observed with dismay and embarrassment that the culture of the ethnic group and that of the mother country did not coincide. Immigrants on the whole spoke their native language badly. Their vocabulary was impoverished; their knowledge of grammar, lacking; their speech, studded with anglicisms and English grammatical structures. They had little contact with high culture and clung tenaciously to cultural forms long discarded in their homeland and ill suited to a sophisticated urban environment. These intellectuals, who were their community's first historians, either glossed over these anomalies or, even worse, whitewashed the immigrants' past.[8] For their part, ethnic groups tended to be very much aware of their "shortcomings" and suffered from what Robert Harney has termed self-disesteem.[9] Over the years, they experienced serious erosion, not to say assimilation, to the extent that many inside observers express serious doubts about the future viability of many ethnic cultures.[10] The reality of the immigrant experience is therefore far removed from the theorizing of the sociologists of ethnicity, from the celebrations of ethnic revivalists, or from the mental gymnastics of government officials who are busily devising new cultural policies based on such intangibles as subjective perceptions, private preferences, or the importation of metropolitan culture.

That reality is best understood by discarding concepts such as persistence and completeness. It may well be that the classical notion of ethnicity is rooted in these concepts: an ethnic group may well emerge and grow from a long and intimate association with a space, from shared experiences and memories transmitted to successive generations, and from a sense of autonomy and cohesion. If so, we are not dealing in North America with classical ethnic groups. The notion of a space is basic to ethnicity. Without it, there can be no shared experiences or memories, nor can a sense of autonomy or cohesion emerge. An ethnic culture cannot survive simply on memories of a distant space. To maintain its distinctiveness and to flourish, it must interact with a real, an immanent space. In North America, however, immigrant groups do not have a space they can claim exclusively for themselves. They are dispersed across a continent and must contend with the ever-encroaching presence of the receiving culture. Consequently, their experience is not that of an ethnic group. This article therefore prefers the terms "immigrant communities" and "immigrant cultures" to those of "ethnicity" and "ethnic cultures," because they capture the changing and evanescent character of the immigrant experience through successive generations.

How is the historian to understand immigrant communities? Robert Harney, who has been in the forefront of such efforts, emphasizes the need to study them on their own terms. Although his comments refer specifically to Little Italies, they have universal validity. "Perhaps nothing . . . epitomized the marginality of being immigrant more than the fact that while the immigrant enclave was being treated as an aberrant and temporary problem for North American scholars, Italian intellectuals dismissed them as an embarrassing misrepresentation of Italian civilization."[11]

These immigrants, Harney insists, are not stereotypical Italians who happen to be living in North America. To begin with, their native culture is particular, bounded by class and region. In some way, it shares in the overall metropolitan culture of the mother country, but cannot be seen as synonymous with it.[12] In fact, Old World intellectuals often have considered this particularistic culture to be an aberration in their own society. Now when this culture is exposed to the New World environment, it becomes profoundly North American in a way which social gospellers and their modern successors, the theorists of multi-culturalism, cannot fathom because they define the term "North American" by the standards of the host society. The institutions and culture which immigrants established here were in response to specific North American conditions, and while they may have retained Old World forms, their content had a peculiarly New World meaning. The immigrants' "American-ness" was immediately apparent to their Old World relatives, but not to North Americans, who dismissed them as aliens while at the same time expecting them to behave as Anglos.

In this context, Frances Swyripa's provocative critique of *All of Baba's Children* raises a false methodological problem. "What is the dividing line," she asks, "between Ukrainian Canadian history and Canadian history?"[13] Ironically this is the same question posed by those who consider immigrant history of little significance to the study of Canadian history. Are not depression stories all the same, whether the actors be Ukrainians or other Canadians? Is Two Hills, Alberta, any different from any other prairie town? Doubly ironic is the fact that this perspective leads Swyripa to a conclusion, tentative though it be, which ultimately undermines the legitimacy of immigrant history. "In future, will Ukrainian Canadian history be increasingly restricted to the ever-narrowing, visible, vocal community, the guardian and spokesman of a distinct Ukrainian cultural identity?"[14] At that point, we may well ask, will anyone care? Swyripa's point of view betrays the conscious or unconscious assumption that Ukrainians in Canada are the remnant faithfully living the true Ukrainian culture defined by "proper" speech, adherence preferably to Orthodoxy, though Uniate Catholicism will do, and other such formal characteristics.

It is necessary instead to broaden this concept of culture to encompass aspects of everyday life which, after all, are its very basis. Immigrant history, it must be stressed, is not about "national" culture, but about popular culture. Fortunately historians have begun to identify these North American forms, rituals, and institutions which, together with the formal structures, give immigrants a sense of themselves and of the world around them. Whether or not these are short-lived is immaterial. The fact remains that they help us to understand key aspects of the immigrant experience as long as there continue to exist, in one form or another, observable communities (not Swyripa's visible and vocal remnant which is self-consciously Ukrainian and disdains things Ukrainian-Canadian). Immigrant culture therefore may not be a permanent historical category, but it is a useful tool to penetrate the complexity of industrial society and to elucidate important chapters of Canadian history.

This historiography of Canadian immigrant groups, of course, has mushroomed in the past ten years.[15] In fact, some observers term it the "new ethnic history" to distinguish it from earlier filiopietistic writings. It remains true, however, that there is a lot of old wine in these new wineskins.

The most visible contribution to the field is the Generations series of monographs commissioned by the Department of the Secretary of State. This project arose out of the legitimate concern expressed by the Royal Commission on Bilingualism and Biculturalism that Canadian historical writing had neglected the contribution of many immigrant groups to their country. The government decided to correct this imbalance by funding the research and publication of monographs dealing with some twenty-five such groups. The intention was certainly noble, but the government has yet to learn that parthenogenesis is not the best means to stimulate the creation of a new field of study. Many of these works were literally virgin births. They saw the light of day without the benefit of extensive and fertile research at the local or regional level and without being tied to specific issues integral to Canadian history. They were expected to be broad syntheses, to be produced by specific dates and, not surprisingly, many were stillborn.

Ill conceived as well was the notion that a standard-sized text should be the format suited to each of the twenty-five groups. Whether or not this was the result of an overly simplistic concern for the equality of all ethnic groups is unclear. But it remains true that some immigrant communities are older than others; some, larger and more developed; some, more intimately involved in key problems of Canadian life. If, however, government guidelines apportion 250 pages to the Scots and to the Arabs, either much will be left unstated or much overstated.

Would it not have been wiser to take a longer-range approach to the dearth of immigrant history in Canada? Funds could have been provided to support less grandiose and more basic research. The results, while less spectacular if judged by the number of books in print, would have been more enduring. The Multicultural History Society of Ontario has, to its credit, followed this tack. The small and unpretentious monographs, the special issues of *Polyphony*, and the conference papers published by the Society have on the whole contributed more to the history of immigrants in Canada than the Generations series.

Of course, the authors are not responsible for conditions imposed upon them. As noted above, their task was often thankless. And yet, the quality of the work produced varies considerably. Of the eight books published so far, four are unmitigated failures — those on the Scots, the Greeks, the Arabs, and the Norwegians;[16] three contain a few good chapters and, on the whole, can be considered fair — those on the Portuguese, Poles, and Japanese;[17] only one study, on the Hungarians, is basically good.[18] The latter will be treated separately. The others, to which can be added a recent work of mediocre quality not in the Generations series, on the Portuguese in Quebec,[19] will be discussed together since they share the same problems.

Their major weakness is a lack of context. While it is true that primary and secondary material was unavailable, the authors were not operating in a vacuum.

American research on immigrants is richer and more developed than in Canada. Had the authors been acquainted with this literature, they at least might have known what to avoid. Ignored as well is the innovative and stimulating research produced by urban, labour, or family history.

More surprising still is general disregard of the Canadian context. To those who read *The Enemy that Never Was*, this may appear as a startling comment. Yet this book is more about Canadian nativism than about Japanese Canadians. When Ken Adachi does describe immigrant culture, he largely ignores the Canadian environment. On the other hand, what saves the books on the Portuguese and the Poles are precisely those chapters on the themes of arrival and settlement which have a definite sense of place. Even discussions of the workplace in these eight studies are little more than catalogues of jobs leading ever onward and upward. The authors do not attempt to analyze what kind of labour market their immigrants entered, or how they took advantage of particular growth sectors in regional and local economies to better their circumstances. Instead, the economic success of the Arabs, for example, is explained by the "Levantine Ethic."[20] If only Max Weber had known! The authors are so fervently convinced that education and social mobility are linked that they seem oblivious to the French-Canadian example, which tends to cast doubts on the equation. It may be objected, of course, that many of the writers in the series are sociologists, not historians. If this comment were to be taken seriously, it would be a sad reflection of the indigence of Canadian sociology.

Another symptom of this eviscerated kind of history is the perfunctory references to Quebec, even though many groups have important concentrations in the province. It seems obvious that their presence in a French-speaking milieu would give rise to particular, if not interesting, problems; but these are not investigated. One may well ask who then will read the French editions of Generations; certainly not Quebeckers, whose existence is hardly acknowledged in them, and certainly not the immigrants who, as we all know, speak English. *Vivent le bilinguisme et le multiculturalisme!* Even *Les Portugais du Québec* largely ignores the Quebec context: its view of French Canadians is based on a now-obsolete study by Vattier done in 1928!

As a result of their shortcomings, these books exhibit the serious methodological pitfalls discussed at the beginning of this article. The reader is presented with immigrants as standard-bearers of their native culture. But in reality, this culture is a museum piece, removed from its natural environment, hermetically sealed in glass, and quite dead. Not even the trumpetings of filiopietists, nor the rose-tinted prophecies of profit, both of which abound in all these works, can raise it up.

Most studies, for example, begin with an outline of the political history of the mother country, devoid of historiographical references. Two books focus instead on early contacts between Canada and the mother country. The inevitable genuflections to ethnic ancestors occur in either case. Did we know, for instance, that Juan de Fuca was Greek, as probably was Christopher Columbus[21] (although my sources tell me he was really Jewish)? Stephan Parmenius, a Hungarian, visited Canada in 1583;[22] but he was upstaged by the Portuguese, João Fernandes, who came almost a century earlier.[23] Still, who could beat the record set by the

Vikings?[24] Even they may have to share the limelight with yet another Hungarian who was possibly a member of Leif Eriksson's crew. All this is sadly reminiscent of Harney's words: "To the most damaging of all North American charges — being new to the land— they responded with long and inventive accounts of the antiquity if the[ir] . . . presence in America."[25]

Would not a more fitting and relevant introduction to these books have been an examination of the social and cultural conditions of the peasantry in the mother country during the nineteenth century, since most non-English-speaking immigrants came from these ranks? In this regard, Paul Body's chapter in *Struggle and Hope* which discusses the macro- and micro-determinants of emigration is a model to be emulated, drawing as it does from migration studies in Hungary and American immigration history.[26]

The core of each study consists of several chapters, as dry as they are static, describing the ethnic culture. Predictably, culture is defined as family, religion, ethnic organization, and language. But rather than considering the family as an economic unit, which might (eventually) have given rise to comparative analyses, most authors present it in structural terms, emphasizing its unique characteristics. These characteristics, instead of being unique, all appear to describe the extended family common to some peasant societies. Still, they allow the writers to reflect yet again on the process of modernization of the family structure.

The topic of religion is presented largely as a set of beliefs and rituals revolving around a litany of feast days. Inevitably, one is subjected to an elaborate list of ethnic parishes and to their vicissitudes; these are as interesting to the reader as are stock-market quotations to the theologian. David Higgs diverges briefly from this model to make insightful comments on popular religion and levels of religious practice, which underscore the importance of viewing religion not as a formal and ossified structure, but as an essentially popular and living phenomenon.[27]

The chapters on ethnic organizations, with their merciless enumerations of professional, business, press, sport, and political associations, invariably represent a monolithic community. Those not fortunate enough to find themselves in that conceptually elusive but very real "mainstream" are either ignored or relegated to the outer reaches of society, if not of sanity. Loken uniformly depicts the Norwegians as earnest Lutherans. Not even the Depression seems to rock this fortress of faith. For their part, Henry Radecki and even N. F. Dreisziger do not ignore, but tend to downplay, the importance of the left in the Polish and Hungarian communities, particularly in the thirties. The former is quite content to view mainstream ethnic organizations as schools for Canadian democracy. Could they not also have been boulevards of political patronage? But this seems to be too controversial a theme to be discussed in public.

Not surprisingly, these studies end with insistent hymns of praise and thanksgiving. Immigrants are shown bleating their contentment in the new land. How do these scholars arrive at their conclusions? It seems that oral interviews and questionnaires are their only tools. These are, however, highly suspect if not used with subtlety and sophistication. Far more eloquent are the authors' underlying assumptions and judgments. Their constant references to upward mobility, based on anecdote rather than on scientific techniques, become incantations to exorcise embarrassing and lingering spirits of backwardness and low socio-economic status in immigrant communities. Some authors, in fact, show implicit disdain for their subjects. Peter Chimbos seems to imply that Canadian society finds little to value in his immigrant culture, unless that culture is expressed in classical Hellenic terms.[28] Similarly, Radecki suggests that the peasant origins of the first Polish immigrants, those who presumably were not members of a distinguished family, explain their lack of enthusiasm for education and their inability to maintain their native language.[29] With approaches as elitist, with attitudes as pretentious and callous as these, it is little wonder that these studies fail to come to terms with the immigrant experience.

Struggle and Hope stands out among these books as a notable exception. The work is by no means perfect. The chapters on Hungarian history and on the Saskatchewan settlement bear little relation to the rest of the text, and display many of the problems discussed above. However, Nandor Dreisziger redeems this study with his own important contribution. He has produced an honest, mature, and stimulating synthesis which will serve as a good springboard for further research. Prospective Generations authors might reflect with profit on his approach. Dreisziger marries social and cultural themes within specific periods of study. Consequently, his discussions of formal culture are neither abstract nor belaboured. He uses a wide range of documentation, including the Canadian census, government documents, Hungarian-Canadian parish and newspaper records, and Hungarian diplomatic reports. The book, therefore, provides a broad picture of the life of the Hungarian immigrants in Canada from the First World War to the revolution of 1956. Dreisziger's Hungarians are not cardboard cutouts, but real people with a historical presence about whom he writes feelingly. They move on a Canadian stage and are shaped by and interact with their Canadian environment. His book should mark a new beginning for an otherwise mediocre collection.

The Generations series is by no means a barometer of the state of the art in Canada. For the past ten years, scholars and writers have been examining different aspects of the immigrant experience, from its earliest manifestations in the phenomenon of migration, to the creation of immigrant communities and their participation in the socio-cultural life of Canada. Their work has lent seriousness and sophistication to a field which Canadian historians can no longer afford to ignore. It is true, however, that the period of first immigration, 1896 to 1913 and the decade of the 1920s, has been better researched. The later period, following the Second World War, is still largely dominated by analyses of public attitudes to immigration, government policies, mobility, and voter behaviour patterns. In other words, for this most recent era, scholars have not considered the immigrant on his or her own terms. No one has attempted to apply the concepts developed for the earlier era; nor has anyone measured with success the impact of later immigration on existing communities.[30] Having said this, we can look at the various components of the immigrant experience and assess the contribution of the many authors to the field.

For many immigrants, abandoning their homeland was an involuntary act. Initially, it took the form of migration and was considered to be a temporary leave-taking. In two excellent essays, Robert Harney looks at the topic both as an individual experience through the eyes of the migrant,[31] and as a process, a business to be exact.[32] He evokes the rural Old World milieu, with its failing economy, its family-centred life, and its strong sense of place. At the same time, he illustrates the extreme porousness of peasant societies at the turn of the century when labour recruitment literature and *padrone* business cards penetrated the most "backward" and inward-looking villages. In this world, the illiterate migrant sought out "educated men" who could mediate between him and the alien world outside his village. A succession of go-betweens entered the picture — from the parish priest, to the notary, the local notable, the steamship agent, the labour bosses; each exacted his pound of flesh.

Harney dispels the romantic image of the migrant as a latter-day Robinson Crusoe. His was not an exciting adventure in which he remade his life in the New World without reference to the Old. The go-betweens and the migrant's work companions who, more likely than not, came from the same area, ensured that the home town was omnipresent in America. Physically too, the migrant was a prisoner of his objectives. The urgency of acquiring cash and the possibility of failure haunted him constantly. Harney movingly describes the migrant's decline into brutishness caused by the deplorable working conditions in the Canadian bush. While there is no reason to idealize the life of the peasantry in the late nineteenth century, the contrast between this closely knit, settled, immanent society and the raw exploitation, the barren isolation of the Canadian North could not have been greater for the migrant. Yet he lived through this experience in a state of suspended animation, knowing that it was temporary and that somehow his objectives would be achieved. Harney's pieces are undoubtedly a high point in the literature of immigrant groups.

The factors drawing this surge of migrants to Canada at the turn of the century were examined ten years ago by Donald Avery.[33] His article revolutionized our way of perceiving Canadian immigration policy. He clearly identified the immigrant's place in the Canadian economy during the Laurier era, as well as the pre-eminent role played by capitalists in fashioning immigration policy. The article was subsequently incorporated in his much-criticized "*Dangerous Foreigners*."[34] Whatever the defects of this book (the lack of thematic unity being its most outstanding), it still makes an important contribution. It is based on solid and wide-ranging documentation and successfully challenges many of the myths surrounding the immigrant.

This work does not, however, deal with the life of the immigrant either in the bush or in the city. Although Anthony Rasporich has insisted on the need to study the immigrant on the northern fringes,[35] little has been written on this topic, probably because of the documentary problems involved. Edmund W. Bradwin's[36] is still the classic study. Two excellent articles, however, merit attention: Ian Radforth's examination of Finnish lumber workers and Allan Seager's article on Finnish miners, both set in northern Ontario.[37] The authors describe very well the sense of community of immigrant workers in the face of harsh and tyrannical employers. This was the north many years after the initial stages of migration; these were in fact settled communities. But one is struck by how immigrants managed in these more remote centres to rekindle the feelings of cohesion and solidarity which they had known in the mother country.

A key figure linking the new workers to the labour needs of the frontier was the *padrone*. Once again it is Harney who devotes attention to this character.[38] The *padrone* was considered by the receiving society to represent the archetypal immigrant: slippery, furtive, ruthless, and violent. He was also an effective scapegoat for residual guilt feelings. In assessing this character, Harney has tried to break away from the moralism of American and Italian historiography by placing him in the overall context of the commerce of migration. He also emphasizes the *padrone*'s vulnerability, dependent as he was on the good graces of Canadian capitalists, on a state of non-belligerence and of grudging co-operation with the many *padroni* of North America, and on the forbearance of government. Although Harney captures the precarious world of the *padrone*, he does tend to downplay the exploitative relationship between labour boss and migrant. No matter how grateful the latter might be for the *padrone*'s protection, no matter how content with his remittances, no matter how exploitative the whole commerce of migration, the *padrone* remained an integral and insidious part of that system.

Jobs in the bush were, of course, seasonal and if, at the end of this period, migrants had not reached their financial goals, they would look for extra work in the cities. Historians have now begun to study some of the urban institutions of the migrant's sojourning culture. The boarding-house was one of these. Harney has drawn us away from seeing it simply as a folksy institution which allowed the transplanted culture to thrive.[39] It was, he insists, an enterprise, and a very organized one at that! For the owner, it was part of a set of strategies to break out of the cycle of low wages. Based on the tradition of the peasant family as an economic unit, it allowed the wife to earn money while she raised her family. For the boarder, the benefits were also primarily financial; but there were also intangible advantages, such as home cooking and the re-creation of the ambience of home. The boarding-house was so crucial that for many migrants no reality existed outside of it.[40] But it also proved vital to the whole immigrant community, since it spawned a host of institutions which became mainstays of the New World culture.

Migrants soon became immigrants and the period of sojourning gave way to that of settlement. When this transition occurred is unclear. It may be, as Harney suggests, that once questions of marriage and inheritance were settled back home, the sojourner put down roots in the new country. This may have happened at the level of the community when women joined their menfolk and when children began to be born in Canada. Still, the concept of sojourning remains illusive because within many immigrant groups it was an ongoing phenomenon, even after the community got settled. Historians too often think of the transition from sojourning to settlement as linear when in fact it is dynamic. However, it is clear that ethnic neighbourhoods soon began to emerge.[41] These were found in areas of cheap housing, usually the urban core, and were not exclusive to any particular group.

We should not see these neighbourhoods in folkloristic terms, any more than we would the other expressions of the immigrant's culture. They were neither static nor monolithic, but rather a curious amalgam of pre-industrial and modern. They were, for example, fragmented by an intense *esprit de clocher* because the peasants' primary loyalty was to their village or town. So strong was this feeling that, as John Zucchi indicates, the Italians of Toronto only patronized merchants from their home town. Immigrants formed organizations based on this intense localism of which the *landsmanshaften* are but an example.

It is impossible to say when a broader identification with the mother country developed. It is undeniable, however, that this wider identity arose out of specifically Canadian circumstances. In part, of course, it may have been a response to nativism. A much stronger force was undoubtedly the participation of immigrants from the same country in common institutions. Still, in communities where immigration is ongoing, the narrower allegiance persists to this day side by side with the larger sense of identity.

Ethnic neighbourhoods were divided not only according to region, but also by rank and status. To some extent, these divisions reflected the peasant society back home with its hierarchies and its sense of deference, but again they were created by specifically Canadian circumstances. A barely literate rustic like Antonio Cordasco could, by artful manipulation, become a *prominente* in his community. The range of services he provided as labour boss, banker, food provisioner, and boarding-house keeper made him indispensable to migrants. Yet, as Bruno Ramirez and Michael Del Balso skilfully demonstrate, this prominence without pedigree co-existed with a more genteel and established one based on mother country standards. The two sometimes clashed, using different sets of symbols and honours to establish their primacy.[42] Whether status was inherited from the Old World or established as a result of cunning, stratification was very real in the immigrant neighbourhood.

How one became a *prominente* is still unclear. But the ability to exploit the needs of recently arrived immigrants, and particularly to control part of the labour market, was important. For example, an immigrant who opened a grocery store moved out of wage labour and took the first tentative steps to prominence. If, as Franc Sturino has shown for the twenties, a grocer could through his contacts with market gardeners provide migrant farm labourers with their first jobs, his rise to prominence was secured.[43] Nor should we neglect contacts with important members of the receiving culture. Jacob Cohen, for example, greatly enhanced his status in the Jewish community in Toronto through his links with the Conservative party and with Colonel Denison, who got him a judicial appointment.[44]

Prominence was not the itinerary of most immigrants. They struggled instead against the vicissitudes of the wage system vividly described in recent Canadian social histories. They devised various strategies to cope with this situation. Immigrants were above all "polyvalent" workers: they were prepared to take on a variety of odd jobs to see them through periods of slackness. Even their houses expressed this adaptability and resourcefulness, since very often there was no clear distinction between living and working space. The pictures in Robert Harney and Harold Troper's *Immigrants* are very eloquent in this regard. Wives and children were integral parts of the family economy. In a stimulating and imaginative article, Bruno Ramirez recently explored some of the devices which made immigrants less responsive to the inducements of the market place. Keeping vegetable gardens and one or two farm animals, processing food at home, exchanging skills and services among kinsmen, building one's house in stages using material discarded (or not) from one's workplace: immigrants used these and other techniques to make life more settled and pleasant at a time when, as Terry Copp showed, real wages were falling.[45] This extra-market production, as Ramirez termed it, should not be perceived only as an economic phenomenon, but as a part of the immigrant's culture.

Slowly material conditions improved. It may be best at this point to consider the concepts of class and social mobility as used in some of this literature. Doubtless it is important to study how immigrants perceived their position within the neighbourhood. There is a danger, however, that the historian will transform these perceptions into absolutes. Harney, for example, is so anxious to move away from the view of the ethnic neighbourhood as the rubbish heap of the American dream that he exaggerates its autonomy with respect to the social structure of the receiving culture. The switch from being a ditchdigger to a grocer may indicate relative mobility, but may not change (perceptions notwithstanding) the immigrant's position in the Canadian class structure. Similarly, Harney abuses a much-abused term by referring to the "ethnic middle class" as a bourgeoisie. It is one thing to note that stratification existed within immigrant neighbourhoods; it is quite another to argue as if these differences in rank were somehow unrelated to an overall class system.[46]

As material circumstances got better, so did the ambience of the neighbourhood. Immigrants, of course, began to make for themselves a familiar landscape soon after their arrival in Canada. Varpu Lindstrom-Best, for example, captures the Finns' spirit of inventiveness as they created a garden out of the cultural wilderness with their temperance societies, their "fist presses," and their theatre.[47] Eventually they institutionalized these early creative impulses by building halls which became centres of political and artistic expression.[48] But most settled communities looked to more formal symbols of their "arrival."

For many immigrants, the church was one of these. What this symbol meant to them, however, is not always obvious. Historians too often interpret it as proof of the peasants' innate religiosity.[49] First, we must bear in mind that North America altered the conditions under which Old World churches operated: here they became voluntary institutions deprived of the coercive power of the state[50] and subject to intense competition from indigenous churches.[51] Second, the phenomenon of religion as a bond between the individual and the local community no longer existed. Harney vividly illustrates this point in citing the example of Italian immigrants from two different villages fighting in Toronto to see which group would carry the statue of St Roch in procession, St Roch being the patron saint of both home towns.[52] Somehow the environment had altered, not to say debased, the meaning of a primitive and vital mother country ceremony. Finally, the most telling point on the religiosity of peasants is made by Ramirez and Del Balso, who looked at the annual reports prepared by the pastors of two Italian parishes in Montreal. These indicated that the immigrants generally neglected their Christian duties.[53] That the church was a gathering place and a focal point for the immigrant community is clear; what it was beyond that requires further investigation.

Ethnic schools were another accoutrement of a settled community, a bridge between the first and second generations. Eleoussa Polyzoi strongly portrays the tension between the Old World curriculum, often filiopietistic, and the New World pupils, underlining the point that these schools were not merely "transplants" of the culture of the mother country.[54]

But formal structures like churches and schools should not mask the more informal institutions of an established community. Ramirez and Del Balso show that Italian grocery stores, which doubled in number in Montreal between 1911 and 1916, not only contributed to the ambience of the immigrant neighbourhood, but were important focuses of community life, serving as meeting-places and distribution centres of news and gossip.[55] More attention must be given to these informal structures, which might be as important as churches and schools for immigrant culture.

Because *The Jews of Toronto* is an extensive study of an immigrant community in an urban setting, it warrants particular attention here. This book is both a social and an institutional account. But the two perspectives are not well integrated and it is the latter which soon takes precedence, to the detriment of the vitality of the study. The pages dealing with the immigrants from eastern Europe, their insertion into Toronto's industrial life, and their confrontation with the older "white" Jewish community over ritual, social assistance, and labour issues are vividly reconstructed by the author. Stephen Speisman in fact touches many of the themes discussed above. However, the book abruptly shifts attention away from the working-class Jews who, the author insistently reminds us, comprised the bulk of the community, to the elite and their organizational activities. It also concentrates almost exclusively on observant Jews and their religious life, making only brief references to the secularists and their organizations. And yet Speisman never indicates clearly how significant an element the religious Jews were within the community. In short, part of the study will be of interest to Canadian social historians; the rest has a much narrower appeal.

While urban immigrants have been the subject of some excellent work, their country cousins predictably have suffered neglect. Examinations of the rural immigrant experience are neither considerable nor very developed. A decade ago, Harold Troper looked at the efforts of the Immigration Department to attract American farmers during the Laurier era.[56] In the same year, Howard Palmer produced a popular account of immigrant groups in southern Alberta, which brought together much interesting information, but which is now dated.[57] More recently, *Canadian Ethnic Studies* devoted an issue to immigrant settlement patterns and the way government regulations undermined their distinctiveness.[58] There is, however, no rural equivalent to the studies of the urban immigrant experience discussed above. Still, two books on Ukrainians in the West by Helen Potrebenko and Myrna Kostash move in that direction.[59]

I should mention at the outset that both books are flawed. Potrebenko adopts a crudely Manichean style, pitting the capitalist exploiters and their Ukrainian lackeys against the hapless, but not helpless, Ukrainian workers and farmers. Her narrative is also marred by a lack of focus: in her frequent accounts of Alberta social and political history, which are intentionally derivative, she does not indicate the specific Ukrainian presence. The book consequently alternates between happenings within the Ukrainian-Albertan communities and broader events in Alberta history without connecting the two. Kostash, for her part, writes a popular history based on her own experience as a second-generation Ukrainian growing up in smalltown Alberta. (It is really quite mysterious, incidentally, why "popular," in this country, should be synonymous with lack of rigour.) The anecdotal style and the presentation of events without reference to historical context and in romanticized tones diminish this study.

Yet both accounts retain a certain power. Particularly evocative are the difficult settlement years at the turn of the century.[60] The terrible isolation of the prairies, caused by the ban on block settlement and the policy of reserved lands which dispersed immigrants even more, contrasted sharply with the rural village life of eastern Europe. Peasants were as resouceful as their urban cousins in confronting these difficult circumstances. They adopted many of the co-operative strategies of urban immigrants to see them through. Yet neither Kostash nor Potrebenko succumbs to a facile Whiggism. Settlement was not uniformly successful, and many farms had to be forfeited because settlers could not meet their obligations. Both authors also describe the almost total absence of social services. The early settlement years left a legacy of high infant mortality, poor nutrition, substandard housing, and inadequate clothing. But what is never clear from these accounts is where the Ukrainians' experience differed from that of other settlers.

Of the two writers, Kostash is both more courageous and insightful. She does not hesitate to broach the anti-Semitic and anti-native attitudes of early Ukrainian Canadians, a subject which seems to be taboo in this era of cultural tolerance. She also alludes to Liberal party patronage in the Laurier years and efforts to co-opt prominent members of the community, a theme echoed by Martin Kovacs in his study of prairie Hungarians.[61] Kostash deplores as well the other-worldliness, the cult of a mystical Ukraine, characterizing most cultural expression in the West. Paradoxically, as her own chapter on culture exemplifies, she still tends to depict Ukrainian-Canadian culture in folkloristic terms: painted Easter eggs, merry wedding feasts, religious holidays and their elaborate celebrations. A broader perspective on this topic has yet to be developed.

The Ukrainian Orthodox Church was certainly a focal point in the lives of many immigrants and was, as Paul Yuzyk shows, a Canadian creation.[62] Yuzyk's study, though, is turgidly institutional. The author insists on going back to the origins of organized Christianity in the land of Rus. He then describes in triumphalistic terms the development of this body in Canada. This study, too, suffers from a Manichean vision. It presents an elite, pretentiously termed intellectuals,[63] leading a backward, inarticulate, unenlightened, and often indifferent peasantry to the light under the twin banners of reason and education.[64] At the same time, the author would have us believe that a democratic spirit suffused the Church! The narrative also contains more than a hint of ethno-centrism: "foreigners"[65] seem bent on robbing Ukrainian Canadians of their heritage and in any case are shown to be incapable of understanding their needs. This pious, smug, and brittle study will be of limited use to the historian of immigrant groups.

The experiences of the rural and urban immigrants come together under the topic of labour. Many worked in the primary sector before settling on their farms or in the cities. The attempt to study immigrants in their working environment has hardly been made.[66] Clearly more work, particularly of a comparative nature, must be done in this area. Historians have instead directed attention almost exclusively to labour unrest in the primary sector. On the immigrant in secondary industries almost nothing has been written.[67]

What has existing research indicated? The myth of the immigrant as a docile proletarian has been seriously challenged. The "foreign worker" may not have had the opportunity or the inclination to participate steadfastly in trade unions, but did not hesitate to use force when pushed to the limit by employers.[68] Immigrants also displayed a remarkable sense of solidarity which overrode their diverse origins.[69]

Ethnic rivalry, however, undoubtedly existed among workers, and employers constantly manipulated it to advantage. Labour historians eventually will have to determine whether these divisions according to country of origin were centripetal or centrifugal forces within the working class. To what extent did groups of workers play on these rivalries to promote their own interests? In the Lakehead strikes at the turn of the century, Jean Morrison contrasts the British workers and their parliamentary methods with southern European labour and its traditions of spontaneous revolt. It is never clear what role cultural determinants play in this depiction. But more fundamentally, in the violent atmosphere characterizing labour relations at the Lakehead, was not the advocacy of due process a way of ingratiating oneself with management? Did not the English-speaking workers have most to gain in this dynamic? The question is important because it is related to Gabriel Kolko's portrayal of immigrants in the United States as an amorphous and rootless *lumpenproletariat* who presumably made the American labour movement what it is today.[70] Were "foreign workers" instead marginalized by an accommodating indigenous working class, or must other factors, such as repression by employers and the police or the Americanization of Canadian trade unions, come into play?

A related question involves the role of immigrants in radical labour movements. Avery, Rasporich, Radforth, and Seager have documented the participation and even the leadership of immigrants in unions from the IWW to the Workers' Unity League.[71] Were these people an insignificant minority in their own communities and among immigrants as a whole in Canada? The question will doubtless have to await further research, but the image of the acquiescent immigrant now must be qualified.

Closely allied to the theme of labour is that of the political immigrant. Recent research has transformed our perception of early Canadian socialism.[72] The important presence of Finns and Ukrainians in Canadian socialist parties is now well established. Lindstrom-Best describes the political culture of Finnish immigrants: their commitment to improving themselves by establishing libraries and disseminating handwritten newspapers; their earnestness in opposing drink and church-sanctioned weddings; and their discipline. She emphasizes as well the active role of women in socialist politics. Norman Buchignani and Doreen Indra, for their part, show the high degree of politicization in the East Indian community of the west coast at the turn of the century.[73] For these immigrants, politics were not only to be talked about but to be acted on. They established institutions based on egalitarian or socialist principles, such as co-operatives, credit unions, and mutual aid societies, most of which endured long after the parties and sects had disappeared.[74]

The individual immigrant radical has attracted a good deal of attention lately, much of it perhaps unwarranted.[75] This was a peculiar breed of immigrant, well-born, highly educated, and politically committed. In most cases, these radicals were forced to flee to the New World because of repression at home. North America made them into misfits. The conservative intellectual climate prevailing in Canada, their own difficulties with the English language, the cultural gap between themselves and their immigrant communities — all these factors conspired to make them marginal. Among Canadian socialists, they were different, outsiders; among their fellow immigrants, they were sophisticated urbanites; in the wider Canadian society, they were just more aliens. The message which they delivered with such conviction in the mother country somehow lost its impact in the new environment, and they seemed incapable of adjusting it to changed circumstances. In some ways, they had never immigrated because spiritually they remained children of the mother country; yet in other ways, emigration abruptly cut them off from rapidly changing and critical events at home. This explains their restlessness, their undisciplined activity, their eclecticism, a striking example of which is Ole Hjelt, the Norwegian socialist who supported Quisling during the Second World War. Only Tomo Cacic does not fit this stereotype. A self-educated worker of peasant origins, he never wavered in his commitment to revolutionary ideology and paid the price, becoming one of the more celebrated victims of the infamous Section 41 of the Immigration Act. But Cacic aside, is there not in the fascination with the radical immigrant more than an element of romanticism? These intellectuals were atypical immigrants, and they did not, as a whole, participate in the life of their local community. Most in fact regarded their fellow countrymen with condescension, if not contempt. Why then accord them such significance? One is reminded here of Kostash's remark: "Is it really necessary to see picturesqueness . . . in the perfectly mundane in order to accord [immigrants] dignity and personality? It is only necessary if you imagined them otherwise."[76]

Immigrants were heavily involved in the Communist Party of Canada during the twenties and thirties.[77] It was very much a passionate affair, blowing alternately hot and cold. Avery attributes the party's success among immigrants partly to its advocacy and use of violence, which appealed to their peasant traditions. Surely this statement requires refinement. Peasants under desperate conditions may have resorted to violence. This does not mean that they were naturally attracted to this tactic. In the early years, Canadian communism was very much part of the fibre of immigrant culture. This also explains its great appeal to new Canadians. Its federated organizations like the Ukrainian Labour-Farmer Temple Association, the Finnish Organization of Canada, and other associations such as the Hungarians' Independent Sick Benefit Association offered them a wide variety of cultural and social services.

Historians have not tried to measure with any accuracy the popularity of the Communist Party in various immigrant communities. Certain indices exist.[78] But this scattered evidence only seems to corroborate the conclusion which, to his credit, John Kolasky substantiated for Ukrainians[79] — the party appealed only to a small minority of the immigrant population.

The party's setbacks among new Canadians were partly self-inflicted, but they were also caused by external factors. Most noteworthy of these was the repression unleashed during the "Red Scare," which reached its apogee in the thirties. This fact cannot mask the party's own mistakes. In an important and well-written book, Kolasky documents how communism lost its vitality and its appeal for Ukrainian Canadians of the left. He portrays a leadership stolidly following the Moscow line, repressing dissent and criticism, gradually becoming a self-satisfied gerontocracy leading an organization without members. The study's only important shortcoming is its failure to situate post-war events in the context of the Cold War, which makes Kolasky's account stilted and one-sided.

The Depression witnessed strong political and ideological polarization within many immigrant communities. In part, these divisions were caused by consular personnel who exploited "their" immigrants in order to advance the diplomatic or political interests of their respective governments. To this end, they organized umbrella organizations which claimed to speak on behalf of the whole community. These should not be seen as unmistakeable signs of the growing maturity of immigrant groups, since the impetus for their establishment in many cases came from outside. The consulates of Finland, Italy, Hungary, Poland, Japan, and Germany took a variety of other initiatives which marked a willingness to intervene in the affairs of the community.[80] Of course, some consular activities were more harmful than others. Finnish diplomats, for example, created a repressive apparatus which sought to isolate Finnish radicals in their work and their communities. As well, the actions of zealous consular officials from Italy and Germany cast long shadows over these immigrant groups during the war. Overall, this diplomatic presence reinforced the organizational structure and the influence of the right in many communities.

To imagine, however, that all immigrants became willing accomplices for consular propaganda, as Lita-Rose Betcherman suggests for the Italians,[81] is to share the consuls' wildest fantasies. There was resistance, in some cases more successful, in others, less, to these attempts to monopolize community life.[82] But more powerful than active resistance was the generalized apathy of the immigrant population for the diplomatic manoueverings of the mother country.[83] Consuls could expect large and enthusiastic audiences at picnics and other such festivities. Properly political meetings, however, only brought together the faithful few. Immigrants were, after all, rooted in a Canadian reality. Those who remained especially blind to this fact were the self-appointed immigrant elite, flattered and seduced by consular attention and favours. More research must be devoted to this group which emerged from the immigrant community, but were not part of it, ambivalent in their identity and allegiances, aberrations rather than representatives of the immigrant experience.

An ironic fate awaited these umbrella organizations so carefully put together by diplomats. During the Second World War, the Canadian government discovered the immigrants' overall lack of enthusiasm for the war effort. Through the Nationalities Branch of the Department of National War Services, these umbrella organizations once again became propaganda vehicles, this time of the Canadian government. In this way, Canada's first multicultural policy saw the light. It was born, as was the second, of crisis and neglect.

Studies on nativism are not within the purview of this article since they really concern the host society. However, scholars have recently paid some attention to the immigrants' response to nativism.[84] In both the Jewish refugee crisis and the evacuation of Japanese Canadians during the Second World War, two communities were helpless in confronting the overwhelming hostility of the host society and powerless because they did not have access to those in authority. Unfortunately, they were also incapable of overcoming their internal divisions. Many members of these communities continued during the bleakest moments to have an abiding faith in government, a faith which for some Jews was cemented by partisan ties. Others sought personal exemptions from the harsh injunctions of government. Still, as Irving Abella, Harold Troper, and Ann Gomer Sunahara show, these communities were not leaderless. Energetic and dedicated people did emerge from these crises, but they were effective only insofar as they could recruit Canadian opinion-makers to their cause. These studies underline the fragility of minority groups and the all-too-human responses of their members in times of crisis. This theme, which has barely been explored, needs further study.

The history of immigrant groups in Canada has come of age. It is not a tale ringing with drums and bugles, nor a stage filled with noble families, intellectuals, or revolutionaries, nor an edifying homily about economic and cultural miracles. The story of immigrants is much more ordinary than the distorted and censored version served up by filiopietists. What it loses in brilliance, and a tawdry brilliance at that, it gains in vitality and realism. This history is an integral part of the Canadian past. It has emerged because of new trends in social, labour, and urban history. Its future development depends as well on the rapidly expanding area of migration studies.

The non-English-speaking immigrants who came to Canada were, as noted above, overwhelmingly of peasant origin. They brought with them a particular-istic culture which they adapted to the Canadian environment. Their communities were neither static, nor monolithic, nor submissive. This is probably not the type of history which "professional ethnics" want to hear recounted. But they should be reminded that self-proclaimed immigrant leaders have not tradition-ally been the best interpreters of the needs of their communities. Immigrants, like many other important groups, have been largely ignored in the past by Canadian historians. It would be a pity if, after these years of neglect, they should again be swept under the carpet by their official historians, anxious to present a favourable image of their group to a wider public.

Recently Harney observed that the attempt to write a pan-Canadian synthesis of an immigrant group would, given Canada's intense regionalism, remain more of an intellectual construct than a reality.[85] Certainly, as this article has suggested, it is the local and regional studies which have best depicted the immigrant in the total socio-economic and cultural context. However, two regions have yet to be explored by the historian of immigrant groups: the Atlantic provinces and British Columbia, which continues to be dominated by studies of nativism. As well, Quebec outside of Montreal, and small-town Ontario remain largely uncharted territories. Still, the history of immigrant groups can only be as good as Canadian history itself. Without more of a regional focus, without more attention being given to popular culture, without more studies of local communities, Canadian history will fail to provide the context which the study of immigrants requires to be fully meaningful. The futures of the two areas are intimately bound up in the same way that the immigrant's fate is tied to that of the country of adoption.

Notes

1. Kogila Moodley, "Canadian Ethnicity in Comparative Perspective," in *Ethnicity, Power and Politics in Canada*, edited by J. Dahlie and T. Fernando (Toronto, 1981), 9. Although disagreeing with this view, Moodley says that it is the current sociological wisdom. The author maintains instead that ethnicity is both an objective and a subjective phenomenon and that the interaction between the two needs to be explored, rather than simply asserting the primacy of one over the other.

2. Nathan Glazer and D.P. Moynihan, eds., *Ethnicity: Theory and Practice* (Cambridge, 1975), 3.

3. Wsevolod Isajiw, "Olga in Wonderland: Ethnicity in Technological Society," *Canadian Ethnic Studies* (hereafter *CES*) IX, 1 (1977): 77–83.

4. J. Dahlie and T. Fernando, "Reflections on Ethnicity and the Exercise of Power: An Introductory Note," in *Ethnicity*, 1.

5. Karl Peter, "The Myth of Multiculturalism and Other Political Fables," in *Ethnicity*, 62. Giving ethnic collectivities power is also a theme found in A. Anderson and J. Frideres, *Ethnicity in Canada* (Toronto, 1981).

6. Rudolph Vecoli, "Contadini in Chicago: A Critique of the Uprooted," *Journal of American History* LI (1964).

7. Raymond Breton, "Institutional Completeness of Ethnic Communities and the Personal Relations of Immigrants," *American Journal of Sociology* LXX (Sept. 1964).

8. Myrna Kostash, *All of Baba's Children* (Edmonton, 1980). Kostash identifies the process of whitewashing and attempts to deal with its consequences.

9. Robert Harney and Vincenza Scarpaci, "Introduction," in *Little Italies in North America* (Toronto, 1981), 4. Apologies for not being able to speak "proper" Italian are a manifestation of this ethnic self-dis-esteem. In the present climate of cultural triumphalism, little research has been done on this vital topic.

10. Many of the authors in the Generations series voice this concern.

11. Harney and Scarpaci, "Introduction," in *Little Italies*.

12. For a succinct discussion of this theme, see Franc Sturino, "Family and Kin Cohesion among South Italian Immigrants in Toronto," in *The Immigrant Woman in North America*, edited by B. Carali et al. (Toronto, 1978), 288–311.

13. *CES* (1978), 60.

14. Ibid., 60.

15. Other historiographical articles include Howard Palmer, "Canadian Immigration and Ethnic History in the 1970s and 1980s," *Journal of Canadian Studies* XVII (Spring 1982): 35–50; Robert Harney, "Frozen Wastes: The State of Italian-Canadian Studies," in *Perspectives in Italian Immigration and Ethnicity*, edited by S.M. Tomasi (New York, 1977), 115–31; Bruno Ramirez, "La recherche sur les Italiens du Québec," *Questions de culture* II (1982): 103–11.

16. Stanford Reid, *The Scottish Tradition in Canada* (Toronto, 1976); Peter Chimbos, *The Canadian Odyssey* (Toronto, 1980); Baha Abu-Laban, *An Olive Branch on the Family Tree* (Toronto, 1980); Gulbrand Loken, *From Fjord to Frontier* (Toronto, 1980).

17. Grace Anderson and David Higgs, *A Future to Inherit* (Toronto, 1976); Henry Radecki with Benedykt Heydenkorn, *A Member of a Distinguished Family* (Toronto, 1976); Ken Adachi, *The Enemy that Never Was* (Toronto, 1976).

18. N.F. Dreisziger et al., *Struggle and Hope* (Toronto, 1982).

19. Antonio Alpalhao and Victor da Rosa, *Les Portugais du Québec* (Ottawa, 1979).

20. Abu-Laban, *Olive Branch*, 109–15.

21. Chimbos, *Canadian Odyssey*, 22.

22. Dreisziger et al., *Struggle and Hope*, 26.

23. Anderson and Higgs, *Future to Inherit*, 5; Alpalhao and da Rosa, *Portugais du Québec*, 46.

24. Loken, *Fjord to Frontier*, 8.

25. "Introduction" in *Little Italies*, 2.

26. "Emigration from Hungary, 1880–1956," in *Struggle and Hope*, 27–60.

27. Anderson and Higgs, *Future to Inherit*, 147–50.

28. Chimbos, *Canadian Odyssey*, 157.

29. Radecki, *Distinguished Family*, 95–99.

30. Radecki and Dreisziger have observed that post-Second World War immigration provided a shot in the arm to their communities, as articulate professionals became available to take up leadership positions in various organizations. They allude to tensions between old and new immigrants, as does Jeremy Boissevain, who probed the attitudes of the two waves of immigrants to each other. See *The Italians of Montreal: Social Adjustment in a Plural Society* (Ottawa, 1970).

31. "The Commerce of Migration," *CES* IX, 1 (1977): 42–53.

32. "Men Without Women," in *The Immigrant Woman*, 79–101.

33. "Canadian Immigration Policy and the Foreign Navvy, 1896–1914," Canadian Historical Association, *Historical Papers* (1972): 135–56.

34. *"Dangerous Foreigners": European Immigrant Workers and Labour Radicalism in Canada, 1896–1932* (Toronto, 1979).

35. "South Slavs on a Northern Margin: The Frontier Experience of Croatian Migrants during Canada's Great Depression," in *Ethnic Canadians: Culture and Education*, edited by M.L. Kovacs (Regina, 1978): 399–410.

36. Edmund W. Bradwin, *The Bunkhouse Men* (Toronto, 1972).

37. "Finnish Lumber Workers in Ontario, 1919–1946," *Polyphony* III, 2 (Fall 1981): 23–34; "Finnish Canadians and the Ontario Miners' Movement," ibid., 35–45.

38. "The Padrone and the Immigrant," *The Canadian Review of American Studies* V, 2 (Fall 1974): 101–18; "Montreal's King of Labour: A Case Study of Padronism," *Labour/Le Travailleur* IV (1979): 57–84; "The Padrone System and Sojourners in the Canadian North 1885–1920," in G. Pozzetta, *Pane e Lavoro: The Italian American Working Class* (Toronto, 1980), 119–37.

39. "Boarding and Belonging," *Urban History Review* II (1978): 8–37; Carmela Patrias, "Hungarian Immigration to Canada before the Second World War," *Polyphony* II, 2–3 (1979–80): 17–26; Robert Harney and Harold Troper, *Immigrants: A Portrait of an Urban Experience* (Toronto, 1975).

40. Lillian Petroff, "Macedonians in Toronto: From Encampment to Settlement," *Urban History Review* II (1978): 53–73.

41. Robert Harney, "Toronto's Little Italy, 1885–1945," in *Little Italies*, 41–62; Varpu Lindstrom-Best, *The Finnish Immigrant Community of Toronto, 1887–1913* (Toronto, 1979); John Zucchi, *The Italian Immigrants of St John's Ward, 1875–1915* (Toronto, 1981); Paul Voisey, "Two Chinese Communities in Alberta: A Historical Perspective," *CES* II (Dec. 1970): 14–57.

42. Bruno Ramirez and Michael Del Balso, *The Italians of Montreal: From Sojourning to Settlement* (Montreal, 1980).

43. Franc Sturino, "Italian Immigration to Canada and the Farm Labour System through the 1920's" (paper presented at the American-Italian Historical Association, St-Paul, 1981).

44. Stephen Speisman, *The Jews of Toronto: A History to 1937* (Toronto, 1979): 249–50.

45. Bruno Ramirez, "Montreal's Italians and the Socio-Economy of Settlement, 1900–1930: Some Historical Hypotheses," *Urban History Review* X, 1 (June 1981): 39–48.

46. "Ambience and Social Class in North American Little Italies," *Canadian Review of Studies in Nationalism* (Fall 1974): 208–24. For a view of post-Second World War mobility, see Franc Sturino, "A Case Study of a South Italian Family in Toronto, 1935–1960," *Urban History Review* II (1978): 38–57. Sturino defines mobility too eagerly in residential and generational terms without taking into account the overall

expansion of the Canadian economy in this period. Moving from "dirty work" to self-employment may not reflect upward mobility but only structural changes in the Canadian economy.

47. See in this regard the excellent special issue of *Polyphony* dedicated to Finns cited above. It illustrates how regional studies perhaps can better represent the life of an immigrant community than can a pan-Canadian approach.

48. Taru Sundsten, "The Theatre of the Finnish Canadian Labour Movement and Its Dramatic Literature, 1900–1939," in *Finnish Diaspora* I, edited by Michael Karni (Toronto, 1981), 77–91.

49. "The churches were still the Old World institution to which immigrant workers were most likely to turn in the first instance in an alien environment" (*"Dangerous Foreigners,"* 46). As for Zucchi's reference in *Italian Immigrants* (15–16) to Sidney Sonnino's depiction of the parish priest as the peasant's friend in the exploitative world of rural Italy, one could cite eloquent passages in the novels of Carlo Levi and Ignazio Silone where the priest forms part of the local notability and oppresses the peasant.

50. Varpu Lindstrom-Best, "The Unbreachable Gulf: The Division in the Finnish Community of Toronto, 1902–1913," in *Finnish Diaspora*, 11–18.

51. L. Petroff, "Macedonians: From Village to City," *CES* IX, 1 (1977): 29–41; also F. Gruneir, "Hebrew-Christian Mission in Toronto," ibid., 18–28.

52. Harney and Troper, *Immigrants: Portrait*, 147.

53. Ramirez and Del Balso, *Italians of Montreal*, 28–33.

54. "The Greek Communal School and Cultural Survival in Pre-War Toronto," *Urban History Review* II (1978): 74–94.

55. Ramirez and Del Balso, *Italians of Montreal*, 34–35.

56. Harold Troper, *Only Farmers Need Apply* (Toronto, 1972).

57. Howard Palmer, *Land of Second Chance* (Lethbridge, 1972). See also Howard and Tamara Palmer, "The Hungarian Experience in Alberta," *Hungarian Studies Review* VIII, 2 (Fall 1981): 149–203.

58. John Lehr, "The Government and the Immigrant: Perspectives on Ukrainian Block Settlement in the Canadian West," *CES* IX, 2 (1977): 42–52; in the same issue, Donald Gale and Paul Korocsil, "Doukhobor Settlements: Experiments in Idealism," 53–71; Richard Friesen, "Saskatchewan Mennonite Settlements: The Modification of Old World Settlement Patterns," 72–90. See as well Hildegard Martens, "Accommodation and Withdrawal: The Response of Mennonites in Canada to World War II," *Histoire sociale/Social History* VIII, 14 (Nov. 1974): 306–27.

59. Helen Potrebenko, *No Streets of Gold: A Social History of Ukrainians in Alberta* (Vancouver, 1977); Kostash, *All of Baba's Children*.

60. Primary documents as well as some excellent photographs on this period have been collected in *Land of Pain, Land of Promise: First Person Accounts of Ukrainian Pioneers, 1891–914*, edited by Harry Piniuta (Saskatoon, 1978). Piniuta's Ukrainians, however, are uniformly unsullied by radicalism.

61. *Struggle and Hope*, 80–82. See also Nadia Kazymyra's mediocre article, "Aspects of Ukrainian Opinion in Manitoba During World War I," in *Ethnic Canadians*, 117–34.

62. Paul Yuzyk, *The Ukrainian Greek Orthodox Church of Canada* (Ottawa, 1981).

63. Surely this term is abused when it is applied to elementary school teachers, and yet it recurs in Yuzyk, Kostash, and Kazymyra.

64. Yuzyk, *Ukrainian Greek Orthodox Church*, 57–58.

65. Adélard Langevin of Winnipeg, for example, is designated as a "French" archbishop. This annoying terminology finds its way, consciously or unconsciously, into Kostash, 90, who refers to the poet Louis Fréchette as a Frenchman.

66. On the subject of women in the workplace, see Joan Sangster, "Finnish Women in Ontario, 1890–1930," *Polyphony* III, 2 (Fall 1981): 46–54; Lindstrom-Best, *Finnish Immigrant Community*.

67. Strikes in the needle trade are briefly described in Speisman, *Jews of Toronto*, 192–95.

68. Jean Morrison, "Ethnicity and Violence: The Lakehead Freight Handlers before World War I," in *Essays in Canadian Working Class History*, edited by G. Kealey and P. Warrian (Toronto, 1976), 143–60; Antonio Pucci, "Canadian Industrialization versus the Italian Contadini in a Decade of Brutality, 1902–1912," in *Little Italies*, 182–207.

69. Avery, *"Dangerous Foreigners."* For Ukrainian involvement in labour disputes, see Potrebenko, *No Streets of Gold*, 43–45, 149–57. For immigrant participation in the Rouyn-Noranda strike, see Evelyn Dumas, *The Bitter Thirties in Quebec* (Montreal, 1975), chap. 2, and A. Rasporich, "South Slavs on a Northern

Margin," in *Ethnic Canadians*. For the Finnish presence in strikes, see the articles by Radforth and Seager cited above.

70. *Main Currents in Modern American History* (New York, 1976), 95.

71. For Ukrainian involvement in these radical movements, see Kostash, *All of Baba's Children*, chap. 12; Potrebenko, *No Streets of Gold*, chap. 6.

72. Avery, "*Dangerous Foreigners*," 59–62; Edward Laine, "Finnish Canadian Radicalism and Canadian Politics: The First Forty Years, 1900–1940," in *Ethnicity, Power, and Politics*, 94–112. In the same volume, see Varpu Lindstrom-Best, "The Socialist Party of Canada and the Finnish Connection, 1905–1911," 113–22; Norman Buchignani and Doreen Indra, "The Political Organization of South Asians in Canada, 1904–1920," 202–32.

73. The authors appear quite hostile to Indian nationalism at the turn of the century and often interpret favourably the Indian policies of British officials in India and Great Britain. Their article depends quite heavily on the reports of a British spy. For a different interpretation, see Hugh Johnston, *The Voyage of the Komagata Maru: The Sikh Challenge to Canada's Colour Bar* (Calcutta, 1979).

74. Mauri Jalava, "The Finnish Canadian Cooperative Movement in Ontario," in *Finnish Diaspora*, 93–100; Kostash, *All of Baba's Children*, 160–62.

75. Jorgen Dahlie, "Socialist and Farmer: Ole Hjelt and the Norwegian Radical Voice in Canada, 1908–1918," *CES* X, 2 (1978): 55–64; in the same issue, D. Wilson, "Matti Kurikka and A.B. Makela: Socialist Thought Among the Finns in Canada, 1900–1932," 9–21, Nadia Kazymyra, "The Defiant Pavlo Krat and the Early Socialist Movement in Canada," 38–54, Anthony Rasporich, "Tomo Cacic: Rebel without a Country," 86–94; Jorgen Dahlie, "From Ringsaker to Instow: A Norwegian Radical's Saskatchewan Odyssey," in *Ethnic Canadians*, 97–107; Donald Wilson, "Finns in British Columbia before the First World War," *Polyphony* III (Fall 1981): 55–64, and by the same author, " 'Never Believe What You Have Never Doubted': Matti Kurikka's Dream for a New World Utopia," in *Finnish Diaspora*, 131–53.

76. Kostash, *All of Baba's Children*, 41.

77. Avery, "*Dangerous Foreigners*," chap. 5; E. Laine, "Finnish Canadian Radicalism . . . " in *Ethnicity, Power, and Politics*, 94–112; by the same author, "The Finnish Organization of Canada, 1923–1940 and the Development of a Finnish Canadian Culture,"*Polyphony* III (Fall 1981): 81–90; John Kolasky, *The Shattered Illusion: The History of Ukrainian Pro-Communist Organizations in Canada* (Toronto, 1979).

78. Donald Avery, "Ethnic Loyalties and the Proletarian Revolution: A Case Study of Communist Political Activity in Winnipeg, 1923–36," in *Ethnicity, Power, and Politics*, 6893; Leonard Sillanpaa, "Voting Behaviour of Finns in the Sudbury Area, 1930–1972," in *Finnish Diaspora*, 101–16, and in the same book, Reino Kero, "The Canadian Finns in Soviet Karelia in the 1930's"; Jules Paivio, "Finnish Canadians during the Spanish Civil War, 1936–1939," *Polyphony* III (Fall 1981): 77–80.

79. *Shattered Illusion*, 22.

80. Varpu Lindstrom-Best, "Central Organization of Loyal Finns in Canada," *Polyphony* III (Fall 1981): 97–103; Roberto Perin, "Conflits d'identité et d'allégeance: la propagande du consulat italien à Montréal dans les années trente," *Questions de culture* II (1982): 81–102; Carmela Patrias, *The Kanadai Magyar Ujsag and the Politics of the Hungarian Elite, 1928–1938* (Toronto, 1978); Benedykt Heydenkorn, *The First Polish Umbrella Organization: The Federation of Polish Societies in Canada* (Toronto, 1978); Jonathan Wagner, "The Deutscher Bund of Canada, 1934–1939," *Canadian Historical Review* LVIII (June 1977): 176–200.

81. Lita-Rose Betcherman, *The Swastika and the Maple Leaf: Fascist Movements in the Thirties* (Don Mills, 1975).

82. See, for example, Angelo Principe, "The Italo-Canadian Press of Toronto, 1922–1940," Italian Section/Northeast Modern Languages Association Conference, *Proceedings* IV (1980): 119–37.

83. Robert Harney has captured the essence of this spirit in "Toronto's Little Italy," in *Little Italies*. See, as well, Perin, "Conflits d'identité et d'allégeance."

84. This issue is addressed pointedly in Irving Abella and Harold Troper, "The Politics of Futility: Canadian Jewry and the Refugee Crisis, 1933–1939," in *Ethnicity, Power, and Politics*, 233–53. See also by the same authors, *None Is Too Many* (Toronto, 1982); Ann Gomer Sunahara, "Historical Leadership Trends Among Japanese Canadians: 1940–1950," *CES* XI, 1 (1979): 1–16. See also Sunahara, *The Politics of Racism: The Uprooting of Japanese Canadians During the Second World War* (Toronto, 1981), especially Part IV.

85. "Frozen Wastes," in *Perspectives in Italian Immigration*, 115–31.

SOME OBSERVATIONS ON RECENT TRENDS IN CANADIAN EDUCATIONAL HISTORY†

J. DONALD WILSON

Canadian educational history has experienced several exciting developments in the past fifteen years, leading one historian to declare that during this period the field of history of education "has proven to be one of the richest fields of critical inquiry."[1] In the process, educational history in North America moved from the periphery of "mainstream" history where it had been before the late sixties into the mainstream where it should have been, a shift both encouraged and predicted by Bernard Bailyn in his provocative *Education in the Forming of American Society* (New York, 1960). Inspired by Bailyn's invocation and prodded by the spirit of the "new" social history, Canadian educational historians shunned the earlier traditional institutional educational history represented by F. Henry Johnson's *A Brief History of Canadian Education* (Toronto, 1968), as well as the presentism of the likes of Charles E. Phillips' *The Development of Public Education in Canada* (Toronto, 1957). Both Johnson and Phillips, by the way, were typical of their era in being educators rather than historians. The "onward and upward," linear interpretation of the rise of universal public education is perhaps best represented by Phillips' clearly stated bias in the preface to his book: "The book is written from an uncompromisingly democratic and rather strongly equalitarian point of view . . . . It is an account of past developments as leading to the present and as judged by the values of the present." And further: "As such it [the book] should be agreeable to adults who need no convincing that life in Canada today is the best kind of life we know, who see better people than themselves in the younger generation, and who look to the future for a golden age."[2] Surely one needs no better example of the sort of "whiggism" Bailyn deplored in the writing of educational history. At the same time one should bear in mind that similar progressive assumptions, particularly in regards to nation-building and national survival, were present in most Canadian histories of the day.[3] Moreover, the educational historians of that period, isolated as they were from the mainstream of the history profession, considered their main professional task to be the training of teachers who, it was felt, needed a legitimating rationale for the importance of their work.

Beginning in 1970 with the appearance of *Canadian Education: A History*, edited by J. Donald Wilson, Robert M. Stamp and Louis-Philippe Audet, Canadian educational historians took up, not altogether successfully, Bailyn's redefinition of "education" as encompassing both formal and informal ways of learning. The

†From Donald Wilson, ed., *An Imperfect Past: Education and Society in Canadian History* (Vancouver: Centre for the Study of Curriculum and Instruction, University of British Columbia, 1984), 7-29. Revised from *History of Education Review* 13, 1 (Spring 1984).

former almost exclusive attention on public schooling was redirected to other agents of education: mission schools and private schools, mechanics' institutes and other forms of adult education, libraries, newspapers and voluntary institutions. Another feature of the "new" educational history was to restore the social and political context to the discussion of educational developments. Previously there had been, as Bailyn asserted, a "wrenching of events from historical context." Now historians strove to see education "in its shifting functions, meanings and purposes."[4] Efforts to ascertain the social context were much aided by the rapid advances in the seventies in Canadian social history. (More of this later.) Another of Bailyn's injunctions, namely that education should be seen "as the entire process by which a culture transmits itself across the generations,"[5] proved well nigh unworkable. One major effort which attempted this anthropological perspective, Lawrence A. Cremin's multi-volume history of American education, was not really successful.[6] As one harsh critic opined: Cremin's work "continued a tradition of triumphantly chronicling the growth of something abstractly called education, uncritical treatment of the school reformers, and failure to ask interesting questions." It was a "pseudoliberation" from the pre-1960 era.[7] No Canadian educational historian ventured down this obstacle-strewn course.

True liberation came in Canada as in the United States not from Bailyn or Cremin, although both continued to be cited, but rather from the influence of the "new" social history and its concern with theory and method. Traditional narrative history came under sharp attack. One of its most severe critics in Canada was American-born and trained Michael Katz whose brilliant leadership sparked a "generation" of revisionist historians in both countries. He conceded narrative history might be "pleasant and sometimes even interesting" but when "uninformed by social or behavioural science . . . it is virtually useless . . . as a way of either advancing knowledge or contributing to substantive intellectual problems." Katz trumpeted the explanatory power of history when approached by recourse to "the systematic use of concepts and the application of intellectual constructs."[8]

As we know, the new social history concerns the history of social structure, mobility, the family, sexuality, and such social institutions as factories (working-class history), prisons (history of crime and delinquency), towns (urban history), hospitals (history of medicine and public health), churches (history of religion), and schools (history of education). While a participant in the early stages of the "new" social history, Katz, like many young historians in graduate school in the mid-1960s, was also influenced by Marxism and the New Left. This feeling of being *engagé* with the bitter social protests of the mid- and late 1960s added an enthusiasm to the writing of Americans like Katz, Clarence J. Karier, Paul Violas, Joel Spring, Samuel Bowles, and Herbert Gintis.[9] Their joint conviction that history could serve reform "by emancipating it from dependency upon an idealized past" led them to conclude that schools as institutions grew over the years "more and more exploitative, more and more repressive, more and more an impediment to change."[10] If in traditional history there was a sense of the inevitability of progress, in revisionist history there was equally a sense of the inevitability of decay and a worsening of conditions over time.

Canadian graduate students, especially those working under Katz at the Ontario Institute for Studies in Education (OISE), were not unaffected by the excitement of ideological commitment and an accompanying sense that history had its part to play in the current debate on public policy and in particular educational policy. Camps began to form up and name-calling ensued. By the mid-seventies the terms "moderate revisionists" and "radical revisionists" came into common use in Canada to designate the two camps.[11] Debates then broke out over whether individual scholars had been put into the correct camps.[12] Although the controversy over revisionism never became as deeply politicized as in the United States, there was certainly an awareness of ideological differences among the various writers as well as differences in research strategy. This element had the decided effect of heating up the debate, and a period of vital critical self-analysis within the subfield was launched.[13]

Moderate revisionists basically accepted the notion that the battles over educational reforms in the past did result in improved public education.[14] Although not uncritical of reformers' motives and methods or of the deleterious effects of many educational policies, the moderate revisionists generally concluded that society over the years had benefitted from public education. Critics might term this a liberal-humanitarian ideological perspective. Radical revisionists, by contrast, lashed out with indignation at what they considered the injustices of the past. Michael Katz described American education by 1880 as "bureaucratic, racist, and class-biased,"[15] and basically concluded that schools have worked out badly. Since he believed that the main outlines of his interpretation applied to Canada as well as the United States,[16] it is not surprising that his students at OISE stressed the class-biased, racist, and bureaucratic nature of Ontario's school system (the focus of their work), and emphasized as well the social-control motives of the school promoters.[17] The latter were pictured as representing middle-class interests which centred on maintaining their privileged class position, creating a disciplined labour force and maintaining a politically passive working class. In the process, the persistent language and religious issues, so fundamental to Canadian educational history, were almost completely overlooked.[18] Their bitterness about past injustices combined with their pessimism about the likelihood of effecting any real changes in the school system led the radical revisionists to quite different conclusions from the moderate revisionists. The danger in all this was, as Sol Cohen warned, that "past ideas and actions may be combined with the moral and social prejudices of the historian to produce a work that distorts the past in an attempt to castigate the past and to lecture the present."[19]

Of course, the two camps of revisionists were also distinguishable by differences in research strategies. Moderate revisionists remained essentially narrative historians. Where they tried to apply the techniques of social science, as in some chapters in *Canadian Education: A History*, they revealed their limitations. One important reason for this was that most moderate revisionists, the products largely of graduate schools in the sixties, had very little training in the social sciences as undergraduate or graduate students. S.D. Clark reminds us that in 1958 there were fewer than twenty sociology professors in the various Canadian universities.[20] In the long run, however, the point is not so much who had social science training and who did not, but rather the historical approach favoured by the individual historian. In the case of the moderate revisionists, they avoided social class analysis and never accepted the notion of social control as a mode of explanation in the way the radical revisionists did.

When one considers the nature of nineteenth- and early twentieth-century Canada, one has difficulty in finding very plausible the social control thesis as applied to Canadian systems of public schooling. This is particularly so when one takes account of the two most common characteristics associated with this thesis, centralization and bureaucratization. To begin with, Canada was overwhelmingly rural throughout the nineteenth century. This point and its influence on schooling is persistently made in the recent work of Chad Gaffield, the late Douglas Lawr and Robert Gidney, and stands in sharp contrast to the "urban outlook" of Susan Houston and Alison Prentice that lulls one into a sense that urban interests predominated in Canadian society as they did in the north-eastern United States of the same period.[21] Until well into the twentieth century, schools were mostly one-room ventures. Multi-room schools were evident only in reasonably sized urban areas. Widespread, rural school consolidation was not effected in western Canada, for example, until after World War II. As late as 1945, 49 percent of all schools in British Columbia were one-teacher schools.[22] Local school boards still exercised a great deal of autonomy over the day-to-day operation of such schools, despite bureaucratic efforts to the contrary.

Secondly, throughout the nineteenth century, government civil service in general and educational bureaucracy in particular remained miniscule, even embryonic. I am reminded of a photograph of the entire British Columbia civil service in 1878: it consisted of nineteen people.[23] The Superintendent of Education, John Jessop, like Egerton Ryerson somewhat earlier in Upper Canada, was virtually a one-man department. Both Ryerson and Jessop personally drafted answers to most of the letters that came pouring into their respective offices. This is hardly the picture of a large, oppressive bureaucracy of the sort Michael Katz drew for Massachussetts of the same era. Local decision making about schools continued despite efforts of the central office to persuade local trustees and school officials to get in line with a set provincial pattern.[24]

Thirdly, the link between industrial capitalism and manipulative public school systems usually made by social-control theorists is either strained or invalid when applied to nineteenth-century Canadian systems. In Ontario the "industrial system" of the day was composed of quite small firms. In provinces such as Newfoundland and British Columbia such a system was completely non-existent. Robert Gidney has argued that urbanization and industrialization cannot account for the timing of educational innovation in Upper Canada.[25] Thus the "correspondence theory" which Bowles and Gintis set forth in *Schooling in Capitalist America* has apparently no validity for nineteenth-century Canada. Any explanation for the widespread acceptance of universal schooling in these jurisdictions obviously must lie elsewhere and not with the emergence of industrialization. One of the most telling criticisms of social control ironically came from one of its former advocates, an OISE graduate, Ian Davey. In an essay reviewing a British book wherein social control figured prominently, he stated:

> the class domination theory implicit in many analyses of schooling as a form of social control is much too simplistic a representation of class relations. It

negates the importance of conflicting ideologies within the ruling class itself at the same time as it characterizes the working class as passive recipients rather than active participants in the formation of popular schooling. Social control, in essence, remains a functionalist concept and downplays the struggle and negotiation within and between classes which is at the centre of the historical determination of institutionalized schooling in the nineteenth century.[26]

Regardless of the limitations of the social-control hypothesis, the work of the radical revisionists represented an important advance in Canadian educational history over the work of the moderate revisionists. New sets of questions were raised and a number of subjects regarding schooling which had previously been ignored or glanced over were singled out for research: the motives of school administrators and reformers, schooling as part of the institutional state, school attendance patterns, literacy, youth and work, gender and ethnicity.[27] In methodological terms, the Katz-led Hamilton Social History Project, with its emphasis on quantitative methods, demonstrated the value of this computer-age approach in reconstituting the lives of ordinary people in a way that narrative historians could not hope to do.[28]

Clio has "an alarming habit of devouring" her followers, as Carl Berger reminds us,[29] and just as the radical revisionists superseded the moderates, so in turn the radicals were soon to be dislodged. Laurence Veysey estimates that revisionism was over in the United States by 1976.[30] In Canada it remained dominant for another couple of years before succumbing before the onslaught of new findings and interpretations in related sub-fields of social history, such as urban, working-class, ethnic, women's, and family history. Over the past decade our attention has been diverted from the public sector to what Carroll Smith-Rosenberg has called "private places" — the household, the bedroom, the nursery, kinship systems (as found in the history of family and childhood) and voluntary associations (ethnic history, women's history, educational history).[31] Following this trend, what educational historians are primarily concerned about today is not the structures of power and how they imposed, modified or streamlined public education (the concerns of the "radical revisionists" in the early and mid-1970s), but rather the human responses to those structures. The concern has been to discover, as Sartre once said, "not what 'one' has done to man, but what man does with what 'one' has done to him." Among other things, these new studies pointed to the primacy of the struggle for survival and security at the very core of individual and family motivation.

The new interpretative framework which I have characterized as "family strategies" was very evident in almost all the papers presented at the founding conference of the Canadian History of Education Association held in Calgary in February, 1980. Susan Houston, a former social control advocate, conceded that the various nineteenth-century institutions, including the school, set up to cushion "the impact of the transition to modern urban society for a large segment of the working class . . . were 'used' in different but equally valid ways by different social classes."[32] Similarly, Alison Prentice from the perspective of women's history stressed that "some women, individually and collectively, have used education and educational institutions to further their own aspirations, despite the inequalities with which they have had to contend."[33] Chad Gaffield in his paper concluded that "the history of education cannot simply be viewed as the imposition of schools on powerless and passive populations . . . . The complete history of public schooling is not only the history of subordination and victimization. Rather [it] is the history of local adaptation and intervention, and of social interaction as much as it is of social control and assimilation."[34] Finally, at the same conference I myself stressed a similar perspective regarding the education of ethnic minorities in Canada: "Ethnic group and host society stood in a dialectical relationship to one another. The space between the two was not fixed . . . . The traditional perspective of oppressor/victim which allows the victim no autonomy for independent action will no longer suffice."[35]

The work of Robert Gidney and the late Douglas Lawr in relation to developments in late nineteenth-century Ontario is also representative of this approach. Their findings show that whenever parental demands diverged sharply from Department of Education policy, it was the latter that was modified or amended. Although the illusion of central control was maintained throughout the nineteenth century, local people were vigorously formulating demands and, moreover, these requests were for the most part being heeded even by an autocrat such as Ryerson, who used his power "cautiously." "For the most part the central authority," Lawr and Gidney remind us, "was moving no faster and often more slowly than public opinion." They underscore the role of the masses in reacting to, even informing, the actions of school board and departmental officials.[36] Similarly, both Harold Silver and Thomas Laqueur have shown how early in the nineteenth century the British working class developed autonomous educational institutions in conscious opposition to those preferred by the middle class. "On closer examination," says Laqueur, "what appears to have been an imposition from above [re bourgeois moral standards] was, in fact, a way in which those who spent their lives in disorder, uncertainty, dirt and disease brought some order into this environment. Cleanliness in body, punctuality, neatness in dress and in one's home, and orderliness in one's lifestyle were very much part of the fabric of 'respectable' working class society and by no means inhibited those engaged in their pursuit from attacking the repressive aspects of the contemporary political and economic system; rather the reverse."[37]

Lawr and Gidney's work is also an important corrective to the radical revisionists' common view of bureaucracy as the engine of middle-class domination. They argue that in the nineteenth century bureaucracy was mutually created. Teachers and local officials alike often saw the advantages of having some uniform rules and a referee to arbitrate. Thus, at least for the nineteenth century, Lawr and Gidney show how a bureaucratic organizational form could be an equitable arrangement serving the interests of all the people, especially teachers, and not just the elite.[38] Of course, it may be that as the bureaucracy became more centralized and instrumentalist by the turn of the century it became less amenable to or tolerant of the wishes of rural-based and working-class people.

By the late 1970s the history of education had witnessed a transition from the creation of school systems as a focus, to ways in which parents and groups of parents looked on schooling in their own self-interest or in terms of basic material calculations. This was as true, as historians began to discover, of non-British immigrant parents as of working-class and rural parents. They all sought to influence the type of education their children received despite the objectives of the dominant group. Much of the work of David C. Jones, for example, underlines the dissatisfaction of rural parents in the twentieth century with the type of education "city folk" thought their children should be getting.[39] Rural parents resented the arrogance of reformers like the Ontario school gardens promoter who said in 1913: "The most difficult part of the program is to get people to want what they should want."[40]

Over the past century, at the very least, the history of Canadian education has been the story of the interplay, or dialogue, between the wishes of government authorities and those of parents over the form and style of education children were to receive. The dialogue was not just one way, as most social control theorists imply. Some time ago Frank Musgrove in *The Family, Education, and Society* (London, 1966) singled out middle-class families as the most determined strategists when it came to their children's schooling. Of course, since their goals and objectives were more likely to be in harmony with those of the state, there was less friction here. Such was often not the case with working-class and immigrant families, resulting in forced submission, or hostility, and defiant behaviour in the face of state bureaucratic pressures. One area in which this circumstance was most apparent was in adjusting the relationship between schooling and work. As Terry Copp and Michael Piva have shown for early twentieth-century Montreal and Toronto respectively, and Ian Davey for mid-nineteenth-century Upper Canada, school was something one went to when other necessities were not pressing.[41] Canadian parents sent their children to school when they could, but when the family's economic condition was suffering, many parents considered that sufficient reason to keep children out of school and did so.

Recent work in Canadian ethnic history underlines the validity of the "family strategies" approach. Many immigrant groups managed to sustain themselves both materially and spiritually without regular recourse to the power structure that dominated them. Most of the histories in the Generations Series published by McClelland and Stewart and the Secretary of State bear out this point.[42] Its truth is amply verified in respect to the ethnic group with which I am most familiar, the Finns, who managed to establish a vast array of voluntary organizations, both political and social, whereby to sustain themselves in a generally hostile environment.[43] Even among the "founding peoples," Chad Gaffield's doctoral thesis and his later work indicate that, throughout the nineteenth century, many French-language schools in eastern Ontario contributed to French-Canadian cultural stability rather than to assimilation. As Gaffield says, "For the most part, classrooms were instructed in French by French-Canadian teachers; textbooks were those used in Quebec; and children went to school only when attendance was in harmony with family responsibilities."[44] Local intervention and control continued even after coercive assimilationist policies were set in place in the early decades of the twentieth century. Similarly, some British-born parents recently arrived in British Columbia early in the twentieth century simply avoided the public school system altogether and supported private, sex- and class-segregated boarding schools such as they had known in Britain. By this means they hoped to preserve language (correct accent), class, ethno-cultural and moral traits, or, in other words, to maintain what sociologists call "ethnic boundary maintenance."[45]

The reactions of various ethnic groups to public school authorities and policies differed from ethnic group to ethnic group. Jorgen Dahlie has demonstrated that Scandinavians, already familiar with schooling in the homeland, embraced the Canadian public school.[46] Others, like Italians, who were suspicious of government in any form, or Ukrainians, who feared for their language in the face of determined assimilationists, were more hostile and recalcitrant. Still others, like Jews, saw the public school as an equalizer, an institution that would assist their children's upward mobility. This perspective thus allows us to see how each ethnic group sought to accommodate itself to government pressure, to use schooling in its own interests, or even stubbornly to react, as the Doukhobors and Mennonites did, against government measures enacted through the schools.[47] The lesson should be clear: ethnic group and host society stood in a dialectical relationship to one another. The space between the two was not fixed; rather it was always shifting in what E.P. Thompson has called the "medium of time."

The one area where the relationship between educational history and other areas of social history has been least ably served to date is probably that of working-class history. Katz's *The People of Hamilton* (Toronto, 1975) and Terry Copp's *The Anatomy of Poverty* (Toronto, 1974), which are notable exceptions, underscore the benefits of linking the workplace and the school. By contrast, the editors of a recent documentary collection blithely assert in their introduction: "we have had to omit some aspects of working-class life — for example, the impact of religion and education."[48] Likewise in his 1973 edition of the *Royal Commission on the Relations of Labour and Capital, 1889*, Greg Kealey omits all the fascinating testimony on education and social welfare. Not surprisingly, he follows a similar course in his award-winning *Toronto Workers Respond to Industrial Capitalism, 1867–1892* (Toronto, 1980), as does Bryan Palmer in his *A Culture in Conflict: Skilled Workers and Industrial Capitalism in Hamilton, 1860–1914* (Montreal, 1979) and *Working-Class Experience: The Rise and Reconstitution of Canadian Labour, 1800–1980* (Toronto, 1983). Do these authors not feel competent to treat education, do they regard it as an unimportant concern of the working class or working-class families, or do they simply find it convenient to exclude this topic from already lengthy manuscripts? The work of educational historians, such as Tim Dunn and Ian Davey, would suggest that such omissions are inexcusable and seriously detract from giving a full picture of working-class life.[49] It would appear that educational historians will have to take the lead in forging links between working-class and educational history. Certainly labour historians have shown no interest in how working people were hired, what educational criteria were used, or how work was learned (whether at school or on the job).

The focus of attention in Canadian educational history in the 1970s was on nineteenth-century Ontario, in particular south-central Ontario. I agree with Rudy Schnell when he predicts that one major area of research in the 1980s will be the twentieth century with emphasis on the interwar years.[50] We have already seen a shift in that direction in the articles published in *Schooling and Society in 20th Century British Columbia* (Calgary, 1980), which signalled a beginning of the revisionism of the received interpretation to date of the "progressive era" and "New Education" in Canada associated with Henry Johnson, Robert Patterson, Robert Stamp, and Neil Sutherland. The articles by Tim Dunn, Jean Mann, and Diane Matters are particularly illustrative in this regard.[51]

Commentators on the progressive era in both the United States and Canada seem to have overlooked or neglected an important point Robert Wiebe made in *The Search for Order*; namely, there were two strains of progressivism in the growing professional class. There were on the one hand service-oriented, welfare-oriented, social reform-oriented progressives, but there were also the business-oriented, management-oriented, efficiency-oriented progressives as well. Dewey represented the former; Thorndike the latter. The same division can be found in Canada, but more work needs to be done. To date, Alberta's H. C. Newland and Ontario's Peter Sandiford have been clearly identified as representative figures of each of these strains — what might be called "social justice" progressives and "social order" progressives respectively.[52] Jean Mann's portrayal of interwar British Columbia makes clear this distinction with particular reference to G.M. Weir, just as Robert Patterson shows H.C. Newland by contrast to be a "social justice" progressive (although he does not use the term).[53]

Similarly, Canada's Cremin, Neil Sutherland and his *Children in English Canadian Society: Framing the Twentieth Century Consensus* (Toronto, 1976) is ripe for revision. Patricia Rooke and R.L. Schnell have already given due warning that Sutherland's "consensus" requires revision. In a recent article they show that Ontario, Manitoba, and Alberta practices regarding foster and boarding homes for child care were still not standardized well past 1920; in fact, in Alberta into the 1950s.[54] Rebecca Coulter has raised similar objections to Sutherland's thesis with respect to the "working young" of Edmonton in the interwar years. She argues persuasively that no consensus existed by 1920 on the place of adolescent youth in Edmonton society. "Unlike other teen-agers," she concludes, "who knew a 'modern' adolescence marked by dependency, protection, prolonged schooling, and an experience of what is loosely termed 'youth culture', the working young entered the adult world early and had to face the world on its own terms."[55]

Often historians of education place too much emphasis on the supposed omnipotence of schooling in shaping the lives of children, as opposed to the other agents of education: church, family, community, media, peers. Thus their histories tend to magnify the historical role of the school. But, as Lawrence Cremin has written, "At any given time different individuals interact in different ways with the various configurations of education, and ultimately with different outcomes."[56] The process of education involves all those formative influences including the family, peer groups, the Church, apprenticeship, and community relations. Histories of shifting attitudes to childhood and adolescence might provide a healthy corrective. Several essays in Joy Parr, ed., *Childhood and Family in Canadian History* (Toronto, 1982), and Patricia T. Rooke and R.L. Schnell, eds., *Studies in Childhood History: A Canadian Perspective* (Calgary, 1982) prove this point.[57] Laurence Veysey suggests that educational historians perhaps should be writing histories of the movies, as they have meaning for both children and adults.[58] Recent studies by Gary

Evans and Juliet Pollard underline the validity of this point. Evans's study of *John Grierson and the National Film Board* (Toronto, 1984) makes clear the role of a combination of documentary film and discussion groups as an important vehicle of mass education. Like the social reconstructionists in the classroom, Grierson believed that film could provide the ordinary citizen and worker with a new collective consciousness.[59] Likewise, Michael Welton's recent biography of the adult educator Watson Thomson reveals the range of non-school educational materials in use in Canada in the 1930s and 1940s. Thomson utilized film, study groups, lectures, and study guides and manuals toward his goal of a new, fully co-operative society, one that was neither completely in the image of the CCF nor the Communist Party of Canada, but stressed communitarian and populist values nonetheless.[60] Both Grierson and Thomson held out the hope for cultural revitalization through informal mass education.

Another promising direction is to approach the history of children through a focus on social policy issues related to children. This perspective focusses attention away from schools exclusively to welfare systems and other institutions designed to aid children. A model of this kind of approach is *Broken Promises: How Americans Fail Their Children* by W. Norton Grubb and Marvin Lazerson (New York, 1982), and for Canada Patricia Rooke and R.L. Schnell, *Discarding the Asylum: From Child Rescue to the Welfare State in English Canada, 1800-1950* (Lanham, 1983). The latter's forthcoming biography of Charlotte Whitton (*Public Figure, Private Woman: The Controversial Charlotte Whitton*) should further enhance our knowledge of children in non-school situations.

Despite the overwhelming influence of social history, the continuing contribution of intellectual history should not be overlooked, although it has been somewhat in eclipse of late in view of the recent prominence of the "history-is-made-by-sweaty-armpits" school of historians. Intellectual history came to be attacked in the sixties as "reflecting the values of elites rather than of downtrodden groups," a major subject of social history.[61] Yet one of the finest books of late in Canadian intellectual history, Brian McKillop's *A Disciplined Intelligence* (Montreal, 1979), has much of import to say about the history of higher education in Canada in the late nineteenth century as well as an explanation of the intellectual, cultural and moral foundations of the Canadian public school curriculum. On a broader plane, McKillop demonstrates that what he calls the Anglo-Canadian moral imperative found its chief expression in education. For literate Canadians, "life at the edge of the forest was as close to the heart of European thought and culture as the nearest reading lamp." Moral improvement, for them, as for Susannah Moodie, "must go hand in hand with increasing literary and scientific knowledge."[62] Similarly, Gerald Killan's award-winning study of *David Boyle: From Artisan to Archaeologist* (Toronto, 1983) has some surprising revelations for educational historians. Boyle, the former Elora, Ontario, schoolmaster who became the father of Ontario archaeology, was a strong advocate of Johann Pestalozzi's radical theories of child-centred learning, which, in part, anticipated the "progressive" educators of the twentieth century. Boyle's convictions about education were, in fact, a strong motive behind his archeological and museum projects carried out for the Canadian Institute Museum and the Ontario Provincial Museum.

The recent segmentation of history into discrete sub-fields whose boundaries are reinforced by similar interest groups at the annual Canadian Historical Association meetings and even by specialized journals catering to labour history, ethnic history, women's history, and the like has had the unfortunate effect of driving apart historians who should be interacting with each other. Increasingly as historians become more specialized, the likelihood of overviews of Canadian history appearing or even of sub-fields of Canadian history becomes more remote. That *Canadian Education: A History*, the standard comprehensive treatment of the history of Canadian education, has not been replaced fifteen years after publication and ten years after it went out of print underlines my point. Post holes descend deeper and deeper but the fence linking them all never seems to get built. Of course, over the same time period, regionalism, that basic fact of current Canadian political life, has intruded into academia as well, resulting in the appearance of regional studies in educational history rather than national ones.[63]

But there are some hopeful signs. The crossovers many educational historians are making to rural history, ethnic history, women's history, and the like are promising, giving firm evidence of a final rupture of the former isolation of Canadian educational historians a generation ago. Such a development is both significant and fortuitous, for educational history should properly draw upon economic and social history, social anthropology, urban and rural history, history of childhood and youth, demography and studies of literacy, linguistics, folklore, literature, and the press. The excitement and controversy of a decade ago may be no more, but freed of both the "pro-school" and "anti-school" myths of the sixties and seventies, we may look forward to a much sounder history of Canadian education in the 1980s.[64]

Notes

1. Chad Gaffield, review of J. Donald Wilson and David C. Jones, eds., *Schooling and Society in Twentieth Century British Columbia* (Calgary, 1980) in *Labour/Le Travailleur* 8/9 (1981–82): 401.

2. Charles E. Phillips, *The Development of Education in Canada* (Toronto: Gage, 1957), xii.

3. Carl Berger, *The Writing of Canadian History* (Toronto: Oxford University Press, 1976).

4. Bernard Bailyn, *Education in the Forming of American Society* (New York: Vintage Books, 1960), 59, 14.

5. Ibid., 14.

6. Lawrence A. Cremin, *American Education: The Colonial Experience, 1607–1783* (New York: Harper and Row, 1970); *American Education: The National Experience, 1783–1876* (New York: Harper and Row, 1980).

7. Laurence Veysey, "The History of Education," in a special issue of *Reviews in American History* (The Promise of American History) 10, 4 (Dec. 1982): 281.

8. Michael B. Katz, *Class, Bureaucracy and Schools: The Illusion of Educational Change in America* (New York: Praeger, 1971), xxv-xxvi.

9. Michael B. Katz, *The Irony of Early School Reform: Educational Innovation in Mid-Nineteenth Century Massachusetts* (Cambridge: Harvard University Press, 1968); Clarence J. Karier, *Shaping the American Educational State: 1900 to the Present* (New York: Free Press, 1975); Clarence Karier, Paul Violas, and Joel

Spring, *Roots of Crisis: American Education in the Twentieth Century* (Chicago: Rand McNally, 1973); Joel Spring, *Education and the Rise of the Corporate State* (Boston: Beacon Press, 1972); Samuel Bowles and Herbert Gintis, *Schooling in Capitalist America: Educational Reform and the Contradictions of Economic Life* (New York: Basic Books, 1976).

10. Katz, *Class, Bureaucracy and Schools*, xxvi; H. Warren Button and Eugene F. Provenzo, *History of Education and Culture in America* (Englewood Cliffs, N.J.: Prentice-Hall, 1983), xv.

11. "Introduction" to Michael B. Katz and Paul H. Mattingly, eds., *Education and Social Change: Themes From Ontario's Past* (New York: New York University Press, 1975), xi-xxxi.

12. J. Donald Wilson and David C. Jones, "The 'New' History of Canadian Education," *History of Education Quarterly* 16, 3 (Fall 1976): 367-375; J.D. Wilson, "Historiographical Perspectives on Canadian Educational History: A Review Essay," *Journal of Educational Thought* 11, 1 (1977): 49-63.

13. An appeal for intellectual rigour in the field was made somewhat earlier. J. Donald Wilson, "Canadian Historiography," *History of Education Quarterly* IX, 1 (Spring 1969): 88-96.

14. Most of the authors, for example, in Wilson, Stamp, and Audet, eds., *Canadian Education: A History* (Toronto: Prentice-Hall, 1970), and a few in *Education and Social Change*, may be termed moderate revisionists.

15. Katz, *Class, Bureaucracy and Schools*, xx.

16. Katz, "Class, Bureaucracy and Schools" in *The Failure of Educational Reform in Canada*, edited by Douglas Myers (Toronto: McClelland and Stewart, 1973), 25. Katz contended: "Canadian and American educational practices have always reflected and reinforced the inequities of the social systems of which they are a part. In the last analysis it is the similarity in those inequities that has sustained a similarity in educational structure." Presumably the same would be true of any "capitalist" society.

17. Ian E. Davey, "Educational Reform and the Working Class: School Attendance in Hamilton, Ontario, 1851-1891" (PhD thesis, University of Toronto, 1975); Harvey J. Graff, "Literacy and Social Structure in the Nineteenth Century City" (PhD thesis, University of Toronto, 1975); Susan E. Houston, "The Impetus to Reform: Urban Crime, Poverty and Ignorance in Ontario, 1850-1875" (PhD thesis, University of Toronto, 1974); T. R. Morrison, "The Child and Urban Social Reform in Late Nineteenth Century Ontario, 1875-1900" (PhD thesis, University of Toronto, 1971); Alison Prentice, "The School Promoters: Education and Social Class in Nineteenth Century Upper Canada" (PhD thesis, University of Toronto, 1974). For recent important articles by Davey, Graff, and Houston, see Neil McDonald and Alf Chaiton, eds., *Egerton Ryerson and His Times* (Toronto: Macmillan, 1978).

18. See J. Donald Wilson, "Religion and Education: The Other Side of Pluralism," in *Canadian Education in the 1980's*, edited by J. Donald Wilson (Calgary: Detselig, 1981), chap. 6.

19. Sol Cohen, "New Perspectives in the History of American Education, 1960-1970," *History of Education* 2, 1 (Jan. 1973): 89.

20. S. D. Clark, *Canadian Society in Historical Perspective* (Toronto: McGraw-Hill Ryerson, 1976), 120.

21. Chad M. Gaffield, "Cultural Identity: The Franco-Ontarians and Schooling in the Mid-Nineteenth Century" (paper presented to the annual meeting of the History of Education Society, 1977), and "Schooling, the Economy, and Rural Society in Nineteenth-Century Ontario," in *Childhood and Family in Canadian History*, edited by Joy Parr (Toronto: McClelland and Stewart, 1982), 69-83; R. D. Gidney and D. A. Lawr, "Who Ran the Schools? Local vs. Central Control of Policy-Making in Nineteenth-Century Ontario," *Ontario History* (June 1980); R. D. Gidney and W. P. J. Millar, "Rural Schools and the Decline of Community Control in Nineteenth-Century Ontario" in *Proceedings of the Fourth Annual Agricultural History of Ontario Seminar* (Guelph: University of Guelph Continuing Education, 1980).

22. British Columbia, Department of Education, *Annual Report, 1970-71*. Chart, "Number and Size of British Columbia Public Schools in Terms of Teachers per School."

23. B.C., Department of Education, *One Hundred Years: Education in British Columbia* (Victoria: Queen's Printer, 1972), 8.

24. R. D. Gidney and D. A. Lawr, "Community vs. Bureaucracy? The Origins of Bureaucratic Procedure in the Upper Canadian School System," *Journal of Social History* 13 (March 1980): 438-457; Timothy A. Dunn, "The Rise of Mass Public Schooling in British Columbia," in *Schooling and Society*, chap. 1.

25. Consult Douglas McCalla, "The Relevance of Canadian Business History: Some Nineteenth-Century Examples," *History and Social Science Teacher* 18, 3 (Dec. 1982): 84-85; Alan Pomfret, "Comparative Historical School Change: Newfoundland, Southern Ontario, and New England," *Canadian Journal of Sociology* IV, 3 (1979): 241-55; David Alexander, "Literacy and Economic Development in

Nineteenth Century Newfoundland," *Acadiensis* X, 1 (Autumn 1980): 3–34; Timothy A. Dunn, "Work, Class, and Education: Vocationalism in British Columbia's Public Schools, 1900–1929" (MA thesis, University of British Columbia, 1978), chap. 2; R. D. Gidney, "Making Nineteenth-Century School Systems: The Upper Canadian Experience and Its Relevance to English Historiography," *History of Education* 9, 2 (June 1980).

26. *History of Education Quarterly* 21, 3 (Fall 1981), 376.

27. A sampling of such work might include Alison Prentice, *The School Promoters: Education and Social Class in Mid-Nineteenth Century Upper Canada* (Toronto: McClelland and Stewart, 1977); Michael B. Katz, "Who Went to School?" in *Education and Social Change*, 271–293; Ian E. Davey, "Trends in Female School Attendance in Mid-Nineteenth Century Ontario," *Histoire sociale/Social History* 8, 16 (Nov. 1975): 238–54; Harvey J. Graff, "The Reality Behind the Rhetoric: The Social and Economic Meanings of Literacy in the Mid-Nineteenth Century," in *Egerton Ryerson and His Times*, chap. 9; Harvey J. Graff, *The Literacy Myth: Literacy and Social Structure in the Nineteenth Century City* (New York: Academic Press, 1979); Alison Prentice, *From Private Servant to Public Servant: Status, Sex and Hierarchy in the Mid-Nineteenth-Century Ontario Teaching Profession* (Toronto: OISE booklet, 1978), and "Towards a Feminist History of Women and Education," in *Approaches to Educational History*, edited by D. C. Jones et al. (Winnipeg: University of Manitoba Press, 1981), 39–64; Ian E. Davey, "The Rhythm of Work and the Rhythm of School," in *Egerton Ryerson and His Times*, chap. 10; Michael B. Katz and Ian E. Davey, "Youth and Industrialization in a Canadian City," in *Turning Points: Historical and Sociological Essays on the Family*, edited by John Demos and Sarane Boocock (Chicago: University of Chicago Press, 1978), s81–s119; Chad Gaffield, "Cultural Challenge in Eastern Ontario: Land, Family and Education in the Nineteenth Century" (PhD thesis, University of Toronto, 1978).

28. M. B. Katz, *The People of Hamilton, Canada West: Family and Class in a Mid-Nineteenth Century City* (Cambridge, Mass.: Harvard University Press, 1975).

29. Berger, *The Writing of Canadian History*, 264.

30. Veysey, "The History of Education," 285.

31. Carroll Smith-Rosenberg, "The New Woman and the New History," *Feminist Studies* III (1975): 185–198.

32. Susan E. Houston, "Late Victorian Juvenile Reform: A Contribution to the Study of Educational History," in *Approaches to Educational History*, 22.

33. Prentice, "Towards a Feminist History of Women and Education."

34. Chad M. Gaffield, "Demography, Social Structure and the History of Schooling," in *Approaches to Educational History*, 111.

35. J. Donald Wilson, " 'The Picture of Social Randomness': Making Sense of Ethnic History and Educational History," in ibid., 34.

36. R. D. Gidney and D. A. Lawr, "Egerton Ryerson and the Origins of the Ontario Secondary School," *Canadian Historical Review* LX, 4 (Dec. 1979): 442–65, and "The Development of an Administrative System for the Public Schools: The First Stage, 1841–50," in *Egerton Ryerson and His Times*, chap. 8.

37. Thomas Laqueur, *Religion and Respectability: Sunday Schools and Working Class Culture, 1780–1850* (New Haven: Yale University Press, 1976), 170; Harold Silver, *The Concept of Popular Education: A Study of Ideas and Social Movements in the Early Nineteenth Century* (London: MacGibbon and Kee, 1965).

38. Gidney and Lawr, "Community vs. Bureaucracy?"

39. David C. Jones, "The *Zeitgeist* of Western Settlement: Education and the Myth of the Land," in *Schooling and Society*, 84. See also Jones, "The Strategy of Rural Enlightenment: Consolidation in Chilliwack, B.C., 1919–1920," in *Shaping the Schools of the Canadian West*, edited by D. C. Jones, Nancy M. Sheehan and Robert M. Stamp (Calgary: Detselig, 1979), 136–151.

40. S. B. McCready of the Ontario Agricultural College, as quoted in Edwinna von Baeyer, " 'A Vision of the New Earth': The Ontario School Garden Movement, 1900–1924" (paper presented to Canadian Rural History Conference, University of Victoria, February 1984).

41. Terry Copp, *The Anatomy of Poverty* (Toronto: McClelland and Stewart, 1974); Michael J. Piva, *The Conditions of the Working Class in Toronto, 1900–1921* (Ottawa: University of Ottawa Press, 1979); Ian Davey, "The Rhythm of Work and the Rhythm of School" in *Egerton Ryerson and His Times*, chap. 10.

42. For a critical overview of the series, see Jorgen Dahlie, "Writing Ethnic History: The Generations Series and the Limits of Pluralism," *Canadian Review of Studies in Nationalism* 10, 2 (Autumn 1983):

299–303. See also Roberto Perin, "Clio as an Ethnic: The Third Force in Canadian Historiography," *Canadian Historical Review* LXIV, 4 (Dec. 1983): 441–467, and reprinted in this volume.

43.   J. Donald Wilson, "Ethnicity and Cultural Retention: Finns in Canada, 1890–1920," *Review Journal of Philosophy and Social Science* 2, 1 (1977): 217–235, and "The Finnish Organization of Canada, the 'Language Barrier' and the Assimilation Process," *Canadian Ethnic Studies* 10, 2 (Fall 1978): 9–21. See also the special issue of *Polyphony* (Bulletin of the Multicultural History Society of Ontario) on "Finns in Ontario," 3, 2 (Fall 1981): 55–64.

44.   Gaffield, "Demography, Social Structure and the History of Schooling," 108–9.

45.   Jean Barman, *Growing Up British in British Columbia: Boys in Private School* (Vancouver: University of British Columbia Press, 1984).

46.   Jorgen Dahlie, "Learning on the Frontier: Scandinavian Immigrants and Education in Western Canada," *Canadian and International Education* 1, 2 (Dec. 1971): 56–66; "Notes Toward a History of Scandinavian Education Initiatives: Glimpses From Saskatchewan's Past," *Review Journal of Philosophy and Social Science* 1, 1 & 2 (Fall 1976): 90–104; "No Fixed Boundaries: Scandinavian Responses to Schooling in Western Canada," in *Emerging Ethnic Boundaries*, edited by Danielle Juteau Lee (Ottawa: University of Ottawa Press for Canadian Ethnic Studies Association, 1979), 117–129.

47.   John Lyons, "The (Almost) Quiet Evolution: Doukhobor Schooling in Saskatchewan," *Canadian Ethnic Studies* VIII, 1 (1976); Frank Epp, *Mennonites in Canada, 1786–1920* (Toronto: Macmillan, 1974), especially chap. 14.

48.   Irving Abella and David Millar, eds., *The Canadian Worker in the Twentieth Century* (Toronto: Oxford University Press, 1978).

49.   Timothy A. Dunn, "Work, Class, and Education: Vocationalism in British Columbia's Public Schools, 1900–1929," and "Teaching the Meaning of Work: Vocational Education in British Columbia," in *Shaping the Schools of the Canadian West*, 236–256.

50.   John H. M. Andrews and W. Todd Rogers, eds., *Canadian Research in Education: A State of the Art Review* (Vancouver: University of British Columbia, 1981), 8–15.

51.   Dunn, "The Rise of Mass Public Schooling in British Columbia, 1900–1929"; Mann, "G. M. Weir and H. B. King: Progressive Education or Education for the Progressive State"; Matters, "The Boys' Industrial School: Education for Juvenile Offenders."

52.   Robert L. Church and Michael W. Sedlak, *Education in the United States: An Interpretive History* (New York: Free Press, 1976), 255–260.

53.   Jean Mann, "G. M. Weir and H. B. King: Progressive Education or Education for the Progressive State," in *Schooling and Society*, chap. 4; R. S. Patterson, "Hubert C. Newland: Theorist of Progressive Education," in *Profiles of Canadian Educators*, edited by Robert S. Patterson, John W. Chalmers, and John W. Friesen (Toronto: D.C. Heath, 1974), chap. 15.

54.   Patricia T. Rooke and R.L. Schnell, "Child Welfare in English Canada, 1920–1948," *Social Service Review* 55 (Sept. 1981): 484–506. See also their *Discarding the Asylum: From Child Rescue to the Welfare State in English Canada, 1800–1950* (Lanham: University Press of America, 1983), 4.

55.   Rebecca Coulter, "The Working Young of Education, 1921–1931" in *Childhood and Family*, 143–159. See also Jean Barman, "Youth, Class and Opportunity in Vancouver 1921–1931" (paper read at Canadian Historical Association Conference, Vancouver, June 1983).

56.   Lawrence Cremin, "Notes Towards a Theory of Education," *Notes on Education* (Institute of Philosophy and Politics of Education, Teachers College), 1 (June 1973), 5. For a more elaborate statement, see his *Traditions of American Education* (New York: Basic Books, 1977).

57.   See in particular the articles by Veronica Strong-Boag, Rebecca Coulter, and Susan Houston in the Parr collection, and by Norah Lewis, Rebecca Coulter, and David Jones in Rooke and Schnell.

58.   For example, see D.C. Jones, "Movies, Censorship and Progressive Education: The Prairies Between the Wars" (paper presented to the Second Conference of the Canadian History of Education Association, Toronto, Feb. 1982).

59.   See also Juliet Pollard, "Movies for the People: The NFB and Rural, Industrial, and Trade Union Circuits," in *Knowledge For the People: Adult Life, Learning, and Social Change in Canada, 1850–1951*, edited by Michael Welton (Toronto: Fernwood Books, forthcoming).

60.   Michael Welton, " 'To Be and Build the Glorious World': The Educational Thought and Practice of Watson Thomson, 1899–1946" (PhD thesis, University of British Columbia, 1983).

61. Laurence Veysey, "The New Social History in the Context of American Historical Writing," *Reviews in American History* 7, 1 (March 1979), 4. A more recent statement on the pitfalls of separating social from intellectual history is Gertrude Himmelfarb, "Denigrating the Rule of Reason: the 'New History' Goes Bottom-Up," *Harper's* (April 1984): 84–90.

62. A.B. McKillop, *A Disciplined Intelligence* (Montreal: McGill-Queen's University Press, 1979), 5–6.

63. Wilson and Jones, eds., *Schooling and Society*, and Jones, Sheehan, and Stamp, eds., *Shaping the Schools of the Canadian West*.

64. The same point is made for the history of American education in Sol Cohen, "Reconstructing the History of Urban Education in America," in *Education and the City: Readings in Theory, History and Contemporary Practice*, edited by Gerald Grace (London: Routledge and Kegan Paul, 1984).

SECTION 3

RESPONSES

BIOGRAPHY IN CANADIAN HISTORY†

ROBERT CRAIG BROWN

As historians we regularly turn to biographies for character sketches to enliven our lectures, our essays, and our books. The analysis of the activities of men and women, of their hopes and of their fears, of their triumphs and of their failures, is what our craft is all about. Donald Creighton, whose work has influenced so much of our thinking about the writing of history and scholarly biography, once remarked that "the historian's first task is the elucidation of character."[1] That task is the fundamental requirement of biography, and without biography we would be hard pressed to record the encounter between character and circumstance that defines our discipline. Today, many historians might not agree with Creighton's order of priorities and its implicit emphasis on biographical studies; but we all use biographies and need them.

Still, we are uneasy about this dependence, and more uncertain about the relationship between biography and history than Creighton was in 1947 when he wrote that "biography is a distinct and special brand of historical writing."[2] In one sense that is still true, at least for historians who write biography. In another sense, because of the continuing influence of social science, especially of sociology and psychology, on both biography and history, the distinction between the two has perceptibly sharpened in the last three decades. Life-studies, as our colleagues in literature call them, now take a multiplicity of forms in attempts at a more precise discovery of a subject's personality. And even in conventional biography the emphasis is shifting more and more towards extended analysis and portraiture of personality. At the same time, J.H. Hexter noted some years ago, ". . . historians are solemnly intent on the quest for underlying trends, basic patterns, significant correlation and deeper meanings."[3] Biography is becoming even more internal and individualistic; history more collective. In the contemporary family of historians the historical biographer is something like an eccentric cousin: a bit old-fashioned in the insistence that individuals can and do shape the historical process we evaluate and interpret in our work.

The search for a redefinition of the role of the individual in history, and of the relationships between biography and history, is clearest, I think, in the development since World War II of the writing of the history of French Canada. Here, as in English-Canadian historiography, the techniques used by scholarly biographers have closely followed the methods and shared the assumptions and purposes of writing history itself. Before World War II French-Canadian history had a decidedly hagiographic tone, buttressed by scores of biographical studies written, in Fernand Ouellet's phrase, "d'une façon édifiante."[4] Soon after the war, with the recognition of history as a distinct discipline in the universities of French Canada, and with the rapid professionalization of historical scholarship in Quebec,[5] the character

†Canadian Historical Association, *Historical Papers* (1980): 1–8.

of historical and biographical writing changed. Extreme selectivity in the presentation of evidence, so much a part of the hagiographic tradition, gave way, in Marcel Trudel's *Chiniquy*, to painstaking research and meticulous analysis of evidence. Guy Frégault, in his biography of Bigot, severed another tie with hagiography with his critical evaluation of his subject's career. Bigot, par exemple, fut "l'un des artisans de la défaite"; "le dernier intendant du Canada," a écrit Frégault, "participe à l'avilissement de son siècle."[6]

Several years later, in 1959, W.J. Eccles, whose work reflects a profound understanding of both traditions of Canadian historical scholarship, published *Frontenac: The Courtier Governor*. Because of the paucity of evidence about the greater portion of the governor's life, *Frontenac* could not be, as Eccles wrote, "a full scale biography."[7] Still, its frank critique of Frontenac's career and character made it the most revisionist biographical study of the period. Many readers were startled by Eccles' approach and a few reviewers were clearly dismayed. "The picture has such dark shadows that the reader inevitably inquires," one wrote, " 'How could Parkman and other biographers and historians have been so misled?' "[8] Frégault, however, welcomed *Frontenac* as "un ouvrage qui comporte une grande part de biographie et une bonne part d'histoire du Canada."[9]

In 1970 Robert Mandrou echoed Frégault's point in an essay on the historiography of French Canada. *Frontenac* reflected the trends and met the demanding standards of both schools of historical writing. "M. Eccles," écrit-il, "réussit à donner non seulement un récit de la carrière de son héros, c'est-à-dire une biographie à la manière si caractéristique des historiens anglais. Mais encore, une évocation pertinente des problèmes essentiels posés aux administrateurs du Canada. . . ."[10] Eccles, like the other biographers of those years, among others, Careless, Kilbourn, and especially Creighton, had achieved that subtle and evocative blend of character and circumstance in his portrait of Frontenac's career which was "si caractéristique des historiens anglais." More than that, Frontenac had another utility for younger French-Canadian scholars. The life of an individual could facilitate "la découverte des structures de la société et . . . l'analyse des mouvements qui accompagnent ou précèdent les changements sociaux."[11]

In recent years the role of biography in French-Canadian historical writing has been made explicit. For Cameron Nish, the study of François-Étienne Cugnet was written to illustrate his subject as a "modèle" "bourgeois-gentilhomme."[12] Andrée Désilets, in her important biography of Langevin, declared that her purpose was "éclairer un visage dans sa vérité individuelle et, au-delà de ce visage, la physionomie d'une collectivité à une étape précise de son destin."[13] Biography, then, could and should inform and enrich the study of the history of the society. But without a clear linkage to social history, biography is incomplete and its utility is vitiated.

Fernand Ouellet, whose portrait of Papineau in the *Dictionnaire biographique du Canada*[14] is among the most sensitive sketches of a person in our historical literature, made that argument in his Presidential Address to [the Canadian Historical Association] a decade ago. His particular reference was to the use of political biography in social history, but I think he would agree that it is equally true of the biographies of men and women in the churches, in business, in labour relations, or any other endeavour.

> Il faudra sans doute multiplier les biographies d'hommes politiques
> influents, mais il faudra utiliser d'une façon plus systématique l'approche
> biographique comme instrument pour détecter les caractéristiques sociales
> des individus engagés à tous les échelons de la politique, pour évaluer leurs
> valeurs et leurs comportements. Ce type d'enquête met en évidence une
> sorte de dialectique constante entre l'individu et la société . . . .[15]

In English-Canadian historiography the redefinition of the relationships of biography to history has been more gradual. Rather than experiencing a sharp break with hagiographic assumptions and goals, the two crafts have steadily refined their techniques and purposes. The early biographies were tendentious and didactic tomes, unburdened by a respect for evidence, in which heroes and heroines could do no wrong. The innovative use of the life and times form of biography in O.D. Skelton's *Laurier* in 1921 was a refreshing departure from this "art of concealment"[16] so assiduously practised by earlier biographers. An official biography, *Laurier* was based on careful research and was scholarly in tone. The novelty of Skelton's approach was not in his portrait of Laurier, which was excessively respectful ("Mr. Laurier") and apologetic. Rather it was in the skilfully documented analysis of the political and economic obstacles confronting his hero throughout Laurier's carrer. Skelton's *Laurier* became something of a model for a generation of biographers of Canadian public men and women.

The problem with the model was that the skilful delineation of circumstance, reflecting new developments in historical and social science research, was not balanced by an equally sophisticated examination and portraiture of character. If the hero became more believable in this generation of biographies, it was because the environment in which he lived, the challenges which he faced, were sketched out with a new and convincing realism. So convincing, in fact, that the subjects of these biographies became, for some readers, depersonalized symbols of great historical causes. The most articulate critic of this development was Donald Creighton, who pointedly argued that this "abstract and inhuman method of presentation" gave us one stylized life of Robert and Francis and Wilfrid Responsible Government.[17] Anyone, or any Liberal, could be squeezed into the mould, glazed with an appropriate constitutional crisis, fired, and taken out as another fragile dime-store figurine commemorating the triumph of self-government. History, he protested, "is made by living men and women, impelled by an endless variety of ideas and emotions."[18] The most persuasive way to demonstrate the axiom, and to challenge the scientism of contemporary historiography, was through biography, biography that centred upon the re-creation of the life of the subject. His own *Macdonald*, Carl Berger observes, "owed as much to techniques derived from romantic history and literature and music as it did to contemporary academic historiography. The most arresting feature of his two volumes was that an entire age and its political history were not merely ordered around Macdonald, but that readers saw the whole scene through his eyes alone."[19]

Creighton's *Macdonald*, like Skelton's *Laurier* a generation before, became the standard against which historical biographies would now be evaluated. But it was a model exceedingly difficult, perhaps impossible, to emulate. The greatness of the book rested upon Creighton's unique artistic talent and a shrewd choice of an unusually attractive, humane subject. Creighton's literary skill needs no elaboration here. But the other half of the equation, the choice of Macdonald as subject, is worth a few more words. Macdonald's time was right and his role in it was perfect for illustrating a great theme, a sweeping interpretation of Canadian history. The tragedy of Macdonald's private life lent itself to dramatic treatment, as did his public personality.[20] No other public figure, not George Brown or J. S. Woodsworth, not Arthur Meighen or Mackenzie King, not even William Lyon Mackenzie or Louis Riel — all subjects of fine biographies in these years — had quite the same proportions of timing and personality, triumph and tragedy, that called for the epic treatment Creighton gave to Macdonald.

Creighton, however, may have gone too far in his attempt to redress the balance between character and circumstance in historical biography. His ardent championship of Macdonald resulted, as Carl Berger puts it, in an "oversimplification of the complexity of political action."[21] Every biographer, of course, runs that risk if he or she is true to his or her subject. That is the bias of biography, and I suspect that every historical biographer has been acutely conscious of it since the publication of *Macdonald*.

But awareness of the problem was also heightened in those years by an unprecedented expansion of graduate studies in Canadian history. A growing number of graduate students elaborated the complexity of historical circumstance in systematic examinations of political and diplomatic history, and moved on to explorations in intellectual, labour, business, social, and women's history. Their work at once helped to dispel any lingering romantic notions about the role of the individual in history and stimulated the search for patterns and structures to rationalize our awareness of the historical process. A few, like Ramsay Cook, whose *Dafoe* is a remarkable analysis of the evolution of a man's public ideas and attitudes, began their work with a more limited form of life study. Others, like Blair Neatby and Michael Bliss, turned to biographies of a politician and a businessman after earlier studies in political and business history were completed. Their biographies of King and Flavelle are fine examples of the sustained appeal of carefully balanced historical biography at its best. Neither subject is given epic proportions, though both men clearly thought of themselves as men of destiny. Both authors have convincingly integrated their subjects' personalities with their careers and their times.

If, then, an attempt to redefine the relationship between biography and history has been made in recent French-Canadian historiography, English-Canadian historical writing has witnessed a gradual process of accommodation of the two crafts over several decades. Beyond a long-standing, general complaint that biography has "dominated" in English-Canadian historiography, little has been written about the relationship between biography and history, and it could be argued that the relationship will unfold as it is destined to do. That, I think, is a counsel of complacency. A few perceptive reviews of the biographies of King and Flavelle suggest that the accommodation has become more and more difficult to achieve. The reviewers, expressing concern about the ability of the *genre* of biography to fulfil the expectations of political and business historians,[22] are not merely carping about the "dominance" of biography in English-Canadian historical writing. Rather, they are expressing a legitimate concern about the utility of biography to the contemporary historian, a recognition, if you will, that a biography of Robert Borden will answer fewer questions for the historian in the 1980s than the biography of John A. Macdonald did for historians in the 1950s.

At the same time, another challenge to the historical biographer comes from our colleagues in literary studies. In literature a revival of interest in the biographical form of writing has developed into something akin to a sub-discipline replete with a generally accepted methodology. With a few notable exceptions both in Canada and abroad, scholars of literary biography argue that psycho-biography is the most illuminating way to explore the life of a poet or novelist. But for the historical biographer, if the experience of our colleagues in the United States is any guide, psycho-biography is as full of problems as it is of promise.[23]

Maria Tippett, in her biography of Emily Carr, demonstrates how rewarding the subtle use of psychological insight can be to the biographer. In similar fashion, Thomas Flanagan's "heuristic biography" has added yet another dimension to the complex personality of Louis Riel.[24] In Canadian historiography, however, few biographers have been tempted to use the methodology of psycho-biography, perhaps in implicit recognition that the adoption of this particular technique to discover the interior life of a subject more often than not threatens to wrest the subject out of his or her historical context. That, in turn, widens the gap between the objectives of the biographer and the historian. Equally important is the observation of Robert Spiller, the historian of American literature, about Leon Edel's majestic five-volume psycho-biography of Henry James. "If we can accept his premises and his method," Spiller wrote, "Edel's interpretation is magnificently enlightening and convincing. Cool reason suggests, however, that although this interpretation may be the truth and nothing but the truth, it surely is not the whole truth."[25]

I stand by the premise that the biographer's task is to attempt to understand and recreate the life of his or her subject in all its parts. Very few will achieve the whole truth. Most will need as much luck and insight as evidence to grasp the bits of truth that are revealed in the accessible aspects of their subjects' lives. Some will find the use of psychological techniques more rewarding than others. Even for those who do, it will not be enough. The biographer has an obligation to do more than evaluate his or her subject's inner life or to relate it to what he or she did.

Motivation, to belabour a truism, is only in part inspired and conditioned by a subject's conscious and subconscious drives. The biographer's subject lived in a society, interacted with other persons and with groups, was influenced by and may well have influenced, in turn, private and public institutions, participated as a producer and a consumer in an economic system, shared or rebelled against the cultural and political norms of his society. It is in this context, as an actor in the historical process, that the biographer's subject assumes significance for the historian. And, as enlightening as the use of psychological techniques may be to the biographer, for most historical figures the questions posed and the discoveries made by the social historian are likely to be far more useful and revealing than the science of psychology. Modern historical biography should not be written to satisfy the particular needs of the social historian. Nor is there a promising future for historical biography in the form of some contorted hybrid of biography and the monograph in social, political, economic, or cultural history. Biography must stand on its own. The biographer needs to use all the insight that can be gathered from psychology and from the whole compass of social history. But, in the end, his or her obligation remains what it has always been: to disclose with sympathy and candor, and with such literary grace as he or she can command, as much as can be discovered of the subject's private and public life. Without historical biography there can be no historical "dialectique constante entre l'individu et la société." And that dialectic, after all, is an essential element not just of social history but of all historical inquiry.

Notes

1. Donald Creighton, *Towards the Discovery of Canada* (Toronto, 1972), 19.
2. Ibid., 197.
3. J.H. Hexter, review of Wallace Notestein, *Four Worthies*, in *American Historical Review* (hereafter *AHR*) LXIII (Jan. 1958): 396.
4. Fernand Ouellet, "L'histoire sociale du Bas-Canada: bilan et perspectives de recherches," *Communications historiques* (1970), 10.
5. See Marcel Trudel, "Les débuts de l'Institut d'histoire à l'université Laval," *Revue d'histoire de l'Amérique française* XXVII (Dec. 1973): 397–402.
6. Cited in Robert Mandrou, "L'historiographie canadienne-française. Bilan et perspectives," *Canadian Historical Review* (hereafter *CHR*) LI (March 1970), 11.
7. W.J. Eccles, *Frontenac: The Courtier Governor* (Toronto, 1959), v.
8. Grace Lee Nute, review of W.J. Eccles, *Frontenac: The Courtier Governor*, in *AHR* LXV (Jan. 1960): 371.
9. Guy Frégault, review of W.J. Eccles, *Frontenac: The Courtier Governor*, in *CHR* XL (Dec. 1959): 345.
10. Mandrou, "L'historiographie canadienne-française," 10.
11. Ouellet, "L'histoire sociale du Bas-Canada," 3.
12. See Peter Moogk, review of Cameron Nish, *François-Étienne Cugnet, 1719–1751*, in *CHR* LIX (June 1978): 222.
13. Andrée Désilets, *Hector-Louis Langevin, un père de la Confédération canadienne, 1826–1906* (Quebec, 1969), 401.
14. Fernand Ouellet, "Louis-Joseph Papineau," *Dictionary of Canadian Biography*. X. *1871–1880* (Toronto, 1972), 564–78. Also see Fernand Ouellet and André Lefort, "Denis-Benjamin Viger," *Dictionary of Canadian Biography*. IX. *1861–1870* (Toronto, 1976), 807–16.
15. Ouellet, "L'histoire sociale du Bas-Canada," 15.
16. See Robert Gittings, *The Nature of Biography* (Seattle, 1978), 35.
17. Creighton, *Towards the Discovery of Canada*, 199.
18. Cited in Carl Berger, *The Writing of Canadian History: Aspects of English-Canadian Historical Writing: 1900–1970* (Toronto, 1976), 220.
19. Ibid., 223.
20. On Macdonald's character, see P.B. Waite, "Sir John A. Macdonald, The Man," in *Empire and Nations. Essays in Honour of Frederic H. Soward*, edited by Harvey L. Dyck and H. Peter Krosby (Toronto, 1969), 36–53.
21. Berger, *The Writing of Canadian History*, 224.
22. See Christopher Armstrong, review of H. Blair Neatby, *William Lyon Mackenzie King*, III, *1932–1939, The Prism of Unity* (Toronto, 1976), in *CHR* LIX (March 1978): 103–5; and Douglas McCalla, review of Michael Bliss, *A Canadian Millionaire: The Life and Business Times of Sir Joseph Flavelle, Bart., 1859–1959* (Toronto, 1978), in *CHR* LX (June 1979): 228–9.
23. See James T. Patterson, "Politics, Personality and Psychohistory," *Reviews in American History* (hereafter *RAH*) I (March 1973): 59–64; and T. Harry Williams, "On the Couch at Monticello," *RAH* II (Dec. 1974): 523–9, for discussions of the problems with psychobiography in relation to Bruce Mazlich, *In*

Search of Nixon and Fawn Brodie, *Thomas Jefferson: An Intimate History*. For the promise of psychobiography, see Chapter 2, "The Fit in the Chair," in Erik A. Erikson, *Young Man Luther* (New York, 1962), 23–48; and William B. Willcox, "The Psychiatrist, the Historian, and General Clinton: The Excitement of Historical Research," *Michigan Quarterly Review* VI (Spring 1967): 123–30. More generally, see the excellent discussions of the subject in John A. Garraty, *The Nature of Biography* (New York, 1964); Gittings, *The Nature of Biography*; and James L. Clifford, *From Puzzles to Portraits, Problems of a Literary Biographer* (Chapel Hill, 1970).

24. The case for heuristic biography is argued by Flanagan in "The Lives of Louis Riel: Conventional, Psychiatric, and Heuristic Biography" (a paper delivered to the Conference on Biography and Canadian Literature, Wilfrid Laurier University, 29 Sept. 1979).

25. Robert E. Spiller, review of Leon Edel, *Henry James. The Treacherous Years, 1895–1901*, in *AHR* LXX (Feb. 1970): 943–4.

THE SECOND TIME AROUND: POLITICAL SCIENTISTS WRITING HISTORY†

JOHN ENGLISH

The troubles for political history began in the 1960s when the traditional came to represent not authority but fustiness or even repression. In Canada, political history was pre-eminently the tradition of Canadian historical writing. "Nation-building" formed character, and politicians shaped circumstances. The historian, indeed, seemed to be the guardian of national tradition. William Kilbourn, for example, suggested in his article on historical writing in the 1965 edition of the *Literary History of Canada* that "Such has been the preoccupation with the question of Canada itself and with a search for a national identity in a nation where it does not exist in as palpable and obvious a way as in Europe and the United States that one is sometimes left with the odd sensation that Canada is nothing but a figment of the historical imagination, a concept nurtured in the minds of a small minority of Canadian leaders in each generation, aided and abetted by a few historians."[1] The young historians had often shared classrooms with future prime ministers and statesmen, and if they did not always share later political affiliations, their style, their companions, and their ethos remained quite similar.

In the 1960s some historians did continue to aid and abet Canadian politicians and those politicians' attempts to define once again Canada's national identity. J.T. Saywell introduced *Federalism and the French Canadians* to English Canada, and Ramsay Cook was the book's leading interpreter.[2] Nevertheless, the setting was changing, as the university became swollen with undergraduates and new faculty. The faculty often came from the United States, either as native Americans or as graduate students returning home to their first job, and they brought with them the American intellectual's suspicion of politicians, an old wariness much enhanced by Lyndon Johnson, Richard Nixon, and Vietnam. For them, and for others whom they influenced, politics had lost their charm; they seemed too much the administration of things and too often sordid. A classical scholar has recently argued that this perception has prevented modern historians generally from understanding—or wanting to accept—the "primacy" of politics in earlier times, when the "polis" was regarded as a memorial to those who had shaped it. In part this inability derives from the expansion of the economy and of the scope of a modern state, which has acted to make the private sphere "the chief locus of human endeavour" for all but a few by limiting direct involvement in the affairs of the "polis." What Plato had deemed the noblest human activity and the ultimate expression of reason, the ordering of the state, became remote from daily experience. The result was resentment and alienation from politics.[3]

Whatever the cause, there can be no doubt that this mood affected younger scholars in their approach to political history. Moreover, there were new approaches

†*Canadian Historical Review* LXVII, 1 (1986): 1-16.

to historical study which promised to open rich lodes which had been closed to earlier scholars. Sometimes these approaches involved technique, as in the case of computer analysis of census material, and sometimes they involved ideological innovation, as in the case of the studies of working-class culture which passed through Britain and the United States to Canada. Simultaneously, young francophone historians were reading from or even studying under French historians of the *Annales* school who had launched the most devastating of all attacks on narrative political histories, the type which Canadian historians had usually written. In Quebec and elsewhere, there was another political ingredient: the attack on Ottawa and "centralization." Among historians this attack fitted neatly into a new focus on "limited identities." In limiting identities, historians normally avoided the political and focussed upon cultural, social, and economic concerns which seemed to offer definitions of these more limited identities more effectively.

Ramsay Cook assessed these new developments as ushering in a "golden age" of Canadian writing, but little of the glitter seemed to emanate from works of political history.[4] Inevitably, the political historians' loss of esteem among their fellow professionals was soon reflected elsewhere. High school teacher Paul Bennett, writing *A Teacher's Guide for the '80s*, commented upon "the decline of political history." Political history, this 1980 Ontario Institute for Studies in Education publication explained, was shunned by "a new generation of younger Canadian scholars" who had found it "sterile, excessively national in scope, too biographical, based on an insufficient understanding of the country's economic and social development, and lacking in an application of the sophisticated tools and methodologies of the social sciences." The rediscovery of political history by students would come when, in the language of curriculum reformers, its experience was made relevant.[5] Or as Mr Dooley had put it more bluntly long ago: "If any wan comes along with a histhry iv Greece or Rome that'll show me th' people fightin', getting dhrunk, makin' love, gettin' married, owin' th' grocery man an' bein' without hard-coal, I'll believe they was a Greece or Rome but not befure."[6]

For a while, Mr Dooley's needs seemed those that many professional historians were most eager to fulfil. To be sure, much political history was written, and some of it tried to move away from the narrative traditions and to employ new social science methodologies. Students of Donald Kerr at the University of Western Ontario and some graduate students elsewhere followed scholars such as Lee Benson and W.D. Aydelotte in applying quantitative methods to historical materials.[7] Others responded by emphasizing political components of limited identities, studying, for example, political developments in Canadian cities. Provincial politics also has attracted new interest for the same reasons.[8] Moreover, for many of the better-known historians, political history has remained the principal mode of historical expression. Works such as J.L. Granatstein's *A Man of Influence* and *The Ottawa Men*, H.B. Neatby's *William Lyon Mackenzie King, III: 1932–1939*, and R.C. Brown's *Robert Laird Borden: A Biography* received professional and popular acclaim. It must be admitted, however, that most of the media acclaim was bestowed upon political history written by journalists such as Christina McCall-Newman and Richard Gwyn, and most of the increasingly numerous prizes awarded by professional historians to other professional historians recognized non-political approaches to Canada's past. In Canada, the journals that are normally deemed exciting or innovative, both at conferences and in common rooms, are explicitly regional and oriented towards social history (the best example being *Acadiensis*) or specific in their social history subject matter (*Labour/Le Travail*). The *Canadian Historical Review*, by contrast, arouses numerous complaints, as the editors heard at a session on "What's Wrong with the *CHR*?" at the Canadian Historical Association Annual Meeting in 1984. One of the most frequent complaints is about a perceived *Review* bias towards "traditional" approaches to history, with "traditional" often identified with political.

It has not helped matters that political history's champions have often chosen conservative grounds for their arguments. In her slashing broadside against the "New History," which is simultaneously a defence of political history, Gertrude Himmelfarb has accused those who scorn political history of "denigrating the rule of reason." By seeking to rescue "ordinary people" from oblivion, the new "history from below" demeans ordinary people, depriving their lives of what had raised them above the ordinary, what had "made them feel part of the polity even when they were not represented in it." This defence, which draws deeply upon the work of Geoffrey Elton, is inherently conservative, both in a political and historiographical sense, and is bound to incense those on the left who regard political history as a bourgeois remnant of a discipline which should be progressive in politics and methodology.[9]

This attitude towards political history on the part of the political left is recent. The Left Book Club of the 1930s and 1940s published an abundance of works that would now be termed old-fashioned political history, and the debates on the left of those times in Britain were firmly grounded in the traditions of British political history stretching back to Clarendon. The same, of course, was true for Canadian socialists such as Frank Underhill and Eugene Forsey who were thoroughly immersed (and perhaps sometimes submerged) in the minutiae of political events. E.P. Thompson's preface to *The Making of the English Working Class* was not the first repudiation of this intellectual orientation towards Parliament, labour parties, and trade unionist politics, but it was certainly the most effective for graduate students of the 1960s and early 1970s.[10] Following Thompson's clarion, many historians began to focus upon the dynamic in working-class culture which acted to "make" the class. The approach has certainly been productive, but it has not been without its limitations, not least in its curious and coy approach to politics. Even sympathetic critics are concerned about this tendency in Canadian works of this genre.

Reviewing the work of Greg Kealey and Bryan Palmer in *Acadiensis*, University of Maryland historian Richard Price has described the focus upon the internal dynamic of working-class culture as "increasingly problematic." "There has been a tendency . . . ," Price argues, "to accentuate what was at the same time the most exciting and the weakest part of Thompson's formulation—that 'the working class made itself' — instead of asking how the other part of the couplet 'as much as it was made' — was to be fitted into the process."[11] That the Canadian state was an agent which made a peculiarly Canadian working class is apparent to any careful reader of *Toronto Workers Respond to Industrial Capitalism* and *A Culture in Conflict: Skilled Workers and Industrial Capitalism in Hamilton, Ontario.*[12] Kealey's study, in fact, devotes many pages to late nineteenth-century political history, some of it ineffably traditional.[13] These are, however, the least effective parts of this book, because the relationship of the political system to the working-class culture is sketchily drawn. Politics seems to intrude, rather than fit, into the analysis. The role of the state, the nature of its autonomy, and related fundamental questions are not explored in the detail that the evidence suggests they deserve. In fact, the obscuring of the role of the state and the shadowy existence of "politics" in so much new history now bring regular complaints from reviewers.[14]

Such questions as the role of the state and the nature of its autonomy have been shunned by many leading historians on the left. Paradoxically, these are the central questions for many political scientists on the left who identify themselves as the "new political economists." In both cases, the paradox can be explained, in large part, by reference to the history of both disciplines.

The tendency to ignore political matters in the new history is unsurprising; in its assumptions and approaches, the new history was much more influenced by anthropology and sociology than by political science.[15] In Canada, as elsewhere, the new historians found little exciting or useful in contemporary political science, and in the late 1960s and most of the 1970s political scientists showed equal disregard for the work of their historical counterparts. The close ties between Canadian political scientists and historians which had marked Canadian intellectual debate from the 1920s through the 1950s withered away as political scientists turned from political theory and historical analyses in favour of voting behaviour, policy analysis, and other so-called scientific approaches to their discipline, approaches which were of limited interest and utility to historians. By the late 1950s what Bernard Crick pejoratively termed the American science of politics appeared to have overwhelmed other philosophical, historical, and institutional approaches to politics in North America.

There was always Canadian resistance to this pressure: George Grant, C.B. Macpherson, Denis Smith, and David Smith were among the notable exceptions. Their voices, however, were often lonely. The coherent and effective first statement of the importance of traditional concern with historical approaches to the study of Canadian politics came from the growth of the so-called political economy group among Canadian political scientists. Influenced by the international revival of Marxist theory and, simultaneously, by a nationalist aversion to the "American science of politics," several young Canadian political scientists looked once again with favour upon an historical orientation to their discipline. Seeking to explain the dependency of Canadian capitalism and what they regarded as the truncated development of the Canadian state, these political economists rediscovered the earlier tradition of Canadian political economy and in doing so associated themselves with a distinctive approach to Canadian history. Thus, what would have seemed a most peculiar pairing in the 1950s — Harold Innis and Karl Marx — became the intellectual stimulus for this new school.

In reviewing recent political history, one is struck by the fact that so much political history is now written by political scientists, not historians. This fact derives largely (but not fully) from the existence of the political economy group and, one might add, the existence of sympathetic publishers and editors such as

James Lorimer and R.I.K. Davidson. It was Davidson of the University of Toronto Press who in 1977 guided publication of two of the most influential works within the tradition of the new political economy: Reg Whitaker's *The Government Party: Organizing and Financing the Liberal Party of Canada 1930–1958* and Leo Panitch, ed., *The Canadian State: Political Economy and Political Power*.[16] *The Canadian State* was a most uneven collection, but attracted considerable attention and soon appeared on course lists throughout Canada. In his preface, Panitch set out the beliefs which, he claimed, united the authors: "In short, concrete historical developments have altered the milieux within which social scientists operate, and this has led, to some extent, to an attempt to attend to certain 'significant problems' which not so long ago were dismissed as archaic in the name of 'pluralism' or the 'unembourgeoisement thesis' or the 'end of ideology' ideology. The renewed interest in a Marxist theory of the state reflects a sense that the concepts and theories of modern political science, and the hypotheses that are derived from them to appropriate reality, are incapable of even addressing, let alone explaining many of the major political questions."[17] Although the essays which followed were too eager to establish a secure foundation of imported theory from such European Marxists as Miliband and Habermas, they did show considerable respect for the work of Canadian historians such as H.V. Nelles and T.W. Acheson.[18] They even took the ideas of Mackenzie King seriously. At a time when many historians were rather consciously avoiding politics and politicians, this new political economy granted such concerns respectability.

The best essay in *The Canadian State* was Reg Whitaker's "Images of the State in Canada." This elegant essay was, in fact, a rejection of narrow determinism and an assertion of the significance of character and circumstance. In a warning which some of his co-authors failed to heed, Whitaker argued that "the mechanical application of concepts drawn exclusively from the European historical experience quickly comes to grief in the North American environment even at the level of economic structures." There was, moreover, the fact that historical specificity is "a *cultural*, as well as an economic phenomenon."[19] The Canadian state and the political sphere had an irreducible autonomy. So too did individuals; "[t]o argue that the individual's behaviour is merely a reflection of his position in relation to the economic base is altogether unscientific, in the absence of any demonstrated concrete linkages between the base and the behaviour of individuals." These views were reflected in Whitaker's *The Government Party* which, seven years after its publication, remains the finest historical study of a Canadian political party.

The Government Party is largely descriptive and is based upon extensive research in Liberal party papers and other manuscript collections. For this, Whitaker does not apologize. In a statement somewhat redolent of the tone of Geoffrey Elton, Whitaker argued that since so little was known about Liberal party organization, "the mere marshalling of the historical evidence from primary sources is of legitimate interest." The evidence was documents; the approach assuredly traditional. After assembling his evidence, Whitaker did conclude that the Liberal party became, under King and St Laurent, a government party which acted to depoliticize Canadian political life by transforming politics into bureaucracy and the party into the state. In this transformation, the importance of an individual,

Mackenzie King, was highlighted. King and his ministers did have "a freedom of action to 'wheel and deal' because they managed to balance effectively the conflicting demands of a corporate capitalist economy and a democratic popular opinion." This argument moved far beyond materialistic determinism and represented, in fact, a strong defence of some aspects of the Canadian political history tradition. Whitaker also implied that while there might be considerable homogeneity within the North American economy, there was a distinctive Canadian political culture. This culture was not merely epiphenomenal, that is, independent of the experience of most Canadians, or regional, that is, a cluster of provincial political cultures; rather, it had to be treated as an autonomous factor, even in the understanding of class formation in Canada.[20]

Unfortunately, not all of the work within the tradition of the new political economy reaches the scholarly level attained by Whitaker. Too much of the so-called new political economy is marked by a scanty knowledge of secondary works, by an overly elaborate theoretical exposition, and by a source-mining which seeks to extract precious historical ore while lacking awareness of the baser metals in which it is found. A book which abundantly illustrates these weaknesses is M. Janine Brodie and Jane Jensen, *Crisis, Challenge and Change: Party and Class in Canada.*[21]

Brodie and Jensen attempt to blend two streams, political economy based upon Marxist class analysis and an historical analysis of voting behaviour. Using quantitative techniques to determine ethnic, regional, and class support for Canada's political parties, Brodie and Jensen seek to prove that "the key to understanding Canada's federal party system is an historical examination of the bourgeois parties' management of the tension between capital and the subordinate classes." Having the key, the authors open only the doors to the past which lead towards their conclusion. As a result, a wealth of historical literature on the party system is overlooked. In the case of the election of 1917, for example, the authors appear to suggest, quite wrongly, that "labour" was overwhelmingly opposed to conscription and even the war. The farmers are portrayed as thoroughgoing anti-conscriptionists who were unenthused about the war. The considerable variations in attitude among farmers, religious groups, workers, and others are effectively obscured. The chapter "1917–1920—Two Parties in Crisis" illustrates the worst traits of some of the history which has been written by political scientists.

Donald Creighton, in his Canadian Historical Association presidential address in 1957, complained that everybody in the university was writing and using history but they were not paying much attention to reading and understanding the work of historians. Today, political scientists like Whitaker and David Smith are certainly reading history, but historians are, perhaps, ignoring the work of political scientists. Certainly few are working with them. This is illustrated in a recent anthology edited by Alain Gagnon, *Quebec: State and Society*, which parallels *The Canadian State* in its strongly historical approach and in the familiarity of the authors with the new political economy.[22] It is less ideological than *The Canadian State* but also less thorough. There is, apparently, no longer a need to refer regularly to European Marxists. The language of neo-Marxist political economy nevertheless endures, and sometimes the growth of this language becomes so dense that it obscures both root and branch. Of course, Quebec scholars came to neo-Marxist language and theory from different directions than did Anglophone scholars such as Panitch and Whitaker. These other sources are described in an essay in *Quebec: State and Society* by Anne Legaré on the contribution made by "leftist intellectuals to the study of social classes in Quebec."

As in English Canada, commitment and scholarship were combined. Legaré explicitly identifies the shifts in scholarly interpretation with political events in Quebec, beginning with the split in the Quebec NDP and the formation of the Parti socialiste du Québec. The "fundamental conservatism" of the Parti Québécois has, according to Legaré, clarified the "sociopolitical context" of the analysis of class in Quebec. In an oddly familiar note, Legaré suggests that the new progressive studies of Quebec political economy recognize that nationalism was an "ornament" for the PQ which served to conceal the party's refusal to satisfy "the general interests of the dominated social classes." Legaré's account of the debate, combined with excerpts from Gilles Bourque, Jorge Niosi, and Pierre Fournier, indicates how class analysis derived from Marxist assumptions influences political analysis in Quebec. Moreover, as with political economy in English Canada, there is a strong emphasis upon historical material in constructing arguments. The sociologist Bourque, for example, presented his earliest analysis of Quebec class formation and nationalism in an historical study of that very popular 1760–1840 period.[23] Despite this reliance upon historical material, *The Quebec State*, like *The Canadian State*, has almost no place for historians. Of the twenty-two contributors only Stanley Ryerson is an historian; he is, in fact, described as "a Marxist historian [and] one of the most praised intellectuals in Canada." Ryerson contributes some brief and rather eclectic remarks on the recent consitutional changes. The article, ironically, is notable for the absence of Marxist terminology and for the traditional nature of its sources. Instead of Poulantzas and Miliband one finds, not even Alfred Dubuc, but rather Donald Creighton, J. R. Mallory, and Peter Waite in Ryerson's footnotes.

Creighton would probably have been no more amused by the new political economy—despite its nationalist tone—than he was by the Marxist enthusiasms of the 1930s and early 1940s. That efflorescence of class analysis carried on by "those party historians, party economists, and party political scientists" associated with the League for Social Reconstruction supplied, in Creighton's view, "an excellent example of how the claims of the Canadian social scientists and the circumstances of Canadian politics combined to induce the historians to accept a doctrine which was alien to their experience and unremunerative for their purposes." In Creighton's view, these early toilers in the vineyards of class analysis brought in a meagre harvest for which they blamed the weather: "Canadians were imperfectly class-conscious, they had had no revolution, and they kept getting politically excited about all the wrong things. Canadian history, in short, was disappointing."[24]

A harsh verdict, to be sure, but one which in terms of the historical literature of the 1930s has stood up fairly well. Some of it fits today's work as well. Nevertheless, there are several reasons why the new political economy will likely have a better fate than its Marxist predecessor.

First, even non-Marxists admit that the introduction of class to historical analysis has illuminated the process of historical change, especially in Quebec. We have travelled far since 1965 when S.R. Mealing lamented the absence of class analysis in Canadian historical studies. One need only look at Terry Copp's *The Anatomy of Poverty* or Kenneth McRoberts and Dale Posgate's study of Quebec social and political change to see how fundamental class is to the understanding of political developments in Quebec.[25] This also seems to apply, but to a lesser degree, with the Prairies, where Larry Pratt and John Richards' *Prairie Capitalism* advances considerably the pioneering Marxist analysis of Prairie politics and society found in C.B. Macpherson's work. Like Macpherson, Pratt and Richards' scholarship is provocative, idiosyncratic, and generally well researched, but, like Macpherson, the analysis often strains the data. Roger Gibbins' work has shown how class analysis can be part of a broader approach to the study of the Prairies which is ultimately more convincing. Nevertheless, the new political economy's contribution to the study of these regions must be recognized.[26]

Second, the new political economy does stress the role of the state, and in accepting the state's autonomy it largely frees itself of the theoretical jumble which affected earlier Marxist historiography in Canada. The expansion of the role of the state is generally admitted to be one of the most significant factors affecting historical change in the twentieth century. Yet Canadian historians have been reluctant to study this subject.[27] The new political economy has been a prod to some historians. A fine example of an historical study influenced by the political economists is Paul Craven, *"An Impartial Umpire": Industrial Relations and the Canadian State 1900–1911*.[28] Craven's study, which focusses largely upon Mackenzie King's early labour activities, is well grounded within the traditions of contemporary political economy and within the scholarship of Canadian political history. King's ideas and their application are treated with sensitivity and seriousness, very much in contrast to earlier treatments by Marxists and non-Marxists alike. Craven, moreover, demonstrates that ideas did affect action and policy. The work locates itself far from economic determinism and rarefied theory. This approach, making use of the best of other disciplines, while simultaneously building upon the work of historians such as Nelles and Traves, is surely a fruitful one for many historians to follow in the future.

Third, the new political economists are, as we have seen, on the political left. Among many historians, the rejection of political history has been motivated by a sense that political history and its practitioners are conservative. This belief has some validity, for the field has been attached to narrative, the traditional historical mode, and most of its leading practitioners tend to fall to the political right of the social historians. Yet the attitude is unfortunate, akin to the aversion to religious history on the part of an earlier historical generation carried away in the first embrace of secular modernism. The work of Whitaker, Pratt, Stevenson, and others has emphasized that the study of political subjects is not intrinsically conservative in an ideological sense. The political economists have accepted much more readily than historians that history is made from above and below and that ideology need not be a factor in the scrutiny of either level. That is a useful corrective.

Fourth, the new political economists are not isolated within their discipline in the attention they pay to historical materials and debates. Indeed, the study of international relations in Canada has been marked by distinguished historical work by political scientists. Historical questions which are the preserve of historians in other nations are the territory upon which some notable debates among political scientists have occurred. Future historians studying such topics as Canada's role in the Vietnam War will probably turn more often to the work of political scientists than to historians.

They will turn very often, for example, to James Eayrs's *In Defence of Canada*. This series, which is a landmark in Canadian scholarship, began two decades ago just as the full implications of the atomic age were being recognized by Canadians and others. Eayrs proposed to trace Canadian decision-making through the perspective of the decision-makers' understanding of what national security meant. The vantage point sometimes obscured important events, and the volumes are far from a history of either Canadian defence or foreign policy, although they do make substantial contributions to both. The most recent volumes, volume IV, *Growing Up Allied* and volume V, *Indochina: Roots of Complicity*, are characteristically well written, strongly argued, and eclectic.[29] They bear the personal stamp of a first-rate mind that roams freely in literary, philosophical, and historical fields and does not fear contradiction. And contradiction abounds, nowhere more obviously than in the most recent volumes.

Growing Up Allied describes the formation of the North Atlantic Treaty Organization, and it is a generally respectful tribute to the architects and their product. *Indochina*, however, is a harsh indictment of the "complicity" of many of these same Canadian diplomats in the entry of the United States into the Vietnam War. Eayrs rejects John Holmes's claim that the Canadian participation in the International Control Commissions was a "rough but useful lesson" of the need to live with paradox and to acknowledge that morality in international politics is "prismatic." Eayrs responds righteously: "Such was Canada's apprenticeship in complicity, whose roots are now exposed."[30]

This exposure, however, has been described as only partial in the recent study of the commissions by Douglas Ross. Ross, a student of Holmes and an admirer of Eayrs, takes strong issue with the lack of context in *Indochina*.[31] Eayrs's dependence on Canadian documentation, his failure to examine in detail the policies of other nations, and his quickness to judge have, in Ross's view, made Eayrs's work a morality play rather than a sensitive analysis of contemporary circumstances. In an earlier volume of *In Defence of Canada* Eayrs chose some lines of C. Day Lewis as an epigraph to begin a chapter:[32]

> Yet living here
> As one between two massing powers I live,
> Where neutrality cannot save
> Nor occupation cheer.

In *Indochina* Eayrs has chosen an Old Testament text; it is Ross for whom Lewis's modernist ambiguity and anxiety are appropriate. Ross's *In the Interests of Peace* describes Canadians pursuing the art of the possible where neutrality was impossible and where the pursuit was a Sisyphean task. This book is a brilliant case study which, by focussing upon a relatively narrow topic, manages to illuminate the broader features of Canada's international personality: it is, indeed, prismatic.

Ross is one of several young political scientists, many of them students of John Holmes, who are familiar with historical materials, aware of international relations theory, but weary of arid theoretical debates and sterile behaviourism. Kim Nossal, another Holmes product, reflects these attitudes in his sprightly overview of *The Politics of Canadian Foreign Policy*, which would be a useful supplement to Stacey in courses on Canadian diplomatic history.[33] What these young political scientists must find odd is the absence of many counterparts among historians. For them, the study of how states interact and how Canada takes its place in such interaction is of fundamental importance, far more so now when Canadians know well that they live between two massing powers in an atomic age.[34]

Despite these promising signs of greater interaction between political scientists and historians, many barriers remain. Political economists have largely focussed on the recent past while Canadian social historians have concentrated upon the nineteenth and early twentieth century. This difference, along with normal disciplinary barriers, has lessened cross-fertilization. Moreover, E. P. Thompson's aversion to theory as expressed in his essay attacking Althusser, "The Poverty of Theory," has affected Canadian historians on the left, and the "culturalist" perspective stands in sharp contract to the explicitly theoretical Marxism one finds in *The Canadian State* and similar works.[35] Disciplinary and departmental separation is further fostered by the nature of the contemporary university.

What this comparison of political scientists and historians suggests is the possibility that the eclipse of political history should be properly seen as a temporary event in the history of the writing of Canadian history. Carl Berger's survey of English-Canadian historical writing was completed in the mid-1970s when the new social history in its many varieties was spreading out to smother traditional approaches to the study of the Canadian past. The "concentration on Canadian national history and nationality," which distinguished Canadian historiography and which led ineluctably to political questions at the national level, seemed to have been broken. So too had "the historical orientation of the political-economy tradition," even though some relics endured in Andrew Hill Clark's geography and James Eayrs's "foreign policy studies." This generation of Canadian historians, Berger pointed out, had turned to the study of class and region as the "more appropriate frameworks for examining the past." Their enthusiasm expressed itself in an impatience with "the exceptional" and "the elevated themes of national history" and in a hankering "after a more authentic description and analysis of ordinary everyday life and the material regularities that shape group existence."[36]

In the decade since Berger wrote this analysis, much has changed. Political subjects and even "the elevated themes of national history" are certainly not shunned by the left; indeed, the political economists now seem to extend to them the most careful nurture. The historical orientation of the political economists, a link between disciplines which Berger thought had been vitally severed, has been reinvigorated. The peace movement and the recognition that the future of Canadians' work, play, life, and love is dependent upon the developments of international politics, or, as it is often put at noon-hour rallies, upon whose finger is on the trigger, have undoubtedly spurred many younger scholars to turn once more towards the study of how states act. That is, of course, a political subject; it is also "elevated" and necessarily deals with the "exceptional." As for the narrative approach, by now nearly all historians know that Lawrence Stone, one of the most distinguished "new historians," has detected "evidence of an undercurrent which is sucking many prominent 'new historians' back again into some form of narrative." Bernard Bailyn has advised them not to resist. Stone's second thoughts extend further. He now believes, for example, that the "new historians" will "undoubtedly be severely criticized for their obsession with social, economic, and demographic forces in history and their failure to take sufficient account of political organization and decision-making and the vagaries of military battle and siege."[37]

One hopes that the criticism is not severe, for it would not be productive, just as the dismissal of political history did not make Clio a more attractive muse for our undergraduates, the general reading public, or other disciplines. It was surely inevitable that in a century whose most significant characteristic may be the fact that the majority of our species is politicized for the first time,[38] and in a country where vast distances and differences make political symbols, myths, and actors one of the few elements of common experience, that political subjects and events would regain their place within Clio's capacious bosom. Never is Clio so charming and instructive as when her brood is large.

Notes

1. William Kilbourn, "The Writing of Canadian History," in *The Literary History of Canada*, edited by Carl Klinck (Toronto, 1965), 497.

2. J.T. Saywell, "Introduction," in Pierre Trudeau, *Federalism and the French Canadians* (Toronto, 1968); and Ramsay Cook, *The Maple Leaf Forever* (Toronto, 1971), especially 23–45. Saywell's contributions to the *Canadian Annual Review* in the 1960s are notable as skilled essays in contemporary history.

3. Paul Rahe, "The Primacy of Politics in Classical Greece," *American Historical Review* LXXXIX, 2 (April 1984), 266 and passim.

4. Ramsay Cook, "The Golden Age of Canadian History," *Historical Reflections/Réflexions historiques* IV, 1 (1977): 137–49. This tone is also reflected in the final pages of Carl Berger's *The Writing of Canadian History* (Toronto, 1976).

5. Paul Bennett, *Rediscovering Canadian History: A Teacher's Guide for the '80s* (Toronto, 1980), 19. Bennett was not yet prepared to inter political history. "Even" political history could improve if it adopted the "scholarship and interpretation" of the "new" history.

6. Finley Peter Dunne, *Observations by Mr. Dooley* (New York, 1902), 271.

7. See, for example, Douglas Baldwin, "Political and Social Behaviour in Ontario, 1879–1891: A Quantitative Approach" (PhD thesis, York University, 1973); Kenneth McLaughlin, "Race, Religion and Politics: The Election of 1896 in Canada" (PhD thesis, University of Toronto, 1975); and the political scientist Donald Blake's "Regionalism in Canadian Voting Behaviour 1908–1968" (PhD thesis, Yale University, 1972).

8. The Ontario Historical Studies Series, for example, reveals a strong bias towards political history in the works published so far. See Christopher Armstrong, *The Politics of Federalism: Ontario's Relations with the Federal Government, 1867–1942* (Toronto, 1981); J.M.S. Careless, ed., *The Pre-Confederation Premiers* (Toronto, 1980); Charles M. Humphries, *Sir James Pliny Whitney* (Toronto, 1985); and Peter Oliver, *G.*

Howard Ferguson: Ontario Tory (Toronto, 1977). The Ontario projects were generously supported by the provincial government. Although this has not always been the case elsewhere, there has been an efflorescence of provincial political history. Great gaps remain, however. Patricia Roy's comment that "From an historical point of view, provincial politics before 1903 are a virtual terra incognita" could be applied to other provinces than British Columbia and to other periods. Patricia Roy, "British Columbia," in *A Reader's Guide to Canadian History*, 2: *Confederation to the Present*, edited by J.L. Granatstein and Paul Stevens (Toronto, 1982), 165.

9. Gertrude Himmelfarb, "Denigrating the Rule of Reason," *Harper's* (April 1984): 89. Both Elton and Himmelfarb are conservative, as are several others of the more prominent defenders of political history. For Elton's defence of political and "traditional" history see his *Political History: Principles and Practice* (New York, 1970); "The Historian's Social Function," *Transactions of the Royal Historical Society*, 5th series, XXVII (1977): 197–211; and his recent debate with R.W. Fogel, *Which Road to the Past? Two Views of History* (New Haven, 1983). See also J.M. Hexter, *Doing History* (Bloomington, 1971), and Oscar Handlin, *Truth in History* (Cambridge, Mass., 1979). See also the letters from John Keep and Robert Daniels to the *American Historical Review* dealing with the interplay between political and social history, LXXXVIII, 4 (Oct. 1983): 1137–8.

10. See Bryan Palmer, *The Making of E.P. Thompson: Marxism, Humanism, and History* (Toronto, 1981), and E.P. Thompson, *The Making of the English Working Class* (London, 1963).

11. Richard Price, "Class Formation in Canada: Some Recent Studies," *Acadiensis* XIII, 1 (Autumn 1983), 180.

12. Greg Kealey, *Toronto Workers Respond to Industrial Capitalism 1867–1892* (Toronto, 1980), and Bryan Palmer, *A Culture in Conflict: Skilled Workers and Industrial Capitalism in Hamilton, Ontario, 1860–1914* (Montreal, 1979).

13. Price makes a similar point in "Class Formation," 175–83.

14. These criticisms now arise from the most sympathetic reviewers, for example, Richard Twomey, review of Eric Foner, *Politics and Ideology in the Age of the Civil War*, in *Acadiensis* XII (Spring 1983): 282, and R.T. Naylor, review of William Melody, Liora Salter, and Paul Meyer, eds., *Culture, Communication and Dependency: The Tradition of H.A. Innis*, in *Acadiensis* XIII (Autumn 1983): 253–4. Naylor criticizes this collection because it "insufficiently" explores "the nature of, and the role of the State." See also Bryan Palmer's admiring comments on Brian Young's biography of George Étienne Cartier and his comments on the need for a "more theoretically poised history, attendant to the role of the State . . . ." in "Town, Port, and Country: Speculations on the Capitalist Transformation of Canada," *Acadiensis* XII (Spring 1983): 136–8.

15. Michael Kammen, ed., *The Past Before Us* (Ithaca and London, 1980), 41–2.

16. Davidson had been an early promoter of John Porter, *The Vertical Mosaic: An Analysis of Social Class and Power in Canada* (Toronto, 1965), which had great influence upon Canadian political economy in the 1970s.

17. Panitch, ed., *The Canadian State*, vi.

18. See, for example, Leo Panitch, "The Role and Nature of the Canadian State," in ibid., 16–17, and Garth Stevenson, "Federalism and the Political Economy of the Canadian State," in ibid., 76–7.

19. Reg Whitaker, "Images of the State in Canada," in ibid., 28 (italics in original).

20. *The Government Party*, 401.

21. (Toronto, 1980).

22. (Toronto, 1984).

23. *Classes sociales et question nationale au Québec 1760–1840* (Montreal, 1970).

24. Donald Creighton, "Doctrine and the Interpretation of History," in *Towards the Discovery of Canada* (Toronto, 1972), 36–7.

25. Terry Copp, *The Anatomy of Poverty* (Toronto, 1974), and Kenneth McRoberts and Dale Posgate, *Quebec: Social Change and Political Crisis*, 2nd ed. (Toronto, 1980). See also Mealing's view in "The Concept of Social Class and the Interpretation of Canadian History," *Canadian Historical Review* XLVI (1965): 201.

26. Larry Pratt and John Richards, *Prairie Capitalism: Power and Influence in the New West* (Toronto, 1979), and Roger Gibbins, *Prairie Politics and Society: Regionalism in Decline* (Toronto, 1982).

27. This has also been true elsewhere. See Raymond Grew, ed., *Crises of Political Development in Europe and the United States* (Princeton, 1978).

28. (Toronto, 1981). Craven was working in a field explored earlier by Reg Whitaker in "The Liberal Corporatist Ideas of Mackenzie King," *Labour/Le Travailleur* II (1977): 137–69.

29. (Toronto, 1980); (Toronto, 1983).

30. *Indochina: Roots of Complicity*, 283. On Eayrs's views on morality and foreign policy see his *Right and Wrong in Foreign Policy* (Toronto, 1965).

31. *In the Interests of Peace* (Toronto, 1984).

32. Quoted in *In Defence of Canada: Peacemaking and Deterrence* (Toronto, 1972), 319. See also Ross's review of Eayrs, *Indochina: Roots of Complicity*, in *Canadian Historical Review* LXIV, 3 (1983), 378.

33. (Scarborough, 1985). For an illustration of the strong historical bent of these younger scholars see the Festschrift for John Holmes, *An Acceptance of Paradox: Essays on Canadian Diplomacy in Honour of John W. Holmes*, edited by Kim Nossal (Toronto, 1982).

34. There has also been a relatively recent efflorescence of interest in international politics in Quebec. Much of this interest derives from the entry of Quebec onto the international scene. Most of this work appears in the various publications of the Centre international de relations internationales at Laval. The historical content, as in English Canada, is strong. See, for example, Paul Painchaud, ed., *Le Canada sur la scène internationale* (Quebec, 1977).

35. In his review of Bryan Palmer's *The Making of E.P. Thompson*, Craig Heron is critical of the limitations of Thompson's "anti-theoretical posture. Countless historians and social scientists — including many Marxists — no doubt share Thompson's (and Palmer's) rejection of an arid, static structural determinism; but many are frustrated by the elusiveness of some of Thompson's analytical idiosyncracies and his persistent unwillingness to consolidate his conclusions and generalizations into anything that might resemble 'theory'." *Canadian Historical Review* LXIII, 2 (1982): 274.

36. Berger, *The Writing of Canadian History*, 259–64.

37. Lawrence Stone, *The Past and Present* (Boston and London, 1981), 74, 81. See also Bernard Bailyn's American Historical Association presidential address, which claims that the greatest challenge now facing historians is the problem of "how to put the story together again" in the form of "dynamic" narratives. "The Challenge of Modern Historiography," *American Historical Review* LXXXVII, 1 (Feb. 1982): 24.

38. William H. McNeill, "The Making of Modern Times," *Harper's* (Nov. 1984): 14.

FURTHER READING

There are several surveys of the background to contemporary historiography. Carl Berger, *The Writing of Canadian History: Aspects of English-Canadian Historical Writing Since 1900* (Toronto, 1986) should be supplemented by Serge Gagnon's two studies: *Quebec and Its Historians: 1840–1940* (Montreal, 1982) and *Quebec and Its Historians: The Twentieth Century* (Montreal, 1985). Carl Berger, ed., *Approaches to Canadian History* (Toronto, 1967) consists of reflections on themes in national history by such past masters as A.R.M. Lower, F.H. Underhill, W. L. Morton, D.G. Creighton, and J.M.S. Careless. Ramsay Cook, *The Maple Leaf Forever: Essays on Nationalism and Politics in Canada* (Toronto, 1971; reprinted 1986) contains two highly critical chapters on the obsession with national survival in both French and English history writing. In two important articles, Fernand Ouellet has subjected past historical writing to statistical analysis ("L'Émergence dans le Canada du XXe siècle de l'histoire comme science sociale," *Transactions of the Royal Society of Canada*, Fourth Series, XX (1982): 35–81), and traced the rise of social history in Quebec ("La modernisation de l'historiographie et l'émergence de l'histoire sociale," *Recherches Sociographiques* XXVI (1985): 10–83). The second article is especially valuable for its full bibliography.

Some of the subjects dealt with by articles in this collection can be pursued in additional studies. On native or ethnohistory, see the first chapters of Bruce Trigger, *Natives and New-Comers: Canada's "Heroic Age" Reconsidered* (Montreal, 1986) and James W. St. G. Walker, "The Indian in Historical Writing, 1971–1981" in *As Long as the Sun Shines and the Water Flows: A Reader in Canadian Native Studies*, edited by Ian A.L. Getty and Antoine S. Lussier (Vancouver, 1983), 340–57. On labour history, see Gregory S. Kealey, "Labour and Working-Class History in Canada: Perspectives in the 1980s," *Labour/Le Travailleur* 7 (Spring 1981): 67–94, and David J. Bercuson, "Through the Looking Glass of Culture: an Essay on the New Labour History and Working-Class Culture in Recent Canadian Historical Writing," *Labour/Le Travailleur* 7 (Spring 1981): 95–112 (both essays are reprinted in David J. Bercuson, ed., *Canadian Labour History: Selected Readings* (Toronto, 1986)). Several useful articles on regional writing include William Westfall, "On the Concept of Region in Canadian History and Literature," *Journal of Canadian Studies* 15 (Summer 1980): 3–15; William G. Godfrey, "A New Golden Age: Recent Historical Writing on the Maritimes," *Queen's Quarterly* 91 (Summer 1984): 350–82; Lewis G. Thomas, "The Writing of History in Western Canada" in *Eastern and Western Perspectives*, edited by David J. Bercuson and Phillip A. Buckner (Toronto, 1981), 69–83; Ronald Rudin, "Recent Trends in Quebec Historiography," *Queen's Quarterly* 92 (Spring 1982): 80–93. Immigration and ethnic communities are treated in Howard Palmer, "Ethnic History in the 1970s and 1980s," *Journal of Canadian Studies* 17 (Spring 1982): 35–50. For women's history, see Eliane L. Silverman, "Writing Women's History, 1970–82: an Historiographical Analysis," *Canadian Historical Review* LXIII (Dec. 1982): 513–33.

Other topics and approaches have been assessed in Duncan McDowall, "Business History as Public History: One of Canada's Infant Industries," *Journal of Canadian Studies* 20 (Feb. 1985): 5–21; A.M.J. Hyatt, "Military Studies in Canada: An Overview," *Revue internationale d'histoire militaire* 51 (1982): 328–49; John Moir, "Coming of Age, But Slowly: Aspects of Canadian Religious Historiography Since Confederation," *The Canadian Catholic Historical Association Study Sessions* 50 (1983): 89–98; and on intellectual history, A.B. McKillop, "So Little on the Mind," *Transactions of the Royal Society of Canada*, Series IV, XIX (1981): 183–200.

An honest attempt has been made to secure permission for all material used, and if there are errors or omissions, these are wholly unintentional and the Publisher will be grateful to learn of them.

J.M.S. Careless, " 'Limited Identities' in Canada," *Canadian Historical Review* L, 1 (March 1969): 1–10. Reprinted by permission of the author and the University of Toronto Press.

E.R. Forbes, "In Search of a Post-Confederation Maritime Historiography," *Acadiensis* VIII (Autumn 1978): 3–21. Reprinted by permission of the author and the journal.

Serge Gagnon, "The Historiography of New France, 1960–1974: Jean Hamelin to Louise Dechêne." From Serge Gagnon, *Quebec and its Historians* (Montreal: Harvest House Ltd., 1985), 53–80, 181–89, being a revision of the article first appearing in the *Journal of Canadian Studies* 13, 1 (Spring 1978): 80–99. Reprinted by permission.

Gerald Friesen, "Recent Historical Writing on the Prairie West." From *The Prairie West Historical Readings*, edited by R. Douglas Francis and Howard Palmer. Published by the University of Alberta Press 1985. Reprinted by permission.

Allan Smith, "The Writing of British Columbia History," *BC Studies* 45 (Spring 1980): 73–102. Reprinted by permission of the author and the journal.

David Gagan and H.E. Turner, "Social History in Canada: A Report on the 'State of the Art'," *Archivaria* 14 (Summer 1982): 27–52. Reprinted by permission of the journal.

Reprinted by permission of Grolier Limited, from *The History and Social Science Teacher*, Volume 17, No. 2 from an article entitled "Historical Writing on Native People in Canada" by Robin Fisher.

Bryan D. Palmer, "Working-Class Canada: Recent Historical Writing," *Queen's Quarterly* 86 (Winter 1979): 594–616. Reprinted by permission of the author.

Kenneth McNaught, "E.P. Thompson vs. Harold Logan: Writing About Labour and the Left in the 1970s," *Canadian Historical Review* LX, 2 (1981): 141–68. Reprinted by permission of the author and the University of Toronto Press.

Gilbert A. Stelter, "A Sense of Time and Place: The Historian's Approach to Canada's Urban Past," revised from "The Historian's Approach to Canada's Urban Past," *Histoire sociale/Social History* VII, 13 (May 1974): 5–22. Used by permission of the author and the journal.

Margaret Conrad, "The Re-Birth of Canada's Past: A Decade of Women's History," *Acadiensis* XII (Spring 1983): 140–62. Reprinted by permission of the author and the journal.

Roberto Perin, "Clio as an Ethnic: The Third Force in Canadian Historiography," *Canadian Historical Review* LXIV, 4 (1983): 441–67. Reprinted by permission of the author and the University of Toronto Press.

J. Donald Wilson, "Some Observations on Recent Trends in Canadian Educational History." From J. Donald Wilson, ed., *An Imperfect Past: Education and Society in Canadian History* (Vancouver: Centre for the Study of Curriculum and Instruction, University of British Columbia, 1984), 7–29. Reprinted by permission of the publisher.

Robert Craig Brown, "Biography in Canadian History," Canadian Historical Association, *Historical Papers* (1980): 1–8. Reprinted by permission of the author and the Canadian Historical Association.

John English, "The Second Time Around: Political Scientists Writing History," *Canadian Historical Review* LXVII, 1 (1986): 1–16. Reprinted by permission of the author and the University of Toronto Press.

1 2 3 4 5   135527   91 90 89 88 87